10629785

THE THIRD CITY

THE THIRD CITY

Philosophy at war with positivism

BORNA BEBEK

Routledge & Kegan Paul
London, Boston, Melbourne and Henley

To Athene, who protects the city

First published in 1982
by Routledge & Kegan Paul Ltd
39 Store Street, London WC1E 7DD,
9 Park Street, Boston, Mass. 02108, USA,
296 Beaconsfield Parade, Middle Park,
Melbourne, 3206, Australia, and
Broadway House, Newtown Road,
Henley-on-Thames, Oxon RG9 1EN

Set in 10pt Baskerville
and printed in Great Britain by
The Thetford Press Ltd
Thetford, Norfolk

Library of Congress Cataloging in Publication Data

Bebek, Borna, 1951–
The third city.
Bibliography: p.
1. Philosophy.
2. Logical positivism—Controversial literature.
I. Title.
B72.B4 1982 100 82-12227

ISBN 0-7100-9042-0

CONTENTS

Acknowledgments vii
Preface ix
Introduction 1

PART ONE: ASPECT AND CONCEPT

1 Dialectic 17
2 Errors of Positivism 33
3 The Critique of Concepts 48
4 A New Materialism 70
5 Plato's *Parmenides* 88
6 The Body of Truth 100

PART TWO: THE THIRD CITY

7 Law of the Heart 129
8 The Ideal World 141
9 Division of Labour 159
10 The Vision of the City 179

PART THREE: *MYTHOS*

11 The Fall 193
12 Curing the City 208
13 The City as the Temple 226
14 Reconciliation 243
Conclusion 248

EPILOGUE

I The Barefoot Philosopher 253
II Immortality 269
III Sentiment 282
Bibliography 289
Index 297

ACKNOWLEDGMENTS

There seem to have been so many people instrumental in the genesis of this work that the designation 'author' is somewhat misleading – 'organizer' might be more appropriate. It was conceived in India, where I was supported by the keepers of Karar Ashram in Puri; further research and transcription took place in Crete, and I would like to thank the Greek government and Ministry of Culture for the grant which made this possible. I am greatly indebted to gurus Hariharananda, Brahmananda and others for hospitality and instruction. The spur to take up formal academic research came from Professor Gadamer of Heidelberg, and the encouragement to persevere came from Professor Morrall of LSE (whose moral character and good nature were a source of inspiration). I am also grateful for the lectures of Sir Fred Hoyle and Peter Park. Euan Cameron and The Bodley Head were the first to assure me I was fit for print, and backed up encouraging words with actions. Platon of Platon's Restaurant in Crete helped me find the cave I believe the son of Ariston wrote about in the dialogues – he and Stelios of Mithi initiated me into the Eleusinian mysteries as they are manifested in the life of Hellas today. Philippa did a marvellous job of deciphering and typing the manuscript; Stratford Caldecott's editing proved invaluable. Santhan and Inran were there to talk to when the going was slow, and Dexter, Igor and Majna to host me when the mood was low. Father Umbala gave the moral guidance, and the builders of the Poseidon temple, Konarak, and the St Nikolaus chapel in Archanes obliged with the architecture.

Peace and honour to them all. *Salve mi professores: salve et vale.*

Borna Bebek
Mithi, Crete
Hellas, 1981

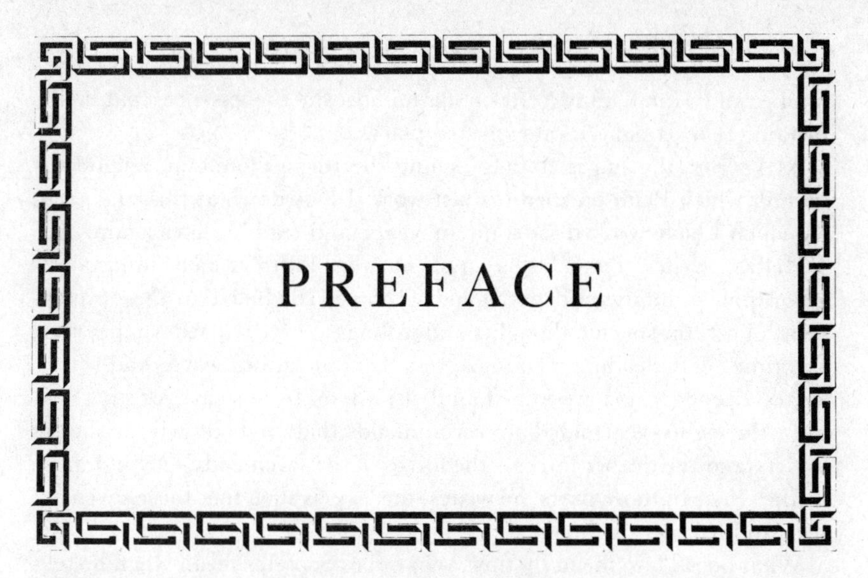

PREFACE

Although I am of Christian background, my family comes from the Muslim-dominated town of Mostar. So Islam to me means early, preconceptual memories of the wailing *Hodga* calling the faithful to prayer. It means rows of bodies swaying rhythmically in tune to an inner corporeal logic, rules which are grasped by the body long before the mind orders these sensations and systematizes them along university lines. In the same way, my understanding of Hinduism is based on the smells, sounds and movements of ritual, and on prolonged non-mental, non-analytic, physical immersion in what amounts to a living organism.

Conventional academics may point out that today's Hinduism or Zoroastrianism is a poor guide to the understanding of the Vedas and Yasnas. Stronger objections yet may be raised against understanding the ancient Greeks or Plato in terms of the mental movements, lights and colours that characterize the Greece of today.

Yet I am not sure. While today's Greeks may not build temples or express themselves in philosophy, anybody who is willing to take the time to observe the self-overcoming, the discipline and the ritual of a Greek wedding banquet, a christening meal or the slow majesty of the Easter procession may yet feel the rhythm of the procession of Panathenea as it was millennia ago. Needless to say such experiences are not to be sought in Bombay or Athens or during a two-week holiday. But in the mountains of the Himalayas the Bhagavad Gita is still being written anew daily, and the reality of which fifth-century BC Athens was a crystallization still exists in the mountains of Crete and of Attica. The spirit of Zen may be observed and experienced through the contemporary tea ceremony; and even the English cup of tea, if correctly made and consumed with due timing and ritual, may contain in microcosm the essence that made Britain great. It hides in unexpected places.

As I write, the sun is sinking behind the Idean mountain, behind the cave in which Plato finished his last work. I look down at this, the *Laws,* on which I have worked for some six years, and read his lines again.

Hellas, writes Plato, is a spot on the Earth which internalizes geographic, climatic and psychological forces conducive to the development of certain specific thoughts and feelings. These will externalize time and time again, leading men to express them in various ways. And yet, he writes, deeper truths are to be found elsewhere. In this cave, or very near to it, the eighty-year-old Plato recommends that anybody who wishes to understand the deeper forces – the forces of the seven gods – should move further east: In those parts, he writes, the 'sky' is such that these seven are seen and felt more strongly.

What does Plato mean by this? What does Socrates mean when he tells Glaucon in the *Republic* that if he is to learn philosophy he must study astronomy, but adds that this astronomy is learned by looking inwards? What does Pythagoras mean when he insists that one must study the numbers within? Aristotle, Plato himself and practically all the subsequent Greek interpreters of Plato repeatedly stress that, for Plato, *Aritmos* (number) was not the object of mathematics. Yet above the entrance of the first and original Academy founded by Plato, there was a sign to the effect that nobody could enter who would not study number. Plato founded the institution so that the facts of number might be known.

Plato and Pythagoras advised that understanding should be sought in the East, where the 'gods are more visible'. This is what I have done. I anticipate sarcastic comments from men grown bitter and cynical through a daily diet of the unnatural and destructive mental exercise of 'logical positivism'. Though I do not feel competent to answer in words some of their expected criticisms of my exposition of Hindu or Zoroastrian thought, concerning Greek philosophy I am prepared to stand behind the statements made: I will welcome any debate in words or print over these matters. As I see it, the case for a 'conceptual' interpretation of philosophical notions such as *Eidos, Logos* or *Periagoge,* is so full of holes that the slightest upset will sink the whole tradition which Western thinkers have carefully built up over the last four centuries. While countless university courses are structured around Plato's theory of ideas, the reader will be hard pressed to find a lecturer in any present-day Academy accounting for the fact that, according to Plato's dialogues, ideas are alive.

Ever since the Renaissance, the bourgeois state has been grooming the 'Greek' edifice to supply respectability and justification to its own institutions. Socialist 'Greek' philosophy is no different, since Soviet and Polish university professors derive their notions from the nineteenth-century Germans, and many Marxists are still too inflexible to open their minds to Eastern or truly Greek thought. In the West, the bourgeois university and democracy is always portrayed as central to 'Western civilization', and as rooted in a Greek model.

'The truth will out', and a lie can be maintained only as long as it is in people's interests to believe it. The 'Greek' myth no longer serves the needs of the dominant section of the European population, for the bourgeois class is no longer a vital force in Europe. From the Renaissance to the twentieth century has been an epoch of merchants, characterized by merchant philosophy and a merchant mentality. Today, a handful of technologues, through their control of the media and the universities, manipulate the world, not by force but by controlling the world's idea of what constitutes the 'good life'.

By determining the music that we hear, the sights and the ideas to which we are exposed, the merchant manipulates our mentality, and consequently our behaviour. While the merchant soul was the dominant mental force of Europe, men could be thus persuaded: however, as matters stand today, the merchant philosophy and the merchant notion of the good life no longer relate to the real needs of England, Germany, Russia or the USA.

This study, however, does not call for a class struggle. The merchant as I shall present him is not a class or a man or a nation. The merchant is within us. The merchant is a particular way of thinking, as present in the Indian Brahmin as he is in the socialist party official. On the other hand, the 'full man', the 'philosopher', the 'Buddha', is also as real and as present in the American coca-cola salesman as he is in the corrupt priest.

In fact, it is in order to stimulate the sense of shame in the businessman who sells us products we do not need, and in order to help induce repentance in the artist turned advertiser that I have written this work. In doing so I have worked to cure myself of the desire for such products, and I hope to affect the reader in the same way. In the words of Socrates, it is to create a stronger conviction in himself that one gives birth to convictions in others. Indeed, as both Hindu thought and Plato make clear, there is no knowledge but shared knowledge: only to the extent that a man creates knowledge in others does he in turn learn, and he is often surprised to find out what his own statement really means.

While every single moment is a moment of change, and every age is an age of change, this particular epoch is one of macro-change, involving a huge shift of mental planes and energies. In such a time of confusion and loss of balance, man looks back, and has always looked back. It is by looking at our roots, at the foundation of that which made us, that we can assess who we are and where we are to go. It is for this purpose that we turn to ancient Hellas, and to that East which, although outside ourselves, is really within.

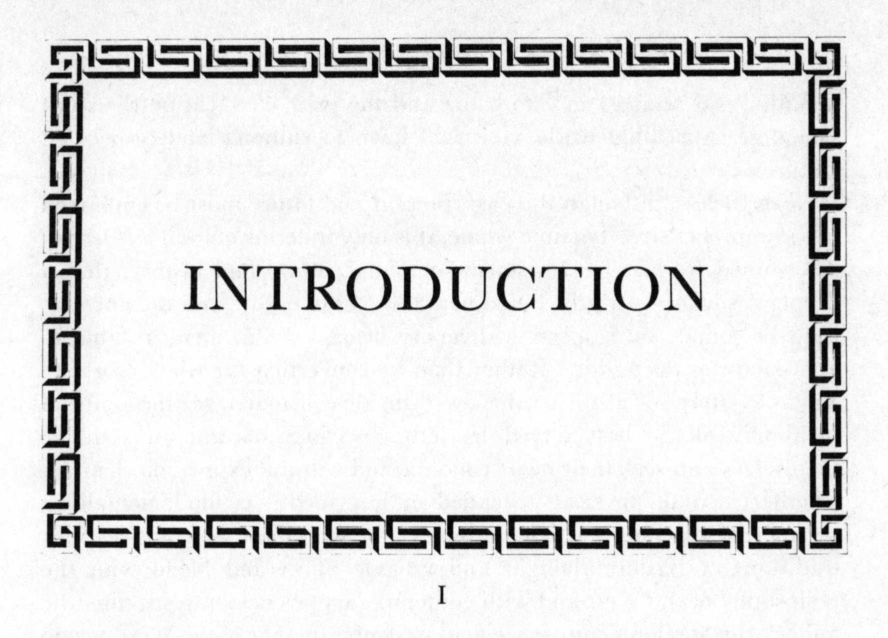

INTRODUCTION

I

The following book is a collage of different ideas. It contains a series of sentences arranged to induce a particular kind of mental activity. That mental activity is the subject, the content and the object of the study.

In order to inject this activity into our own and into social consciousness, I have used as my vehicle themes from ancient Greek and oriental philosophy, and some popular notions of contemporary science.

Although in the course of the study many contemporary notions are criticized, it is not intended as a refutation or critique of any contemporary doctrine, philosophy or set of ideas. It does, however, criticize the mental activity *behind* contemporary systems. In other words, what is wrong with man today is not so much what he thinks as *how* he thinks. Thus, while this work contains some formal ideas and a world view, the world view is not important. To talk we need to use words; to walk we need a direction. Eventually the direction of the author may be discarded: the important thing is to walk gracefully and with dignity.

In order to convey this mental movement, I have resorted frequently to 'foreign', 'distant' and 'ancient' ideas and words (the more unfamiliar being in italic). The view taken here towards the culture and traditions of the East and antiquity does not see them as something 'there', separate from us 'here'. Economically, politically or climatically, the cultural, physical and moral activity exercised in location and period A is not simply a local matter, for it affects the balance of the world at large. Fred Hoyle has pointed out the meaninglessness in astrophysics of 'near' opposed to 'far', or of 'before' opposed to 'after'. What happened in the Crab Nebula millions of years ago affects droughts in the Sudan, famines in India, war strategy in Cambodia and the price of wheat on the stock exchange. A healthy world view will have to embrace and respect all cultures.

Nevertheless, although the past, present and future must be embraced in a comprehensive, dynamic whole, it is only in terms of local *differences,* determined by historical moment, climate, culture and history, that a deeper resonance with the fundamental forces of nature and the universe is to be found. By respecting diversity of expression, men are able to approach this deep unity. Rather than by converting the whole world to Yugoslav-style socialism or the Swedish idea of marriage, the unity of mankind will be best served by letting various natural units define themselves and seek their own economic and cultural expression. Unity – whether mental, physical, extended or imagined – is fundamentally a product of diversity. Although this study will show how the various traditions of Eastern thought and religion affect and blend with the philosophy of the West and with contemporary science, in respecting the 'other', the 'foreign', culture we neither denigrate that of the West nor do we minimize the importance of local tradition.

There is a paradox involved in this. Human psychology in some ways necessitates that man should regard his own set of beliefs as universally valid. Yet there is no need for cynicism: the paradox is conceptual and cannot be avoided. It is not possible to be objective with verbalized beliefs and opinions, and this study is not objective either. Man is condemned to the perspectives of his culture and experience, and to attempt to override them is hubris. The brotherhood or unity that one may hope for is not an objective common ideology, nor a common profession of belief or non-belief in one or another God. All that holds the deeper unity together is a specific 'sentiment'. What this sentiment might be and what it entails is the subject of the study.

Although I shall jump from Niels Bohr to Lao Tzu to Socrates, the point developed is that by studying the thought or discipline of any of these men one can reach compatible, and in some sense identical, conclusions. Thus the method and the conclusions of this study are also in some sense paradoxical: there is a need to keep one's interest within one's own domain and tradition, and yet a need to transcend these; there is a need for formality, but only to enable the over-stepping of formality. I shall not attempt to resolve these contradictions between the law and the heart, the yang and the yin, formal and informal, specialization and diversification – indeed their existence provides the very energy for life, and they will be resolved in different ways by each person in the context of particular situations.

II

One of the assumptions on which this work is based is that the flow of history, rather than being continuous and uninterrupted, takes place through the alternation of well-defined periods, each characterized by a specific mental activity. The twentieth century signifies the end of such a period, which began with the Renaissance and was characterized by the type of thinking I am calling conceptual. The energy that maintained this epoch, as I shall argue, has exhausted its potential: it has fully, or almost fully, expressed itself.

Correspondingly, any science (social or natural) that bases itself on this type of thought relates to a reality that is no more. For this reason the new physics and biology have broken out of the mould, and are based on non-conceptual thought. Artificially preserved by the forces of the State and the market, positivist conceptual thought lives a shadow existence within universities and the research and development departments of industry. Its objective is to produce goods and ideas which do not fulfil any real needs, mental or material.

It is in view of the inadequacy of the tools and methods of contemporary and recent philosophy that I have turned to other cultures and other epochs. Ancient sources may appear a questionable basis for a study in a 'new' kind of thinking. All transitional periods, however, are marked by a certain retrogression: the European barbarians of the centuries shortly after the advent of Christ were in some ways more backward than classical Rome; the Renaissance itself looked back to the Greeks. Indeed, in a transitional period a culture can do nothing else but look for reference in obscure places. We cannot rely on conventional authorities when the 'conventional' is no longer adequate or even relevant.

That Taoists and Hindus are outside the conceptual tradition will, I assume, be readily acknowledged. However, objections may be raised to my seeing the ancient Greeks in this way. Greek thought as taught by the positivist thinkers of Western universities is a conceptualized modification of nineteenth-century scholarship, and is based on the post-Renaissance view of Greece. In other words, notions such as the Platonic ideas, Aristotelian *Hyle* (matter), the Heraclitian *Logos,* are conceptualized modifications bearing no meaningful relevance to the original Greek notions – which I shall interpret by cross-cultural reference to similar notions held by the contemporaries of the Greeks.

III

Another assumption of this study is that in all humanity there exists a set of common characteristics which – although changing – participate in a unifying set of principles which can be called the sentiments.

The particular world view or philosophy which I am using as a vehicle to present these sentiments has been variously described as Philosophia Perennis, Eternal Truth, Saanthana Dharma, Tao *Tien* and the Way of Heaven. In its caricatured form, it is supposed to be presenting two worlds: one the true world of ideas, and the other the perceived world of actuality. While Saanthana arguments have often been used by idealist philosophers in this sense, they have also been used by the materialists. Both idealism and positivist materialism are caricatures of Saanthana.

Since the dominant philosophers after the Renaissance have been either idealists or positivist materialists, one may confidently state that Saanthana thought has not had a major spokesman in the field of philosophy for the last several centuries – even though the tradition has been carried on in spurts, and by isolated individuals, within and without the academic milieu.

The thinkers representing the Saanthana tradition have often been identified, yet the majority of commentators seem to have been unable to determine what holds them together. The essential, unifying principle of all their philosophy is a common ethical 'emotion' – which can also be characterized as a pattern, or as the organizational principle of the universe. This principle has been called Tao in China, *Ahmra* by the Semites, *Ahuna Varya* by the Zoroastrians, AUM by the Hindus and *Logos* by Heraclitus.

All the Saanthana-oriented thinkers posit this Tao as the organizational principle both of the whole universe and of each individual thing. Throughout this tradition it is held that each atom in some sense reflects the entire universe, and that each man is potentially the perfect man, and is made in the image of that perfection. Similarly a city is a microcosmic picture of a State, which itself is a macrocosmic picture of man. Thus there is a Tao for each being and there is a Tao for all. On the individual or micro level, Plato has taken this notion of Tao, as the essential unchanging characteristic which instantiates in time as a particular entity, and called it *Eidos*. It is this *Eidos* which was later misunderstood by Aristotle and radically transformed by the Renaissance to create contemporary concepts of 'idea', 'idealism', etc.

Another way of seeing the *Logos* as a feature of the Saanthana philosophy is in the paradigmatic city. This definitive or model city may take many forms, such as St Augustine's City of God, or Lao Tzu's

Tao-structured family, province or town. It is one of the misunderstood aspects of Saanthana thought – misunderstood because it is necessarily both the absolute, the only, the immediate actuality and yet is also projected into conceptual externality. It is this fact of projection that causes it to be misunderstood. The sage, the philosopher or the prophet must necessarily project the model into externality, for such are the rules of language. Yet the grasp of the model must be immediate and non-conceptual.

Confucius projects his ideal community into the past. Plato projects it into the realm of theory: hence *Bios Theoreticus* or *Vita Contemplativa.* The Vedantic Yogi synthesizes it into a contemplative symbol, such as a complex lotus pattern. In Hindu thought, both Vedanta and Advaita Vedanta project the perfect model into a realm out of time, whereby the realized city instantly reconciles and combines all the perfect instances (incarnations) of the actual cities which have illusorily been seen as reincarnating in history. The New Jerusalem is projected into heaven: in Zen the same reality is projected into inner consciousness as Samadhi. More recently, idealogical thinkers have projected the state of perfect non-alienation or realization into the perfect State of the future.

The distinguishing idea behind all these models is not that the good, the true, the authentic life will take place in the future or in heaven. The paradigmatic model is only a conceptual externalization of an existing inner reality. For the man living in the paradigmatic city, 'there' is already 'here'. These notions are only contradictory in so far as one attempts to understand them conceptually: the 'new' thinking can reconcile them, for it will use a 'different' part of the 'brain'. Indeed the fact that these notions cannot any more be reconciled conceptually proves the need to move into the new mental era, that of noetic thought.

It must be pointed out that, following an initial few decades or centuries, this new way of thinking will again reconceptualize itself, and ideas will again solidify into concepts. Such is the historical circle, and it is this process whereby a burst of creative emanation is followed by a gradual rigidification that characterizes every epoch. Yet circularity does not mean that events repeat themselves. The new conceptualizations will be slightly different: the circular locus is an up-reaching spiral.

IV

To write this study in the form of an interpretation of religion, science and philosophy, as if explaining what Socrates or Jesus – or Fred Hoyle – 'really meant', would contain a dangerous element of idolatry. It would risk leaving the impression that something is 'true' not because the reader or author feels or finds it to be true, but because the author is successful in persuading the reader and himself that he is an authority on the subject.

An alternative to externalized authority would be to appeal to the rules of logic. But in *practice*, the rules of logic – just like the official interpretation of an ideology – reduce, as will become clear, to a few rituals guarded by a particular interest group or political party, imposed either by the police or through control of the universities and the academic media.

'Logical positivism' for example, is a particular brand of tyranny exercised by the industrial state. The industrial market is not opposed to any idea or product which can be packaged and sold. If Yoga means selling Yoga magazines, health food and meditation lessons (an absurdity, like paying an entrance ticket to be allowed to pray), then the logical positivist is not opposed to Yoga. However, any activity which might produce non-commercial vibrations in the brain will be labelled by the same logical positivist as unscientific, false and illogical. For he is not guarding any particular doctrine or idea, but a particular manner of thinking, which in itself is an expression of the market or of the merchant soul in man.

The efforts of contemporary psychologists to make Westerners accept this condition, and feel at peace with the situation, will fail, and have failed. The basic premises are false. These are that man is an individual entity, and that human happiness is increased by maximizing individual consumption, whether of cars and liquor or of ballet, opera and Yoga lessons. The very notion of what it is to be a human is contemporarily based on a conceptual formula – a formula which avoids the ethical dimension. This very manner of thinking is wrong.

It must be emphasized that the word 'positivist' is being used in a projected sense. As already stated, the positivist – called by Plato a sophist – is in fact an internal dimension to each man: a particular sophist – i.e. a sophist in the formal sense – may well be a good fellow. But the internal sophist does also take external expression. In fact, the typical Western thinker of today, whether a psychologist, economic commentator, sociologist or city planner, is just such an external expression of the archetypal logical positivist. Given the 'pluralistic myth', a Western university department employs a token Marxist, a token existentialist, etc. But since it is the logical positivists that control the institution, the person chosen for this role is often a congenial thinker who happens to specialize in Marxism, Buddhism, anarchism or existentialism. For such 'anarchists' and 'Buddhists', being one or the other is indicated by wearing the appropriate clothes and adopting a jargon. Hence the colourful world of the American university, where in the campus café one drinks coffee with Zen Buddhists, Manicheans and dialectical materialists, all appropriately dressed and affecting the corresponding mannerisms. However, beneath the Zen exterior there hides the true-to-form logical positivist, who will – possibly unconsciously – act in such a way as to ensure that no Zen-oriented thought enters the realm of his university work. The typical attitude of a long-haired American 'Zen Buddhist' professor of psychology may be expressed in such statements as: 'I don't care what you write in your final paper – you may be a Trotskiist or a Maoist or argue that Haile Selassie is the second Jesus. But – the paper must contain 5,000 words. It must have an introductory section stating the intention. The argument must be developed so and so. Further, the claims must be supported by data and research stemming from such and such sources. Further, statistical evidence must support any claim. Further, the evidence must be presented in such a way as to be susceptible to cross reference and verification by a Fortran-language-based computer. Since at Amherst we use Fortran and not Cobal, Cobal-oriented data will not be acceptable.' Thus in the USA whether one studies philosophy or psychology, physics or mathematics, one is always studying statistics and the principles of operational research and presentation.

Logical positivists have always shared an assumption that truth can be ascertained by 'positive', exterior criteria. In sociology, truth is therefore the number of ticks in a gallup-style poll; in philosophy, adherence to an arbitrarily constituted matrix called the principles of logic. In Plato's time it was the amount of wealth and power one could amass; in so-called totalitarian states, truth is measured by adherence to the party line.

As opposed to the external criterion of truth – whether holy writ, party line, bank balance, logical matrix or mathematical formula – there stands the internal criterion. Whether something is true or not is determined by inner psychological factors, which as I shall argue are both objective and subjective, both social and individual. This criterion is based on real needs and their satisfaction, needs which may be described as 'material' only if we depart from the positivist conception of matter.

The dogma that the logic and science of the logical positivist is the only true wisdom is nothing more than a period-specific, local opinion. The notion of matter as the ultimate reality belongs to the nascent years of physics and science: the Platonic, Hindu and Taoist view of matter is much more 'scientific', and, indeed, leading contemporary scientific figures are beginning to admit their indebtedness to Eastern thought. Thus Niels Bohr (1958, p. 20) observes:

> For a parallel to the lesson of atomic theory [Bohr is not referring to Dalton's out-of-date positivist atomic theory], we must turn to those

> kinds of epistemological problems with which already thinkers like Buddha and Lao Tzu have been confronted when trying to harmonize our position as spectators and actors in the great drama of existence.

Similarly, J.R. Oppenheimer (1954, pp. 8–9) writes that all the general notions about human understanding 'which are illustrated by discoveries in atomic physics are not in the nature of things wholly unfamiliar, wholly unheard of or new. Even in our own culture they have a history, and in Buddhist and Hindu thought a more considerable and central place.' Heisenberg, too, sees Eastern cosmological views as closer to those of contemporary science than the views of positivist conceptual thought.

Pre-Fregean and even pre-Aristotelian systems of logic, such as the four systems of the Rig Veda, or Platonic logic based on the vibration of the soul matrix, are also more sophisticated, and more helpful, than the limited logic of the positivist social sciences, and they will be found to suit the needs of the new type of thinking that lies behind the emerging physics. For them, the ethical factor is inseparable from the truth-validity of a statement. A contemporary physicist, Fritjof Capra, opens his book *The Tao of Physics* by observing that if a method is a 'path without heart' it is not true: again a sweeping statement, but one which anybody who has been exposed to Eastern thought will immediately understand. On this criterion the path of much contemporary thought is fundamentally and finally false.

The positivist philosopher is not actually *living* in the world: nor will his philosophy help anybody else to do so. His task is to interpret the world rather than participate in it. Hence Marx's statement: 'Historically all that philosophers have done was to interpret the world – the point, however, is to change it'. For reasons elsewhere elaborated, I find the concept of 'changing' the world to be nineteenth-century specific, and have substituted the notion of 'living philosophically', or 'actively participating in the world'. The Pythagorean brotherhood not only developed mathematics and the arts of music, war and city planning: they were active politicians, and came to rule Sicily, Croton and many city states. The idea of the ruler-philosopher is of course central to Plato's thought, and an analysis of Plato's institution – the Academy – will reveal it responsible for rulers of all kinds: generals, tyrants and democrats. The idea of separating secular from spiritual power is a post-Renaissance development, integral neither to Europe nor to Christianity: correct philosophy or logic is instantly practicable and applicable, in one's own life as in affairs of State: the separation of theory and praxis is a bourgeois invention.

Active participation in the world does not necessarily mean practical interference in the everyday affairs of men. Socrates and the recluse monk are actively engaged in the 'actual' life of the *Polis* because they are umbilically and psychologically connected to it, whereas the isolated conceptual university philosopher is not. The conceptual thinker is on his own: conceptual thought is self-gratifying and, as such, in the deepest sense sterile. While physically separate, a recluse monk through his erotically and noetically based 'thought' is emotionally and mentally an inseparable part of the *Polis,* and is conditioned by it. What he thinks affects the *Polis,* whether the *Polis* likes it or not, and he suffers and is affected by the thoughts and ideas of the *Polis.*

An Indian sadhu living and meditating in the Himalayas is not running away from the world. He withdraws into solitude to integrate himself with the world. On the other hand, a conceptualist theoretician or an ivory-tower philosophy professor is a fugitive from the world: he is made so by the very nature of his isolating mental activity. Conceptual thought stuns the ethical faculty in the mind: the exercise of his skill serves to sever the bonds that bind him to his city, his family, the fishes in the sea and the trees in the forest.

It is this empirical necessity that makes it essential to almost entirely dismiss the post-Renaissance manner of thought, and to seek the roots of the 'new' kind of thought elsewhere. As pointed out by Chuang Tzu, to jump you must retreat to gain the ground.

The epoch dominated by logical positivism is spent. In music, it culminated in the eighteenth and nineteenth centuries; in painting it reached its peak even earlier, and in literature it climaxed with the nineteenth-century novel. Developments since then have been a gradual fall into decadence. The last aspect of the conceptual era to peak was technological, and its high points were reached in the USA, culminating in the moon shot. To land men on Venus will be an effort as anticlimactic as an attempt to outdo Beethoven in symphony, da Vinci in painting or Hegel in conceptual philosophy. Modern philosophy, like modern painting, opera or poetry (with some honourable exceptions), in the main reduces to drawing moustaches on the Mona Lisa, and at worst to pornography.

The ancient Romans saw progress as the endless improvement of the quality of roads, aqueducts, transport, building techniques, trade – activities in which they excelled. For them it was inconceivable that the way of savage barbarians, the Germanic, Slavic and Romanic tribes, could be superior. The Romans' failure lay in their inability to grasp that their marvellously sophisticated aqueducts, trade mechanisms, book-keeping and legal structures were all rooted in the slave-owning system. It was the core, the root, the basis of the system which was spent.

So it is with the conceptual era. The mental energy, the mental activity which has characterized and given birth to it is almost fully realized. It has expressed itself in music, in art, in technology: it desires no more expression. It has to go: it is gone.

V

Before concluding this introduction and beginning the exercises conducive to the new way of thinking, we should consider more closely the brand of inclinations that brings together the thinkers of the Saanthana tradition.

In this work it is not our intention to prove specific points, such as that Greek philosophy is essentially Zoroastrian. Rather, in the words of the English poet-philosopher Cornford (1948, p. 176):

> Whether we accept or not the hypothesis of a direct influence of Persia on the Ionians in the 6th century, no student of Orphic or Pythagorean thought will fail to see between it and the Persian religion such close resemblances that we can regard both systems as expressions of one and the same conception of life, and use either of them to interpret the other.

Cornford's suggested 'influence of Persia on the Ionians' is precisely the kind of generalization I want to avoid. In the case of Greek, Persian and Indian thought, Boyce (1979, p. 17) argues that 'these often identical myths, symbols, words and philosophies do not necessarily indicate copying, borrowing or intellectual exchange, but rather are a result of common cultural background.' Preferable, perhaps, is Mircea Eliade's (1958) attribution of similarities in myth, ritual and dogma between the various religions to 'certain universal climatic, astronomical and psychological constants', rather than to cross-cultural influence. In the hope of bringing this out, quotations will be drawn from Taoist and Confucian as well as Middle Eastern and Indian sources. Stress on common etymological roots for *Asha, Ṛta,* world order, justice, Dharma, *Humen,* Amen, AUM, *Amete* can sometimes distract attention from a deeper, non-etymological universality of ideas.

The aspectual thinkers who represent this universality are all religious, in some sense of the word. But unlike linear thinkers, who subscribe to the local notion of God (i.e. God as the unit of notional currency of their particular culture and period), the hallmark of a Confucius or a Kierkegaard is a certain attitude towards life, not a verbal profession of faith. Shared by all religious philosophy is the hidden, perhaps unsubstantiated, assumption that life is not what it should be; that man is fallen, estranged or alienated. Further, the religious thinker assumes that there is a basic pattern to man, who should be guided to come closer to its full realization. The religious attitude also requires a cosmology where every individual gain is a common gain, and every loss a common loss. Merlan (1970, p. 24) attributes an extreme version of this doctrine to Plotinus, and calls it the 'Unicity of the cosmos whereby all its parts are in sympathy'; he goes further, to see this as explanatory of paranormal phenomena, telekinesis, etc. Merlan's argument is based on the *Timaeus* (34, 35), where Plato describes the cosmos as one living organism. Neoplatonism apart, the central point stands quite independently of any hylozoistic intimations, and it affirms simply that individual and general interests always coincide. This co-incidence of interest, however, takes place on a higher plane: to perceive this plane, and to integrate into it one's action on the lower level, is the objective which unites St Augustine's philosophy with that of Ramanuja or Valmiki.

None of this implies that 'linear' philosophy has other than ethical objectives. Plato states explicitly that *all* striving is striving for the good, and a perceptive mind will value all philosophy as the rational expression of this striving. However, to reconcile the thought of the contemporary language analyst or the nineteenth-century utilitarian with that of Ramanuja or Zoroaster would require some considerable conceptual and notional facility. The philosophies of Plato and Ramanuja, by contrast, need not even be called 'different' ways of expressing the same thing: most of the time they are the *same* ways of expressing the same thing. Blocks of passages or whole chapters of their writings could be readily intermixed or blended – given philological rather than conceptual flexibility.

Having established that these thinkers are persistently making the same point, and in more or less the same language, I shall generally tend to refer to Plato. This is not because he is an authority: Plato was just an encyclopaedist of various ideas present in Greece. These ideas are also the ideas of Pythagoras and of the Zoroastrians: in fact in Plato's Academy it was claimed (by Eudoxus) that Plato was Zoroaster in his sixty-sixth reincarnation. In the same way, the Indian thinker Ananda assumed that Plato was one of the six gurus of the Sikh tradition. Islamic thinkers assumed that Plato was Moses talking Attic: the leading Islamic theologians based their studies in theology on Plato, and it was through them that Renaissance Europe rediscovered him.

Plato was not, however, welcomed by the Muslims because he was particularly persuasive: neither did St Augustine create the dogmas of Christianity through having been 'persuaded' by Plato. The Muslims used Plato only because they realized that he was saying what they believed in anyway.

Apart from his role as spokesman for Philosophia Perennis, Plato is of little interest to anyone: indeed he is of no interest to himself – hence the works he wrote *as Plato* were not kept by history, nor did he make any effort to ensure that these were preserved. He did as a young man write poetry and drama, and even won prizes for it: it is these works that he signed and considered his own. As for Plato's philosophy, his dialogues, it was others who attributed them to him. Plato attributes all his arguments to Parmenides, Protagoras and primarily to Socrates. Some scholars maintain that Plato used Socrates and others as spokesmen to project his own views, but I do not agree. He himself tells us that the ideas are not his own, and for anybody who has busied himself with the particular manner of thought behind the dialogues the reasons for this will be clear. The responsible writer of this type of philosophy is always the one who best manages to suppress his own views, rather than to expound them. (To emphasize the fact that Plato wrote in dialogue form – and the ever-present danger in quoting out of context – I have left quotation marks around the extracts from his work.)

The Saanthana tradition is characterized by a division of labour. There are two kinds of people: the paradigmatic thinkers, and the writers or compilers of their thoughts. Socrates, Buddha or Lao Tzu, Vijasa (responsible for the Bhagavad Gita), Valmiki (the Ramayana) or Zoroaster (the Yasnas) – none of these were authors. The paradigmatic thinkers do not write: they inspire others to do so. Behind the name Zoroaster there are probably five or six people writing and editing, as for any of the others. Socrates gives birth to a notion: Plato writes it down. In the case of Plato, we happen to know the name of the editor, though not through any effort on Plato's part. In the Saanthana Dharma tradition, the compiler always attributes the argument to the Eudaimonic Perceptor – the true giver of arguments. We do not know for sure who the people are who wrote down the Gospels: nor is it important.

To some extent, of course, it was not possible for Plato to deny himself completely. It is for this reason that his arguments sometimes fail. Plato's objections to democracy and his aristocratic prejudices are examples of his own personality breaking through, and there his arguments are correspondingly warped and invalid. The following study will also be warped and deviate from Saanthana thought in so far as the present editor was not able to control for his own personality: it is my own only to the extent that it is false. It is not easy to deny oneself, and not everybody can do it: it is only to paradigmatic thinkers that thoughts come effortlessly – 'they fall off by themselves, like ripe fruit'. This is why Plato so admired Socrates, and was fascinated by the ease and grace with which he produced his arguments. The paradigmatic thinker, being free from pride, greed and desire, is given his insight painlessly: rarely is he educated or highly qualified in any formal sense. Not suffering from any desire to prove that he is clever, he adds no unnecessary verbiage to his speech, or unnecessary education to his life experience. Socrates not only refused to write as a matter of principle: we learn from Xenophon that his spelling was that of a child – he could barely read or make out letters. Jesus may well have been illiterate, as was Mohammed: but their lack of formal education did not hamper their ability to deliver their message.

Paradigmatic thinkers are few in any age, but there are many highly educated men like Plato ready to record their thoughts. It is enough for the paradigmatic thinker to sit down in the square and talk to the grocer: some Plato will inevitably turn up to write down and organize.

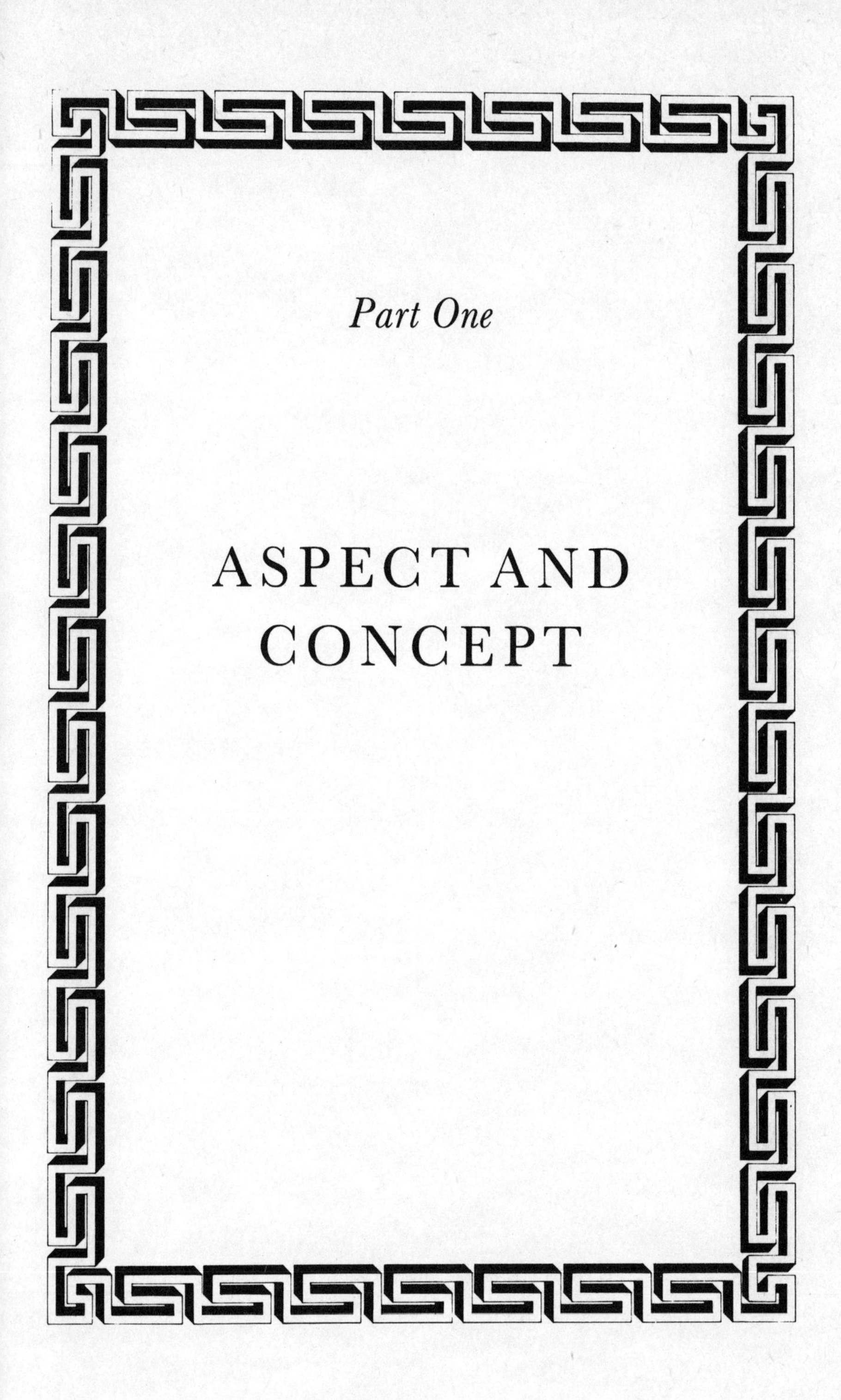

Part One

ASPECT AND CONCEPT

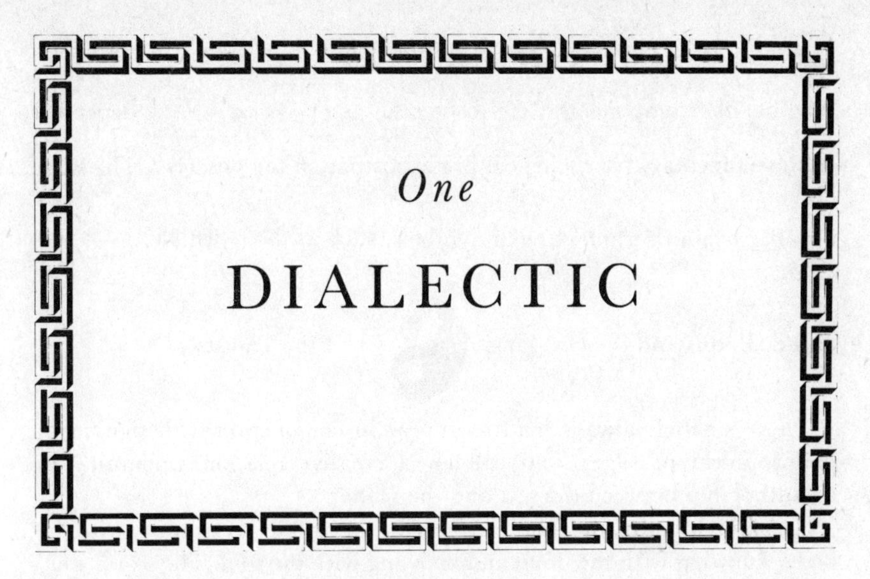

One
DIALECTIC

This study will examine some factors affecting and regulating our processes of apprehension.

Broadly speaking these processes may be seen in three basic sets of relationships. Although one may be loose and flexible in one's wording when describing them, the factors behind them are neither loose nor relative. Indeed, it will be claimed that these three different kinds of knowing are rooted in fundamental universal realities relating to the three kinds of time, and apply equally to the forces constituting the psychological and the physical universe.

The triunal divisions are subtle, and cannot be specified in a single introductory sentence for reasons which will become apparent as the study unfolds. Stated briefly, the three constitutive principles and corresponding cognitive faculties range into one another in such a way that any one can stand for any of the other two at any moment. As they take place in three kinds of time, the relations are in fact a set of $3 \times 3 \times 3$ permutations. The decision as to which particular relationship is being considered demands an active participation by the reader, and cannot be subject to a single definition. This point was illustrated by the meanders at Delphi: the patterns surrounding the sign 'Know yourself' were such that the apprehension of shapes and direction were to be determined 'aspectually':

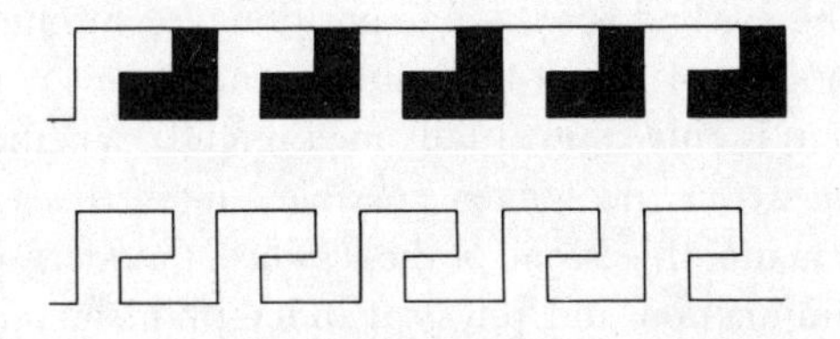

Whether the components were to be seen as or depended on the momentary psychological predisposition of the observer. The same idea lies behind certain circular symbols, such as the swastika

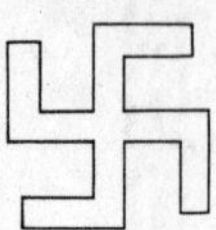

of the Hindus and the yin–yang

of the Taoists.

These symbols always tend to appear in conjunction with significant philosophical passages, and call for a creative relation amounting to co-authorship between the text and the reader.

Speaking broadly, the three modes of knowing refer to knowing with the body, knowing with the mind and knowing with the soul. The word 'soul' is somewhat unfortunate, yet to refer to 'psyche' or '*Jiva*' may at this early stage prove equally misleading. Knowing with the soul and knowing with the body are the legitimate ways of knowing, whereas knowing mentally refers only to the reconciled representation of the first two. This relationship holds for a correctly functioning cognitive apparatus: otherwise the three are at odds.

Within the tradition that I shall follow, the body and mind are in a sense equal; seen from a different aspect, so are the body and the soul. In order to avoid the ambiguities stemming from these divisions, it is necessary at first to resort to some simplification. The body-knowing faculty will be fused with that of the soul to create a single cognitive mode. This fused entity will be counterposed to the faculty of the mind. The division and the fusion are only conjectural and contextually valid. Reducing the triple cognitive matrix to duality in this way will give us a basis for rediscovering the triunal relationship. Only then will we be in a position to see the cognitive faculties in terms of a procedural unity. (The technique of provisional isolation for the purposes of definition, while observing interrelationships within a system, is called *Diaresis–Simploke* (disjunction–conjunction) by Plato, and takes the form of S-matrix interpretation in quantum physics.)

Provisional definition may seem unsatisfactory to a mind grown accustomed to the methodology and expositional techniques of the epoch of conceptual thought. It must be pointed out, however, that 'progress' (another word that is only contextually meaningful), whether in science or philosophy or in art, is no longer possible unless this epistemological breakthrough is made: this is one of the lessons of modern physics.

The Delphic injunction and physical indeterminism both call for the observer to make constant adjustments in his understanding: through redefinition the actor/spectator corrects and adjusts for the interference created in the system by the very fact that it is being analysed. Unlike Descartes, who assumed that the I which asks questions about itself can, while doing so, remain fixed and unchanging, its nature and existence deducible from objective self-observation, this study will define its units only in terms of tendencies.

I

Man's two cognitive faculties are referred to in the Upanishads as *Buddhi* and *Manas*, while the Greeks call them *Noesis* and *Dianoia*. Plato defines *Dianoia* as thought based on abstract images and symbols, while *Noesis* is thought rooted in true entities (*Republic,* 510–511).

There is a particular tendency that is specific to all *Logos*-oriented philosophy: provisionally it may be called the principle of teleological or end-oriented aspectuality. The word 'aspectual' (or transaspectual) seems appropriate, because noetic activity is concerned with creating notional unities from the different dimensions, or aspects, of conceptually separate phenomena. The word 'principle' may unfortunately be misleading when applied to the activity itself, which is a tendency or conation, but can be used here in connection with this tendency to the extent that the argument of this study develops a 'rhyme' or a 'conviction' that this aspectual 'flow' should indeed replace the unnatural mode of apprehension. Thus aspectual apprehension can be regarded both as a prescriptive principle of thought and as a tendency; as the latter it can be seen as a confluence of *constant and fixed entities;* these entities will elsewhere be defined and described in some detail as the sentiments.

In speaking of the sentiments, I shall not use a single word but alternatively *Pathos, Logos,* Tao, *Pneuma,* depending on the tradition within which the notion is being examined. Rather than specifying my notional currency through definition – writing, for example, as someone has, that apprehension is a 'cognitive process which consists of the mental synthesis of data supplied by the senses so as to create objects' – I shall try to avoid definitions as much as possible, for it is precisely such techniques that characterize the mode of thinking which I accuse of being deficient. My meaning will be contextually and rhythmically determined.

As an example, the word 'rhyme' as used above (to suggest knowing rhythmically, rather than by conviction or persuasion) will probably prove startling to the reader: instead of going forward or back in search of a definition of 'rhyme', he should simply accept the half-developed connotation and the ambiguity, which should resolve itself elsewhere. A look at Zen literature will show it to contain various unexpected and undefined words which create a deliberate tension (a Koan in Buddhist thought, *Tonos* in Heraclitus). These tension-building paradoxical insertions are not intended to confuse or arrest the flow of thought; for the reader is expected gradually to develop his own definitions.

On the other hand, unlike the work of a poet or creative writer, this study does not make use of invented words, nor does it resort to bending the language to create a specific effect. Such procedures require great insight, for if these deviations are to be valid they need to be based on a deeper truth. For the most part, the words and notions I use have a long history of meaning. To know rhythmically was the object of education in *Li,* practised in ancient China. As we learn from Confucius and Cratylus, even the sounds and letters that compose words are not arbitrary but relate to material and psychological constants. (Rectification of government, argues Confucius, must be preceded by rectification of names.) However, it is only those people who are sensitive in a particular way who can sense the rhythmic meaning of the letters of a word and correctly translate or transcribe it. Unable to do this (i.e. to render the old words correctly), I will use a variety of the original words and original sounds, 'machine-gun style', in anticipation that one of them, or a combination, may hit the mark and activate the reader's deeper layers of consciousness.

Occasionally, where appropriate, some of the implicit arguments are summarized and presented in a more closely structured form. These 'definitions' tend to demand the participation of the reader. In fact, the reader may disagree with them. My purpose was to bring together specific mental movements arising in various periods and traditions. In doing this, I could only synthesize and organize them by following certain individual, and thus prejudicial, inclinations: I am more likely to be close to Lao Tzu or Plato when simply imitating their style of exposition than when actually summarizing their message. Thus, although throughout this study conclusions are drawn, these conclusions are not necessarily correct.

But I am not saying simply that each reader should form his own conclusions, all conclusions being equally valid or truth subjective. Quite the contrary: as Socrates has established, were words not objective, we could not talk. The perennial philosophy is not mere relativism.

Nor should the reader feel frustrated or overcritical if a specific explanation or definition does not occur at a particular place which he finds appropriate; for it is also possible that it is he, not the author/editor, who is rhythmically out of step. Indeed, the meaning of a statement is radically affected by its positioning within a broader argument. Sometimes ambiguous placement is called for.

The technique of inserting paradoxical words or arguments, and relying on rhythm as the organizational factor in psychological logic, is developed to its limit in the Koran. There one finds at various places different unintelligible words and sounds, such as *Alif, Lim, Mim.* To this day nobody has discovered their objective meaning, nor is anybody trying to do so – they are understood subjectively and contextually. Again, the Koran does not follow a chronological development of exposition, nor are the surahs organized by conceptually defined themes or subjects. A discussion on immaculate conception is suddenly interrupted, to be followed by the rules regarding trade and ritual washing, yet picked up again in some other surah which was revealed to Mohammed perhaps several years later.

It is incorrect to assume that the style of such compositions is random or subjective. As Lao Tzu says, he that would listen ought to be yielding, and follow the flow of water: this flow, we learn from Plato, is an inner flow of consciousness. By relaxing the conceptually conditioned mind, a contemporary reader may enter into a resonance with the rhythm of the Koran or Tao Te Ching. As the theory of lasers has shown, a coincidence of crests and amplitudes in light waves creates a highly coherent and potent beam of light. And so it is with noetic brain-waves. A relaxed reader of Buddhist or Hindu sutras will feel a sudden coincidence of his mental activity with the rhythm of the text, instantly comprehending and verifying issues which might otherwise prove obscure. This coincidence in pitch is called by Plato *Diarithmesis,* while the (rhyming) technique of writing in a rhythmically logical way can be called 'corybantic'. This technique induces a movement in the mind, as do the visual patterns in a Zen garden; these issues will be dealt with in due time.

This study consequently makes use of the specific rhythmical expositional technique that is variously referred to in the East as the spiral or the wheel, and used in music and speech, in mantras and in city construction. Ravel took the technique over from the Arabs, and grafted it on to a Western piece of music to create the work called *Bolero.* In terms of music, the Bolero technique involves the reamplification of the main theme, which is introduced by a single instrument, relying on a 'linear exposition'. The theme is repeated by two instruments. As more instruments are added, the linear harmony dissolves. Careful listening will reveal that no single instrument carries the tune any more, and many are in fact playing different tunes: even so, the listener, if sufficiently concentrated, hears the same tune.

Ravel, working within the Western tradition, could follow the technique only thus far. The mantric or Bolero development, when properly executed and properly received, leads to the listener's perceiving one tune as several tunes and vice versa. It is only on the objective level that one can claim that the same mantra is being repeated over and over again. Subjectively experienced, however, by variation of pitch, rhythm and melody, a single mantra can express the unity of the cosmos.

Plato resorts to this technique in his corybantic or mantric dialogue, the *Parmenides.* There he repeats a single notion in nine different ways, each time becoming less and less intelligible, and culminating by writing nonsensical sentences such as 'One is and is not both young and old but is neither young nor old, nor is he not young or not old, nor is it not here nor is it not there,' etc., eventually concluding that:

> 'whether there is or is not a one, both that one and the others alike are, and are not, and appear and do not appear, to be all manner of things in all manner of ways with respect to themselves and one another' (*Parmenides*, 166[b]).

Since the method of exposition determines the content of that which is exposed (such is my thesis), I was necessarily led to employ such techniques, even though mistakes may have been made. Owing to inexperience on my part, jolts will be felt even by rhythmically sophisticated readers. But imperfect as this attempt may be, it seemed best in view of the subject matter to avoid following the laws and rules of conceptually constructed studies.

II

In the Upanishads we learn that all thoughts and things are made of the same stuff, and that the formation of both thought and 'concrete' things follows the same principles. Lao Tzu observes that 'One begot two. Two begot three. And three begot the ten thousand things' (Tao Te Ching, XLII). Likewise, knowledge is universally seen by noetic thinkers as generated from the conflict of two factors variously described as the 'stiff and the loose', yang and yin or *To Peras* and *Aperion.* Although Plato does not assign gender to them ('the one and the indefinite', also known as 'limit and unlimit'), Aristotle (1965, 987–988) refers to them as male and female principles. They are associated with right and left respectively, and it is interesting that the contemporary political connotations of right and left, even though claimed to stem from different sources, carry compatible notional connotations.

This dialectical view was imperfectly simplified by Hegel, who used it to interpret history. Plato and Confucius had stressed that the dialectical relationship should not be one of the temporal succession of the 'right and left', but rather a perpetual simultaneous reconciliation. Hegel, on the other hand, while professing to have learned the secrets of dialectic from the dialogue *Parmenides,* horizontalized it: whether in speech, in politics or in philosophy, there arises first of all a specific formulation or 'thesis' which takes a certain amount of historical time. After it is opposed by an 'antithesis' there is a new development – the synthesis. After another passage of time the synthesis becomes a thesis. In some sense Hegel has captured the yin–yang, left–right dynamic; yet in trying to make it conceptually attractive and objectively presentable he has simplified it almost to the point of irrelevance. For noetic thought, the *To Peras–Aperion* dialectic involves the whole cosmos: each and every cell and molecule. It is the dialectic between earth and heaven, and between two types of time (mental and cosmic). Seeing it in terms of historical, i.e. mental-conceptual, time, Hegel has captured but a vague glimpse.

A further simplification of the dialectical principle implies that this historical conflict of opposites is to be resolved at some unspecified date in the future. The noetic tradition from which Hegel borrows his model sees this resolution (elsewhere called the Omega point) as a model or an instrument of reconciliation between *Ekei* – there (*Tien,* heaven) – and here. To imply that the reconciliation takes place 'then' and not now is to misunderstand the whole tradition. There cannot be a reconciliation 'then' or 'there'; the whole point of reconciliation is that yang should meet yin, *there* should meet *here*, 'Thy will be done on earth as it is in heaven'. For noetic thought, dialectics cannot involve an Aristotelian or Hegelian maturation in time. The reconciliation is always in the 'now'. Indeed, even the notion 'now' is misleading, for it implies a stage inserted between there and then, tomorrow and yesterday.

Since noetic thought does not grant legitimacy to tomorrow and yesterday, neither can it grant legitimacy to now. 'Existential' notions such as the dictum that 'There is nothing but now,' so that we are free of obligations to our children, and also free of obligations to history and tradition, are as foreign to Confucius as they are to Socrates. Confucius sees within each man a unit comprising all his ancestors, and Socrates sees in himself the unity of all the men who are to be born. Indeed, for noetic thinkers living does not take place then, there or now.

We may well ask when and where men do live. The answer is that they live in the future and in the past and now, or all at the same time; or, more correctly, that when they live at all they live out of time.

Naturally, such a question often faces noetic thinkers. (The paradoxes raised provide a momentum for the type of thinking that eventually forces the mind to start operating aspectually.) But noetic answers cannot easily be conveyed in writing, and most noetic thinkers have refrained from expressing themselves thus. Lao Tzu, the so-called father of Taoism, never taught by positive instruction, nor was he willing to put any of his teaching into writing unless forced to do so. Buddha never wrote, and, apart from writing with his finger in the sand (before the woman taken in adultery), no report has been given of Jesus ever having written. Mohammed, of course, did dictate a book; but this was composed rhythmically and corybantically. That is why the Koran cannot be translated and has to be read – or sung – by rhythmically sensitive readers. The most important messages cannot be verbalized.

To explicate this notion we turn to the 'maieutic' (birth-giving) technique used by Socrates. Rather than conveying a positive message of his own, Socrates was interested in assisting at the birth of each man's insights (*Theaetetus*, 149^{a-e}), clearing the mental obstacles and breaking the conceptual rigidities that arrest the 'aspectual' manner of thought. For example, in the dialogue *Sophist*, Plato is particularly concerned with diagnosing the nature of the incorrect manner of thought. The uncreative, 'non birth-giving' mind is seen as operating in terms of ready-made semblances, or *Eikones* (*Sophist*, 235^{c}, 266^{d}). These *Eikones*, or concepts and opinions, are frozen blocks of observations which are used indiscriminately on the false assumption that they are universally applicable. False thinking, according to Socrates, consists in using a set of conclusions which came to birth in one precise and unique situation in conjunction with another situation (*Sophist*, 269^{a-e}). It is for this reason that Socrates 'refutes' his interlocutors, to rid them of those false and preconceived assumptions that tend to arrest the autonomous process of thought. The 'unrefuted' mind thinks mediately in terms of ready-made images, using as currency not real entities but arrested mental semblances: *Eikones* and phantasms (*Sophist*, 266^{b-e}).

We can assume on the evidence available from Xenocrates and Aristophanes that the historical Socrates conducted his dialogues in the sense described here as aspectual; that is, he was concerned to actively demonstrate the inadequacy of a mode of apprehension based on pre-formed conceptualizations in favour of a process of self-generated insight. We should expect the failure of any attempt at written re-creation of such activity, whether through the literal transcription of questions and answers or by the use of definition. Literal transcription may descriptively illustrate the 'outer' dimension of such discourse, but it does not enact the aspectual dimension.

Generally speaking we can assert that a transposition in media, from thought to conversation or from an actual conversation to drama or literature, necessarily forbids literal rendering, if its objective is to convey a non-formalistic content as well as to indicate the activity behind the content. In aspectual philosophy, the characteristic elements are the process by means of which the search for solutions is to be conducted, and the nature of the solution itself. The progeny of this activity differ radically from those of the conceptual search for a philosophical definition, such as, 'Matter is substance permanently extended in time and space'. An aspectual type of conclusion has no extra-contextual validity. Thus the aspectual solution is unique, for one time only, and may be grasped only instantaneously within the movement of the argument itself. Indeed, stated in any other context, the conclusion transgresses the limits of attention.

III

Throughout this study the reader must bear in mind that in freeing themselves from conceptualized, frozen units, noetic thinkers are not deobjectifying the process of thinking. The mind, in order to operate, needs to grip on something; it needs rules, guidelines and a currency. Noetic thought does not perpetually invent new rules; the rules are there all the time. The mind (to use imagery from the Vedas) is like a lake which is constantly being covered up by weeds and algae, which seal off the surface, cut off the sun and stifle the life within the lake. The weeds, the blockage, the debris that imprison the mind are the frozen images, and these must daily and diligently be cleaned and weeded out. Once freed from the debris, the mind can perceive the *true* rules which are always there. The rules which regulate the correct working of the mind are, as stated, certain psychological constants. These rules are firmly related both to man's essential needs and to the laws of physics.

In other words, the correctly functioning mind operates in harmony and according to the constants governing the flow of blood and the workings of the human body. The correctly functioning mind will not appreciate ideas or activities that are damaging to heart or liver, or to the family, society or the cosmos at large. The correctly functioning mind interprets and operates in terms of the essential needs of man as he truly is. To perceive one's deeper interest is to think correctly.

Any insight-giving discourse incorporates a temporal and rhythmic dimension of its own. Further, to have relevance to our deeper interests, it must be rooted in the realities by means of which we can satisfy these essential needs. Much contemporary thought has tended to see satisfaction as subject to the development of external givens, such as the means of production or changes in the environment. Saanthana thought incorporates change, and weds it to a deeper, inner, psychological reality. Thus the growth rate of corn, the rate of fission of an atomic nucleus and the roll of the waves on the sea reduce to constant, fixed and objective mathematical functions. The spread of electrons and the branching of nerve currents within the cortex of the brain are likewise subject to the same mathematical functions, the log of e, so-called natural numbers and a score of other rhythmic constants. The operations of the mind, the rate of seasonal interchange, the seven-day week and the rhythm of daily work are all subject to fixed values.

In a scientifically based study of the patterns of nature, P.S. Stevens surveys the constants ruling the construction of the universe. He bases his work on that of Zimmermann ('How Sap Moves in Trees'), Strahler's erosional topology, the Reynolds Number, various studies in the dynamics of fluids and quantum theory. All these are used to demonstrate a basic thesis: that the creation of all units, biological, mental, microcosmic or galactic, is subject to a limited number of constants. Thus Stevens (1977, p. 3) is led to observe that 'Nature acts like a theatrical producer who brings on the same players each night in different costumes for different roles. . . . Nature uses only a few kindred forms in so many contexts.'

Our deeper needs and psychology, and these same cosmic constants, determine how we create notions and concepts and how we construct our logic. While our conceptual grasp of the world changes from age to age, the process of apprehension itself does not change, and it is this that is under examination here. The way we satisfy our needs changes, the needs themselves vary slightly, yet there is a dimension of them that remains constant. In this connection it is observed by Marx (1952, p. 67) that 'Natural laws can absolutely not be abolished. What can change in different historical states is only the form in which these laws take effect.' As the Koran says, 'Every age has its scripture', yet 'His is the eternal Book'.

There are two sets of human needs. First, there are the needs of man ontologically considered as an individual entity; second, the needs of man considered as a social being. The man determined by the former criteria is a man determined positively and empirically. His needs, and correspondingly his thinking and his logic, are rooted in the conceptual mind, *Manas*. The thinking of *Manas* is determined by the 'stomach', or rather by the stomach-based soul. This curious Hindu designation is repeated by the Zoroastrians and by Plato, who likewise sees the mind (*Dianoia*-based thought) as controlled by the *Thorax* (soul) and by *Epithumia* (meaning desire – Hindus use the word *Kama,* which means desire, greed or lust).

'Stomach' logic is of two types: (1) the direct, immediate, healthy logic of the real body, and (2) the 'aberration logic', which is its mentally perverted image. Aberration in the satisfaction of any need is the satisfaction of that need through a non-corresponding organ or activity. A modern parallel is the search for the satisfaction of the need for companionship through the consumption of material goods – food, cars, etc.

So lower-body logic is only a mental interpretation of bodily need. It is through the interjection of the mind into the body that healthy needs are mentalized and formulated into *Eikones.* To put it another way, the craving, unsatisfied body projects its genuine needs into *Manas.* Deflected by greed these needs mutate, creating a man who is falsely constituted. Objectified as mental rules, rhythms and images, needs are reduced to fixed, familiar conceptual patterns, constantly recognized rather than newly created.

Opposed to this, there is the aspectual way of *Elenchos,* which is not based on instantly recognizable patterns. *Elenchos* constructs discourses according to a set of rules which I shall define as the rules of number, sentiment and human interest – where the human being is not empirically and individually determined. For a discourse to be creative, it must follow these rules.

(This study makes considerable use of the word 'sentiment', and at the outset we must avoid misunderstanding by establishing what sentiment is not. Moral and ethical factors must be instrumental in the creation of thought. Sentiments are vehicles or modes of communication with the ethical element of our psyche. They are not to be equated with emotions or passions: such are the currency of poets and artists. Emotions are only the body mind's or body soul's reflection of sentiments. Sentiments are noetic creations, and are concerned with the aspect of the psyche which is called by the Hindus and by Plato the ruling or cephalic (head) soul. The objective of this study is to point to the deficiency of objective, positivist thought: the intention will misfire if it is seen as favouring the emotional, i.e. poetic, approach to knowledge. Passions are 'parekbasitic' aberrations – i.e. similar but counter-images – of sentiment. For all the reasons given by Plato, artists and poets are irresponsible people, and indeed they must be so to be effective: they stun the noetic part so as to be more receptive to the passions. Thus they must be controlled and directed, for their sentiments are not operating.)

H.G. Gadamer (1973) notes that insight-generating dialogues have a relational validity: they are not to be understood without reference to compatible issues and to the broader themes that move beneath. Such dialogues are movements that transcend a particular verbalization, and must be interpreted in reference not to a narrow but to a broader context. Similarly Herman Sinaiko, (1965, p. 285) writing of Socratic dialogues, suggests that these be grouped around theme, or participants' setting, or method. The relational principle, however, goes further than this. The central feature and distinguishing characteristic of the aspectual tendency is that the organizing principle of the process of apprehension is the particular interest with which we approach the entity to be comprehended (while subject to certain fixed procedural limitations). The manner in which we constitute a unity, be it a concept or a sentence, is to be determined by the nature of our interest.

This apparent subjectivity does not involve the absence either of restraint or of objective rules. To quote J.N. Findlay (1974, p. 156) of Yale, who calls himself a hylozoist:

> (The collecting and dividing aspect of Dialectic often merely traverse the same territory in an opposite sense, but it makes a difference whether one's interest lies in discovering a common pervasive Eidos, or whether it lies in dividing such an Eidos into sub-species.)
> Socrates-Plato emphasizes the non-arbitrary character of the division into species: it should be determined by what is divided, not by the predilections or whims of the carver. A good dialectician must cut his material at its natural joints.

Jurgen Habermas also points to the fact that although the way man organizes his thought will be subject to his interest, this interest will itself be subject to a particular constraint: in his view, the means of production. While he finds it necessary to stay close to this particular terminology, it is contextually clear that what he means, or ought to have meant, is simply that there is a divergence between egoistic and social consciousness – i.e. non-alienated social interest – the nature of which is determined as one integrates, through work, into the larger community.

It is precisely this underlying unity of human needs and interests which enables us to move abruptly from one epoch to another, from the tradition of the Greeks to that of the Indians. The technique may at first create some notional problems. Environment, for example, may be referred to in one place as 'productive materiality', and elsewhere as the 'supportive actuality of the *Polis*' or the 'externalization of the *Vaisya* soul' (the aspect of the soul concerned with survival). Sometimes these notions will be qualified, and it will become obvious that they are not arbitrarily conglomerated.

IV

Nature constructs in accordance with a few basic patterns, and so does the mind. Thus whether we speak of the three aspects of the soul as the priest/Brahmin soul, the self soul and the desire soul, or as *Sattva, Rajas* and *Tamas,* or as Plato's *Logisticon, Thumos* and *Epithumia,* we are not transgressing the limits of comprehensibility. I shall start by qualifying some of these terms according to Vedic psychology.

The human being on this earth, writes Krishnaswami (1901, pp. 158–9), may be said to consist of seven constituent parts. Three of these parts constitute the human soul; they are

1 The spiritual soul or *Budhhi*, 'which is the highest discriminating principle in man'.

2 The higher *Manas*, which is the intelligence of the mind – reason and consciousness.

3 The lower *Manas*, which is the animal soul – 'being the seat and totality of the purely animal instincts, passions and desires'.

Over and above these three there is the 'spirit of Atma, the spark of the divine – a piece of Godhood'.

The cosmic, social and individual levels of the soul are tied by Plato to the ruling, the executive and the appetitive principles. *Logisticon* refers to light, and *Epithumia* to darkness. In Zoroastrian and Pythagorean thought these principles are heaven and earth, light and mass, right and left. Life and the perceived universe are a mixture of light and mass, of visibility and corporeality, given the living spark through fire. The object of Yoga, Tai Chi acupuncture, Vedic psychotherapy and all Saanthana thought is the reconciliation of heaven and earth, in such a way as to bring them together in a third. Plato's *Republic* is an exposition of methods of bringing harmony to these three principles.

In the Bhagavad Gita (XIV,1, 3), Lord Krishna describes the whole universe as ruled by three powers of nature: 'I will reveal again a supreme wisdom, of all wisdom the highest: . . . In the vastness of my Nature I place the seed of things to come; and from this union comes the birth of all beings.'

Sattva is the divine quality that inspires one with the highest knowledge, and it characterizes the godly part of the soul: its corresponding cognitive agent is *Buddhi*. This *Logisticon* is the ruling quality of the soul of the philosopher.

The second psychological quality, *Rajas*, manifests in activity and physical execution. If *Logisticon* is the ruling part of the soul, then *Rajas* – or *Thumos* – becomes the executive, the soldier, the enforcer, the policeman; or in other words the practical extension of the ruler, his feet and arms. The Gita defines the attributes of *Rajas* as courage, fierceness in battle and enterprising activity in general; enterprising, that is, in the worldly sense.

The third universal force, *Tamas*, is the aspect of the soul dominated by *Kama*, or acquisitive desire. It is *Tamas* which is described in the Gita as clouding over knowledge. *Epithumia* also means desire, and obscures cognition. This perversion, however, manifests itself in the *Thumos,* the mental element.

'As there are three different kinds of soul, so there are three different paths to God', declares Krishna. 'In any way that men love me in that same way they find my love: for many are the paths of men, but they all in the end come to me' (Bhagavad Gita, IV, 10). The Gita teaches three basic paths: (1) Gnana Yoga, the path of wisdom and knowledge – this, of course, was the way of the philosopher; (2) Karma Yoga, 'the way of doing', i.e. doing everything in such a way as to make it an offering to God – this in a sense is the path of Islam; and (3) Bhakti, the way of love, where one allows the love of the Word to guide one's actions through purity of heart – this corresponds to Christianity.

For the Hindus, these three paths represent three different cosmic vibrations of one and the same word: AUM. They are received by centres of consciousness (*Chakras*), again situated in the head, the heart and the stomach. (See also *Timaeus,* 69–70.) We perceive something similar in Zoroastrianism, where the three commands of Ahura Mazda are right thought, right speech and right action – and a trinity of the same kind pervades much of Sufi thought.

The division into head, heart and stomach cannot be equated with thought, feeling and greed. The head in this tradition refers to the soul. As for the mind, it can ally itself with the stomach or with the heart (the mind is contextually passive). Heart-stomach aspectuality is dramatically portrayed by the Muslims. When speaking of their heart they touch their stomach, and attach great importance to it in other ways too – for example touching it when taking an oath or greeting somebody.

According to the Upanishads, the Zoroastrians and Plato, the soul is like a chariot. Its driver is the divine spark, 'the centre of the soul', the true self. The desiring part of the soul is symbolized by two horses, one black and one white. The white horse can be equated with the 'higher *Manas*', i.e. legitimate desires; while the black horse is to do with the lower kind, i.e. false desires. It is a common mistake to equate the higher desires simply with those for culture, philosophy, etc. and the lower desires with those for sex and food. As usual, the division is aspectual. Higher desires are *legitimate* desires, whether they be for culture or sexual gratification. Such desires stem from the man defined as a constitutive part of the cosmos. The gratification of higher desires serves to integrate a man with his wife, family, society and the cosmos in general. The false desires stem from a man's false self-identification.

In satisfying such false desires, whether these are for food or for career advancement, one uses the environment as a means to self-gratification, and hence isolation. This is the Hobbesian view of nature: in a universe where food is scarce, an individual can only eat at somebody else's expense. For Saanthana thought, however, to be a successful father or a successful mother does not necessarily mean to be well fed. In order to fulfil herself as a mother, a woman will not necessarily have to eat her children's food. In fact, given specific circumstances, she becomes what she is (a mother) by forgoing consumption: to satisfy her need means to feed her children, even though this may entail self-sacrifice.

In order to differentiate between the desires of man socially and individually defined, I shall speak of the former as interests and of the latter as desires. A desire and its fulfilment therefore constitutes a false man. The particular inclination which dominates the soul at any given moment defines a man at that moment, both his thought and his activity, the way he is understood and the way he understands, whether noetically, conceptually or erotically.

To define man in terms of his relation to the means of production is valid, but not exclusively so. How we classify things in our mind will be determined both aspectually and teleologically (that is, with respect to intention). Commenting on this, Professor Clark (who has lately interpreted Aristotle in the light of contemporary psychology and Buddhism) writes of difficulties in locating generic kinds unequivocally: 'As subclasses of larger kinds, are birds flying land creatures or feathered sea creatures?' Are we to suppose, asks Clark (1975, p. 34), that there is a final solution to this or similar problems? He answers his own question by observing that in a world 'where bats are bats and eels are eels . . . there is surely no solution which is more than a decision on our part'. Truth , it is implied, is decisional: yet decisions are subject to moods, desires and interests which may be harmonious or not. Considering decisions of the type, 'Are whales mammals or fish?' Clark writes: 'We label them according to our current interest, and there is no sense in asking for the "correct" label'. But there is a correct label. For the noetic tradition, every decision with regard to a current interest is ethically determined, i.e. the way in which we decide to comprehend is ethically teleological (Cushman, 1958, p. 113). In deciding what it is we want to know, to eat or not to eat, to kill or not to kill, we are deciding whether and how to know, eat or kill in a correct manner: meaning in a manner such as to preserve or restore the basic ethical order that characterizes man as man.

V

Another insight into 'aspectuality' may be gained by investigating the manner of thought marked by the absence of any such tendency. The term 'knowledge' cannot be properly applied to perception-based thought, to the kind of thought which we call making judgment or to the kind of thinking associated with opinions, whether these are right or wrong. For perception, judgments and opinions deal with entities differentiated in time and with their predications. Things as they are in themselves are not predicated, they are not subject to verbal description – or at least not in such a way that they derive their being from, or are entirely exhausted by, such predication. We put into description aspects of things: exhaustive predication would require transmodal predicates, applying to the aspects of a thing considered in all its ontological realms (e.g. being in an absolute sense, and being as becoming or as given by the senses). If we are to reduce knowledge to perception, or to judgment in accordance with fixed concepts, then no knowledge is possible. In the *Theaetetus* (160–191), Socrates argues that things are not seen or written about as they are. The Hindu sage, when asked who he is, tells a disciple he ought to close his eyes.

Husserl points out that it is not possible to prove empirically that one is seeing any given individual. Nor are ontological generalities, such as the 'nature of man', empirically deducible: man is not what he is in a specific place between times A and B; he is continuously unfolding in individuals. And the same applies to every individual entity, which unfolds in a series of moments. Empirically, in the positivist sense, we can never know anybody.

According to the kind of thought that has been dominant ever since the time of Kant, a thing is judged a thing on the basis of a coincidence between a mental concept and empirical data. This cognitive process is exposed to weakness on two sides. Our original data-gathering and concept-forming process may have been false; and the current data-gathering process may also be false (e.g. in the dark a stump of wood may look like a man). From the noetic point of view, what is false is the whole empirical-positivistic tradition.

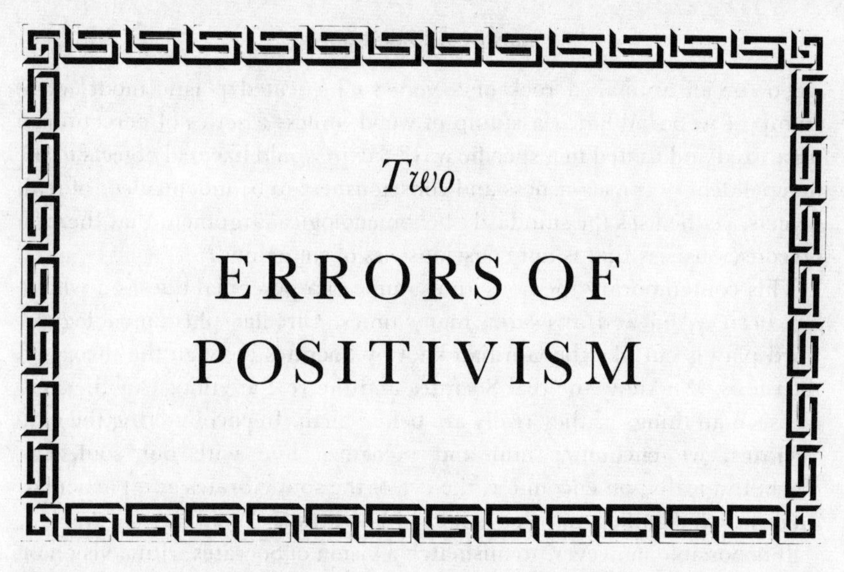

Two
ERRORS OF POSITIVISM

'Positivism' may be examined through the work of a few representative thinkers, the distinguishing factor in whose philosophy is not a content but a method, the type of mental activity engaged in. Naturally, any criticism of these philosophers' conceptual failings will be tongue in cheek.

I

Sartre may be taken here for a token existentialist, and his thinking as representing the sentiment of an entire generation. Formally considered, his unelaborated assumptions bring to focus an important point. Even those philosophers whose philosophy does not account for the existence of absolutely real things base their thoughts on the implicit assumption of such realities. Concerning the question of true and false perception, Sartre imagines himself in *Being and Nothingness* observing what he thinks is a man in a wood. It is twilight, and the 'man' turns out to be the stump of a tree. Sartre asks himself whether he had confused the actual stump with the mental image of a man – but like Socrates in the *Theaetetus*, he decides against this possibility. Real things cannot be confused with mental contents, such as images; rather, 'I perceived an object but had misinterpreted its nature'. In this way, Sartre and Heidegger too reject Husserl's claim that we perceive mental representations, not real things.

The criticism of Husserl is valid, given the assumption made here by Sartre that real objects are real even apart from any empirical knowledge of them on our part. Sartre does not, however, give the criterion for reality. How am I to determine that the stump of wood was in fact a stump of wood, and not my friend Theaetetus masquerading as a stump of wood, or an animal, a rock or a very sophisticated plastic model of a stump of wood? What *is* a stump of wood, unless a series of perceptions organized and united in a specific way? Sartre would like real objects to be independent of consciousness and consciousness to be independent of real objects, yet he uses the standard phenomenological argument that there is no consciousness that is not consciousness of something.

This contemporary theme is an example of a perennial question which has been asked and answered many times. Circular phenomenological word play is cut like the Gordian knot by Socrates through the theory of *Anamnesis*. We know the real Socrates and the real anything, for the soul has seen all things as they really are before birth. In encountering the real Socrates, we encounter him and recognize him with our soul, i.e. diarhythmically; on encounter, the eye of the soul vibrates at a particular pitch which signifies that this is indeed Socrates.

It is possible, however, to mismatch a vision of Socrates with a vision of Theaetetus, for in perceiving a person one never perceives the totality. We only know aspects of Socrates: his profile, or his back, etc. It is possible to think that $8+5$ is 12, for we do not know all the ways of expressing 12; at best we know some of its aspects, such as 2×6 or 12×1 or $10+2$, but we do not know aspects such as $\sqrt[3]{((160\times28)\div\frac{dy}{dx}2x)-8^3}$. No image, no verbal description or concept, can cover the totality of a thing's identity: at best it can cover one legitimate aspect. Others are inexhaustible: 12 as a function of log e, Sartre masquerading as Heidegger or the stump of a tree – there are endless possibilities.

Thus we are brought to a realization. If no differentiated entities can be truly known, then things as commonly regarded are possibly not things at all, but sectionalized flows of perceptions. Or, if things do exist, how it is that they are constituted, and what it is that they are, lies outside the realm of judgment, opinion or perception. The negatively insinuated, or implicit, conclusion is that the organizing principles around which the mind constructs its pictures can only be conjectural. The mind creates entities which cannot, by the very nature of their construction, correspond to true entities. If what the mind, and reason based on the mind, tells us is true, then all things are perpetually changing, and hence properly speaking there are no things. If, however, the mind and the reason based on it are falsely operating, then there possibly are things, but no such 'things' as are perpetually changing, i.e. no things that correspond to the entities believed to be things.

Stumpf (1966, p. 477) describes Jaspers as concluding that:

There can never be an objective knowledge of being. Objective

> knowledge or science deals only with the objective aspect of an object; however, the reality of an object is not exhausted by its objective predication. By definition sciences divide up reality into objects. To think scientifically then is to have access to only one kind of data. . . . But the content of being, total reality, existence, is not limited to objective data.

One could dispense with such complications and simply state that everything we see is false – trees are not trees, horses are not horses: only transcendental horses are true, and these are in the separate world of ideas, bearing no outward resemblance to the phantasms commonly referred to. This simplification is typical of the type of interpretation popularly associated with nineteenth-century idealism, with Indian philosophy according to Schopenhauer, and with Kant, or rather Kantian interpretations of Plato. Possibly believing the Greeks to be incapable of summarizing the unstated assumptions behind their arguments, the Kant-Marburg inspired scholarship has drawn a whole series of such reductions, creating a 'straw man' Greek philosophy with a life of its own.

(Even though *Logos*-oriented thought may be hinting at something resembling the doctrine that real things are ideas and perceived things are false, no representative thinker positively expresses it. I, too, shall abstain from all such direct statements, and be concerned with formulating a series of aspectual counter-positions, each of which, if expressly posited, would contradict the others. Despite speaking implicitly, however, I shall hint at a comprehensive notion typical of aspectual thought.)

Apart from the fact that aspectual thought opposes positivist philosophical formulae as a matter of principle, conceptual simplifications are quite objectively false. Even if perceived unities are not things, the things we perceive are not necessarily unreal. They may have legitimacy on grounds quite independent of the process of perception itself, based on a higher process, the nature of which is not the immediate subject of our discussion. But before establishing what the true things really are, we are interested to establish what they are not.

As with Sartre, while contemporary Western thought may see in Kant a thinker specific to eighteenth-century Germany, I will take him here as representing an ever-recurring historical phenomenon, voicing opinions that have been put forward time and time again. According to Marx, as a society moves from the aristocratic to the mercantile stage, or, as in Plato, from the honour-seeking to the property-seeking stage, there arises a corresponding manner of thinking (*Republic,* 547[a]–565[b]). In response to the shift of power from aristocrats to merchants, there arises a need for the separation of religion from practical life. The bourgeoisie or the merchants desire a religious element as the basis of social stability, but prefer a primarily world-oriented religion, one that will not place restrictions on commercial operations in this world. In contrast with these 'stage-specific' speakers and thinkers are the representatives of Philosophia Perennis, who voice an opinion which reconciles at a higher level different aspects of period-specific thought, though subject to variations in the manner of exposition. 'The form must be the same, but the material may vary . . . whether made in Hellas or in a foreign country there is no difference' (*Cratylus*, 389[e]).

According to Plutarch, decisions to expand the Greek timber industry and to build both a fleet and an empire were closely connected to philosophical developments of the time: Aristotle saw such philosophical expressions of commercial interest as one of the causes of the fall of Athens. Owing to interpretational gaps and notional shifts, the philosophy of the original sophists is not easy for us to approach: Kant, being closer, will serve us better as the merchants' spokesman. For the cyclical view of history places him, too, as an agent in the transition from an honour-oriented to a commercial State, through the secularization of thought – the separation of philosophy and religion. The historical Kant, of course, had other interests, but the intention here is not so much to compare different schools of philosophy as to explore one, the perennial, using Kant.

All noetic thinkers, from Valmiki to the Buddha and Nagajuna, have taken pains to lead one (negatively) to the conclusion that perception can never be the basis of knowledge. For Kant, in contrast, it was precisely perception that provided such a ground. He opens the First Critique by observing: 'It is beyond doubt that all our knowledge begins with experience. For by what should our faculties be roused to act, if not by objects that affect our senses?' (Kant, 1881, p. 115.)

He argues in this First Critique that perceived reality conforms to objective and fixed rules, to categories over which no one thing or person exercises authority. Indeed the fact that a thing is perceived as a thing, or that a person is aware of himself or another as a person, is determined by the synthesizing activity of the mind itself. Categories of perception determine both the identity of the perceived and that of the perceiver. Rejecting the idea that the mind conforms to an independently objective reality, Kant's (1881,p. 29) 'Copernican inversion' postulates that reality conforms to the processes of the mind.

By this postulate, however, Kant has created a duality between the perceived world and the thing in itself – between the world of here and now and the transcendental world of things as they are for themselves. It is the rationalists, i.e. the conceptualists, who are the dualists, and not the Vedic or Zoroastrian thinkers or Plato. The Saanthana philosophy's division between here and there is not dualistic, for it does not posit two worlds, 'here' and 'there': it posits only one world that can be conceived in different ways. Neither does it separate man as man from man as cognitive agent, the knower from what is known. It is precisely this sort of separation which creates the division into 'subject' and 'object', into 'me' and 'the world'.

Such a division is necessary for the merchant, since the merchant's (epithumic) soul will necessarily see each individual as an ontologically separate unit, requiring the separate satisfaction of his needs through the intermediate market. Bourgeois thought must create an individual unit of consumption so as to cater to its newly created needs. Thus it is necessary for Kant to interject between man and his fellow man, and between man and the world, the divisive cognitive faculty. We cannot know the world or our fellow man directly, for such knowledge is false; rather, we must first learn to know through the cognitive faculty – then we can see what it is that we know. Kant has put the cart before the horse: he is saying, 'Let us know how we know before we know.'

This inconsistency has not passed unobserved by Hegel, and is also criticized by Habermas (1972, p. 7), who writes:

> [Kant's] critical philosophy demands that the knowing subject ascertain the conditions of knowledge of which it is in principle capable before trusting its directly acquired cognitions. . . . What is demanded is thus the following: we should know the cognitive faculty before we know.

II

For the conceptualist, it is the mind, or the mental product (the concept), or the linguistic expression of this (the language), that functions as the organizing principle of apprehension. For all *Logos*-oriented thought it is an inner, essentially ethical faculty that acts as the organizing principle.

This organizing principle in Hindu thought is called *Buddhi*; Plato calls it *Logisticon*. In both cases, it is preceded by an ethical element, surprisingly called by the same name both in the Upanishads and by Plato (*Republic*, 518): the 'inner eye of the soul'. From the Gita we learn that knowledge is synthesized by the *Buddhi* faculty situated in the head, but the workings of *Buddhi* are controlled by the heart: hence Patanjali writes that knowledge is obtained 'by meditating on one's own divine light, situated in the heart'. The 'heart' that Patanjali is referring to is not the heart characteristic of the lower soul: the highest soul has its own heart element, i.e. the sentiment of love.

Thus *Logisticon* participates in desire, but desire of the highest kind – man's genuine interest. I have argued that conceptual thought stems from the desire of the lower, epithumic soul, the body; yet I have referred concepts and the merchant to the second, mental, executive faculty. The ambiguity is not incidental. The merchant caters to excessive desires, to needs which are not genuine and not rooted in bodily needs. Indeed, we may define the merchant and the market as that excess which is brought into existence after genuine needs have been catered for.

A merchant is therefore aspectually defined. A grocer, or a manager of a huge factory, becomes a merchant at that point where his activities exceed catering to genuine needs. Hence people are only partly merchants. This point is made by Jesus, who did not come for respectable people but for thieves, tax collectors and their like. To interpret Scripture to mean that Jesus came *only* for the poor or *only* for the tax collectors is a simplification. Jesus came for the sick aspect of each man. It is the 'tax collector' in each man that he calls to repentance.

The merchant aspect of a philosopher causes him perennially to twist the meanings of words, turning things upside down. This is why Confucius calls for the constant rectification of names. However, as soon as a philosopher rectifies a word, there will be a 'merchant thinker' who will find ways to turn it upside down.

The paradigmatic example of word inversion concerns the needs of the body. As we have stated, there are three cognitive faculties: (1) the cognitive faculty of the soul, (2) that of the mind and (3) that of the body. The needs of the body are for such food, drink and sleep as are advantageous to it. The merchant calls the 'desires of the body' the desire for excessive drink which will ruin the liver, or the desire for excessive food which will turn a healthy body to fat. These are not needs of the body: at the point where desires become excessive, they are mental. Perversions with regard to food, sex or drink are never perversions of the body, but rather of the mind. The grocer caters to the body; the merchant does not. The merchant caters to false mental needs, and is hence a product of the mind. Thus although it originates in the lower soul, excessive desire is in fact *thumetikoid*, i.e. mental.

For Kant, the categories of the real are fixed, objective and, even though 'of mind', in some sense autonomous, since they cannot be influenced by any individual. Indeed the categories precede the individual, who becomes conscious of himself as a unity only indirectly, in the act of organizing and cognizing other things as unities. For noetic thought, on the other hand, the individual precedes the mental cognitive activity in every sense, logically and temporally. *Logisticon,* 'the centre of the soul' and the executive faculty, is entirely independent of, and superior to, the activities of the mind (cf.*Phaedrus,* 247). To use Kantian terminology, the self chooses its own sets of categories and constructs reality according to its own innerly determined and varying predisposition.

What distinguishes the views of Kant from that of Philosophia Perennis is the radically differing account of what it means to be an individual. For Kant the individual is equated with an entity fixed by objective givens: birth, circumstance, objective environment. For *Logos*-based thought, not only is the psyche or *Logisticon* autonomous in the way it synthesizes data to create objects, but this noetic element is free to choose any or almost any personality (e.g. *Republic,* 617[c]–618[a]). For example, pre-Protagorian man exercises a choice in the way he perceives 'external' things: whether he perceives a horse as a virile black deity, a pulsating mass of energy or a thing that pulls the plough; whether the concept white (*Leukos*) means swift, quick or light yellow, white or any lighter shade of black, was a matter of ethical choice for the sixth-century Athenian.

The notion of free choice, later to be developed by Kierkegaard and the existentialists, is central to all Saanthana thought. What we think and how we think may be modified and conditioned by objective categories, yet in the final analysis the deepest, noetic thought transcends words and concepts and reduces to an ethical movement – *Elenchos*. The deepest cognition is simply the cognition of the good, and of how any action, word or thought relates to the good. To Kant it was the sense of Ego – as in the transcendental unity of apperception – that accompanied all our perceptions; to *Logos* thought, it is this constant ethical choice. In this connection Boyce (1979, p. 20) writes of the permanent choice revealed to the Zoroastrians – for every act and thought man chooses between *Vohu Manu* and *Angro Manyush* – and Kierkegaard (1962, p. 12) links the notion of *Anamnesis* to man's ever-present and primaeval decision.

For Kant there existed only one ontology, one epistemological system and a single way of organizing perception, i.e. the conceptual activity of the mind. For Plato there existed at least three distinct ontologies, corresponding to the erotic, the noetic and the conceptual realms: 'Thus in *Phaedrus,* being is seen as the object of love . . . in *Republic* . . . being is seen as the object of knowledge . . . and in *Parmenides* being is seen as the object of discourse' (Sinaiko, 1965, p. 284). In Vedic thought, the equivalent realms are those of Karma, Gnana and Bhakti.

Aspectual thought resorts to several methods of creating notional unities. Its distinguishing feature is that it freely ignores the limits set by temporal and spatial proximity. For transaspectual thinkers, centaurs could (for those so interested) be as real as perceived individuals. Even the so-called empirical individual could (for those so interested) be perceived as part woman, part man, part animal, part living today, part living yesterday. The latter notion is, of course, that of reincarnation. The idea is of the unity of all life and being: in the course of our many incarnations we all participate in bees and birds, in sinners and saints. Likewise, the notion of communism entails that one can today in some essential way identify one's individual being with that of the beings inhabiting the non-alienated, perfect city of the future. All the above notions presuppose a non-individual, social, transdimensional, unfolding essence to man. Opposed to this stand the bourgeois thinkers with their sense of the individual 'I'.

III

In order to gain a clearer understanding of the process of creation of the bourgeois sense of 'I', let us turn to the thought of Descartes, by whom the conceptualization of the ego was begun. If we examine the apparently disinterested *Meditations*, we shall discover them to be yet another expression of the market-oriented individualization of human nature. The Cogito argument itself is formally false: the conceptual thinker inevitably breaks his own rules.

A full exposition of the Cogito argument does not seem to be called for, and can be found elsewhere. Briefly, Descartes wanted to find something of which he could be certain, and this something turned out to be a specific sense of 'I'. Simplified to its bare bones, his argument was that 'I can be certain only that I am uncertain' – i.e. I doubt everything, even that I doubt. In all this doubting, the one thing I can be sure of is that I doubt: even when I doubt that I doubt, I doubt. From this, Descartes concludes that since I cannot doubt that I doubt, therefore I exist.

While the argument is clever, it should be obvious that Descartes starts with the assumption of that which he sets out to prove: in stating that he doubts ('I doubt') he has already decided that an 'I' exists, that it is the 'I' which is doubting. There is, in fact, no justification for this: all we can legitimately infer is that there is thinking and there is awareness of the self. This awareness of the self is not the same as an 'I' conceived as a being separate from 'thou', and separate from my body. In other words, the 'I' of Descartes is a loaded I, and is different from the instantaneous, self-generated and non-conceptual awareness of the self. A (mentally) correctly functioning person does not doubt that he exists; it is only the already alienated mind that sets out to prove the existence of 'I'. In other words it is only somebody with a specifically formulated sense of 'I' who could and would set out to prove the existence of 'I' rather than of the self.

In proving that there is 'I', Descartes borrows this sense of self and grafts it on to his reflection.

Further, as Husserl argued, Descartes has no valid grounds – even on the conceptual plane – for moving from the conscious self to the notion of an extended substance, a body; coupling the thinking subject with an objective, differentiated piece of extended reality. In doing this Descartes creates a mind-body dualism. Ungrasped by Husserl is the fact that only by giving the thinking subject such extension can Descartes grant any differentiated being to the Ego. In the final analysis, we realize that it is not through Cartesian arguments that we become aware of the sense of I; this sense exists independently of such arguments.

What Descartes has done is to legitimize the false activity of *Dianoia*. By supposedly legitimizing the existence of I, Descartes legitimizes a method. It is this method which creates a specific I, for how we think determines what we conclude. Thus conceptual thought creates the conceptual individual: 'I' separate from 'thou' and the world.

Just as the relation between mass, energy and light has been postulated time and time again, so have the stock ontological or cosmological arguments, which turn up with mechanical regularity at corresponding stages of societal development. The Cogito argument was made in its valid form by a Hindu thinker, Samkara, probably between AD 788 and 820. Unlike Descartes, who uses it to create dualism, Samkara's Cogito argument was employed to formulate the so-called non-dual Vedanta position. No doubt Samkara himself was reacting to, or rather correcting, a stomach-soul based argument of some Hindu 'Descartes'. Hence his argument: 'All means of knowledge exist only as dependent on self experience, and since such experience is its own proof there is no necessity for proving the existence of self'; or, as formulated by Radhakrishnan, 'The objects of knowledge may be open to doubt, but the doubter himself cannot be doubted.' The argument parallels that of Descartes except that there is no word 'I'. The Hindu self and the bourgeois I are radically different, for the self is not here equated with the mind:

> It is undifferentiated consciousness and it persists even after the mind perishes . . . the self (Atman) is existence, knowledge and bliss. It is universal and infinite. The object world is dependent . . . we perceive objects; we do not invent the corresponding ideas. The world perceived is as real as the individual perceived (Radhakrishnan, 1957, pp. 506–7).

For Descartes, I become the mental 'I' as opposed to the bodily 'I'. I am different from my body, your body, everybody. As will become apparent it was this 'me' and 'cosmos', subject – object separation which created the atheistic world view. 'Atheism' for the Buddhists, for example, would be not a profession of disbelief in God but the separation of the knower from the cosmos; while to be pious in Buddhist thought means to reintegrate oneself into unity with the objects of perception, apprehended as the environment within which one exists as an organic whole.

> On the premise that subject and object are not identical, knowledge by understanding is possible only when our original synthesis brings the manifold of given representations under the unity of apperception. The synthesis of representations is brought about by my representing to myself the identity of consciousness in these representations. This occurs in self consciousness. Thus in order to show the possibility of a cognitive faculty divided into sensibility and understanding, Kant must assume a faculty that combines all my representations in a self consciousness. We ascertain this 'spontaneous faculty of imagination' in the experience of the ego being identical with itself. . . . According to Kant, pure apperception produces the representation 'I think' which must be able to accompany identically all other representations, without this representation itself being able to be accompanied and reflected by a further one (Habermas, 1972, p. 37).

In fact Kant, like Descartes, borrows the immediately obvious sense of the self, and by supposedly proving its existence defines the self as a specific I, as something given mediatively through the process of apprehension. The result of all this is that although without Kant I know *that* I am, I am persuaded as to *what* I am by him.

It is in this way that the presence of 'I' in any perception-based activity legitimizes both itself and the perception. Yet both are logically false. Like Descartes, Kant breaks the rules of his own method and commits a logical fallacy. In order to account for the conjectural 'I' of 'I think', the 'I' is forced to create a further 'I' in terms of which it can qualify both the conceptualized 'I' that accompanies the perceptions of other things, and the 'I' that accompanies self-perception. This, however, is an endless process, since the I is forced to create a procession of further I's to account for its own identity and knowledge of itself. (Not that such arguments are important. Kant is first of all methodologically false: his most serious falsity lies in the nature of his mental activity, rather than in any content or conclusion.)

Practically all this criticism levelled at Kant and Descartes might have been aimed at Wittgenstein, or any language-oriented analyst. Wittgenstein's thought is a repetition of the same theme in another key, carrying the process of abstraction from the conceptual to the linguistic stage. Kant had attempted to determine what can and cannot be thought: Wittgenstein took these arguments a stage further to determine what can and cannot be said. Just as the post-Hume Kant suddenly realizes that it is not reality that determines the structure of our thought but vice versa, so likewise the post-*Tractatus,* 'mature' Wittgenstein determines that it is not the structure of reality that determines the structure of our language, but the structure of our language that determines our grasp of reality.

IV

We have seen how non-aspectual thought leads to conceptual mismatching, as a result of its attempt to achieve objectivity in a realm where no such objectivity is possible. In contrast, being free from this search for conceptual objectivity, aspectual thinking can define a single notion in many different ways. For such thought, whether something is true or not is to be determined teleologically and within a context: truth therefore is aspectual.

Parallels will continually be drawn to show how all these notions relate to the way we construct scientific theories and divide up work and society in general. As pointed out earlier, for noetic thought, to be contemplated, things need also to be isolated and defined: noetic thought is not identical with the fluidity of wordless meditation. The difference between noetic and conceptual definition is that for the former, definition is in relation to a broader system: it needs to be interreacting to be meaningful. This method is also followed by contemporary physics; hence S-matrix interpretation and Stapp's Rule: 'The observed system is required to be isolated in order to be defined yet interreacting in order to be observed' (Stapp, 1971, p. 1303).

The Renaissance and post-Renaissance period found it necessary to investigate nature, man and society by effecting a specific division of labour. Biologists concerned themselves with biology and not with ethics. Atoms were independent, autonomous elements; matter was divided into organic and inorganic. The same principles were applied to all aspects of human life, as well as to philosophy. The philosopher of today is a highly specialized individual, relating to likeminded professionals using a specialized language that no lay person can possibly understand. Church has been separated from State, God from man, husband from wife. Marriage, citizenship and the membership of any community are all seen as legal and temporary associations of independent, autonomous units. All organic wholes – in philosophy, science or the family – are divided into fundamental, fragmented building blocks: atoms or individuals.

Originally, of course, atoms and matter were 'invented' by Aristotle and Democritus as philosophical abstractions with relative validity. The less flexible thought of Descartes and post-Renaissance science assumed these atoms and atomic selves to be real entities, and proceeded to create social institutions based on the fundamental reality of the atomization of each and everybody. The ultimate culmination of this process, were it allowed to continue, would be the breakdown of all ethics and philosophy, since 'ethical for me' and 'true for me' are axioms which are fundamentally irreconcilable with the true state of nature or human existence.

Water is not simply two atoms of hydrogen and one atom of oxygen. Water is as legitimate an entity as an atom. Indeed water is more legitimate, since it can be used and observed, whereas nobody has ever seen an atom. In the same way, nobody has seen an individual. What we see is a Frenchman, or a son of Ariston, or a husband of Xantippe and a citizen of Athens. An individual is none other than a participant in broader systems.

Noetic thought accepts the above in principle, but goes further. It operates in terms of two processes – *Diaresis* and *Simploke,* division and synthesis. While an individual can only exist as a son of so-and-so, such divisions do not necessarily parallel deeper divisions yet. In other words, an individual is to be defined by more complex criteria. These rules apply to all definitions, and to the creation of all entities.

The criteria which determine the meaning of a definition are for noetic thought context-relative. Absolute truth exists, but we cannot speak of absolutely right or wrong statements or philosophies: on their own level, they can only be relatively right or wrong – relative, that is, to the assumptions that underlie them and to the 'language game' in which they are set. It is only when philosophy is made to descend to the level of mechanically universal rules that issues become either simply true or false. Aspectual thought follows a different technique, that of the resolution of conflict by means of reconciliation in a synthesis raised to a higher noetic plane. The vehicle of that synthesis is the sentiment.

V

Having criticized Plato for basing his metaphysics on the 'pure air of hypothesis', Kant (1881, p. 119) had himself in the conclusion of the Second Critique justified his own ethical imperatives by reference to unspecified feelings of duty and obligation, and compared them to the feelings conveyed by 'the awe of the starry heavens'.

What Kant derived from the starry heavens was the feeling or moral sentiment of awe; what the Hindus, Plato, the Pythagoreans and the Babylonians derived was something nebulous they refer to as *Namas, Aritmos, Kephr* – the number. There is, of course, a possibility of some relationship between number and moral sentiment, though what this might be is not immediately obvious. But before examining 'sentiment' in terms of either the Pythagorean exactitude, determined by ratio and pitch, or the more fluid Platonic notion of *Aritmos,* let us first approach the notion of sentiment in its popular form – that is, interpreted as emotional feeling.

In the introduction to Stewart's *The Myths of Plato* (1960,p. 45), G.R. Levy writes that for Plato 'the test of truth is the feeling of wonder and awe'. 'In looking for truth', Levy writes, 'it is good . . . to appeal . . . to this deep-lying part of human nature as to an oracle. The responses of the oracle are not given in articulate language . . . their ultimate meaning is the feeling which fills us beholding them.'

In the *Symposium* (186^{b}), Socrates reports the views of the famous Athenian physician Eryxymachus, who says that the body comprehends love in its very nature. In the *Gorgias* (481^{c}), Socrates tells Callicles that were it not for shared emotions, men could not communicate them. Pseudo-Theages declares that he never learned any formal doctrine or philosophy from Socrates; rather, what he learned was a particular mood or manner of apprehension, and he learned this simply by being next to Socrates, observing him, sitting beside him and being touched by him (*Theages,* 2,8,24).

In *Greek Philosophy,* Burnet (1950, p. 168) writes of 'emotive intelligence' and observes that 'intelligence was for Socrates something touched with emotion'. In his *Theology* Jaeger writes that he is 'impressed by the continuity of the human mind'. He is referring to the relation between Christian religious thought and the philosophical thought of Greece; the latter however, as Jaeger (1947, p. 9) points out on the authority of Aristotle, is rooted in its origins in *poetic* thought, i.e. experience as grasped by the early poets. These poets understood the cosmic forces in terms of sentiments. (These religious poets are not the same as Aristophanes and his like. Greek poets were of two kinds – noetic and passionate.)

In the *Phaedo* (99^{c}), Socrates repudiates objective scientists, for 'they do not think that anything is really bound together by goodness and moral obligation'. Cushman (1958, p. 159) finds the validity of an argument is not to be found in the formal resolution of a syllogism culminating in a conclusion, but rather in its *Koinonia,* its correspondence, with a particular feeling which reduces to ethical knowledge.

Josef Pieper, in *Leisure the Basis of Culture,* sees truth as consisting not in any reduction to formal parameters, but rather as 'godly sentiments', 'feelings of awe'. According to Pieper, the Middle Ages drew a distinction between intellect and reason (*Ratio*), whereby the intellect was intuitive and emotive. Thus sentiment can function as a criterion for judging the validity of a philosophical position or the correctness of an action (this becomes apparent in the thought of Aquinas). It is for this reason that noetic thinkers create mental movements, moods and verbal exercises rather than doctrines, formulae and definitions. As Sinaiko notes (1965, p. 8), knowledge in the form of the mere possession of a definition, e.g. of justice, is not going to help its possessor either to perform just acts or to judge the acts of others as just; what one needs is the *feeling* of justice. Thomas Aquinas also distinguishes between two ways of knowing: the moralist (who is not necessarily a good man) 'knows' the good 'per cognitionem', whereas the good man knows and does good 'per connaturalitatem'.

These observations lead us to a major difference between *Logos*-oriented thinkers and the rational conceptualists. For Kant, the criterion for judging an action good is the intention behind the act. The essence of the conceptualists' position rests upon the separation between the modes of apprehension concerned with 'this' and 'the other' world. In separating the modes of apprehension, Kant-Descartes creates two worlds, 'this' and 'the other', the empirical world and the world as the object of metaphysics, which previously were one. Analogously, the 'good intention' criterion implies the separation of means and ends. The hidden assumption entails a preference for a 'good' or 'desirable' outcome.

For noetic thinkers, in contrast, the only criterion for judging an action good or bad is the sentiment in which the action is undertaken. This, however, entails no preference for outcome, hence no 'good intention'. In Plato's *Laws* (863[e]–864[a]), for example, 'right is that which is of noble sentiment', i.e. which is undertaken in the sentiment of good wish, the mastery of the soul by good desire. The sentiment exists prior to the desire for an outcome; indeed the sentiment determines what is desired, as sentiments precede any intentions. And in the Mahabharata we learn that a good man is not necessarily one who does charitable acts; rather the good man, the truly wise man, is he who abandons all hope of any outcome, and does all simply for love and in tranquillity.

For the noetic thinker, it is quite imperative never to assume that ends justify means, for we never know – and should never think that we know – what is good for us or for other people (*Laws*, 875[d]; Bhagavad Gita, VI, 4; Tao Te Ching, LXV). The distinction between intention and sentiment is parallel to the crucial distinction between aspectual activity and an arrested, static image – the difference between a notion and a conceptualization.

Hence in the Tao Te Ching (XII) we read that 'the sage is guided by what he feels and not by what he sees'. The noetic thinker is not interested in intentions or in actions, but in the sentiments in which actions are undertaken. In a Biblical parallel, Jesus equates looking lustfully at a neighbour's wife with adultery. Although Jesus himself does not make the claim, from the Koran one learns that looking lustfully at one's own wife is also forbidden: the issue is not the doing but the sentiment. This notion is echoed in I Thessalonians, IV, 4–5, where Paul writes that 'each one of you [should] know how to take a wife for himself in holiness and honour'.

While it is a common accusation that Muslims are ritualists, to whom morality signifies particular acts rather than sentiments, this is not in fact what is enjoined by the Koran. Concerning those who give positive advice of a kind reducible to formulae for good action, 'Mohammed' writes in the Koran (IV,114): 'There is no virtue in much of their counsels: only in his who enjoins charity, kindness, and peace among men. He that does this to please Allah shall be richly rewarded.'

In the New Testament, the heart is the only criterion for deciding which acts are good or evil. Hence in Matthew, XV, 17–21 it is only evil sentiments of the heart – 'evil thoughts' – that can defile us. We shall later see how all such sentiments, whether those of the Zoroastrian Yasnas or the Islamic surahs, reduce to fixed groups and quantities that are neither subjective nor arbitrary, and are subject to cosmic fixities which are instrumental in physical creation as well as in the creation of thought and notions. Suffice it for the moment to establish that sentiment – here still loosely considered – is instrumental in the formation of thought.

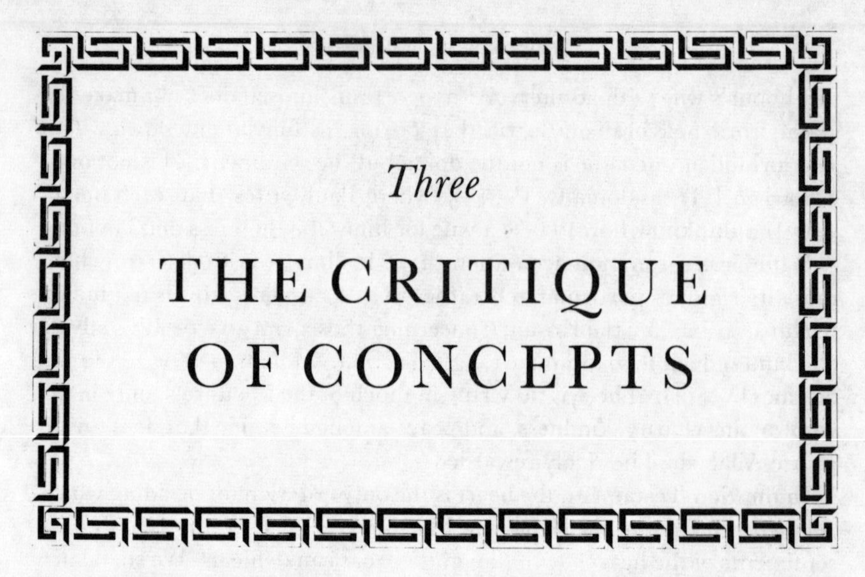

Three

THE CRITIQUE OF CONCEPTS

The foregoing suggests some ambiguities as between specific injunctions, such as those of religious and secular law, and ethical demands determined by the sentiment. It will become obvious that my intention is not to diffuse these tensions, nor to be critical of them, but to switch sides, arguing or seeming to argue formalistically, only to reverse this position elsewhere. The purpose is to create the so-called *Tenos*, a corybantic paradox.

The use of paradox is not specific to pre-sophist Greek philosophy or to Plato; indeed all the Philosophia Perennis schools eventually lead to a confrontation between two conceptually irreducible statements. In Zen this is called a Koan, and takes expression not only as a clash between two conceptually irreconcilable doctrines, but also in various actions, musical patterns, unexpected visual disharmonies and so on. A pious master may end a wise tale with a piercing scream, or he may unexpectedly violently strike his favourite disciple on an occasion which requires praise and commendation. This is the method of the Rinzai school to precipitate satori – the higher-level reconciliation of contradictory opposites. The regular pattern of a Zen garden is suddenly interrupted and the observer sees an apparently random collection of lines and paths, until suddenly he discovers a new organizing pattern and the garden paths appear again to be harmonious, yet this time the pattern is not objectively apparent.

In Hinduism, man is required to renounce all his desires; yet the highest realization lies in the reconciliation of the paradox created by the obligation not to strive, work or wish for renunciation in any way. One must renounce the renunciation in order to renounce.

The corybantic paradox in Islam is the demand to worship the transcendent (negative) God, yet by submitting to a positive law and ritual. As against this, Christ – or Paul – points to the absurdity of calling things clean and unclean. Paul stresses that it is wrong to assume that the way to God lies in observing or not observing the Sabbath, or eating or not eating pork. These Pauline anti-formality arguments appear particularly sensible and intellectually attractive as opposed to Muslim ideas of salvation through regular prayer and abstinence from pork. To Christians, such rituals may appear idolatrous; yet the paradox in Christianity, as Muslims will readily point out, is the conceptually nonsensical claim that Christ is both God and man.

Islam and Christianity have both produced 'philosophers' who would resolve the paradoxes and make the religion conceptually (dianoically) attractive. It is claimed by more than one Islamic author that the consumption of pork was forbidden only because there was no adequate refrigeration in the time of Mohammed – today, however, there is no need for such rules, and the law may be abandoned; and likewise for Ramadan (the fast), etc. Such scholarship is applauded in the West, just as some Muslims would no doubt applaud the repeated 'philosophical' claims that Christ was not really God.

The hard core of any religion rejects such conceptual reconciliation. While religious claims may be myths, the whole point of these myths is to create the corybantic paradox, the tension which projects man into noetic rather than conceptual reconciliation. Even the 'Godless' philosophy-religion of Buddhism relies on the renunciation-of-renunciation paradox. As for a contemporary ideological *Weltanschauung* such as Marxism, this also employs the paradoxical notion of a completely non-alienated society – the perfect state of communism – projected into the future so as to exact specific forms of behaviour in the real-actual world of today.

While a competent 'philosopher' could perfetly well argue for the necessity of corybantic paradox, in practice we may observe that his verbosity will not help him to accept it himself. The final requirement for a philosopher is that he should humble himself in favour of those who do understand. It is for this reason that Plato, having persistently ridiculed and exposed the myths of religion and of seers and mystics as unreasonable and immoral, nevertheless finishes his dialogues by beating a sudden retreat, and bowing his head to 'the men of old who were better and wiser than us'. Hegel, on the other hand, takes the 'philosopher king' idea literally, and imagines himself to be a superior being, competent to create reality and to pass judgments on the 'true nature' of the Absolute.

Hegel's idealism as a consequence has no practical relevance, for it is not based on the reality of the cosmic myth but simply on the conceptualization of such a myth. Myths can take different forms and be given different names, but essentially they must be based on eternal fixities such as the Fall, the Cross, the curse of realization through toil and so on.

One may reject the concept of the Fall and call the basic human condition 'alienation'. One may deny that man realizes himself by daily picking up his cross and consecrating his toil to Christhood, and write instead that man realizes his essence himself in non-alienated labour – or indeed that man becomes truly man by defining himself through labour. Further, one may reject the Second Coming and replace it with non-alienated communism. Such a world view 'works' in so far as it is based on the cosmic truths; when it strays away from them, it ceases to work.

I

It has been suggested by some scholars that concepts and conceptual thinking are a relatively recent phenomenon. Thus we may note Heidegger (1968, p. 213) claiming that both 'concept and system alike are alien to Greek thinking', and this applies even more to Hindu and Taoist thought.

Of course Greek texts and the Tao Te Ching may be read conceptually; and as a result one can derive interpretations of Hinduism in which 'all is illusion'. Likewise, a market interpretation of Taoism would be a call for the unlimited gratification of desire. The mistake is typically modern, but it is not true that the ancients never made it themselves.

Before turning to these issues, some preliminary investigation of the term 'concept' itself seems due. The *Shorter Oxford Dictionary* defines it as 'the result rendered permanent by language of a previous process of comparison' (W. Hamilton). The key phrase here is 'rendered permanent'; that is, a concept is fixity as opposed to a tendential movement. It is to this characteristic that Heidegger makes his objection.

Further, as pointed out by the phenomenologists and Heidegger, the concept-forming mind operates with a specific notion of time. Concepts are seen as being made from different stuff and in a different manner from ideas. I shall refrain here from looking at the stuff of which ideas are made, and attempt to see what process lies behind concept formation.

Conceptual thought, as well as the conceptual notion of time, sees both the process of thinking and the flow of time in terms of a string of points located on a continuous line. Thoughts as well as matter are created from tiny building blocks. Opposed to this stands Kierkegaard's account of actuality as a non-concretized flow of non-existent entities, which if arrested are rendered vacuous. As an example he uses a group of soldiers communicating a password. The soldiers are standing in line and whispering the password from one to another. Each soldier forgets the password as soon as he has communicated it to the next one. Thus the password exists, if at all, as a movement – an activity – rather than anything that can be pinpointed and arrested. Likewise, noetic activity is the activity behind the aspectual principle: as such it does not create concepts – instead it tears down the arbitrary walls which concepts create. In addition, the correct performance of noetic activity is dependent not on a particular conclusion but on the thinker's ability to make categorial divisions along the natural and contextually appropriate lines (Findlay, 1974, p. 156).

> 'It seems probable to me that God in the beginning formed matter in solid massy hard impenetrable movable particles, of such sizes and figures and with such other properties and in such proportion to space as most conduced to the end for which he formed them; and that these primitive particles being solids are incomparably harder than any porous bodies compounded of them; even so hard as never to wear or break in pieces (Newton in Crosland, 1971, p. 76).

This study is emphasizing the interconnection of man, cosmos, matter and thought. Whether a culture appreciates food by tasting it with the upper frontal taste buds or the *Katic* tastebuds (the ones at the back of the throat) – sipping wine or gulping beer – determines whether a man understands or swallows meaning. The Koran, the Laws of Manu and Plato point to the fact that man's understanding and vision is determined by such 'details' as whether he wears a hat or works at night. It is not for tradition's sake that Muslims cover their heads. How we view matter or the world influences how we form our thoughts. A man who thinks in the conceptual manner, in terms of building blocks, forms a specific world view. According to Galileo, the centre of the universe was 'there' in the centre of the sun, not here on earth. Further, Galileo was of the opinion that prior to the invention of the telescope, these matters could not have been properly studied. Kant embraced these views enthusiastically and called his own revolution in thought Copernican, extending it to all fields of knowledge. Nothing could be known prior to the sensual encounter and to understanding in terms of categories (Kant, 1881, p. 115).

We, on the other hand, can deduce from the analysis of primitive art that the notional unities embracing certain phenomena are not necessarily formed simultaneously with man's sensual encounter with them. The abstract art of seventh-century Athens portrays this preconceptual state of mind. This is not to argue that a man whose thought is not conceptual has no knowledge or opinion concerning things he has not formulated in terms of objective images (concepts). It is only when the mind attempts to treat opinions as facts of externally objective knowledge that it is forced to lend reality to the previously undifferentiated building blocks on which these opinions were based. Or, simply, although Democritus created the atomic theory and Protagoras saw the mind and not the soul as the final cognitive faculty, the Greeks did not treat these postulations as final truths.

Abstract postulations, then, if treated merely as abstractions do not give rise to concepts. They are simply meaningful or not, depending on factors external to their genesis. In treating such abstractions as objective knowledge, however, the mind is stirred into reflective, causally oriented reckoning. In order to justify its behaviour by retrospective reference to rational rules, a person or his mind is forced to lend reality to elements that previously had no mental existence. Concepts are thus always retrospective; conceptual thought is likewise retrospective.

Prior to the concepts, we noted, there were notions. These notions may still be valid while based on undifferentiated entities. They become concepts when the mind attempts to re create them in terms of first elements, i.e. as legitimate autonomous sub-unities. Concepts, however, are not valid unities and should not be differentiated as such. In granting unity to concepts the mind is simply arresting the flow of thought, building illegitimate walls and creating grounds for various kinds of falsity.

This applies to the creation of all things. The idea that thought is made of building blocks gives rise to the corresponding idea that matter is made of tiny building blocks – elements. Yet as pointed out by Socrates, in either case this 'idea' is false:

> 'Do you remember, then, my dear Theaetetus . . . that no account could be given of the primary things of which other things are composed, because each of them taken just by itself was incomposite and that it was not correct to attribute even existence to it, to call it "this" or "that"?' (*Theaetetus,* 205c.)

Or, in the words of a contemporary physicist: 'Subatomic particles do not *exist* with certainty at definite places but rather show tendencies to exist, and atomic events do not occur with certainty at definite times but rather show tendencies to occur' (Capra, 1975, p. 137). As for Socrates, he does not deny that the mind does lend existence to the building blocks of conceptual thought or of matter: the point of the argument is not to deny that perception, belief and judgment – or physical things – are thus constituted; the process is illegitimate only if treated as knowledge. The manner of thought that treats building blocks as real entities creates the possibility of a conceptual mismatch, putting the concept of the Theaetetus who really is together with a Theaetetus who is flying, who really is not. In this way we can account for the fact that one may claim that $7+5=13$; for only in attempting to see the unity 13 as composed of $7+5$ units does the possibility of mismatch arise.

The process of conceptualization therefore directly relates to the view that a conceptualist thinker has of time. Since this problem of time and matter will be dealt with at some length later, all that should be pointed out here is that the view of the existence of elementary particles necessitates the view of time as a series of points and of matter as extended building blocks.

This conceptualist view is not adequate. Contemporary science is handicapped by conceptual thought, and by the 'logical' language of the positivists, as is contemporary philosophy. Though physics has broken through this barrier, the tight lid held by the logical positivists on philosophical thought has so far stifled the inevitable breakthrough. Concerning this matter, Heisenberg (1963, p. 177) observes in relation to physics:

> the most difficult problem concerning the use of language arises in quantum theory. Here we have at first no simple guide for correlating the mathematical symbols with the concepts of ordinary language; and the only thing we know from the start is the fact that our common concepts cannot be applied to the structure of atoms.

'Non-logical', non-conceptual thinking, far from being unscientific, is in fact in tune with the realities of our time. Capra (1975, p. 71) states:

> Quantum theory thus reveals a basic oneness of the universe. It shows that we cannot decompose the world into independently existing smallest units. As we penetrate into matter, nature does not show us any isolated basic building blocks, but rather appears as a complicated web of relations between the various parts of the whole. These relationships always include the observer in an essential way. The human observer constitutes the final link in the chain of the observational process, and the properties of any atomic object can only be understood in terms of the object's interaction with the observer.

II

Noetic principles are as relevant to art as to physics: elaborate technology confers no great advantage in approaching them. But the relation of the artist to *Aritmos* is of a particular nature. According to Plato, he is an inverted mirror-image of the noetic thinker. Each operates under a kind of spell (*Mania*). These spells however are of three kinds: the noetic and the two 'lower manias'. While the 'lower mania' divides into two – positive and negative – noetic mania, as *Theia Moira,* is always single and positive. The cognitive agency of the soul, *Logisticon,* is such that it is entirely truth orientated, and as such it can only fail in so far as it ceases to operate: it cannot malfunction. Artistic inspiration, on the other hand, stems from the heart and the stomach; and unless these two are controlled by the noetic faculty, they inevitably do malfunction.

While the normal individual ought to keep in balance the three cognitive faculties – those of the soul, mind and body – the artist, in those moments in which he operates as an artist, stuns his other faculties so as to be receptive to the passionate aspect of the soul. In this sense the artist is different from other people, for in order to be productive, he tends to maim the balance of his own soul. The artist in the moments when he acts as an artist may resemble an irresponsible child, and must not be left to his own devices.

It may be disturbing to the contemporary mind, yet history empirically testifies to the fact that 'great' art was produced in service of the community. The great artists were subject to control and censorship. Such control was not necessarily exercised by a human agency – the environment at large and the materials used could be the controlling factors.

In other words, for art to be effective it needs to meet resistance and opposition. The traditional Hindu artist is bothered and inconvenienced by the poor quality of his paint compared to the non-drip paint of the modern painter. The flute player in Pakistan is inconvenienced by the restrictions of his instrument. Even so, by making the execution of art easier in the material sense – by constructing electronic organs and 'perfect' paint – the art is not improved. Art is in fact the art of overcoming the restraint of the given situation, whether considered in terms of materials or of other, social constraints. Art can be defined as a symbolic, publicly observable and graceful way of overcoming the friction of *Anangke.* Ballet dancers could leap higher if they were to be given little jet propulsors, yet the beauty of a ballet leap lies precisely in that the restrictions of gravity are defied. Advancement in technology does not *in any way whatsoever* lead to advance in art. The same principle may be applied to a limited extent to formal restrictions of other kinds. While Beethoven and Michelangelo found it distressing that they were subject to censorship by the Pope and the State, it was in fact in the controlled climate of the Vatican, the Hapsburg court and the Florence of the Medici that 'great' art flourished.

Too much control stifles the black, passionate horse of the soul; hence there is less art in times of excessive repression. On the other hand, to allow the lower mania a free rein leads to the disappearance of 'good' art.

Such a view may be unusual to the contemporary mind, yet it can be objectively verified. A look at any period of repression of art or of its unlimited expansion will show a reduction in the amount of 'good' art. These matters will be taken up elsewhere, and are to be understood in terms of *Pleonexia* – the psychological desire for unlimited expansion – which also manifests as a phenomenon known to physics as 'negative interference': light waves if not in harmony will cancel themselves out.

Before turning to these issues, let us establish how art relates to the formation of concepts.

In every period, the conceptual thinkers create time-specific philosophies to which later generations cannot relate. While Socrates, Lao Tzu or Ramanuja were not the 'established' or 'famous' thinkers of their age, we do not know who these established or famous thinkers were, since their thought is not of interest to us.

Though texts such as the Tao Te Ching or the Mahabharata are constructed in accordance with 'foreign', non-conceptual rules, members of other cultures and epochs may – if willing to relax and to concentrate – find them interesting and meaningful. The reason, of course, is that these texts relate to fixed, deeper needs: they are constructed in accordance with the ethical or religious sentiment, and this is why we can understand them.

If no amount of concentration can help a non-specialized citizen to understand a contemporary work of philosophy, the indication is that such philosophy no longer relates to reality.

The same objection applies to non-conceptual disciplines such as contemporary music and art. The reasons why a non-specialized individual cannot always relate to these are of an ethical nature, and are given in relation to music by J.S. Bach. Bach expresses himself by using a notion – that of 'God' – which is meaningful to him, yet his observation is valid even for those who do not accept his terminology. Thus he writes that all music which is not written in the spirit of God is false, and is not music but an imitation of it. He points out that when the ethical sentiment – which he calls 'God' – is abandoned, the arts can freewheel for a while, but only for a while.

Unlike the social sciences, contemporary art is not always conceptual: yet there is no merit in abandoning conceptual rules unless one reintroduces the ethical element as the organizing principle. In all cases 'true' art as well as 'true' philosophy will be found in the dialectical relationship between the two elements. Linear art freewheels; linear, non-creative music replays the patterns already created by the conceptual mind.

It is for this reason that Parmenides and Heraclitus – despite their differences – both warn against the habit-conforming mind, and it is in the light of this warning that one is to understand what it is that Plato is hinting at with his continuous references that one is not to forget Oceanus' and Thetys' axioms that all things are perpetually flowing (*Theaetetus,* 152[e], 180[d]; *Timaeus,* 40[e]; *Cratylus,* 402[b]). One may also understand how it is that Plato is said to have combined both Heraclitian and Parmenidean traditions. If thought is arrested by the nature of conceptual activity, then reality indeed becomes flux – the rivers of Oceanus and Thetys pass man by. In recognizing this fact, man unbalances the conceptual arrest and learns to flow with the rivers: viewed in this sense, reality can be observed as unchanging.

For example, the dialogue between Socrates and the sophists can be seen as the struggle between thought and the arrest of thought. Words and language can be used either as triggers to notional flow, or as sources of autonomous meaning arrested in these very verbal formulations. This issue of flow versus the arrest of flow is the subject of the dialogue *Cratylus. Episteme* – knowledge – can be interpreted as *Epetai* – the movement of things (412[a]): this is the 'tender' use of language. *Episteme* can also be taken as *Stenai* – stopping or standing still (437[a]).

True meanings cannot be arrested in words or definitions. Language is only a tool to help us recollect. Treating a word or definition as a source of reality lends a unity and permanence to conceptual thought which it does not possess. This principle also applies to things as mentally put together. As Findlay (1979, p. 218) notes, Cratylus 'rejects the basic premise of the Wittgensteinian theory of language: that there is no understanding or percipient grasp of ideal natures prior to the use of linguistic expressions'. Thus neither language nor the rules of logic or reason determine reality, despite various claims to the contrary voiced by philosophers from Kant through Hegel to Wittgenstein.

The difference between the sophist and the philosopher can be seen as the difference between a man who uses language to persuade and a man who uses speech to discover. In creating a concept, the mind had already made a statement and chosen a miniature philosophy, and it seeks to persuade others. As pointed out in the *Gorgias* (520[a], 521[e]), the sophist enters a courtroom armed with a set of definitions; he 'knows' prior to the facts and context what justice, wisdom and knowledge are. Against him stands Socrates, the stingray, stinging the lazy horse back into activity, not allowing thought to stand still, and insisting on treating each instance as new (*Meno,* 80[a–c]).

III

Noetic thought does not lay stress on arrested definitions, whether arrested in a single-word sentence or in a philosophical doctrine. Extended to the field of ethics, concepts materialize as laws – so noetic thought attempts to minimize reliance on the law in the courts as well as on definitions in philosophical discourse. These principles extend further into the region of man's ideological and religious beliefs. Noetic thought minimizes beliefs that are based on images, words, doctrines and *Eikones*.

According to Lao Tzu, 'Good men do not argue' (Tao Te Ching, LXXXI); the true teaching is the 'teaching without words' (XLIII). What he means is that a man cannot be persuaded to a true belief. By persuading a man to accept a particular creed, one has only captured a non-essential aspect of the man. The profession of faith in a creed, if a matter of persuasion, is likewise of little value.

This is borne out by Jesus' parable of the two sons. A man had two sons and asked them to work in the vineyard. One rejected the words of his father; yet for reasons which are not analysed, it was in fact this son who went and cultivated the vineyard. The other son accepted – i.e. conceptually accepted – his father's words, but did not cultivate the vineyard: 'he answered, 'I go, sir,' but did not go. 'Which one of the two' – asks Jesus – 'did what his father wanted?' (Matthew, XXI, 28–31). Elsewhere, Jesus says that he himself, the Son of Man, may be rejected, but not so the sentiment that he represents – the Holy Ghost: 'whoever says a word against the Son of man will be forgiven; but whoever speaks against the Holy Spirit will not be forgiven' (Matthew, XII, 31).

Though Mohammed calls upon all to be Muslims and to accept 'the Book', one should not be too quick to understand this 'book' literally. Thus in surah IV,153, he writes of the people who look for God in scripture: 'the People of the Book ask you to bring down for them a book from heaven. Of Moses they demanded a harder thing than that. They said to him: "show us Allah distinctly." And for their wickedness a thunderbolt smote them.' Mohammed does not mean by this that the Koran is dispensable. However, elsewhere he writes that Allah has sent messengers to all nations to tell them his word in their own language; thus Christians, Sabaeans, Jews, etc. should all do well: 'As for those that believe in Allah and His apostles and discriminate against none of them, they shall be rewarded by Allah' (IV,152).

There is of course a paradox here, for one cannot be both a Christian and a Muslim, yet both insist on exclusivity. Mohammed himself accepts – and preaches – this paradox, for above the paradox, which is conceptual, there stands the *Logos:* it is in fact the 'Islam' – submission to the will of Allah – that is decisive. Pickthall writes (n.d., p. 33), 'All through the [second] sûrah runs the note of warning, which sounds indeed throughout the whole Koran, that it is not the mere profession of a creed, but righteous conduct, which is true religion.'

This point is carried to an extreme by the Sufi mystic who, when tortured to death by Christian crusaders, spoke thus to his torturers: 'If you believe that you strike for Allah, then strike harder so that we shall meet in heaven.'

The point is also illustrated by Kierkegaard (developing an idea also found in the Mahabharata). A knight is a knight by virtue of his noble conduct in battle. A knight when fighting in the fog may in fact be fighting on the opposite side to the one he thinks, yet – notes Kierkegaard (1962, p. 20)– this is not the point: when the fight is a noble one any side is the right side.

The contemporary ideal of an all-embracing resolution with the absence of all paradox and conflict sounds (conceptually) pious, yet is not of *Logos*-based thought.

Krishna speaks to Arjuna before the battle – 'Slay and be slain': the Kshatrias on both sides are equally dear to God. Likewise, Mohammed writes: 'Had your Lord pleased, all the people of the earth would have believed in Him. Would you then force faith upon men?' (Koran, X, 95.)

St Paul cannot be assumed to be writing of historical 'Jews' and historical 'Gentiles'. Jews are those who have accepted the formally true religion – i.e. that of the one God – and Gentiles are those who have not.

> For he is not a real Jew who is one outwardly, nor is true circumcision something external and physical. He is a Jew who is one inwardly, and real circumcision is a matter of the heart, spiritual and not literal (Romans, II, 28–9).

My argument, however, is not against formality. Unlike Californian gurus and pop singers, I do not urge people to rise above environmentally determined givens or parties, religions, creeds, etc. In saying that all men are brothers, neither Buddha nor Confucius was advocating that men should abandon the particularity of belief, custom, philosophy or religion necessitated by the historical moment. 'Faithful *in abstracto*' pop stars and professionalized humanitarians may be successful in drawing universal approval by preaching 'peace and love' platitudes in such a way as to reduce them to simplified images bearing no relation to reality; but the ways of *Logos* are not susceptible to conceptual simplifications. Behind the 'let's do away with divisions' slogans lies the hard materiality of the bourgeois machinery. The divisions these entertainers would really like to do away with are those halting the spread of the market: few pop stars or Californian gurus have seriously proposed to eliminate economic divisions, or given away the money they earned by preaching anti-formalism. The complexity of real life situations is given in the Mahabharata. The general rule of conduct is abstention from injury by act, thought and word in respect of all creatures, yet a few lines later in the text we read that 'no person in the world can support life without injuring other creatures. The very ascetic in the depths of the forest is no exception.'

While noetic thought stresses that a particular manifestation is not the truth, it does not pretend that it can do without such manifestations. An icon is not a god but a picture of God. Likewise, man is not God but made in the image of God; yet for man there is no God except as manifest in man.

Positivists would have us believe that we can know what man is by studying an existing, particular man or group of men. Yet no man can exhaust manhood. This does not mean that for every actual man there is a real man in the world of ideas. Even though the tangible is not the ultimate truth, there is nothing but the tangible. Although the actual man is not the man himself, there is no man but the actual man. Behind Taoism or altruistic socialism there does not exist a transcendent, 'true' philosophy of *Logos,* even though we may be forced to make the conceptual assertion that there is such a 'thing'. There is nothing but the actual: in taking away the actual manifestation of a particularized religion or philosophy without replacing it by a new one, one takes away everything there is. Thus man will never be able to do away with nations, ideologies and so forth: even though one might do away with nations based on territory, language or race, people would form groups and associations on a different basis. The same principle applies to thoughts, words, actions, houses – all of these need to take expression by resorting to some actual form.

The noetic thinker is obliged to differentiate between the symbol (which is fixed) and the meaning (which is loose). Anything becomes what it is through the marriage of the fixed and the loose, the limit and the unlimit. The noetic thinker does not deny the ability to connect things through the unifying activity of the sentiment, which transcends the various manifestations which take place in time and space.

But if Kant and Stenzel were wrong to equate the ideas of true things with concepts, and if concepts are illegitimate entities anyway, then where are valid forms to be found? Similarly, if atoms – or any tiny building blocks – are not the real constituents of things, what are things made of? Noetic thought claims that thoughts and things, bodies and souls, are all made from the same material and range into one another. Before we identify this material, let us examine the formation of thoughts and concepts in more detail.

IV

Contemporary thought in the West appears unwilling to give up the view of ideas as concepts, though it is quite prepared to replace 'concepts' with a different word. Sir David Ross prefers 'universals'. He writes: 'the senses present us with a world of particular events, but in Reason we have a faculty by which we transcend the flux and synthesise universals' (Ross, 1966, pp. 225–6). Ross bases his understanding of universals on the Aristotelian paradigm or master instance which, to him, becomes the idealized concept. Crudely understood, this means that through seeing many horses, we eventually form a picture of the universal horse. He considers that 'the best example we have of this power is to be found in mathematics.' Ideas, in this interpretation, become abstract and theoretical, like the rules and objects of mathematics.

This is not the view of noetic thinkers. In the *Republic* (511^{a-e}), for example, Plato claims that mathematics is entirely limited by the lower epistemic activity, which is expressed as an hypothesis derived from sense data. This is different from the idea-oriented activity called *Noesis,* which is entirely independent of the calculative reason of the mathematical (i.e. theoretical) sciences.

In view of Egyptian, Babylonian and Pythagorean thought, we could ask whether it might be *numbers* that are the currency of noetic thought. In associating numbers and mathematics with universals, Gaiser, Ross and those like minded seem to base their views on certain Pythagorean strains in Plato's thought. While such views are currently being exploited at length by all kinds of unexpected authorities, it must be remembered that Aristotle (*Metaphysics,* $987^{a}29$–$988^{a}17$) writes that the numbers Plato and Pythagoras are talking about are not the objects of mathematics. The numbers that are constitutive of reality have little to do with mathematical universals. For the Egyptians or for the Brotherhood at Croton, 'mathematical thinking' is not the correct currency for apprehending reality.

Numbers, according to Plato, are forms – or like them – and as such quite above thought: even the purest thought cannot be equated with the universal. The realization that ideas transcend ordinary thought is not easily made, and may have been hotly disputed in the Academy itself. This is possibly why in the dialogue *Parmenides* the old philosopher finds it necessary to point out this peculiarity to Socrates, who is described as 'young and inexperienced' in observing that ideas are thoughts. 'But Parmenides,' asks Socrates, 'may it not be that each of these ideas is a thought which cannot exist anywhere but in the mind?' Parmenides refutes this, for it would imply that there have to be thinkers everywhere present, otherwise the universe would consist of thoughts being thought by nobody.

While attempting to diagnose the false way of thinking, I have so far been less explicit concerning the nature of correct thought. (It is of course a part of *Logos*-based philosophy that positive conclusions should be implied rather than formulated.) I have called the correct manner of thought 'aspectual', and described it as a 'flow' of entities. I have emphasized that these entities are not concepts.

Even though it is not etymologically correct, Hamilton's equation of *Ratio* with concept and *Nous* with notion seems philosophically apt. The word 'notion' as a counterpart to 'concept' serves to suggest both the '*Noein*'-forming process and its product. The sage's mind 'flows like water' (Lao Tzu) or 'like smooth oil' (Socrates in the *Theaetetus*), but Chuang Tzu speaks of fools recognizing things by referral to a string of pictures, and Confucius advises the rectification of these pictures when they are arrested in words, according to the rhythms of *Li*. If concepts are defined as universalized words or pictures derived through the senses and imprinted as models on our minds, then we do not have far to look for them in Plato's dialogues: 'It appears to me that the conjunction of memory with sensation together with the feeling consequent upon memory and sensation may be said to write words in our souls' (*Philebus*, 39[a]). This passage seems to be a description of the process of concept formation. However, if we are to follow Hamilton's definition, for a concept to be a concept it must be rendered permanent: 'Then please give your approval to the presence of a second artist in our souls . . . a painter who comes after the writer and paints in the soul the pictures of these assertions that we make' (*Philebus*, 39[b]).

Concept formation is also similar to the process outlined by Socrates in the *Theaetetus:* sense impressions are imprinted on a 'block of wax', to be used as a fixed symbol or universal by means of which one can recognize other instances (*Theaetetus*, 191[c]). Socrates likens the possession of 'concepts' to the possession of token birds held captive in the aviary of our minds. When sensually encountering an unrecognized 'bird', the mind turns to the token collection and seeks to grab hold of an identifying representative (*Theaetetus*, 197[c]). However, the use of such knowledge is of limited value to Socrates: all these attempts to account for such knowledge lead to eventual bankruptcy, since they allow for the possibility of false judgment. If something is known, argues Socrates, it can never be matched against an unknown and different thing and judged to be the same. The very fact that conceptual mismatching occurs proves that conceptual 'knowledge' is not knowledge but conjecture (*Theaetetus*, 200[b]).

Opposed to this there is the aspectual flow. 'To know like a river' is a standard form of imagery much used in Vedic, Taoist and Platonic thought. 'Notion' is defined by the *Shorter Oxford Dictionary* as an inclination, a tendency, a flow: and it is the word 'flow' that we here distinguish as characteristic.

In the *Symposium* (207^{b}–208^{a}), Plato gives us a detailed account of knowledge as a flow of births:

> 'Everything including man is continually changing, and this is true not only of the body but of the soul, [yet] what happens with pieces of knowledge is even more remarkable. . . . Each individual piece of knowledge is subject to the same process as ourselves. When we use the word "recollection" we imply by using it that knowledge departs from us; forgetting is the departure of knowledge, and recollection, by implanting a new impression in the place of that which is lost, preserves it and gives it a spurious appearance of uninterpreted identity. It is in this way that everything mortal is preserved: not by remaining for ever the same . . . but by undergoing a process in which the losses caused by age are repaired by new acquisitions of a similar kind.'

Notions cannot be defined positively – that is, statically – for they only trace that from which they separate, and which is forever being born anew.

Aritmos is the organizing principle of noetic thought. Its general meaning apart, it also has a number of specific meanings: this plurality of meaning is perfectly legitimate if in each case it is determined by context. Faced with the words arithmetic, reason, *Logisticon, Techne,* science, astronomy, the contemporary mind automatically reduces a pre-conceptual terminology to conceptual units: but a knowledge of *Aritmos,* it is repeatedly argued by Plato, is necessary in the ordering of one's affairs, of one's own soul and of the affairs of State (*Laws,* 737^{d}–738^{b}; *Epinomis,* 979^{a-b}). He placed a sign over the entrance to the Academy, stating that 'those not schooled in *Aritmos* need not enter'. In contemporary terms, he was saying that practical science may increase the standard of living, and that excellence in theoretical science may win social recognition, but the study of number is that which 'facilitates the conversion of the soul' to true values, which are ethical (*Republic,* 525^{c}). (For those who are of the opinion that contemporary science has surpassed the thinking of the Greeks, it may be worth pointing out that Dalton obtained his atomic theory from Democritus. The debate over the wave and particle theories of matter was just as active in the Academy as it is today. Plato rejected the particle theory on the same grounds as those recently used by Bohr and Rutherford. The popular belief that Galileo discovered that the earth is round and that it was he who posited heliocentric theory is just a myth: all this was well established in Greece. Plato rejected the heliocentric theory of Aristarchus on ethical grounds, while being fully aware of the empirical evidence in favour of it.)

Findlay (1974, p. 345) draws attention to the word Diarithmesis, and writes concerning it: 'Our sense of the just and noble always depends on a subtle numbering that we use to persuade ourselves and others.' He adds, 'Without this we should only have correct opinions and could convince no one.' Diarithmetic vibration is in fact the test of truth. Without this sentiment, we can persuade people only on the basis of concepts and opinions: we appeal only to the mind and ignore the logic of the body and that of the soul. The difference between persuasion and the creation of sentiment is the difference between the sophist and the philosopher. The sophist does not speak to a man as an integrated body, soul and mind; he structures his words, beliefs and institutions around images and concepts. The philosopher, on the other hand, verifies the validity of a particular construction – whether a sentence or a legal constitution – by comparing it to the underlying reality which manifests itself in a certain *Aritmos,* the ratio defining a unity of body and soul (*Epinomis,* 978[a–b]).

It may be difficult to calculate the numbers involved in these ratios, but several ancient systems of philosophy were structured around them, and so are the notions of contemporary physics, since they reflect and are consonant with the forces ruling the universe. Sentiments correspond to the aspectual notional movement, and follow the changing flux while maintaining an *inner* fixity and objectivity which is not touched by outer change. Sentiment, therefore, is that objective quality which legitimates the fluid aspectuality of noetic thought, and rescues it from the ethical subjectivity of the positivists.

In short, then, there are three different uses of the word *Aritmos:* (1) in the ordinary sense of number as in counting; (2) in the quasi-eidetic sense, as an object of theoretical mathematics or defined ratio; and (3) in the completely non-empirical sense, where it functions as the subjectively felt cognitive element, or divine sentiment, whereby one understands the rhythmic substrata of the ethical cosmos.

In this tradition, the universe is constituted, apprehended and governed by rhythm. 'Not only for plants that grow from the earth but also for the animals that live upon it there is a cycle' (*Republic,* 550[a]). This must be true for men as well; the qualities of the rhythmic divisions ruling any group in a city – and the city itself – ensure 'the common sentiment' (*Laws,* 745[e]). These qualities of measure and proportion are what constitutes beauty and excellence (*Philebus,* 64[e]). Indeed it is rhythm, ratio, proportion, as apprehended by a correct motion of the soul, that constitutes all noetic differentiation. In this light, one can understand better how it is the nature of our sentiments that determines the way we construct not only our own persons and identities but all other entities, inner and outer. With Solmsen (1942, p. 169) we can see Plato's laws as reflective of 'basic spiritual and moral forces in fact deriving their strength, appeal and power of persuasion from intimate contact with the deeper layers of human existence.'

V

To summarize the whole discussion so far, we have seen two principles around which an autonomous, conscious entity constitutes knowledge. In the first case, the constitutive activity was expressed in the creation of entities differentiated by their extension in time and space, and organized into unities called things. The force bringing these unities together was parekbasitic *Epithumia, Kama,* desire. As an indirect product of this activity, the 'discerning agent' was generated, i.e. the person who becomes conscious of himself as a unit through his reflective awareness of the above process. Through such activity, man separates his mind from his body and his body from his soul. The individual is equated with his mind, and as such separates himself from the environment at large – the cosmos – and his immediate environment, his body. Opposed to this mentally constituted individual there is the aspectually perceiving psyche posited by *Logos*-orientated thought. The differences between these two are rooted in a difference over the nature of the organizing principles of thought.

For Kant, whose thought was taken as an archetype counterposed to noetic thought, the principle behind all reasoning is the categories of the mind. In choosing this principle, Kant (as also Protagoras) chose to accept a particular set of scientific beliefs which were predominant in his time. In Kant's case, the views concerned were of matter as consisting of material particles, and the centre of the universe as being external to man – i.e. not the earth.

The sophists accept Democritus' view of all matter as composed of indestructible little elements – atoms – and of thoughts being composed of summarized, fixed images or *Eikones*. Further, they accept the heliocentric theory of Aristarchus. All this is rejected by the noetic thinkers – Socrates, the Pythagoreans and in particular Plato – who, while familiar with the arguments of the astronomers, reject these views on ethical grounds and propose an alternative way of seeing the universe. The assumptions of heliocentric theory are now held as provisionally true. In the local sense, the views of Newtonian mechanics hold: the object with the larger mass will be central to rotation. However, as far as observational evidence goes precisely the same observations will be made whether the sun is orbiting around the earth or vice versa: in fact the observations will conform to the locality of the observer.

Protagoras, like Kant, never denies the existence of the 'almighty mover'; both thinkers, however, make the origin of movement external to man. In order to define man, Protagoras externalizes the divine. Kant follows the same procedure, except that he claims his intention is to be better able to define God and religion. They both turn the man-cosmos or man-God relation upside down: by externalizing God in man, Kant also externalizes man. The essence of man is seen as external to the actual man, and is given by the categories of apprehension. Protagoras summarizes all these views in his famous dictum that man is the measure of all things. For 'man' read 'man's mind as given by external criteria' (*Theaetetus*, 154^{b}–171^{b}); hence for the paradigmatic sophist, external pattern is the measure of all things (*Theaetetus*, 160^{d}).

Against this view stands Socrates, for whom it is the internal pattern – God – which is the measure of all things; God is conceived of as 'divine mind' or 'the true divine reason', *Logos,* which is different from mental, *Dianoia*-based reason (*Philebus,* 22^{c}). This divine reason can be provisionally equated with the set of internal criteria I have labelled sentiment. Thus the criteria for God, which in positivist thought are external to man, are in fact internal or humanistic; and the conceptually 'internal' criteria become external.

The Kantian, so-called humanistic, man-oriented conception inevitably leads to the 'dehumanizing' conclusion that man is preceded by abstract entities called categories. The noetic notion starts and ends with man, or rather an aspect of man, the *Auto Kath-Auto* (*Timaeus,* 57^{e}–58), the infinitely flexible self-determinant or self-mover, which precedes any constitutive entities. The divine aspect of man here chooses the organizing principles by its own changing inclinations. The organizing activity itself is 'teleologically aspectual'. I have chosen the word 'aspectual' since such activity transgresses the aspects or dimensions delimited by time and space, and does not compose unities according to sensually perceived units of shape and temporal succession, nor according to Newtonian mechanical causality; rather, unities are determined by a particular inclination or affection of the soul, and are governed by a specific *Aritmos* or ratio. I have used the word 'teleological', since both the manner in which something is discerned by the soul and the nature of the soul's eventual conclusion is determined by the nature of its interest.

The constitutive blocks of the 'things' discerned by 'categorial' thought were labelled concepts, and atoms or elements. Against these were posited notions and *Aritmoi,* being the flux of sentiment-structured thought and of things. This distinction between the two sets of organizing criteria has led to a further distinction, between things as functions of time and space and things as functions of number or sentiment.

While introductory definitions such as 'by man we shall mean so-and-so' are the currency of the conceptualist, a definition may be employed by a noetic thinker in order to summarize a set of movements. Having gone through such a set of movements, the reader may compare how his own positive grasp relates to that of the author: the true definition lies in the dialectic between these two.

Thus we may generalize, and claim that a human individual is never this or that, but is always a flow of decisions. In other words, there are many possible I's, and the true I is created in the relationship between the chooser and the environment within which he chooses. Logically the chooser precedes the chosen I, but the precedence is only logical, not temporal.

In the course of his life a man is constantly redefining himself. While the choices are infinite, conjecturally we may reduce them to a choice between two kinds of I. In every thought, in every action, in every desire, one chooses between these two selves. One of them is integrated and noetic, and defined in a positive symbiotic relation between the larger cosmos – the universe – and the immediate environment of one's family, city and own body. Such an I instantly resolves the clash of any interests, whether of body-mind or soul, and fuses them all into a single entity. As against this there is the individualizing I, which is the desire that makes us smoke even though this may be bad for our body: it creates body-mind conflict. Further, the individualizing I sees its own interests as independent of the immediate environment and of the cosmos at large.

VI

The mind-knowing faculty, if not operating in conjunction with the body-knowing faculty, and if separate from the knowing faculty of the soul, necessarily creates false thinking. The objection to mental thinking is not an objection to a particular doctrine or a content – the objection is to the activity itself. The mind is ultimately a conjectural abstraction: there is no mind, but simply the brain which feels pleasures and pains. The mind is a mechanical, passive instrument, which when divorced from noetic control seeks to avoid pain and maximize pleasure in the most immediate ways.

The mind is capable of perceiving that certain pleasures taken today may bring pain tomorrow, since these relationships follow the cause-and-effect laws of mechanics, which are also the laws within which the mind itself operates. The mind, however, is not able to grasp how damage done to the environment, i.e. to entities other than the self conceived by the mind, will also bring pain to the self and to all other selves – since the interrelation between the self and the cosmos does not follow the principles of mental thought, temporal succession in causality, the categories of time and space and so forth.

The mind therefore is incapable of being good. A mentally rational man can only be expected to be good to his fellow man if he can be shown that if he behaves in this way to others, others will be good to him. Thus parents are expected to love and care for their children only in the expectation that they will be cared for by the children in their old age. If such 'market' relationships can be institutionalized, e.g. through social security and old people's homes, then love becomes unnecessary. Thus the market replaces love.

Noetic thought maintains that love is its own reward. For a parent to love and care for a child is rewarding in itself, for in loving a parent becomes what he is. So too for a citizen and his duties towards his city. In a complicated way such individuals *are* rewarded, although the manner and the nature of the reward cannot be grasped by the mind: it is grasped by the soul and by the body – by the heart.

The individual who is rewarded by acts undertaken in the sentiment of love is not the same individual as the one synthesized by the categories of time, space and causality. Kant, realizing this, calls on men to do not what they would like but what is their duty. This is the inevitable result of conceptual thinking: action either becomes self-gratifying or self-sacrificing. We dislike serving king and country but it is our duty; and so also for duties towards children, parents and God.

Eventually one becomes tired of all these duties. It is unreasonable to expect people to act in a certain way because they are daily persuaded that they ought to, even though they don't like it. And it is unreasonable to accept that they can be forced to behave in a socially acceptable way merely through the creation of an efficient police force and law courts. In the long run, a conceptually organized society – market, law, police – is unbearable.

Rather than the 'stick and carrot' techniques of the market and the law courts, noetic thought uses sounds, rhythms and ideas to educate the individual to perceive himself differently. Thus activities which are seen as painful by the conceptual I appear enjoyable to the noetic I.

Views such as this are also advocated by conceptual thinkers, but without realizing that mental philosophy is not enough. For the object of noetic writing is not to draw conclusions such as the above, which are themselves conceptual: the object is to create the sentiment.

Were one to draw philosophic distinctions according to the nature of the mental activity behind a philosophy, one could fruitfully posit a dichotomy between idealists and noetic thinkers. The idealists, 'the friends of ideas', may take the 'religious' view as their intellectual starting point, but their view is itself rooted in an idea of the mind – i.e. it is a thought. Idealists like Hegel are forced to deny objective reality to the external empirical world, and to see it as a product of the mind. Though apparently at odds, the idealist and empirical positions are identical with respect to the mental process through which the world view of each is derived. Their conclusions are, of course, different: the idealists assert the primacy of mind over matter and the empiricists assert the reverse. Noetic thought rejects both positions as based on object-subject, inner-outer divisions which are incompatible with its own world view. Such divisions do not occur in aspectual thought. For the aspectual thinker, the world is the body of the deity: and the deity is within and without, in matter and outside it. Thales writes that all things are full of God. There are in the Saanthana tradition no discussions of the type on which post-Cartesian philosophy is based: noetic thinkers do not ask questions such as 'Do I exist?' or 'Who am I?' Having never asked such questions, noetic thought never provided answers to them.

As against noetic thought, conceptual thought is parekbasitic – it turns things upside down. When he wrote that Hegel ought to be turned right side up, Marx was not being clever with words or coy. The conceptualist inversion of reality is an ever-recurring phenomenon. As Plato argues in the *Parmenides,* wherever the conceptualist uses an 'is', the philosopher should substitute an 'is not'.

The sophist is in fact a mirror image of the philosopher, for he is exactly the same, except that what is on the left for the one is on the right for the other. Indeed the notions 'left' and 'right' in contemporary political jargon are based on yin-yang, heaven-earth, male-female divisions and are correspondingly inverted. Inversion or *Anatrope* will be explored further below; let us for now take a last look at how it relates to the paradigmatic bourgeois thinkers, Kant and Descartes.

These two, while formally claiming to be religious, in fact present a sentiment and a manner of apprehending the world which is in the long run fundamentally irreligious. They present an externalized entity and call it God. This 'theoretical' God however is not a living God; it was only a matter of time before it was negated by Nietzsche and others.

Kant would have us believe that in destroying God as within man, and externalizing it into the transcendent world of 'things as such', he has made true religion possible. Arguments apart, history has shown the result of Kant's activity (in the words of Jesus, 'by their fruits you shall know them'). Kant is afraid to verbalize what Nietzsche, in a sudden bout of courage, screams from the cliff of Engadin – 'God is dead and we have murdered him!' A formal disbeliever, Nietzsche proves more ethical and religious than the formally pious, clerical Kant – proving once again that formal notions or the profession of faith in God are not decisive.

Nobody can believe in a conceptual God, and nobody does. A conceptual, external God is a projection of fears, prejudices, fantasies and wishful thinking. This is what the God of the nineteenth century had become: opium for the masses and the intellectuals. While God as an intellectual concept seems to be different from the God of the superstitious, icon-worshipping, ignorant idolater, both notions are in fact the same: both are externalized, fixed icons or pictures, and, as such, subject to all the criticisms of Freud, Nietzsche and the others.

All these criticisms apply only to God as conceptualized. In denying this external God, the mental-intellectual idol, Nietzsche, Freud and other conceptually atheistic philosophers make room for the re-emergence of the 'new', the internal God. Whether this internal God will be *called* God again will depend on how soon the negative, conceptual connotations of the word can be removed from the European consciousness; until this happens, it is possibly better to call God by other names.

As I shall argue, any progress, in art, music or science, necessitates the radical banishment of conceptual thought. Contemporary physics has already moved in this direction. Given that activity and motion are the essential properties of matter, the concept of 'dead' physical atoms and external forces which push them around can no longer be maintained. Let us look now at the substance of the new and living cosmos that will replace it.

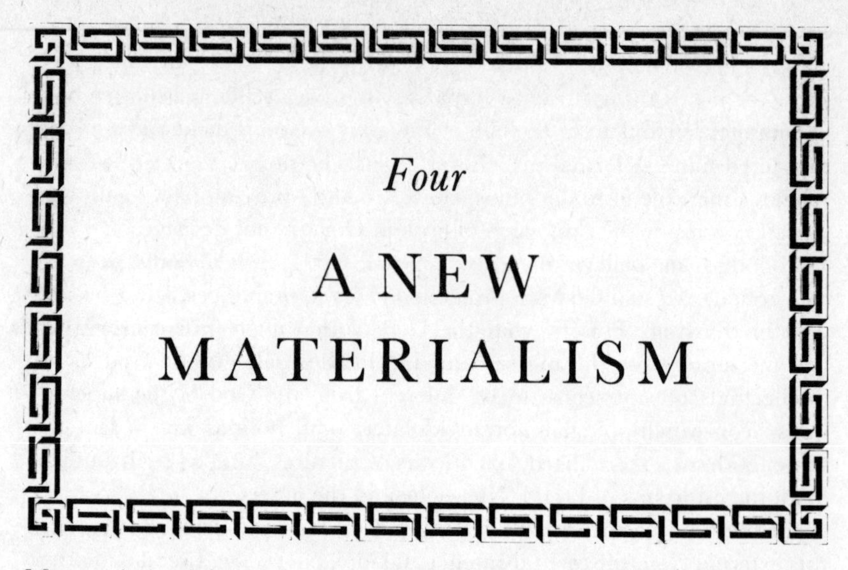

Four

A NEW MATERIALISM

Matter, it is claimed by Bohr, de Broglie and the quantum theorists, moves itself – it has its own forces and laws. Plato's definition of 'real' is that which can move and be moved, which can affect and be affected. For the Greeks, for Hindu and Chinese thinkers, the whole cosmos was alive.

The new microbiology likewise abandons the organic-inorganic division, and so does the new chemistry. While the social sciences are continuing their march toward further and further specialization, and while sociologists can no longer meaningfully communicate with psychologists and lingual philosophers, these principles of specialization are in fact already bankrupt.

History creates strange alliances, and it is not surprising to see physics merging with philosophy and biology with political science. On a large scale, the new alliances will fuse tax merchants and 'sinners', atheists and priests. New affinities and new common interests will be found in surprising quarters. Sentiment cuts across ideological, racial and professional divisions.

Dramatic examples of this can be found. While the mainstream of philosophy today is either logical positivism or anarcho-existentialism, there is appearing a small group of thinkers from various schools who suddenly grasp a common affinity and realize that, although they are classified as philosophers by the various university departments, they share neither the language nor the interests of their so-called peers – the positive philosophers and social scientists. Instead, they socialize and converse with physicists, biologists and members of the 'other camp'.

Similarly, there is a split between the main body of applied science (the technologist and the market scientist) and an avant-garde group of physicists, biologists and chemists. Industrial chemists can meaningfully talk to industrial sociologists and to logical-positivist philosophers, while the same individuals cannot grasp the ideas of contemporary mathematics or physics.

The new, noetic biologists converse freely with the new chemists, and the one science ranges freely into the other. Men like Bohr or Einstein were not particularly impressive as students of conceptual mathematics, and the latter found considerable difficulty in stunning his mind sufficiently to follow its fixed rules. Park finds that he can never remember the formulae necessary to solve quadratic equations, and creates a new formula every time this algebraic problem presents itself. More than one scientist has observed that the theory of relativity is more likely to make sense to a philosopher than to a professional (i.e. industrial) mathematician. This theory cannot become a law precisely because it cannot be objectively verified – if by 'objectively' we mean by the mechanical application of preformulated rules, such as those followed in conceptual mathematics. It is as a result of this that many leading physicists have turned to Eastern and ancient philosophy for inspiration, exchanging their ideas with philosophers, biologists and chemists of the noetic variety, and turning the established division of labour upside down.

Before long questions will be raised about the naturalness of dividing biology from chemistry and physics. Leaving these issues aside, let us turn to a related topic: the division between idealism and materialism.

I

While the word 'materialism' is widely and popularly used, its validity and meaning may be doubted, whether it is scientifically or philosophically considered. 'Matter' may be saved if it is modified to include motion as internal to it. I prefer, however, to use a new word. The 'matter' which reabsorbs the externalized idea of motion no longer exists: in the sense of *Esse* it is no longer the matter of Descartes. The new word is *Chora,* and its manner of 'existing' is actuality. Matter exists, but *Chora* is actual. So the new materialism is better called actualism. Of course, to call it 'new' is misleading. It is not new; it was essential to Greek, Taoist and Buddhist thought.

As a result of post-Cartesian views on substance and post-Aristotelian views of matter, Kant and subsequent scholarship misread the Greek view of the formative medium of 'things' and their ideal models. This misapprehension involves the assumption that the ideal – the entity called the *Eidos* – is the perfect instance behind the imperfect manifestation of a thing: seeing many different horses, a man develops a view of a perfect horse. This 'Aristotelian' rendering is almost diametrically opposed to what noetic thinkers have in mind when positing notions such as *Eidos*. It implies that he who wants to know horses ought to see as many horses as possible, study them, compare them and thus form an idea of the true horse. If we were to caricature noetic thought, we could by inversion say that, for the Orphic Greeks, a man who wants to know what a horse is should rather close his eyes every time he sees one. For within such thought, instances are not true entities.

In saying that perceived objects are shadow-copies of true objects, Ramanuja or Plato is not emphasizing the fact that they are copies and hence imperfect imitations of the real thing; only that they are other than real, they are not true. An instance can, and indeed ought to, serve to trigger a recollection of a true unity, but it is not the empirical dimension that activates such recollection. In other words, the empirical horse bears no empirical resemblance to the true horse. The knowledge of a horse comes through the noetic activity and psychic rhythm involved in using and experiencing a horse as a means of satisfying certain of one's essential human needs. There is a 'horse' aspect to each man, and it needs to be fulfilled in a certain way for a man to be a man.

In short, it is not the horse in time and space which reminds one of the true horse; but this does not mean that an actual horse cannot be used to gain knowledge of a true horse, for actual or visible things have a dimension which is out of time. In fact, as soon as one perceives the flux as flux, i.e. as soon as one recognizes actuality for what it is, one is no longer deceived, and can no longer be said to be perceiving things in time even though one is perceiving sensible reality.

It is only in conceptual thought that things are seen as isolated entities ('a stone is a stone, a river is a river'). Noetic thought, being out of time, sees a stone in a thousand years from now, when it will be earth, sees a river as rain or cloud. Indeed, noetic thought insists that there really are no such things as stones or rivers. Where does the Indian Ocean become the Pacific, where does the Pacific become the Atlantic, and where do all these become different from rain? It is the mind that isolates them.

Kant was correct when he pointed out that the mind does not exist before its encounter with the sensible environment. Prior to mental perception, there are no things or individual persons, and there are no objects. There are, of course, noetic objects as constituted by *Aritmos,* but these are not the same. Heisenberg has described the world as divided not into objects but into 'groups of connections' determining 'the texture of the whole'. The mind is simply a set of motions which has the ability to constitute mental images – objects – and in turn to constitute itself:

'the universe really is motion and nothing else. And there are two kinds

> of motion. Of each kind there are any number of instances, but they differ in that the one kind has the power of acting and the other of being acted upon. From the intercourse and friction of these with one another arise offspring, endless in number but in pairs of twins. One of each pair is something perceived and the other a perception, whose birth always coincides with that of the thing perceived' (*Theaetetus,* 156[a,b]).

This is, of course, the correct version of Kant's argument, and it does not claim that the individual is composed thus: the soul faculty, *Logisticon,* has its own rules and movement.

Plato makes clear that there is no other than conjectural distinction between perception and what is perceived. Matter or the thing-in-itself does not 'cause' sensations, which the mind unifies to create perceived objects. The sensation and the thing – what we see as the chair and the chair – are coequal, a pair of twins springing to life in the intercourse of the two motions.

Later in the same dialogue, Plato continues this argument and states: 'Nothing has any being as one thing just by itself, no more has the agent or patient, but as a consequence of their intercourse with each other' (*Theaetetus,* 182[a]). This statement, caricatured, is taken to mean that a tree in the forest cannot fall unless some conscious entity is there to perceive it: or simply that there is no tree prior to somebody perceiving it as such. However, since 'the offspring' (actuality) always come in pairs, just as there are no trees, chairs, tables, bodies or matter prior to being perceived as such by someone, there is likewise no 'someone' prior to perceiving something: 'For there is no such thing as an agent until it meets with a patient nor any patient until it meets with an agent' (*Theaetetus,* 157[a]).

It is in terms of these two motions that we can understand Plato's One and the indefinite dyad, or the Pythagorean male-female principle. All things are a creation of the intercourse between them, yet the One and the dyad are not in themselves actuality – they spring into existence and can be understood only through the offspring of their intercourse. As shown in the *Parmenides,* the unqualified unity, the non-predicated One, while alone is perfectly real: as such it is completely beyond thought, it is out of time and place and can only be conceived of negatively: indeed it cannot be conceived, but one posits it in order to account for things that can be conceived. Everything that can be touched, seen or even thought of is the progeny of the encounter between that One and the dyad, *To Peras* and *Aperion.* The progeny is *Chora* and is in *Chora* – it is all things.

II

Contemporary thought abounds with conceptualized 'Eastern mystics'. Common to all of them is the externalization of the verifying criterion. This externalization may take many forms. For example, contemporary research into the physical aspect of marital love gauges the superiority of a particular kind of relationship according to criteria devised in the laboratory; yoga is a useful discipline since it helps one keep a desirable figure and meditation is valid since it produces certain effects on an oscilloscope. The philosophy of a logical positivist is 'true' if it adheres to a specific logical matrix. In the so-called totalitarian states, a particular interpretation of an ideology or of a particular philosophy is 'true' if it adheres to the matrix laid down by the ruling party.

Logos-oriented thought radically avoids verification by any such criterion. To use a few more examples, the popular cliché that meditation brings peace of mind is no more than a cliché if one is referring to the empirical mind, *Manas*. This is pointed out by Jesus, with the words, 'Do you think that I have come to give peace on earth? No, I tell you, but rather division; for henceforth in one house there will be five divided, three against two and two against three . . . father against son and son against father'(Luke, XII, 51–53). Many saints were torn by psychological conflicts and suffered correspondingly. The popular notions of smiling gurus and self-satisfied practitioners of Hindu meditations living in blissful indifference have little basis in fact. The experiences of the aspirant after enlightenment are more likely to be those of the hero of the Bhagavad Gita, Arjuna, who, when faced with the realities of the real battle – i.e. real yoga – 'is overcome by grief and despair'; he is, in fact, participating in the cosmic experience described elsewhere as the hour of Jesus in the garden of Gethsemane. It is for this reason that the hero of the yoga of resignation says, 'In the dark night of my soul I feel desolation. In my self-pity I see not the way of righteousness' (Bhagavad Gita, II,7). Not that the yoga of the Bhagavad Gita does not bring peace – but 'My peace is not such as the world gives': the fruit of the resignation to the sentiment of Krishna is not any peace, health or indeed anything that can be registered on a electroencephalograph.

Apart from the reigning positivist orthodoxy, the late twentieth century has also seen the growth of a 'spiritually oriented' dissident group which attempts to blend the spiritual with the scientific. The activities of such people range from the deeply philosophical and scientific to funfair charlatanism; what they all share, however, is the assumption that since one cannot differentiate between the body and the soul, the soul itself ought to be an empirically verifiable entity. While one may sympathize with their broad intentions, Saanthana-oriented thought cannot possibly endorse their approach. All attempts to communicate physically with the soul – to photograph it, to induce it to speak, to register its presence on a geiger counter or any such device – are essentially foreign to this kind of thought. While Saanthana philosophers do assert that the body and soul are one, they do not claim that the soul is physical in any way whatsoever.

In other words, the soul, absolute Being, Brahman and Atman, reality, are wholly negative entities. The essential I is not an entity composed of extremely fine particles. God is not a field of electrical force. The way of *Logos* thought is the *Via Negativa:* there is no soul and there is no God, so long as 'is' – *Esse* – is used in the time-space sense as it is in normal speech. 'The kingdom of God is not coming with signs to be observed; nor will they say "Lo, here it is!" or "There!" for behold, the kingdom of God is in the midst of you' (Luke, XVII, 20–21). Neither the soul nor God nor the kingdom of God can ever be photographed. In saying that there is no soul, *Logos* thought uses 'is' in a very specific way. The notions 'is' and 'is not' will be dealt with in some detail elsewhere: suffice it to establish for now that a noetic being is never to be confused with one existing in time and space.

Perhaps it is now safe to begin a discussion of space and matter. It should be clear that the fact that the view of space, time and materiality in the contemporary natural sciences is essentially that held by Buddhist and Zoroastrian thought, the fact that Bohr and Rutherford derive this view from *Logos*-based thought and their theories can help to send men to the moon and create laser beams, is no proof of its validity. That validity is known in a different fashion.

III

More than one scientist has expressed amazement at how it was possible that, without the scientific tools of the astrophysical observatory, the Eastern thinkers could form sophisticated theories about the creation of matter and the life-cycle of the universe. Park, in his lectures on quantum theory and time and space in Plato, observes that there must be some universal constants inspiring such thought. Less qualified but more fantasy-orientated authors have assumed that there must in the past have been extra-terrestrial visitors passing out sheets of information on the creation of matter, space and time, for only in that way can we account for this uniformity of views. These apart, a serious answer can be given. It lies in the fact that *Logos*-orientated thinkers do not differentiate between space and themselves – between the far and the near. The notion that the galaxy a million light-years away is *far* stands up only for the conceptual thinker. Against this, contemporary astronomers observe that in astrophysics the notions of far and near are not meaningful, they are simply conjectural; i.e. conceptual views of the universe do not correspond to reality. What is near determines the behaviour of what is far, and what is far directly conditions what is near. What is true here is only true in so far as there is a specific 'there': in this sense, there is here. Fred Hoyle (1970, p. 304) observes:

> Present day developments in cosmology are coming to suggest rather insistently that everyday conditions could not persist but for the distant parts of the universe, that all our ideas of space and geometry would become entirely invalid if the distant parts of the universe were taken away. Our everyday experience even down to the smallest detail seems to be so closely integrated to the grand scale features of the universe that it is well nigh impossible to contemplate the two being separated.

Compare the Hindu view of the world, where each unit contains as a microcosm or a macrocosm all other units. Vyasa's or the Delphic dictum 'Know yourself' (*Knothi Seuton*) implies that in knowing yourself you know everything that is, for 'Tat twam asi' ('That art thou'). This is, of course, Plato's view, and his method is based on it. He taught that in order to learn about anything one must learn astronomy; yet he never failed to point out that astronomy is studied by examining oneself. 'Internal' and 'external' are for Saanthana-based thought conjectural, and so is limitation in time and space. The formation of the Crab Nebula can be studied here and now by examining the microcosmic 'Crab Nebula' contained within each man. It can be studied as it was millions of years ago or as it will be in millions of years' time. These notions are as startling to the author as they must be to anybody brought up in the conceptualist tradition: they are, however, the views not only of Plato but also of any thinker of the Hindu or Vedantic tradition. Indeed the notions of the inseparability of observed and observer, of matter as non-extended in time and space, of the elementary unit as both a wave and a particle, are all beyond conceptualization.

From all this the scientifically orientated mind may gain further insight into what it is that the Saanthana tradition means when it affirms that in order to know we must first decide what it is we ought to know. How we decide to know will determine what it is to know. There is no such thing as an objective concept or an objective atom or electron or neutron for science – only the logical positivist and the party idealogue use the external authority of science to discipline dissenting opinion. There is no objective, positively determined 'I' for sociology: in pretending to be objective, by turning to a set of criteria such as polls and laboratory observation, the positivist scientists have merely decided in advance on the nature of the person they are investigating.

J.A. Wheeler (in Mehra, 1973, p. 244) is led to observe:

> Nothing is more important about the quantum principle than this: that it destroys the concept of the world as sitting out there with the observer safely separated from it by a 20 centimetre slab of plate glass. Even to observe so miniscule an object as an electron, he must shatter the glass. He must reach in. He must install his chosen measuring equipment. It is up to him to decide whether he shall measure position or momentum. To install the equipment to measure the one prevents and excludes his installing the equipment to measure the other. Moreover the measurement changes the state of the electron. The universe will never afterwards be the same. To describe what has happened one has to cross out that old word 'observer' and put in its place the new word 'participator'. In some strange sense the universe is a participatory universe.

This is, of course, the famous Heisenberg principle which has revolutionized contemporary physics. The noetic thinker agrees, and points out that twenty-five centuries ago Plato (*Sophist,* 248[e]) wrote:

> 'If knowing is to be acting upon something it follows that what is known must be acted upon by it; and so on this showing, reality when it is being known by the act of knowledge must insofar as it is known be changed owing to being acted upon.'

While Plato and Heisenberg speak the same language when writing of the universe as consisting of nothing but a set of motions, and when describing the properties of matter, Plato goes further by introducing a yet higher dimension. Here he is closer to Bohr, who understands both Taoism and physics as subject to rules which can only be described as ethical. De Broglie, Bohr and indeed the whole team that formulated the quantum theory unanimously point out that the observer/observed relationship cannot be externalized: that its rules are internal, derived within an integrated system and valid for that system.

The principle of the externalization of evaluative criteria is one which distorts not only scientific theory but also society at large. By externalizing criteria and calling them 'the high standard of living', 'the satisfaction of material needs' and so on, positivists are sundering man and universe. This separation is unethical: indeed 'unethical' means that which differentiates the individual from the social interest.

The ideas of contemporary sociologists, psychologists or physicists may appear to be new, but the idea of linear time and hence of 'historical progress' is itself time-specific, and when analysed breaks down to the interests of corporate multinational capitalism. This study does not deny progress, yet the nature of progress for Saanthana-based thought is altogether different from the 'progress' posited by bourgeois sociologists. All notions – whether of time and space, or of progress – are not true or false in themselves: it is the manner in which they are understood and the nature of man's relation to them which makes them true or false. At a specific moment in history, the separation of man and cosmos may have been legitimate for the thought specific to that period. Thus in order for Heisenberg to be able to observe that the observed and the observer are one, it was necessary for Newton and Galileo to have held otherwise: hence 'progress'. *Logos*-based thought, however, operates differently: Plato's views of the formation of galaxies do not differ from those of Lama Govinda or of contemporary astrophysics. For noetic thought there has been no progress: in other words, while the noetic thinker applauds the scientist for concluding that the external and the internal are one, he did not need a scientist to tell him this.

> The Buddhist does not believe in an independent or separately existing external world, into whose dynamic forces he could insert himself. The external world and his inner world are for him only two sides of the same fabric, in which the threads of all forces and of all events, of all forms of consciousness and of their objects, are woven into an inseparable net of endless mutually conditioned relations (Govinda, 1973, p. 93).

To be in harmony within oneself one must be in harmony with the external world. The bourgeois assumption of 'me and my needs' as opposed to 'you and your needs' is thus fundamentally false and unethical. For *Logos* thought, 'true' and 'ethical' are the same.

Preconceptual Greek language was better equipped to serve these purposes than English, but the relevant Greek words have atrophied. In turning to Plato we cannot speak of 'matter'; we must somehow attempt to grasp the notion of a 'formative medium'. It will not do, however, to equate this formative medium with that of quantum physics. Contemporary physics has only touched on the edges of *Noesis*. *Logos*-based notions of the formative medium are elaborate and more complex, for they include biological, microbiological, ethical, political, religious and scientific aspects.

Science proceeds from hypotheses which change from age to age. Every epoch is characterized by its own Newton and Galileo, founding fathers who set up the basic framework, which in its early stages is both noetically and empirically derived. To break away from the sophists, the Greeks seem to have turned to the Zoroastrians for inspiration. In the Middle Ages, philosophy, algebra and geometry all entered Europe primarily via the Arabs in Africa and Spain. In attempting to break through the rigidifying conceptual cloud which was stifling creative thought in Europe, Bohr, Heisenberg, Chew and others have reached still further East.

But eventually the noetic element is always discarded: it is only in times of change that such faculties can be used to the full. We can expect that our physics, too, will eventually be 'rebourgeoised' and reconceptualized, its revolutionary theories adapted to the satisfaction of epithumic needs. While the process may take several centuries, if history is *Magister Vitas* then this development is inevitable. However, unlike scientific and ideological *Weltanschauung*, *Logos*-oriented thought itself is not a conceptual framework, and therefore not subject to these fluctuations. It is rooted in needs which are constant, and the ideas of physicists are quoted here only because they may be found suggestive.

IV

Let us turn to the question of 'matter'. As a noetic thinker, Plato does not posit a fundamental underlying entity enduring in time and taking on various predications. For him there is no Aristotelian 'ideal essence' such as 'oakness' maintaining its 'oakhood' while taking on its many cloaks from the acorn to the mighty tree. It is only conceptualists who operate with abstract essences. Though Y. Bonnitz has argued that it was Aristotle who created the idea of a nonchanging essence as something apart from what is perceived, calling it *Hyle*, other scholars have suggested that this was above all a hypothetical exercise in order to solve a logical problem. Only subsequently was it concretized into a theoretical dogma that has, over the span of centuries, acquired the solidity associated with material reality itself.

Before approaching Plato's notion of the formative medium of reality, one ought to dismiss all such notions as 'matter' or 'substance', whether abstract or concrete, visible or invisible. For Plato there is only one formative element, and all visions, thoughts, souls, ideas, feelings and things are made from, or rather in, that medium. And although Plato only introduces this notion in his later dialogues, one cannot thereby simply assume that he reached this conclusion late in his life; rather, such was the nature of this formative medium that a great deal of negative mental refutation was necessary before the notion of it could be introduced.

The main assumption which had to be undermined was the idea that there is a difference between being made 'from' and being made 'in'. The container or crucible in which all things are made is called *Chora*, and this is also the stuff of which they are made (*Timaeus*, 52b). While *Chora* in some ways functions as matter, it is not the same as 'matter' considered as substance extended in time and space: the notion is much broader, since not only material but also abstract things such as concepts, notions and images are made in and of *Chora,* and so are moods and sensations (*Timaeus,* 48^{e}–52^{b}). Cornford (1937, p. 181) writes: 'there is no justification for calling the receptacle 'matter' – a term not used by Plato'. However, if by 'matter' we understand only the permeable stuff of which 'things' are made, then Plato quite distinctly does treat *Chora* as matter. In *Timaeus* (50^{b-c}) he explains:

> 'Suppose a man had moulded figures of all sorts out of gold, and were unceasingly to remould each into all the rest; then if you should point to one of them and ask what it was, much the safest answer in respect of truth would be to say 'gold', and never to speak of a triangle or any of the other figures that were coming to be in it as things that have being, since they are changing even while one is asserting their existence. . . . Now the same thing must be said of that nature [*Chora*] – it appears to have qualities, it receives all qualities, but it itself is always the same, never changing.'

So *Chora* is not matter, or at least not matter in time; thus it cannot be the stuff of which conceptually constructed things are made. But it is the stuff of which all real things are made, and it is called 'matter' by Aristotle (*Physics,* 207^{a} 29–32) and Callicles, and identified as such more recently by Crombie (1971, p. 223). Cornford, denying that *Chora* is matter, equates it with space. However, while the word may be thus translated, this 'space' is of a particular kind.

Although everywhere, *Chora*-space has shape: it is curved. Cornford (1937, p. 188) observes that 'according to Plato, space has a shape of its own, being co-extensive with the spherical universe'. Conceptually, Plato, like Einstein, found it difficult to account for the fact that space is everywhere and yet is curved. Plato's answer was that *Chora*-space exists in pockets. Particles large or small, galaxies or grains of salt, are all formed by the condensation of *Chora*. This condensation creates solidity and visibility – mass and light – and, when intense, forms a solid body perceived as a particle.

The empirical view of body and shape is given by Socrates as 'shape is the limit of a body'; yet the correct view does not reduce bodies to dense concentrations of weight. Thus from Proclus' commentary on the *Timaeus* we gather that the space-matter which solidifies as a star does not end with the first degree of condensation: any solid particle is in fact a collection of concentric spheres of condensation. The centre of a star contains a super-dense kernel, 'where weight and light are densely crowded together'. Around this kernel, space solidifies in the form of 'earth' – a less dense crowding of *Chora*. Beyond the limit of the perceived shape there is another layer, called 'ether' (not to be equated with what we call the atmosphere – air), where the crowding of *Chora* is still less dense. Beyond this there is another envelope of very rarified space, and then the void: nothing. Therefore space exists only around bodies. Since each little body resembles each large body, each has its own ethereal envelope. This is the case with atoms, where the kernel is a densely packed nucleus of protons and neutrons, surrounded by less densely packed electrons. Likewise the universe at large curves its own space, and has its own aura.

Thus *Chora* is everywhere, and yet it is curved and has a shape. Beyond *Chora* is nowhere. Einstein (1969) working within an entirely different tradition, concludes:

> We may therefore regard matter as being constituted by the regions of space in which the field is extremely intense. There is no place in this new kind of physics both for the field and matter, for the field is the only reality.

Unlike the modern physicist, Plato applies this same principle to spiritual entities, so that each soul also creates its space, i.e. curves its field of extension: this is how a true individual is constituted.

In Proclus' commentaries, the true individual (like the true body) is brought together by the gravitational pull of the sentiment. Wherever there is *Logisticon,* there will be a series of outer layers constituting the various aspects of the individual. The perceived body is simply a less dense aspect of the kernel-soul or *Logisticon;* and beyond the perceived body as limited by extension there are further, even less dense aspects of the individual. This does not refer to a physical aura, as it has been simplified by gnostic interpreters: the less dense aspects of the individual may be scattered in other people, in other times and so on. The layers of the individual are not next to each other in a 'time and space' sense; only if considered noetically is the body – *Chora* – of an individual concentrated and curved around the kernel *Logisticon.* (This is, of course, why the true individual cannot be photographed – for such an individual exists only in the noetic sense. It is also where the present work parts ways with the contemporary popular body of literature that works from the same sources – Pythagoras, the Vedas, Proclus – but draws different conclusions.)

Just as the body is only aspectually different from the soul, so space is only aspectually different from time or from matter. While Einstein does not extend the micro-macro analysis beyond that which he can mathematically support, he also comes to the conclusion that space is curved, and that matter and space cannot be separated:

> In general relativity these two concepts can no longer be separated.

> Wherever there is a massive body, there will be a gravitational field, and this field will manifest itself as the curvature of the space surrounding that body. We must not think, however, that the field fills the space and 'curves' it. The two cannot be distinguished; the field *is* the curved space! (Capra, 1975,p. 218.)

It is this fact of the curvature of space that invalidates both Newtonian mechanics and Euclidean geometry. A triangle drawn on a sphere is no longer a 180° triangle. The shortest distance between two points is no longer a straight line. Time is similarly affected, and stretches and bends in accordance with the pull of gravity.

Plato's *Chora* is the container of creation and the matter of it: 'it creates a home for all created things' (*Timaeus,* 52^{b}) and it 'assumes a form like that of any of the things which enter into it' (*Timaeus,* 50^{b-c}). *Chora* is a 'nurse and mother' of all creation (*Timaeus,* 49^{e}), not only of concrete visible things but of anything that can be thought of.

Things are organized into unities following the rules of *Aritmos* or sentiment. An activity is a flow of instances; it is not a collection of sections of time synthesized into blocks. Reality is not conceptually perceived, but grasped in an instant which is itself free of temporal considerations. Taylor (1928,p. 332) is led to observe that while the world as a function of *Chora* may be perceived as phenomenal, *Chora* itself is non-phenomenal.

In trying to explain what *Chora* is, Plato uses the examples of fire and water occurring in space to make it clear that such nouns as 'fire', 'water', etc. should not be mistaken for anything substantial or permanent. One must be careful, however, not to assume that there is something else which *is* permanent, and thus bring back the idea of substance or essence enduring in time. The conceptualist's mistake has to do with the understanding of 'permanent' as opposed to 'transient'. 'Permanent' in conceptual thought means 'that which endures in time'. Plato, however, points out in the *Parmenides* (155^{e}–156^{e}) that the meaning of 'permanent' is closer to that of 'instant': both are out of time altogether.

Fire *as seen* is true fire; it is not an illusion. The illusion sets in only in the infinitesimally short period (not an instant, which has no duration at all) of interpretive interjection. The visible world is real; what is false is the assumption that behind the visible there is a 'real' hidden entity, a perfect instance enduring in time, of which the visible is a false image. These images are not false: 'the forms [i.e. the images of the visible world] which enter into and go out of her [*Chora*] are the likeness of eternal realities modelled after their patterns in a wonderful and mysterious manner' (*Timaeus,* 54^{c}).

It is thus misleading to translate *Chora* as space, if this is confused with a Kantian category. For Plato, space is also matter. *Chora* is 'that in which all elements grow up and appear and decay. [*Chora*] alone is to be called by the name "this and that"' (*Timaeus*, 50^{d}); everything that is seen or thought of is both in and from *Chora*. Obviously the notion is much wider than that of quantum physics: we ought to look for further parallels and different words.

Can it be maintained that the twentieth century mind has no word to match this notion? I think not. While it is possible for certain notions to be without ready words, *Chora* is too basic to human experience ever to lack a word: it includes anything of which any entity or thing is made. The word that comes to mind is 'actuality'. While actuality has been defined in many ways, and Husserl's notion of it as 'that which quite literally is, without the aid of intermediate interpretation by the organizing mind', seems adequate, we need not feel restricted by such definitions. While words change in meaning and so do concepts, there is a hidden substratum of notions which does not change; actuality, despite its over-use, appears to me far closer to Plato's *Chora* than any other contemporary word.

V

In the *Timaeus,* for fire to be fire it must endure in time; however, this 'time' is not a string of points. It is a fusion of instances, no longer distinguishable as separate from each other. In other words, in *Chora,* time and space are fused.

This same view was proposed by Minkowski in 1908 (his theory was at the time regarded as 'surprisingly' similar to that of Plato but has now been generally accepted):

> The views of space and time which I wish to lay before you have sprung from the soil of experimental physics, and therein lies their strength. They are radical. Henceforth, space by itself and time by itself are doomed to fade away into mere shadows, and only a kind of union of the two will preserve an independent reality (in Einstein, 1969,p. 53).

Minkowski, according to my view, is unduly optimistic. It is only in transitional periods (such as the twentieth century) that science becomes noetically based; inevitably it slips back into *Dianoia,* and the technicians take over and reconceptualize its assumptions. It is only Saanthana-based philosophy which does not change its views from epoch to epoch, but persistently repeats one message.

But how does this empty space-*Chora* create objects? Let us again turn to Einstein for his view. According to Wheeler (in Stevens, 1974, p. 6):

> Einstein, above his work and writing, held a long-term vision that there is nothing in the world except curved empty space. Geometry bent one way here describes gravitation; rippled another way somewhere else it manifests all the qualities of an electromagnetic wave. Excited at still another place the magic material that is space shows itself as a particle. . . . matter, charge, electromagnetism and other fields are only manifestations of the bending of space.

This is as far as science can go. But *Chora*, although it is all that is, is for Plato beyond all that is. This is what Taylor implies: all manifestations of *Chora* are phenomenal, but *Chora* itself is non-phenomenal. The world taking place in *Chora* is only a duplication of the noetic, non-phenomenal world (*Cosmos Noetus* – the cosmos which 'is' not).

Why and how *Chora* solidifies – what stimulates, guides and creates the electron – is not the subject of physics. Modern physics is still not *Aixos,* the science where inner and outer, psychological and empirical observation is merged, as it was for the Greeks. While the indications are that science is about to break the wall by which it has unnecessarily been divided from the inner science of man, this breakthrough has not yet been performed.

The organizing principle of *Chora* is, of course, *Aritmos* – which is the very object of science as *Aixos*. While *Aritmos* has an objective dimension, this is not all. Concerning the 'public' aspect of *Aritmos,* Findlay (1970, p. 256) remarks:

> being water or earth or air, wood or gold or purple or angry or intelligent or a man or a dwarf star or an electron are all basically a matter of specific proportions or quantitative measures.

And a contemporary physicist affirms: 'rather than a concrete particle, an electron is simply a field in space. . . . there is no such thing as one and the same substance of which the electron consists at all times' (Weyl, 1949, p. 171). Whether this electron creates atoms of hydrogen or carbon is all a matter of the organizing principle, number.

The Plato scholar, W.K.C. Guthrie (1950, p. 337), writes:

> There can be no essential difference between a tankful of water and the delicate organism of a racehorse or a human being. Since both are formed of some ultimate matter [*Chora*], the cause of their difference lies elsewhere, and it is there, said Plato, in the principle of organization by which the matter has been differentiated, that the true philosopher will look for explanation.

Sri Aurobindo, (1957, p. 337) puts it like this:

> The material object becomes . . . something different from what we now see, not a separate object on the background or in the environment

> of the rest of nature but an indivisible part and even in a subtle way an expression of all that we see.

And Heisenberg (1963, p. 96): 'The world thus appears as a complicated tissue of events, in which connections of different kinds alternate or overlap or combine and thereby determine the texture of the whole.'

While the friends of Buddhism might be more convinced were we to rely more on Buddhist texts, and the scientific reader might prefer more from Bohr or de Broglie, the intention in using such quotes is not to rely on outside authorities. In the final analysis, all theories will change, and can be differently verbalized. But introducing them in a particular way may create a meaning in this context which does not depend on what the original author said or did not say.

VI

The noetic thinker does not intend to convey a particular picture of the world. Seen cyclically, the noetic impulse occurs at the end of an epoch, to give an impetus to theories which will only later take forms specific to the historical givens of the moment. Theories, rules and models are a function of specialists. The noetic thinker's intention is to see things, or to make men see. Given a healthy society, healthy food and a healthy life, seeing actuality is simple. A healthy shepherd sees nothing but actuality, and needs no noetic thinker to point it out to him; most likely such a person sees actuality even more clearly than did the people who wrote down the sayings of men like Socrates (who was, according to Xenophon, practically illiterate). Yet, for the citizen of a sick city it is not so easy, for the mind interjects and perverts the vision. Actuality is not a sum of mentally interpreted images. These difficulties came to the fore in the last century, where philosophers – foreseeing the end of an epoch – attempted to present a better world by painting beautiful conceptual models and abstracting the needs of the body. This was, of course, the failure of the idealists.

The nineteenth century had great difficulties in defining matter. Some thinkers called their world view materialist, yet they did not define matter in terms of irreducible tiny particles. Why should anybody assuming matter to be 'non-material' call himself a materialist? Given the reigning orthodoxy of the century – such as Hegel's idealism – a 'materialist' label for the counterposition becomes understandable. Idealists see the world as a creation of the mind: to Hegel, in particular, 'real' means 'rational'. Matter, however, is a reality existing outside or rather beyond the mind (that is, beyond mind as *Manas*). In positing a reality external to the mind, a *Logos*-based thinker means external to the 'mind' of Hegel.

Noetic thought sees reality in some ways as being internal to man, but not 'internal' in the sense of being created by the human mind. Man – Atman – is not mind. The material world is internal in so far as man needs the material in order to fulfil his needs. Thus the external is internalized.

Actuality – and/or the materiality of essences – can also be defined in terms of the forces of material production and social intercourse, within which societies and individuals satisfy and realize themselves. Of course, the notion of 'material production' is too readily abused. It should mean more than just the production of so many kilowatts of electrical energy, or so many tons of grain. For Plato, materiality includes social intercourse, thought and actions: material needs are also social and cultural. Indeed, given the nineteenth-century connotations of the word 'matter', 'actuality' seems far more useful. Actuality is thus materiality, where 'matter' is not composed of concrete particles, and it takes form in time, where 'time' is not composed of a string of points.

The world of sense is thus twofold. There is actuality, which is perceived in an instant, and there is the world of becoming, which is perceived in time. The difference is inner: it is a psychological difference. The world of instantiation is described in the *Parmenides* (156^{d}):

> 'There is no transition from the state of rest so long as a thing is still at rest, nor from motion so long as it is still in motion, but this queer thing the instant is situated between the motion and the rest; it occupies no time at all, and the transition of the moving thing to a state of rest or of the stationary thing to a state of being in motion takes place to and from the instant.'

This realm of instantiation is separate from that of becoming, and hence from the interpretive activity of conceptual thought – which always necessitates an extension in time. And it is this realm of instance which corresponds to *Chora*.

Actuality is that ever-present reality which is grasped without recourse to intermediate interpretation by the mind. It is defined by Plato as that which is 'apprehended when all sense is absent by a kind of spurious reason' (Jowett's translation, *Timaeus,* 52^{b}). Taylor translates the kind of reason by which we apprehend *Chora* as 'bastard reason'. The word 'bastard', though possibly a negative emotive characterization, seems a telling one, and better than Jowett's 'spurious'. The word 'bastard' does not imply an inferior product; the bastard offspring may be of excellent quality – it is just that its generation is unconventional. This interpretation is also given by Crombie. Why is such reasoning 'bastard', he asks? 'Not, I think, because the inference is illegitimate, but because the mind cannot grasp and understand the entity which it has to postulate' (Crombie, 1971, p. 217).

The word for apprehending Chora is *Apsastai,* 'grasping'; the activity itself is reflective of the mental process I have called *Diarithmesis.* Findlay (1974, p. 345) connects *Diarithmesis* with grasping, and Cornford (1967, pp. 76–7) equates grasping with the cognitive activity that involves the immediate apprehension of actuality by a 'leap of mind'.

Although in some way derivative of reality, actuality is not far removed from it. Actuality, rather than the realm of becoming, is made in the image of true being. Concepts, as we have tried to show, are the stuff of thought. *Chora* is grasped by a process parallel, though not identical, to *Diarithmesis,* which I have equated with sentiment. Sentiment is the 'stuff' of actuality: '*Chora* is the immediate reflection of reality,' writes Crombie (1971, p. 218) commenting on the *Timaeus,* 50[d], and Robin (1908, p. 475) argues that *Chora* is the stuff of which number (*Aritmos*) is made. Sentiment and number, in this light, are the two sides of the same coin, *On* or *Ens*. Perceived through the 'reason' or intellect, *Ens* is number. Perceived through the immediate emotive consciousness of the third part of the soul, the thorax soul (through a process to be described later), number is sentiment.

In between sentiment and number there lies the whole intermediate world of interpreted perception, called variously the flux, the becoming, *Saṃsara, Maya,* etc. Neither actuality nor reality, but only their intermediate interpreted counterpart, becoming or *Samsara,* is illusory. Since the conceptualists have failed to differentiate between the two worlds of body-sense and conceptualized sense (mental sense), *Samsara* has been translated as the world of sense. Since then, a body of Western-educated Indians have been convincing the world that in Indian thought the world of sense is not an illusion. Owing to the fact that the world of sense and the conjectural world have been one for the West, there has been a whole series of such cross-purposed East-West dialogues. As a result we have Western Buddhism, which like the nineteenth-century God is a conceptualized idea with no root in the body-mind, nor in the inner eye of the soul: just another move in a game of conceptual chess.

The above discussion has been restricted mainly to the lower two (becoming and actuality) of the three ontological realms. Let us now move on to the nature of the first realm, that of being.

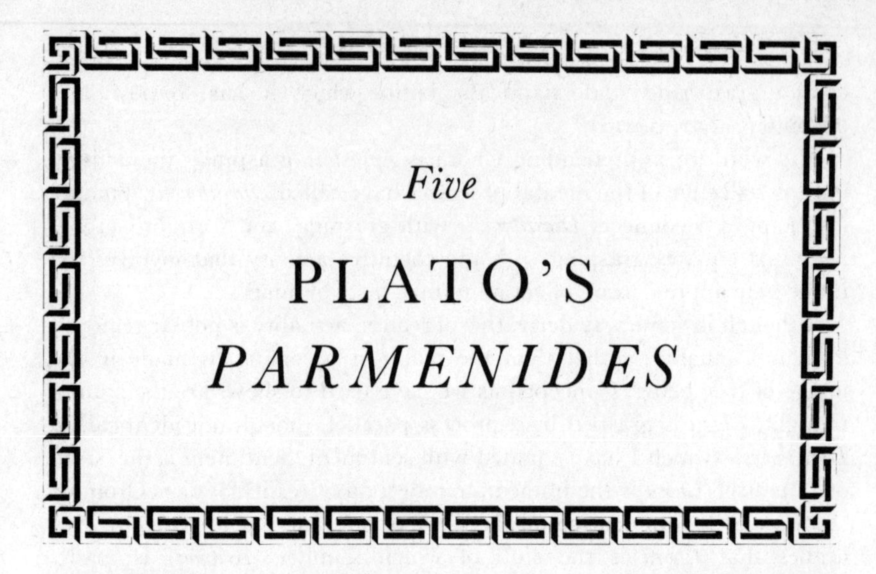

Five PLATO'S *PARMENIDES*

In the dialogue *Parmenides,* Plato has attempted a 'one time only' discussion of the true nature of being. Such is the nature of this being that it is unchanging and eternal. Plato's intention is to show that such a reality cannot be philosophized about or constructed by human reason. Here he differs from idealist philosophy: the idealists consider the unchanging as an object of thought, and hence as an object of reflection and philosophy (*Sophist,* 248[a]). For Plato, however, that which truly is cannot be predicated, that is, it cannot be given verbal predicates and spoken about positively (*Phaedrus,* 247[c]).

If the existence of real entities cannot be proved philosophically, then it might seem that all the authors of the Upanishads and the Orphic philosophers of Greece could hardly justify the time they have devoted to their tasks. The solution is that being or reality can be *insinuated* through philosophy. It is in order to use words in this insinuating manner and thus to account for the 'Beingly Being' (*Usia Ontos Usa,* or Brahman) that Plato creates the curious mental exercise referred to today as the *Parmenides* dialogue.

I

The object of the *Parmenides* is to drive away all positivist representations of true being. Its author will outperform the atheists and the sophists, and destroy the last conceptual residue of this true being, which he refers to as the One. His intention is to construct a dialogue that will force the mind to grasp the unsaid. In driving away positive representations, the author makes the reader participate in the authorship by forcing the identification between author and reader in a common movement. Thus he makes the mind receptive to a conclusion which is not stated, but generates itself. The mental exercise is so constructed that the mind consciously realizes that absolute, real things – here called 'forms' and translated as 'ideas' – cannot possibly be thought about, and that the infinite cannot possibly be conceived: yet we do think of both. Inevitably the mind is forced to ask, from where do we derive these 'ideas'?

This principle, applied in connection with the absolute unity of being, gives rise to the only correct version of the ontological argument. It is the perfect version of this argument precisely because of its negativity; St Anselm's and the Cartesian versions have, by their explicit verbalization of the implied, made the argument subject to all the objections raised by Kant.

Conventional Greek thought alternatively relies on three basic types of exposition:

1 So-called indirect or negative description – speaking of things in a roundabout way so as to allow the reader to come to his own conclusion. Negative description is used by Heraclitus, and is also related to the Socratic method: in Hinduism it is the *neti neti* approach – 'not this, not that'.

2 More conventional philosophical discourse employing discursive reason (*Logos*) treats knowledge as the object of definition (see, for example, the discussion of justice in the *Republic*, or the philosophy of Aristotle).

3 Myths and scientific allegories (*Aixos*) can be literally imagined, painted or in some way imitated. Examples are stories of heroes, references to the sun as the good and soul as a chariot or the 'scientific' accounts of the world as an animal in Plato's *Timaeus*.

The use of these three methods is not arbitrary. In treating their subject matter as (1) things negatively predicated, (2) objects of definition and (3) pictures or imitative models, the Greeks are referring to the three different realms of being, becoming and actuality. Each one of these methods – useful as it may have been at times – is shown in the *Parmenides* to be inadequate if the purpose of the exposition is to convey a meaningful account of real entities such as the living ideas themselves. Even such sophisticated devices as the negative description cannot convey knowledge of true entities if used in isolation from other methods.

Things as they really are can be grasped by simultaneous referral to three different realms. Things as spoken about, however, are reduced to only one aspect of their nature, or to several aspects perceived within a single realm. No philosopher can present all three sides of reality at the same time; rather he presents them alternatively. Various horizontal ('monodimensional') sections are stringed in a sequence that should lead the reader to grasp them 'vertically', all at the same time.

Any philosophical argument calls for creative synthesis on the part of the audience. If a philosopher wishes to be absolutely coherent in the linear, verbal, logical sense, he can achieve this coherence only by eliminating an essential dimension of the issue under discussion. A noetic thinker does not wish to eliminate that dimension; it is for this reason that he uses several – in fact, three – systems of exposition, as will be described below.

The creative activity exercised by the reader is that of seeing the issues under discussion in terms of 'extended references'. He synthesizes the positive, mythological picture with the *Logos* and with the negative definition, seeing all three as a unity otherwise scattered by the noetic philosopher throughout his work. These extended references are discovered as the reader restructures the argument in his own mind, unbalancing the subject-predicate relationship he had previously established. What is and what is not becomes dictated by the contextual rhythm and flow of the exposition, connecting with an inner psychological rhythm which is both objective and universal. It is only towards the end of the exercise that the reader realizes that the author meant something other than what had to be postulated to elevate the discourse on to a higher plane.

Notions are formed in terms of grasped units. These units filter into conscious thought and unravel the concepts of linear philosophy. 'Normal' philosophical discourse – that relied on by linear thought – pretends that it can effect sharp definitional distinctions and deal with things in a single realm only. However, the mind carries the 'transdimensional residue' from one realm into another and from one argument to another, raising corresponding contradictions. Rather than try to control for this by using stricter qualifications, the noetic thinker relaxes the contextual rules and allows things to manifest themselves in all three realms according to a presupposed inner logic.

II

Throughout this study I have attempted to interpret central philosophical notions primarily in terms of the Western tradition, but the nature of the dialogue *Parmenides* is such as to lend itself readily to cross-cultural comparison. (Of course, the technique of extended reference may well have been as common in pre-Parmenidean Greece as it was in Indo-Iranian thought. Whether Plato learned the *Sat-Asat* (beingnonbeing) method from Eudoxus, was following an indigenous tradition or independently discovered it, it is not possible to establish.) In order to avoid misrepresentation through a literal rendering of the ancient wisdom, Indo-Iranian tradition has forbidden that it should be written down. (Plato also makes reference to this idea, e.g. *Phaedrus,* 275[a]; *Letter VII,* 334[c].) The wisdom was to be interpreted by recourse to three referential systems, called in the Vedas three ways of using language. Issues under discussion were to be examined either (1) by a single reference, literal narrative; (2) by a cross-reference; or (3) by a combination of the two. The latter was difficult and its exercise allowed only to the initiated keepers of the scripture. Writing on this topic in *The Myth of Invariance,* McClain (1978, p. 21) calls these different methods 'systems of logic': 'The *Rig Veda* has been written in keeping with four different systems of logic, or rather four different ways of using language'. Of these four, we are interested only in three (the fourth is only the reference to the other three). Each of these ways is concerned with an 'is', an 'is not' and their combinations: (1) *Sat,* the language of existence (of 'is'); (2) *Asat,* the language of nonexistence (of 'is not'); and (3) their combination in the third by cross-sectional reference, where the predication by 'is' or 'is not' is relative to each and every part of the exposition.

As today, in ancient Greece there were already conceptual thinkers equating ideas with concepts, while others were seeing them as existing things. Parmenides' objection to all these is that 'forms' cannot simply be treated as existents, conceptuals or non-predicables. They cannot be treated as existing things,

> 'for if like things, then other things cannot partake of them as parts nor as wholes, for as parts they would by participation suffer diminution, and if as wholes when they would become separate from themselves' (*Parmenides,* 131[e]).

Nor can they be conceptual models which other things imitate, for in order to account for a relation between a thing and a model, a further model would have to be posited and so on *ad infinitum* (the Third Man argument, *Parmenides,* 133[a]: this is also Kant's problem with his mental sense of 'I'). Nor can the forms be treated as abstract negative universals in a separate, non-predicated world of their own, for then they would cease to have significance for us (the separate God-for-himself-in-heaven, or Master-Slave argument, *Parmenides,* 133[e]–134[a]).

Parmenides makes it clear that in spite of all this he does not insist that ideas do not in some sense exist or participate in each of the three realms, or that they are not such as the refuted assertions held them to be. Parmenides' explicit statement is that the forms cannot be treated separately if their treatment is restricted as in ordinary discourse.

However, 'a man of exceptional gifts will be able to see that a form or essence just by itself does exist in each case' (135^{a}).

Having refuted Socrates' method rather than his position, Parmenides is to show Socrates the new kind of discourse. Before the exercise was begun we were told of three ways in which ideas could exist – i.e. as actual, conceptual and negative entities. Consequently, the argument that follows has three distinct stages: (1) of things as if they are (136^{a}); (2) of things as if they are not (136^{a}); and (3) 'Let us take the argument yet a third time' – as things which appear to exist (156^{e}–157^{e}). The dialogue terminates as follows:

> 'To this we may add the conclusion. It seems that whether there is or is not a one, both that one and the others alike [1] are, [2] and are not, [3] and appear and do not appear, to be all manner of things in all manner of ways with respect to themselves and one another' (*Parmenides*, 166^{b}).

What this means is that real things can be seen in three ways: as being eternally; as being in time; and as being in an instant.

The dialogue uses the *Sat-Asat* technique, and – Heraclitian fragments apart – it is the only written account of this technique in the Western tradition. The exercise treats the three realms cross-referentially: whenever an 'is' is evoked, it can refer to either becoming, being or actuality. In other words 'is' can mean 'is not', and vice versa. All predication is in reference to the whole: the dialogue must be 'raced through' (Parmenides is like a racehorse in Ibycus – *Parmenides,* 137^{a}), or read in a single attempt, and cannot be broken down into sections. Treated as a linear piece of writing it becomes what Wilamowitz called it: a lark, silly pedantry, *Schulfuchserei.* Misinterpretation occurs when, like Taylor, one both assumes it to be a serious piece of writing (which it is) and treats it as a normal piece of philosophy (which it is not). Parmenides clearly warns, first, that it is not for a large audience, and second, that 'is' and 'is not' are interchangeable: 'You must make a supposition that such and such a thing is and consider the consequences; you must also make the supposition that the same thing is not' (*Parmenides,* 136^{a}).

From the account in 142^{b}–155^{d}, we can gather that whatever is in time is becoming, and whatever is becoming is changing. The change takes place not in spurts but continually: becoming is an uninterrupted change. Nothing extended ever properly exists, as we also learn from the *Timaeus* (38–39). The fact that Parmenides, as must anybody, uses 'is' to refer to things that are becoming is an unavoidable characteristic of speech. Ideas have an eidetic content which is beyond any participation, but even those who 'know' cannot help using these words in referring to something. As we learn in the *Sophist* (252^{c}), even forms differentiated within speech cannot be referred to without recourse to predication by existence.

In contrast with the Socratic negative argument used in the *Theaetetus,* the argument of the *Parmenides* is doubly negative, since it denies the denial by adding a third qualifying element: 'seems both to be and not to be'. Things are not denied but seem to be denied, and things are not but seem to be, yet they both are and are not. Qualification is based on the following referential implications of is: (1) 'is' for things which truly are (i.e. out of time); (2) 'is not' for things which are in time; (3) 'is and is not' for actuality (seeming both to be and not to be).

(It would be fascinating to learn from where the Greeks derive this technique. Plato attributes it to Parmenides, which may indicate Zoroastrian origins; quite definitely it is not Socratic, since Plato explicitly says so. Both Plato and Parmenides would have been familiar with Egyptian techniques, since both had studied these in Greece and one presumes in Egypt too, for it is hardly likely that Plato went to Egypt for the sole purpose of sightseeing. I am inclined to think that the technique is that of the historical Parmenides. Plato never used it in any other dialogue, and had he falsely attributed it one assumes somebody would have recorded an objection. As it was, antiquity has not corrected Plato nor claimed that he was distorting the historical Parmenides – a man whom Plato held in the highest respect.)

'Is' is differently understood when using reason (*Logos*) and when using the thinking mind. The mind inverts the correct subject-predicate relationships. If one is thinking with *Logos,* then 'is' refers to things which are unchanging, i.e. to things which are out of time; 'is' refers to that which is real, and not that which is becoming. The mind, however, operates in terms of concepts, things which are functions of time. Hence to the mind, 'is' refers to that which is not, which is becoming. That which is, cannot be apprehended by the mind, for it cannot be verbally qualified. It can only be apprehended by reason, *Logisticon,* in an immediate, non-conceptual way, for it has no properties (such as colour or smell); it is not in time and space; and it alone is the object of all true knowledge (*Phaedrus,* 247[c–d]).

Against the true being of the forms, there is the realm of actuality. As stated, actuality is the mirror of reality, i.e. in some ways it also is: it is not changing, it is not becoming, therefore it is. However, the duration of actuality is infinitely short – instantaneous – so it is not out of time in sense of persisting for ever. Actuality both is, since it does not become or change, and is not, since it has no durability. In so far as it 'is and is not', Plato refers to it in *Parmenides* (166[b]) as that which appears to be.

Although becoming (*Samsara*) has no noetic validity, it is not free of all rules. Becoming has its own rules, those according to which the mind constructs its illusion. In the realm of becoming there can be false as well as true judgments: Theaetetus cannot fly (*Sophist*, 263[d]) nor can $7+5=13$. Parmenides therefore accomplishes the following:

he establishes the three realms of being, becoming and actuality;

he accounts for false judgments, i.e. the matching of that which is with that which is not;

and he accounts for nothingness, which has no existence whatsoever.

III

In the dialogue, Parmenides is in fact asking three questions concerning the nature of unity. Beforehand, he has not bothered to define what is meant by unity, nor has he asserted that there is such a thing. In speaking of it, he relies on the existence of an underlying notion which he shares with his audience. This notion is no longer part of contemporary Western secular thought, yet it is readily met with in the East: 'All things have their life in this Life' (Bhagavad Gita, VII, 6). Whether or not Plato believed in this notion of unity, Zeno certainly expressed it, echoing the historical Parmenides. In the dialogue, Parmenides' three questions regarding this unity are:

1 If there is a unity, what if anything can be known about it, if it is not in any way conceptualized, i.e. predicated by pictures, things verbal or mental? This relates to the realm of being.

2 If we insist on conceptualizing this unity, (i) how is it changed by being described in terms of words and things, and (ii) having granted this conceptualized unity to perceived phenomena, in what way, if any, have we affected the phenomena that we call things? This relates to the realm of becoming.

3 Is it possible that the unity may somehow be used to give immediate identity to actual things without conceptually predicating these things by the unity? This relates to the realm of actuality.

In asking the second of these questions, Parmenides may be seen as examining the mental effects of the principle contemporarily known in science as Heisenberg's: how is the observed changed by the fact that it is observed? In Plato's equation there are three participants: the unity, which is sum and substance of all reality; the perceiving individual; and the things perceived. If there is no interaction at all, nothing can be known.

For the mind, either all is change, or there is no change at all: these two are the positions of the idealists and the empiricists, both rooted in the mind. Parmenides will have both change and rest, so he posits the realm of the instant.

Nothing considered in time could ever make the transition from rest to motion unless it itself passed out of time: 'But there is no time during which a thing can be at once neither in motion nor at rest' (*Parmenides,* 156[c]). Parmenides' conclusion is not that things are therefore either *only and always* in motion or *only and always* at rest, but rather that all things considered beyond all change or else in time are conjectural: the actual state of nature is that things are simultaneously in motion and at rest, and this is the realm of instantiation – it cannot be thought of, but it is grasped by every conscious man or animal, as actuality. Nothing can change without making the transition from rest to motion and vice versa; yet for Plato, unlike Parmenides, change is real:

> 'On the other hand it does not change without making a transition.' 'When does it make the transition, then?' 'Not while it is at rest or while it is in motion, or while it is occupying time. Consequently, the time at which it will be when it makes the transition must be that queer thing, the instant' (*Parmenides,* 156[c–d]).

Actuality relates to the flow of births and deaths; it is continuously born anew and it passes away (*Symposium,* 207[a–e]). Thought, or rather grasping to apprehend, must likewise follow this process of continually passing from motion to rest. This is the very nature of aspectual thought. Yet this transition is not taking place in time, for only conceptual motion is in time, whereas the grasping thought and actuality are for ever in-between, passing from motion into rest. Plato writes:

> 'The word "instant" appears to mean something such that *from it* a thing passes to one or other of the two conditions. There is no transition *from* a state of rest so long as the thing is still at rest, nor *from* motion so long as it is still in motion, but this queer thing, the instant, is situated between the motion and the rest; it occupies no time at all; and the transition of the moving thing to the state of rest, or of the stationary thing to being in motion, takes place *to* and *from* the instant' (*Parmenides,* 156[e]).

He is arguing that true things are not sections of the perceptual flux-in-time, synthesized by the mind into units. The elements of thought and of matter can only be considered as concrete particles instantaneously. Yet the instant is not a very, very short duration in time – it is out of time. On the other hand, if we consider thoughts or matter as a flowing continuity, then thinking is not fragmented and *Chora* is not made of particles: it can be grasped only as an undifferentiated flow.

Writing of the location of atomic particles during moments of change, Oppenheimer (1954, pp. 42–3) observes that at the moment of transition the particle is neither in motion nor at rest; yet it is only at this time that it is a material particle, i.e. that it can be observed as such:

> If we ask for instance whether the position of the electron remains the

same, we must say 'no', if we ask whether the electron is at rest, we must say 'no'; if we ask whether it is in motion, we must say 'no'.

Operating within an entirely different tradition, Bergson reaches compatible conclusions, pointing to the inadequacy of treating time as a series of moments. He criticizes Zeno's argument that the arrow does not really move, since it at each instant occupies a single point in space and is therefore at rest in each. Bergson, of course, misunderstands Zeno, who makes his argument tongue in cheek: in fact, Zeno acts like a Zen master who creates a paradox precisely in order to stimulate the disciple to posit his own solution. Bergson, like Marx, has in refuting Zeno reached precisely the conclusion Zeno intended. Zeno's intention is suggested by Plato, who – almost unobserved by scholarship – reports a conversation between Zeno and Socrates in which Socrates suddenly realizes that Zeno is, in a negative way, arguing precisely the same point as Parmenides: 'You seem to be opposed, yet your arguments really come to very much the same thing – this is why your exposition and his seem over the heads of outsiders' (*Parmenides,* 128^{a-b}). Greek thought is full of such paradoxes. One may well wonder how often in refuting Heraclitus one is in fact reaching the conclusion Heraclitus intended; these philosophers did not wish to win arguments but to convert souls.

IV

There are three kinds of time: cosmic time, as defined by the movement of the stars and the 'sun's movement around the earth' (this is Plato's position); biological time, or the cycle which regulates the growth, feeding and reproduction of living beings; and finally mental, conjectural, psychological time, or time as mentally experienced. This latter kind is only felt as a resistance or friction when the mind is at odds with biological and cosmic time. In the sick city this is a permanent condition: hence perceived things are not true, they are in flux. For the mind flowing in rhythm with biological and cosmic time, the flux is no longer flux: hence actual entities are perceived.

This notion is not easy to grasp. Being in tune with cosmic time does not mean being in tune with the calendar: the calendar is certainly based on stellar movements, but these movements are empirically observed: a picture of a picture. This kind of 'cosmic time' can easily be conceptual (mentally false). It is not the object of thought that determines the manner of thought, but the latter that determines the nature of the former. Thinking about God does not make one pious; thinking about man, or anything, in a godly way is to think of God.

It is when the three kinds of time and the three kinds of 'is' coincide that actual things are perceived. In this coincidence time is in fact abstracted, since one moves with it. The actual entities are constituted out of time and space (i.e. in *Chora,* which is both).

Parmenides points out (155[c]):

> 'if there is a One such as we have described . . . it follows that since it *is* one, it has existence at some time; and again since it *is not* one, at some time it has not existence. And since it cannot both have and not have existence at the same time . . .'

This is the Koan or corybantic paradox, and it is precisely the question faced by Bohr and Heisenberg, who – having broken away from the concept of atoms – tried to account for the existence of real constituents of matter which both were and were not particles. Like Plato, Bohr and Heisenberg concluded that these things in fact have 'existence' out of time.

So what, then, of space and time, and things constituted in space and time? Parmenides' answer is that these are simply the product of limitations of language and conceptual thought, which operates in terms of lingual symbols. They appear to take an 'is', yet they should be referred to as 'is not'. It is not the things taking shape out of time and space that are unreal, but time and space itself. This is expressed by the physicist Mendel Sachs (1969, p. 53) – 'relativity theory implies that space and time coordinates are only elements of the language that is used by an observer to describe his environment' – and in an ancient Buddhist text: 'O Monks . . . the past, the future, physical space . . . and individuals [meaning individuals as in time and space] are nothing but names, forms of thought, words of common usage' (Murti, 1955, p. 198).

Actuality is a string of instants – but not in the conceptual sense. All real things take form in the realm of instants or *Chora;* individuals take existence and can be seen only when the time-space division is abstracted.

> 'Athough we speak of an individual being the same . . . every bit of him is different and every day he is becoming a new man, while the old man is ceasing to exist. . . . And the application of this principle to human knowledge is even more remarkable. . . . when we say we are studying we really mean that our knowledge is ebbing away . . . and we have to study to replace what we are losing so that the state of our knowledge may seem at any rate to be the same as before. . . . This, my dear Socrates, is how the body and all else partakes of the eternal – there is no other way' (*Simploke,* 8).

Diotima (a Hetera, or highly cultured courtesan – possibly a mistress of Pericles) adds that this principle applies to all kinds of knowing, thinking and seeing: a man must see instantaneously all the time. Conceptual interjection, even though extremely short in duration, nevertheless takes that fraction of a fraction of a second – long enough to feed the mind with a flow of illusions. Concepts are always retrospective, for they refer to previously held models. Actual things are seen forever anew.

IV

It has been suggested that the technique used by Parmenides is doubly negative. In positing the realm of instance, the 'is and is not' realm, Plato denies validity to conceptualized perceptions; he is also negating the existence of abstract universals. As such, the dialogue becomes a refutation of 'abstract' idealism (the two-world theory). For there are not two distinct worlds – that of ideas and that of material things – rather, there is one world, or simply all there is – the One, Brahman – which we can conceive in three separate ways. So far in this study I have been primarily concerned with differentiating between the realms of actuality and of becoming, since it is these two that are least well distinguished in contemporary philosophy. The main objective in the *Parmenides,* however, is to elaborate on the nature of the One. The realm of the One is that of reality. To understand its deeper meaning, an inclination in sentiment is required: 'for those whose temperament finds the procedure of this sort of thought congenial' (*Sophist,* 265[e]) it is a matter of deeply-felt certainty that that which is finally and ultimately real is God, and it is for this reason that the neo-Platonists and Anselm equate the One of Parmenides with God. It may very well have been Plato's assumption, also, that anybody who could conceive of the One would not fail to identify it with God ('I am the one that is'): but, unlike Plotinus or Anselm, Plato did not feel that such an identification should be 'provided' for the reader. As a matter of principle, Plato will not positively identify the Good itself (*Letter VII,* 241[c]); whether it meant God for him or not cannot objectively be determined from the dialogues. (For hints as to his private views on this matter, see *Letter XIII,* 363[b]; *II,* 312[e]; *VII,* 340[c]; *VIII,* 365[e].)

While Plato sees fit to argue for the immortality of the soul (e.g. *Phaedo,* 85; *Laws,* 959; *Meno*), he does not argue in the same way that there is a One; indeed in the *Parmenides* he explains why. He eloquently shows that there is nothing in the mental sphere, *Dianoia,* to lead one to infer either its existence or its non-existence. However, if there is anybody in the audience who still maintains (as does Zeno) that there is a One, Parmenides will show him not what that One is, but what it is not. It is this negative description of the One which will be considered below.

The non-predicated One 'has no beginning nor end; it has no limits'

(*Parmenides,* 137[d]); 'it has no shape, it is not round or straight' (137[e]). Further, such a being, by being everywhere, is in no particular place – it is out of space, not extended (138[a]). It cannot have an age, for that would imply being older or younger (140[e]–141); hence it is out of time: 'we may infer that the One, if it is such as we have described, cannot even occupy time at all' (141[a]).

The concluding paragraph serves not only to delineate what being is not, but also what becoming is – since becoming is everything that being is not. Becoming is in time, it has properties, it is in space and so on. Consequently, if the One has nothing to do with time, 'it never has become or was becoming . . . or will be becoming' (*Parmenides,* 141[e]): it is not in time and place (141); we cannot speak of it (142[a]); it has no properties. Conclusion is by grasp; it cannot be thought of.

Parmenides has a specific purpose. The One which has no existence in time and space also has no existence for thought. Therefore if the non-predicated unity is what truly is, then what truly is is literally beyond thinking (*Dianoia*). This conclusion is the object of the dialogue.

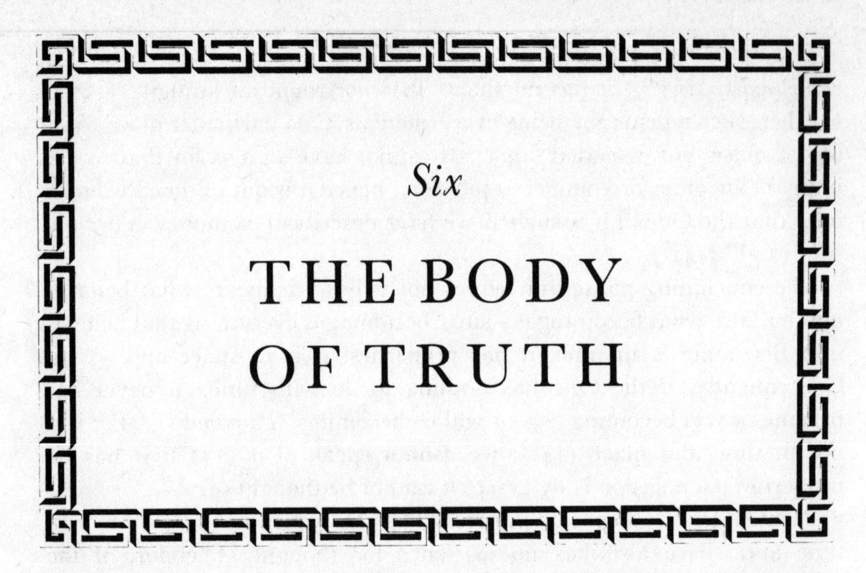

Six

THE BODY OF TRUTH

Taoism, Plato and the Upanishads are not simply expounding compatible doctrines. Much more than this, their imagery, their choice of words and their rhythmic construction is essentially identical. This is not because of borrowing or copying: any highly disciplined and concentrated mind faced with sets of conceptual paradoxes will resolve them in a similar way.

What is important is not the empirical content or the method, narrowly understood. One may concentrate on the symbol of the lotus or gaze at the infinite expanse of a moonlit sky; one may feel music deeply or lose oneself in the love of mankind: the decisive factor is the level of this concentration. It must be intense enough to absorb egoistic, conceptual impulses, and allow the noetic mind to flow freely. Conclusions thus reached will be verbalized in a certain way. To make them accessible to others who do not think noetically, they are further translated into time-specific imagery. These reductions do not render the original vision meaningless. While it may be useful to undermine these second-order verbalizations when they grow sterile, it is mistaken to assume that all formalization is bad. Like the idealists and materialists, the antiformalists and ultraformalists are equally misguided, and not surprisingly of the same psychological make-up.

The extreme antiformalist Bible fundamentalist will argue that there is no mediator between God and man save for Jesus Christ, and that there is no need for priests, vicars, churches, etc. If it is pointed out to him that there is no Jesus Christ or New Testament save for Matthew, Mark, Luke and John, he will inevitably answer, 'Yes, but when we read Luke we do not hear or see Luke – we see beyond Luke; we listen, in fact, to Jesus Christ.' In this he may be right; yet Luke was also an actual person, who according to his own account received the teachings of Jesus second-hand,

and was as such no different from a contemporary priest. While Luke may be simply a channel to Jesus Christ, so likewise is a Hindu Brahmin or even an icon: there are no teachings other than mediated teachings.

This is not intended as a formulation of anti-anti-formalism. 'There is no mediator between God and man but X, Y or Z' may well lead many men to good thoughts, feelings and acts, so let it be. Yet as an idea it is just as reasonable – or unreasonable – as the idea that the holy water of the Ganges cleanses all sins, or that no pork-eater may reach heaven. As Kierkegaard said, any belief of man formalized into a doctrine becomes false. Yet if a doctrine serves only as a trigger for grasp by love, then that doctrine (even though formally false) is a useful stepping stone. The same principle applies to anti-doctrine doctrines and to this study.

Let us look critically at the philosophically attractive and conceptually plausible statements of men like Heidegger, Russell and indeed Einstein, who believe in God, but not in Jesus or Krishna or the Talmud. Their attitude may be philosophically sophisticated, yet Plato and, in a different way, Zoroaster both show that such statements can become meaningless. To believe in an abstract God, in God as nothingness only, is to believe in nothing – it is not to believe. According to Christ, 'no one comes to the Father, but by me' (John, XIV,6); and Krishna makes similar statements in the Bhagavad Gita.

The contemporary Western notion of a transcendent God of Islam versus an immanent God of Hinduism is also false: both are transcendent and immanent. To be a Muslim it is not enough to believe in an abstract Allah: one must accept his prophet Mohammed. To be a Muslim means to accept Mohammed and 'his' Book.

I am not arguing here that there cannot be a belief in God without organized religion, but simply that there cannot be a belief in nothingness, neither can there be ethics, an idea or an ideology, without it taking some positive expression – although such positive expression is not itself truth, but a trigger or vehicle to an inner grasp in terms of sentiment. Even Marxism – as practised in Eastern Europe or China, not the 'transcendental' Marxism of Western intellectuals – necessarily resorts to icons, 'saints' and ideals similar to the garden of Eden or the Second Coming: the notion of a land 'beyond', to come in the future. This is not sarcasm: woe to any communist or Muslim or any nation that dismisses these organizing 'myths' – its inevitable fate is anarchy, immorality, rampant egoism and finally collapse.

The cynic will observe that I am recommending the invention of myths and beliefs in order to create social cohesion. Quite the contrary: I am asserting that all myths are true in so far as they have a common basis, i.e. that of the essential brotherhood of all men, the unity of the cosmos and its essential harmony. These facts are not relative but absolute truths. The fact that societies and individuals who submit themselves to such rules prosper is due to the fact that they behave in accordance with the real nature of the cosmos: since this is good, goodness is their reward.

A particularly successful exponent of anti-formality writes best sellers on the theme that all government and all other organized social units such as the city and the family should be done away with. This view would be correct were it not presented as a positive doctrine, as a literal truth. As it stands it is a simplistic view, comparable to the zeal of fanatical Muslims who attack the Hindus for worshipping cows, failing to realize that the cow is simply a symbol, as is turning to face Mecca; or like the Hindus who attack Muslims for 'reducing religion to ritualism'. The quasi-intellectual attack on external aspects of a foreign creed are always a self-defensive fight to preserve some domestic brand of orthodoxy. In some sense this may be necessary; yet the self-righteous would-be doer away with the formalities of creed ought first to take the log out of his own eye. . . .

The same applies to sophisticated anti-formality arguments such as those of Hume. Not that in criticizing 'religiosity' Hume is without merit; however, he does take his own argument too seriously. His objections, valid as they are on the conceptual level, do not touch noetic faith. Just as I have advocated replacing the notion of 'matter' with *Chora* and 'actuality', so I am tempted to use new words for 'faith' and 'belief', 'gods' and 'God'; instead, I shall follow Plato, who advises philosophers to leave these matters alone, and retain the word 'faith', although I cannot emphasize too strongly the difference between faith as a concept of *Dianoia* and faith as noetic belief based on the corybantic paradox.

Bohr and Rutherford testify that it was the absolute and unbridgeable conceptual paradox between light as particles and light as waves that required the leap of 'faith' (the faith of *Noesis*) into quantum theory. Quantum theory itself is transconceptual: it cannot be conceptualized, yet it can be believed. It is this kind of faith which is *Noesis*.

The conceptual notion of faith is of a blind acceptance of testimony: one may accept on the basis of factual statements that the population of a certain city is a certain number, without having counted its inhabitants oneself. Faith in this sense means the acceptance of the probable, without having to verify the facts. It is this kind of faith in God which is criticized by Hume, and quite correctly so. Indeed Hume may have been a deeply religious man without knowing it (conceptually). *Noesis*, or the faith proposed by Kierkegaard, is the mental leap beyond two conceptual paradoxes, an active and logically coherent act of reconciliation between two conceptual opposites leading to a resolution on a higher plane.

In this light we may look at the way in which the Greeks solved conceptual paradoxes. The older, pre-sophistic Greeks had no problem in grasping that 'spirit' and 'matter' were one, that the mover and the moved were inseparably bound yet not identical. Thales writes that 'all things are full of gods' – or in other words, that 'matter' is spiritual. Plato pointed out that the perceived thing and its essential 'spiritual' quality are not the same. (The word 'spiritual' of course is as misleading in this context as 'matter'; as usual we are condemned to use other people's words.) This conceptual ambiguity is overcome by noetic grasp: hence we read in the Brihadaranyaka Upanishad (III,15) of 'He who dwells in all beings, yet is other than all beings, whom all beings do not know, whose body is all beings. . . .'

To argue that the moving principle is eternal, or that ideas are reabsorbed into the things which they are the ideas of, is not to say that perceived things are the same as the ideas of them. The ambiguity cannot be presented conceptually, and must be grasped by an ethical leap. Faith does not mean blindly accepting implausible statements such as that there is a God in a place called heaven. Rather, it means the ability to stun the conceptual mind and grasp the deeper logic – the deeper kind of thought, *Noesis* – which moves on ethical grounds. Even a first-class dianoic brain such as that of Aristotle was incapable of such a leap. He could not grasp how it was that Plato insisted that ideas were in things and yet were other than things: for him, this necessarily meant that ideas were apart from or external to things, and it is in this way that Plato has been interpreted by almost everyone who pays their attention to commentaries on Plato rather than the text itself.

I

The purpose of Plato's dialogue *Parmenides* is to induce in the reader or hearer a noetic grasp of the relationship between the One and the many. I observed in the last chapter that Parmenides shared his notion of the One with the East, though this observation was not adequately supported at the time. This final Being is seen by Plato (*Timaeus*, 51,52) as:

> 'that one kind of being the form of which is always the same, uncreated and indestructible, never receiving anything into itself from without, nor itself going out to any other, but invisible and imperceptible by any sense, and of which the contemplation is granted to [noetic] intelligence only.'

And in the *Phaedrus* (247[c]) it is described as 'without colour or shape, that cannot be touched; intellect alone, the soul's pilot, can behold it, and all true knowledge is knowledge thereof.'

This, to Plato, is *Usia Ontos Usa* – the Beingly Being, the Indivisible One which the Upanishads call Brahman and which is described in the Svetasvatara Upanishad (VI,11–12) as 'the One God, hidden in all beings, all-pervading, the [Self] existent within every being, the surveyor of all actions, dwelling in all creatures, the witness, the spirit, the unique, free from attributes.'

Before we too hastily draw a linear-style deduction, and conclude as did the historical Parmenides that all is one, we turn back to Plato's *Parmenides* and observe with him that although if it were not for the One there could not be anything at all, yet in order for it to be a One for us it must of necessity have some kind of extension, whether this be simply a verbal predication or merely a notional one. The One to be a One needs some kind of a body, concrete or abstract.

The complications involved in conceiving of the One, i.e. Brahman, are further elaborated in the Svetasvatara Upanishad (VI,12): he is the One, Controller of a passive multitude', that is, he 'makes his one seed manifold'; and in the *Parmenides:* 'Thus he is both one and he is many, or rather he is one that seems and seems not to be many.'

The problem of the many being one lies in the separation between the observer and the observed. Heraclitus remarks that when you are awake, you cease to be one, you are embraced by the many and embrace the many in yourself, so that there is nothing without and nothing within.

> Just as a man embraced by his beloved wife does not know what is outside and what is inside, likewise the person, when he is embraced by the conscious [Self], does not know what is outside and what is inside. . . . Being just Brahman, he goes to Brahman (Brihadaranyaka Upanishad IV,3,21; IV,4,6).

Likewise, to know oneself becomes to know the one being, 'for all knowledge is the knowledge thereof' (*Phaedrus,* 247) and 'the knowledge of all is that which you are – *Tat Tvam Asi.* '

We find echoes of this in Tillich's (1951, vol.1, pp. 72f) formulation of 'ontological reason' – reason which perceives the ideal pattern of the being itself and its repetition in the structure of human intelligence.

We find Lord Krishna instructing Arjuna that knowledge is the perception of the one in the many. He says:

> When one sees Eternity in things that pass away and Infinity in finite things, then one has pure knowledge. But if one merely sees the diversity of things, with their divisions and limitations, then one has impure knowledge. And if one selfishly sees a thing as if it were

> everything, independent of the ONE and the many, then one is in the darkness of ignorance (Bhagavad Gita, XVIII, 20–22).

Ignorance is not just a perceptive deficiency: it has an ethical dimension, for it is the same as egoism and selfishness opposed to knowledge.

Thus religious, philosophical, scientific and even mundane practical knowledge manifests itself through the activity of gathering the many into one, and vice versa. Or in the words of St John's gospel (XVII, 11–23):

> Holy Father, keep them in thy name, which thou hast given me, that they may be one, even as we are one . . . that they may all be one; even as thou, Father, art in me, and I in thee, that they also may be in us. . . . The glory which thou hast given me I have given to them, that they may be one even as we are one, I in them and thou in me.

This relationship pervades all noetic thought, and is based on the assumption that one is indeed many – but not just any kind of many, or infinite kinds of many, but a specific, ordered kind: the many become one only in so far as they are ordered according to a specific pattern. To be, therefore, means to be in a specific place and to execute specific actions: to be is to be in order.

In religious philosophy, this principle extends from the formation of individual words themselves (as in the *Cratylus,* 389), to sentences, to philosophies and to cities, leading to man's integration into the body of Brahma, Jesus or the *Shariah.* This is conveyed in I Peter (II,5): 'like living stones be yourselves built into a spiritual house'. St Paul taught that the church is the body of Christ.

We become what we are meant to become, or what we 'really are', when we function 'as we should', harmoniously with respect to both planes: 'Thy will be done on earth as in heaven.' Through 'knowledge', the nature of this functioning is made manifest on both planes. St Paul (Ephesians, IV, 9–16) writes:

> ('He ascended', what does it mean but that he had also descended into the lower parts of the earth? He who descended is he who also ascended far above all the heavens, that he might fill all things.) And his gifts were that some should be apostles, some prophets, some evangelists, some pastors and teachers . . . for building up the body of Christ, until we all attain to the unity of the faith. . . . we are to grow up in every way into him who is the head, into Christ, from whom the whole body, joined and knit together by every joint with which it is supplied, *when each part is working properly,* makes bodily growth and upbuilds itself in love. (My emphasis.)

This perennial order, this universal truth and pattern which St Augustine writes always has been and always will be, is characterized by the Vedic *Rta* – meaning the world order, the law and pattern to which all the cosmos must conform. Confucius calls it Tao *Tien* which Noss (1974, p. 243) defines as 'the pre-established pattern into which all things ought to fall if they are to be in their proper place and do their proper work'.

The Zoroastrian *Asha* is described by Boyce as a 'natural law which ensured that the sun would thus maintain its regular movement and that the seasons would change'. She adds that 'the concept of *Asha* had ethical implications also in that it was thought that it should likewise govern human conduct. Virtue belonged to that natural order and vice was its betrayal. *Asha* is a difficult word to translate.' And she writes of 'order where the concept refers to the physical world, truth and righteousness in connection with the moral one. The principle of falsehood ... which was opposed to *Asha* the Avestan people called drug – Sanskrit *Druh*' (Boyce, 1979, pp. 7,8).

This same concept – i.e. the lie – is called in the Koran *Druj*, and opposed to the holy order, the law, called *Ashariah* or simply *Shariah*. The way of the gods or Tao *Tien* is, in Confucius's words (cited by Smith, 1973, p. 65), 'the way a man ought to travel, because it is ordained by Heaven that he should walk in it. It is fundamentally the way of Heaven, and only becomes a way of man because all wise and good men follow it.'

All these models see the individual as walking on two paths: one as an individual integrated into the *Asha, Rta,* Body of Christ, world order; and one as an individual separate from it.

In between order and the false self there is always a door – there is necessarily a positive intermediate vehicle or model. I shall later call this model the paradigmatic city (the New Jerusalem, the City of Ayodha, the cosmic Athens). It may also take local form as a person – 'I am the way, the door, the truth,' etc. – or as law. The 'City of God' concept is an important prerequisite of noetic thought, being on its lower level a social representation of the eternal *Rta-Asha*. The model is triple in nature, for its function is to represent the way in which the fixed ratios and relationships of the unchanging order particularize down into the sphere of social existence, taking concrete form within the context of a particular culture. The city of God never *is;* for it to materialize, all men would have to accept the law of *Rta* and behave accordingly. None the less, it has a function.

II

This study began with an attempt to distinguish between two different modes of apprehension, *Noesis* and *Dianoia*. Corresponding to these we posited two cognitive faculties, one the mind and the other *Logisticon* or *Buddhi* ('greater than the mind is Buddhi' – Bhagavad Gita, III, 42). Associated with these two cognitive faculties were two realms of being. The body perceives a world of sense, yet it is not this world that is mediated by the conceptual mind. As we have shown, the conceptualist differentiates between things and sensations. To the conceptualist, an orange is a synthesis of roundness, redness and sweetness – all the manifold qualities that the mind synthesizes as an orange. Likewise, a horse is a synthesis of blackness, four-leggedness and so on. Sometimes the horse is regarded as something behind all these sensations, and it is never taken in immediately.

If we could peep into the mind of a Hsia dynasty peasant (as indeed we can, through the art of that time), a horse appears as a pulsating bundle of energy, virility, warmness and various other impressions that cannot be conceptually deduced. Rivers are the blood vessels of dragons, hills can be male or female and caverns are the orifices of a cosmic animal. To the Greek preconceptual mind waterfalls are imprisoned lions that roar; the sound of a gong is for Pythagoreans the sound of an imprisoned giant. The presophist Greek calls white and quick by the same name (*Leukos*); Platnauer argues (tongue in cheek) in *Classical Quarterly* that the lack of correspondence between words and colours would indicate that the ancient 'Greeks were insane or colourblind'. His point is that the pre-seventh century BC Greek world is non-mental: it is grasped by a cognitive faculty other than the mind. Proclus, too, distinguishes between reality which is grasped and reality which is seen mentally. The equation of the mentally interpreted with the grasped universe is false. The two can coincide but need not.

Both, of course, are rooted in perception. We have already considered a third realm which is altogether independent of sensual perception. It must, however, be immediately stressed that the realities of this third realm are not different from the realities of the grasped world. By positing an intuitive world, we are not creating a dualistic position. The ontological distinction of the world of sense and the world of intuition is a necessary conceptualization, but it is conjectural. World A is not different from world B, the inner from the outer, though they may be differently perceived. The realm of *Eidos* or *Logos* and the realm of grasp and actuality, though in some ways separate, are essentially one: subject and object are only aspectually independent.

For Plato, what is and what is not external or material is a highly complex question. The problem is grasped by several more recent thinkers:

Here externality is not to be understood as sensuousness that

> externalizes itself and discloses itself to sensuous man. This externality is meant here as an alienation, a fault, a weakness that should not exist (Marx, *Mega,* I,3, pp. 171f).

This 'otherness' appears in existentialist philosophy and psychology as the principle of falsehood and inauthenticity. Psychological-existential authenticity becomes 'wholeness': the return to the unity from which one originally stems. The same principle of alienation from unity and the return to it likewise crops up in microbiology: in the creation of new organisms, DNA formation controls the evolutionary development of Dictyodora – the spiralling movement of shells, horns and galaxies (see Thompson, 1942). It also surfaces in contemporary cosmology, in the Big Bang theory, where the One explodes into the many, and history is a gradual return to the One.

III

The earlier chapters have used the words 'horizontally' and 'vertically' in a connotative manner which can now be explicitly elaborated.

It was suggested above that the 'Left' and 'Right' division in popular political terminology stems not from the seating divisions in Parliament but reaches far back into history, and is as present in Plato's Athens as in the thought of Confucius. 'Left' signifies soft, liberal, yielding, earthy, feminine: its negative connotations are dark, crooked, devious, untrustworthy. 'Right' – being associated with maleness, catharsis, purity, rigidity – stands for the opposite qualities. As we gather from Lao Tzu (Tao Te Ching, XXXIV), the eternal Tao does not differentiate but rather incorporates left and right. Plato, likewise, was at great pains to reconcile and avoid these divisions; for it was as a victim of these factions that Socrates was condemned to death.

The theme of the left and right and their reconciliation is of paramount importance to *Logos* thought. It is symbolized by the Tai Chi symbol chosen for his coat of arms by Niels Bohr, who himself accounts for things in terms of the creation of yin and yang, or positive and negative charges in the life of subnuclear particles. The two can be viewed as the two ways of perceiving the world – sensually and intuitively. (The intuition of Bergson, of poets or of the nineteenth-century Romantic movement, while a valid form of apprehension, should not be equated with noetic thought. As there is Eros and Agape – love of the lower and higher Aphrodite – and as there are two kinds of divine madness, so there are also two different types of intuition, to be treated elsewhere.)

To divide the world poetically, empirically, scientifically and erotically presupposes a (unified) conceptualist vision characteristic of the age of specialization. Such an age does not manifest itself only in the actual division of labour; the principle spills into all areas of life. So at the height of a conceptual era, men specialize in the ways they perceive the world; further, they specialize into 'serious' and 'unserious', employed and unemployed, workers and non-workers. Poets are paid to poetize, scientists to scientize, singers to sing. When the scientist wants to participate in music or art he does so via the mediation of the market: in other words he buys a record. Singers similarly buy the products of the scientist. Man is therefore conditioned to consume things in packages. This principle of pre-packing applied to thinking results in piecemeal apprehension.

In view of this, I can declare what I mean by the notion 'horizontal' in a single sentence. Whenever the being of anything is presented through an exposition of separate aspects, that presentation is horizontal. The 'left and right', 'being and becoming' divisions presented above are all horizontal in this sense.

Aspectual thought, on the other hand, operates in vertical units, that is, it simultaneously grasps the three aspects of entities which have been identified as the realms of being, becoming and actuality. These vertical units do have a horizontal dimension: a form can be spoken about, a God can be painted. The tension between vertical and horizontal lies behind the word play of the Vedas, and accounts for the apparent rivalry of Lao Tzu and Confucius.

Broadly generalizing, noetic philosophy can be seen in terms of an intersecting set of trichotomies, which come into being in the course of interaction of the vertical and horizontal duality called by Pythagoreans the limit and unlimit, or *To Peras* and *Aperion* (the One and the indefinite), and by Homer Oceanus and Thetys. Thus 'all things . . . consist of one and many and have in their nature a conjunction of limit and unlimit' (*Philebus*, 16^{d}).

The horizontal element of anything is that which can be seen, touched or thought about; it is that aspect of being which admits to more or less, heavy or light (*Philebus*, 24^{e}–25^{a}; see also Aristotle's *Metaphysics*, $998^{a}8$ and *Physics*, $207^{a}8$ and Simplicius' *Comments on Physics*, $207^{a}29$–32). In a way, we can follow Speussipus and Aristotle in claiming that it corresponds to the process whereby the concept – the content of the mind – becomes also a kind of body: 'The being which is distributed or parcelled out by the limiting factor of unity is the indefinite dyad' (Aristotle, *Physics*, 209^{b}; see also Simplicius *On Physics*, $187^{a}12$), the horizontal element of being. In thus equating the indefinite with matter, we need not subscribe to the absolute Aristotelian division between matter and separate ideal essences (*Metaphysics,* 987[a]–988): it must be emphasized that even God and Form have a horizontal element, for they too can be painted, spoken about and thought of. Although it is the horizontal element that can be sensually perceived, in itself it is held in existence by the vertically defined limit; thus even the action of conceptualization (as any action) is derivative of both the limited and unlimited principles.

The vertical element is the hierarchical aspect of a thing, its ontological structure. The indefinite element progresses horizontally and is distributed among bodies (*Timaeus,* 359). The conceptual 'body' is its verbal predication. To give body a conceptual unity is to give it a predication, a word: and this unity of predicated conceptualization is other than itself:

> 'If the One is, it cannot be and yet not have a being. So there will also be the being which the One has, and this is not the same thing as the One: otherwise that being would not be its being' (*Parmenides,* 142[c]).

This simply means that in conceptualizing anything we must give it a tangible aspect, even if this be the concept or the word itself. This element is 'the being distributed among the bodies' (*Timaeus,* 35[a]) which Aristotle identifies with the indefinite, and which we have called considering things horizontally. Horizontally seen, being is known, becoming is understood conceptually and actuality is grasped. Vertically seen, any single thing exhibits the three aspects of being, becoming and actuality.

Nothing could be seen or thought of were it not held in place or contained by the horizontal element; in order to be known, the One has first to emanate, alienate or in some way separate or contradict itself; but then the contradiction must be resolved into a unity. Hegel turns this principle upside down and creates the idealistic dialectic; Marx turns Hegel upside down and creates dialectical materialism; yet the mechanics stay the same: the non-alienated, the One, the thesis, followed by the historical process of alienation, *Entfremdung,* the emanation away from the normal, the dyad.

This alienated, externalized principle is referred to in Taoism and the Upanishads as the 'illusion', as the material or perceptual veil, *Maya,* the cause of all suffering and all evil. In Zoroastrianism it is called 'the Other': it can be variously portrayed either as a psychological principle (*Angro Manyush,* Ahriman), or as a conjectural principle opposed to the true and real (Vohu Manu). It can also be regarded as nothingness: the devil is frequently portrayed as an absence of reality by pseudo-Dionysius, St Augustine and St Thomas Aquinas. For pseudo-Dionysius, existence is the fusion of being with nothingness. 'Nothingness' can also sometimes stand for true being (non-conceptually considered): thus conceptual or empirical being can be called an emanation from nothingness returning to nothingness. The Advaita school of Vedanta take the view that nothingness is being, while perceived (atomic) matter is conjectural.

And Lao Tzu writes:

> The Tao begot One. One begot two. [These two are yin and yang, the male and female principles which create the third, their offspring.] Two begot three. And three begot the ten thousand things. The ten thousand things carry yin and embrace yang. They achieve harmony by combining these forces (Tao Te Ching, XLII).

Triunity is, of course, the essential characteristic of Christian theology. The One – the Father – creates the world through his word, the *Logos* ('through him all things were made'), and reconciles duality into unity by means of the all-comprehensive sentiment of the Holy Ghost. Here we shall tend to concentrate on the schematic outlines of the philosophical aspect of this process.

Mythologically, the Hindu God is a unity – the One, alone – 'with whom was the word'. The creative word – AUM – emanates from the One, and by its various vibrations creates the extended universe. A Tibetan Lama cited by Alexandra David-Neel (1936, pp. 186–7) sees all things as:

> aggregations of [tiny entities, atoms] that by their movements produce sounds. When the rhythm of the dance changes, the sound it produces also changes. . . . Each atom perpetually sings its song, and the sound at every moment creates dance and subtle forms.

A contemporary 'field theory' of matter sees it as originally existing as a non-differentiated frequency ('nothingness' in the sense, not of a void, but of not being other than itself), which becomes differentiated by the concentration of energy. All atoms, elements and so on are simply more or less dense rhythmic vibrations of this primal substance. Material particles are created by the symmetrical interaction of two kinds of movement, that of positive and negative charge or matter and antimatter, during which energy and momentum are conserved. Such models are daily re-examined; they vary from laboratory to laboratory, from age to age and from culture to culture. Yet whenever we look for the dual triunity we may be sure it will be there.

IV

We have so far considered the ontological realms and their corresponding epistemologies. Vertically considered, being, becoming and actuality correspond to knowing, thinking and grasping. Hence the two philosophical divisions, the epistemological and the ontological. There is, however, a third broad division, which concerns souls, and is a *psychological* division.

Psychologically and vertically considered, the soul can be seen as a tripartite hierarchy of *Logisticon, Thumos* and *Epithumia (Republic,* 435–442, 580[d]), or *Sattva, Rajas* and *Tamas* (Bhagavad Gita, XIV, 5). It must be emphasized that whereas a man *dominated* by the 'highest' soul quality, *Logisticon-Sattva* (Bhagavad Gita, XIV,18), can be considered to be superior to a man dominated by *Epithumia-Tamas* (Bhagavad Gita, XIV,17), such superiority does not ascribe a hierarchy of worth to the three qualities themselves when taken out of their instantial context. *Thumos-Rajas,* when correctly functioning, is no more than a psychological quality, and as such as good as any other. Considered vertically, *Sattva, Rajas* and *Tamas* are coequal; indeed to claim anything else would be like claiming that a piece of paper with a painting of a gold coin on it was by virtue of its subject worth more than a painting of a silver coin. These qualities are, then, precisely like paper money: coequal in their objective worth (i.e. as pieces of paper), yet acting as tokens for the symbolization and perception of objective value-relations between goods other than themselves.

Thus, considered as a psychological quality, *Logisticon-Sattva* can be seen as that part of the soul concerned with thought and reflection in the epistemological dimension called knowing (*Noesis*); ontologically it corresponds to the realm of being. *Thumos-Rajas* is that executive element of the soul concerned with activity, and hence with the realm of time and extension; it corresponds to becoming. The third element, *Epithumia-Tamas* has no negative connotations: it is defined by Proclus (1820, XI) as a 'tendency or appetite to be filled with something present, to be disposed according to some sensitive energy', hence it corresponds to the psychological dimension of grasping. The grasping soul apprehends immediately: it is filled with impressions without the intermediate function of opinion or thought. It is made clear by Proclus, through reference to the Pythagoreans, that a negative judgment about any of these psychological qualities can be made only as a result of their mutation or aberration, they are no longer functioning within their assigned places. The Arab philosopher Averroes (1956,p. 162) also opposes the two 'active' qualities of *Logisticon* and *Epithumia* with the *Rihd,* which is like *Thumos* in a sense passive or lacking independent impulse; and he assigns no qualitative predication to these three parts of the soul. The Indian caste corresponding to *Rajas* (i.e.*Thumos*) is that of the warriors: their duty is to fight, yet not to originate the causes of wars, nor to dwell on issues – not to reason why. *Kshatriyas* who fight well reach heaven regardless of the side on which they fight or the issue.

We are now in a position to clarify further the functioning of the horizontal dimension. The epithumic soul has a cognitive function which we have called grasping and whose object is actuality. Graphically, this relation can be portrayed as follows:

Actuality ——— Grasping ——— *Epithumia*

(horizontal or indefinite)

All things consist of both the One and the unlimited, i.e. vertical and horizontal elements; therefore actuality itself can be considered vertically. Portrayed graphically, this vertical element of actuality is the triunal being, as below:

Being
|
Becoming (Vertical)
|
Actuality

In order that these two creative forces, the One and the unlimited (vertical and horizontal) can create a progeny, they must be brought together graphically. This marriage is shown in Fig. 1.

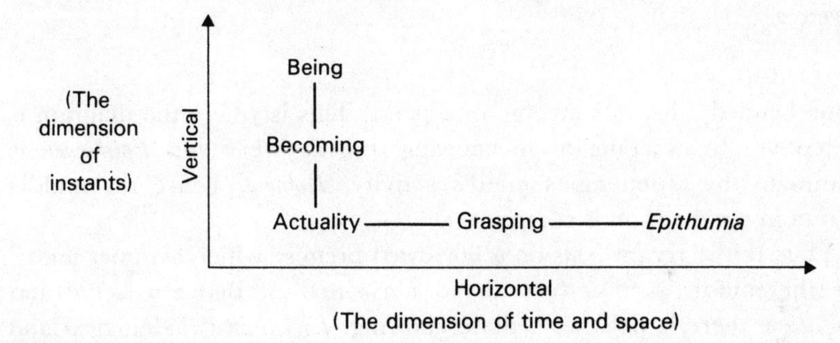

Figure 1

Reality, we said, is constituted by an intersecting set of ontological trichotomies (psychological, ontological and epistemological), brought together through the interaction of a vertical and horizontal duality (*To Peras* and the indefinite *Aperion*, or the two rivers Oceanus and Thetys). Bringing the intersecting trichotomies together, the matrix of Fig. 2 results.

The horizontal aspect imparts corporeality and tangibility, whether mental or physical, for it can only operate by creating extension in time or space. The vertical aspect confers instantaneous unity through a noetic grasping or 'intellecting' of three aspects in one.

In actuality or reality, the One and the indefinite dyad, when correctly

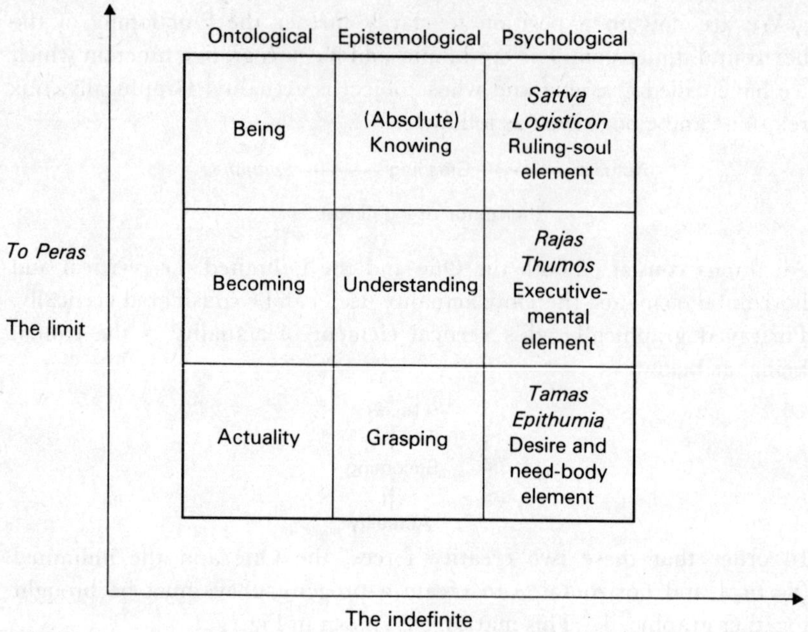

Ontological	Epistemological	Psychological
Being	(Absolute) Knowing	*Sattva* *Logisticon* Ruling-soul element
Becoming	Understanding	*Rajas* *Thumos* Executive-mental element
Actuality	Grasping	*Tamas* *Epithumia* Desire and need-body element

To Peras

The limit

The indefinite

Figure 2

apprehended, always converge in a point. This is where the diagram is deceptive. In grasping or in knowing, the *Logisticon* and *Epithumeticon* eliminate the autonomous mind's activity, *Dianoia:* hence the middle region in the diagram is conjectural.

Thus this diagram rests on a borrowed premise which assumes an 'is' for the middle section (considered horizontally). Between being and *Logisticon* there is no intermediate knowing: *Logisticon* is axiological and comprehends itself; knowing is being (*Ens*). Likewise, considered vertically, there is no becoming between being and actuality (see Fig.3). The aspects of the mediative 'cross', from the perspective of reality, become mere conjectural creations.

The diagram in Fig.2 can be seen as portraying the three different modes of apprehension. When attempting to apprehend the notion 'grasping', the mind should abstract the middle cross, and connect the opposites in one movement. Looking at the diagram: between the square representing being and the square representing actuality there stands a square representing becoming; the same relationship is true of knowing, understanding and grasping (see Fig. 4). Knowing is only aspectually different from understanding. Knowing, if considered mediatively (e.g. between being and *Logisticon*), becomes conjectural. *Logisticon* compre-

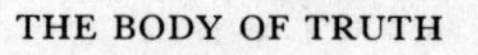

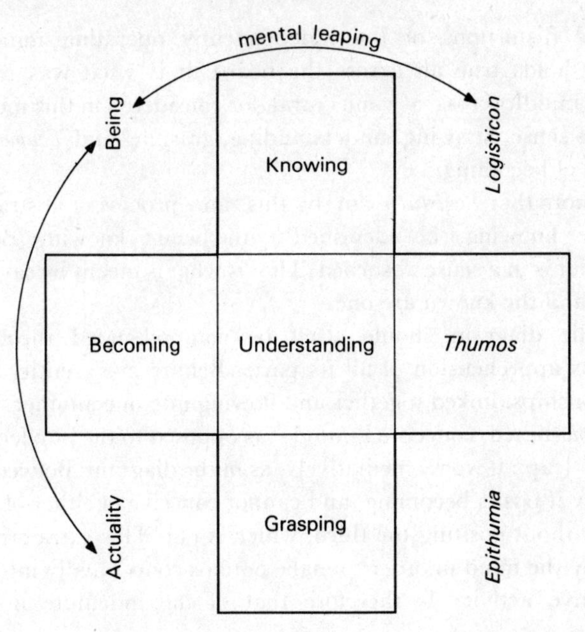

Figure 3

hends (is) being. Knowing, in this horizontal sense, ceases to be knowing. The grasping mind, when moving between knowing and grasping, abstracts the square in between – the process of understanding. This is precisely what 'grasping' means in our context: the ability to abstract the

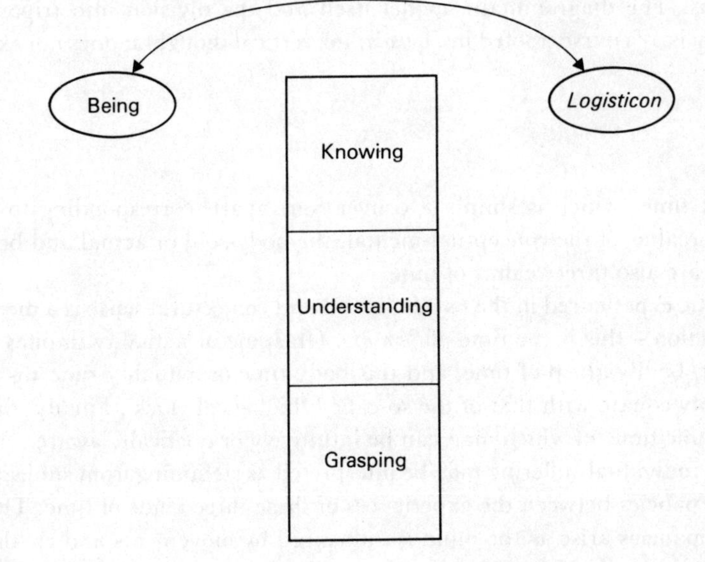

Figure 4

intermediate distortions of the independently operating mind. This relationship holds true all across the board: it is what was meant in positing the middle 'cross' as conjectural, for considered in this mediative, middle-cross sense, knowing, understanding, grasping and *Thumos* are all of the realm of becoming.

We may note that *Logisticon* can, by this same process of abstraction of intermediate knowing, be identified with being; knowing does not disappear, but is in a sense absorbed. That is what is meant by saying that the knower and the known are one.

Ideally the diagram should itself be comprehended through the simultaneous apprehension of all its parts. Behind every entity hide all these relationships, linked together and flowing into one another.

The *Dianoia*-based, conceptual mind – as opposed to the intellect – does not grasp or 'leap': it works mediatively, as in the diagram. Between being and actuality it posits becoming, and cannot conceive of either of the two which are without positing the third, which is not. This extra creation is grafted on by the mind in order to make notions conceptually intelligible. The mediative activity is therefore that of the indefinite horizontal element.

We can define *Noesis* as the simultaneous grasp of the three ontological aspects of being – not in the sense of stringing them one alongside the other, but by abstracting any such division. *Noesis* is 'vertical thinking'.

Dianoia, on the other hand, uses as its currency symbols and images, and can consider its objects only by seeing them as within one of the three realms. The diagrammatic model itself and the division into tripartite reality is, of course, rooted in *Dianoia:* for vertical thought it does not exist.

V

Clock time (which is simply a convention) apart, corresponding to the three realms of the conceptual-mental, the body-soul or actual and being there are also three realms of time.

Time experienced in the psychological and conjectural sense is a mental projection – this is the time of *Samsara.* Grasping or actuality implies the direct, bodily grasp of time, and this body-time or actuality-time we can roughly equate with that of the so-called 'biological clock'. Finally, there is cosmic time, of which man can be intuitively or noetically aware.

All individual suffering may be interpreted as stemming from subjective discrepancies between the experiences of these three kinds of time. These discrepancies arise as the mind is influenced by movements and rhythms which contradict that of the cosmos.

The mind is in a sense drugged to such mismatches. False music, false philosophy, false eating all drug the mind. One of the symptoms of intoxication is a distorted sense of time, and to understand this phenomenon, we must look at the origin of this sense.

Noesis involves the constant overcoming of inertia, and this friction gives rise to the psychological experience of time. The experience is intensified in moments of acute suffering. Pain can be overcome by abandonment to the cosmic rhythm; but it can also be avoided through drugs. False music creates a false feeling that life is friction-free. A potent drug such as heroin temporarily blocks the friction of *Anangke* or the Cross (notions to be developed later) by distorting the sense of time. The use of heroin may be felt as pleasant to the conceptual mind, yet the body's biological system is being destroyed: inevitably the pain of destruction is felt after a period of some days. It is the fact that body-time and mental time diverge that causes the suffering.

The same applies to evil sentiments such as sadism. The torturing of animals or of human beings – even if by mutual consent in sado-masochism – inevitably causes psychological and mental damage to the practising individuals, and to the society at large, even if the practices be discrete or unknown. This is why the bourgeois idea that all is permitted given consent falls flat, for this 'consent' is given on the conceptual plane by the conceptual mind. True consent involves a simultaneous agreement in all three realms. Any arousal of evil sentiment causes damage on the bodily or mental plane.

The evil that men do is only possible because of the delay in inevitable punishment. The punishing agent has often been externalized into a vengeful God: a more appropriate conceptualization is to see the punishing agent as some inner entity. To say that the individual punishes himself may be misleading, for there are two 'individuals' concerned: the true individual punishes the false one. 'Punishment' is again an incorrect word, for it implies vengeance. There is no vengeance. Pain stems from the restoration of imbalance, and all pain is self inflicted. A man actually cuts into his own flesh when he steps out of body or cosmic time, for in doing so he no longer feels what is painful, and hence 'unwittingly' commits evil acts on others – and on himself, since he is in others. (Mohammed: 'Whosoever committeth a sin committeth it against himself.' Socrates: 'One can only commit injustice against himself.')

If a man were to perceive the three realms of time simultaneously, he would be perfect. In the moments when he does, a man *is* perfect: biological and mental time are reconciled in cosmic time, and therefore disappear. Perfect time – cosmic time – is in a sense no time; man is projected on to a higher plane, where he is out of time.

Likewise for all real entities: contemporary physics bears out that the conceptual constituents of so-called 'real' things – things in time – are in fact abstractions. These abtractions – atoms and other primary elements – are not adequate, for they can no longer account for the universe as empirically given. The 'particles' in conceptual time and space are not true: true particles take form out of time and place. We read this in the Chandogya Upanishad (VI,12,1):

> 'Bring me a fruit of the fig tree!'
> 'Here it is, sir.'
> 'Break it open!'
> 'There it is, sir!'
> 'What do you see?'
> 'These fine seeds, like tiny particles.'
> 'Break one open!'
> 'There it is, sir.'
> 'What do you see?'
> 'Nothing at all, sir!'

These invisible particles are not nothing – they are invisible because they are out of time. The 'out of time seeds', as the sage goes on to observe, are in fact the constituents of all that really is: 'This finest element, which you cannot perceive [in time and space] – out of this finest element, my dear, comes this big fig tree! That which is this finest element, the whole world has for itself'(Chandogya Upanishad, VI, 12,2–3).

As pointed out earlier, in order to be 'that', it needs to take a body. In fact, 'that' is the synthesis of the body and 'that' – prior to this synthesis, there is neither 'that' nor the body. According to Socrates, *all* is nothing but pairs of movements – yet even these movements *are* not until there is a synthesis: 'there is no agent before it meets a patient, and no patient before it meets the agent.' The mind operates by the same rules.

In view of the foregoing we can understand the complexity of the relationship between *Noesis* and *Dianoia*. This can only imperfectly be graphically portrayed in our matrix; the two merge into one another by means of the intermediate area. The intermediate area of becoming, i.e. conceptual understanding, can be apprehended in several different ways. If it is understood for what it is, it is in a sense abstracted; it is absorbed into knowledge. As we have argued of actuality–*Chora*, the container and the contained, the receptacle, space and the stuff of which the universe is made, merge into each other – there is no more container and contained.

Conceptually, *Chora* itself can be considered as an object (and so can *Noesis*, for a process is also a thing), which is discerned as such either by word or by thought, once it has been differentiated as an entity by granting it a unity. The intelligible *Noesis* itself takes on tangibility, i.e.

conceptual unity: 'the one in order to be thought of as one must take a being which is other than itself'. In other words, *Noesis* is divided into *Noesis* and its body (*Dharmakaya*).

All things are constituted by the One and the indefinite dyad (*Philebus,* 16[d]), by on the one hand the eidetic content, the being of the being, and on the other the kind of being distributed among bodies, apprehended by opinion jointly with sense (*Timaeus,* 52[a]). *Noesis,* considered as a process – a thing – therefore has both a vertical and a horizontal component: horizontal as a concept or a word, for words and concepts have a being (*Cratylus,* 386[e]); considered vertically, a notion. The vertical aspect is knowledge considered as its own object, the realm of form, and as such it is called *Noesis*. The horizontal component represents knowledge apprehended as an opinion of itself, and is represented by the 'one section of it which the soul is compelled to investigate by treating things as images' (*Republic,* 510[b]): this dimension of *Noesis* is called *Dianoia*.

Let us consider two sections of Fig.2, understanding and knowing. Considered aspectually, each of these likewise has a component which could in turn be called knowledge or understanding – just as a god, a man and a piece of dirt each have a form and extension (*Parmenides,* 130). In order to avoid the infinite internal regression to which the ontological matrix is subject conceptually, we add the third dimension – grasping. The object of the subdivision is not to create a new and independent class of knowledge, but rather to illustrate the relations of the two basic entities (conceptuals and knowables). We are not dealing with three classes of knowledge, but with knowledge viewed aspectually, 'knowledge' viewed conceptually, and knowledge as grasped.

Dianoia is thus not a 'second-best' kind of knowledge: it is not knowledge at all, but a picture of knowledge. The distinction at hand is between objects and pictures of these objects. Pictures can be considered both as pictures of objects and as objects – as they indeed are, considered for themselves.

VI

The intention here is not merely to distinguish between an object 'knowledge' and its *Eikon* 'opinion'; this distinction is readily acknowledged. The more important distinction relates to the conjectural thinking characteristic of those people commonly considered as 'thinkers': mathematicians, positivist philosophers, scientists. I aim to diagnose the nature of the mental activity that would today be called positivist thought, and to show it to be different from the mental activity of the dialectical thinkers.

Noetic activity escapes positive elaboration, since it starts from principles that cannot be positively derived, and it uses no pictures to make progress. In the *Republic* (511[c]), Glaucon states:

> '[I understand that you mean to distinguish reality and dialectic from] the so-called sciences and arts whose assumptions are arbitrary points. And, though it is true that those who contemplate them are compelled to use their understanding and not their senses . . . you do not think they possess true intelligence about them, although the things themselves are intelligibles. . . . And I think you call the mental habit of geometers and their like, mind or understanding and not reason. . . .'
> 'Your interpretation is quite sufficient,' I said.

Thus, simply, *Noesis* is an act of apprehension independent of concepts or images. *Dianoia* is abstract or discursive thinking, dependent on images which are conjectural. This is also observed by K. Oehler – to whom I am indebted – and by Cornford (1967, pp. 76–7):

> *Noesis,* as opposed to *Dianoia,* is the intuitive act of apprehending by an upward leap . . . for this *Apsastai, Katidein, Feastai* etc. are usually substitutes [grasping, direct vision]; [whereas] *Dianoia* means generally abstract thinking. . . . as opposed to *Noesis, Dianoia* is the downward movement of understanding . . . the uncertain state of mind of one whose so-called knowledge consists of isolated chains of reasoning.

The distinction between *Noesis* (Oehler's term for which is *Empfangen*) and *Dianoia* is not the distinction between thinking about 'higher' entities (such as forms, gods, morals, ideas) and thinking about 'lower' entities. It is between a valid and the invalid manner of apprehending the same things. Conceptual thinking is invalid; *Noesis* is valid, and it is not thinking. It is a common but mistaken assumption to see the *Noesis-Dianoia* distinction as derivative of a distinction between objects of thought; this was Kant's mistake. Cornford (1967, p. 76) notes: '*Noesis* is not the realm of apprehension to do with moral ideas, as for Kant, and *Dianoia* is not the realm of mathematicals.' It is the manner and not the object of thought which distinguishes the two activities.

The implications of this statement may be obvious, yet they are far-reaching. *Noesis,* it will now be clear, is essentially an ethical way of knowing: to know noetically is to know 'Sattvically', i.e. diarithmetically through the vibration of the soul which is controlled by the heart. For Kant, the sense of 'I' is present and conditions all categorical perception; for noetic thought, it is the sentiment which conditions all apprehension. The point is well developed in the Upanishads. Faith in the One is not to believe in this or that, for the One is never this or that. However, he who thinks noetically, through the sentiment of the One which is Love – is always in the One. And Krishna says in the Bhagavad Gita (XI, 53–54):

'Not by the Vedas [i.e. formal religion] . . . or ritual offerings can I be seen as thou hast seen me. Only by love can men see me, and know me, and come unto me'.

Noesis is knowing through faith. The knower voluntarily surrenders the mental 'I', and in so doing creates and perceives a different world and a different self.

A man who is apprehending correctly makes limited use of the conceptual mind, and relies instead on the vibrations of the soul. For the simple, healthy shepherd, this process is natural and comes as a result of proper upbringing and inner moral goodness (*Laws,* 679[c]; *Republic,* 372[b]; *Phaedrus,* 275[b–c]). For the citizen of a fevered city, the same process may be realized only after the limits of thought have been understood and exhausted, or by *Theia Moira* (*Meno,* 100[b]; *Republic,* 519[b]).

Having attained this realization, a noetic thinker does not cease to talk or to think. Rather, he develops techniques of using words, thoughts, and discourse not in order to create further concepts, but to create a philosophy which serves to agitate the soul. The soul has its own movement, and it is eager for the words which will stir it into activity. Words and speech become charms; this is expressed by Socrates in the *Charmides* (157[a]) and commented upon by Cushman (1958, p. 22):

> Words of the right sort are charms which heal the soul . . . and if words of the right kind induce wisdom in the soul, Socrates is not averse to being an enchanter. . . . He is prepared to excite a kind of ravishment, namely a moral sensibility, *Alidius* – shame or reverence for goodness.

If we cannot see Socrates as a teacher of specific thoughts or concepts, we can see him as a creator of sentiments. This idea is conveyed by Xenophon's (1923, vol.3, lines 25–31) observation: 'for I never heard Socrates say that he taught philosophy, neither did I know any who ever did hear him'. In the *Symposium* (209[c]) a man seeks a companion so that each of them should educate the other not by persuasion, but by the mutual creation of 'noble sentiments', by giving birth to correct movements of the soul. Also in the *Symposium* (175[c]), Agathon requests Socrates: 'Come and sit here beside me, Socrates, and let me by contact with you enjoy the discovery which you made in the porch.' That Socrates' method was not that of any of the concept-employing philosophers is further borne out by Alcibiades (*Symposium,* 217[e]–218[a]): 'There never was anybody like Socrates, unless you compare him to satyrs.' 'Socrates' philosophy stirs the soul'; 'it is like a bite in the heart'. It 'clings like an adder to any young or gifted mind' (*Symposium,* 218[a–b]).

The extreme example of knowing through absence of thought is given by the 'wise' dogs of the *Republic* (375[e]), who know instantly by recognition their friends and foes (whatever is known instantly, by recognition or 'remembering', is true, and to know thus is to know the truth): 'An exquisite trait, and one which shows [dogs'] true love of wisdom'. 'How I ask you can the love of learning be denied to a creature whose criterion of the friendly and the alien is intelligence and ignorance?' (*Republic*, 376[b]).

The taciturn Spartans are called 'the most talented among philosophers', but their philosophic activity is hidden and secret: they use no medium of thoughts and words (*Protagoras*, 342[a]). In the *Protagoras* (343[b]), Plato states that the Spartan, non-elaborated wisdom was for the ancients 'a characteristic expression of philosophy'. The activity of the philosopher thus seen is primarily to silence the mind, in order to make it reflective of the sentiment. Having made himself a medium of the perception of sentiment, the philosopher can then assist others. The philosopher does not teach a philosophy that needs to be thought of. Quite the opposite: he conveys sentiments and arrests thought.

St Augustine (1952, IX,p. 25) expresses the same view:

> Could one silence the clamorous appetites; silence his perceptions of the earth, the water and the air; could he silence the sky, and could his very soul be silent unto itself and by ceasing to think of itself transcend self consciousness . . . could he entirely silence all language and all symbols . . . so that we might hear His word [*Logos*] not through human language nor through the voice of an angel nor through any utterance out of a cloud nor through any misleading appearance, but might instead hear without these things the very Being himself. . . .

In *The Silence of St Thomas*, Pieper describes the development of Aquinas' thought as leading to final silence. This was manifested in a literal sense: Thomas indeed ceased to speak or write of his final experiences, and in the last part of his life simply affected his fellow monks by his behaviour, his composure and presence.

Plutarch describes the mind of Socrates as perfectly still and free of thoughts. Philosophers, unlike thinkers, become like people whose minds are asleep – for 'Sleepers see and hear although there are no sounds or pictures'; and the method of Socrates is to induce this absence of thought:

> There is no voice heard, but fancies and notions as to particular words reach the sleepers . . . only sleepers receive such conceptions in a real dream because of the tranquillity and calm of the body in sleep, whereas in waking moments the soul can hardly attend to greater powers, being so choked by thronging emotions and distracting needs that it is unable to listen and give its attention to clear revelations. But the mind of Socrates, pure and passionless and intermingling itself but little with the body for necessary purposes, was fine and light of touch and quickly changed under any impression. . . . the words of spirits

pass through all nature, but only sound for those who possess the soul in untroubled calm (Ferguson, 1979, pp. 224–5).

In the light of this view of the philosopher, perhaps we can understand why in the Potidean campaign Socrates stood fixed in place without word or movement for twenty-four hours, from dawn to dawn, a 'story which, if true', writes Guthrie (1971, p. 34), 'is hard to explain without some element of trance'. Before commencing his discourse in the *Symposium*, Socrates likewise retreats to a neighbouring porch, and stands fixed and silent throughout the first part of the banquet. That these are not isolated instances is shown in the *Symposium*, 175[b]:

> 'And there he stood, said the man [informing Agathon that Socrates will not move or speak]. This is very odd, said Agathon, you must speak to him again. . . . But here I broke in: I should not do that, I said. You'd much better leave him to himself. It is quite a habit of his you know; off he goes and there he stands, no matter where it is.'

In the final passage of the *Republic* (618[c]), Plato concludes not by recommending that one study philosophy as such (i.e. thinking, doctrines, etc.) but rather

> 'it should be our main concern that each of us, neglecting all other studies, should seek . . . if in any way he may be able to learn of and discover the man who will give him the ability and the knowledge to distinguish the life which is good from that which is bad.'

Chuang Tzu's paradigmatic teacher teaches by silence; he mirrors the Tao: 'The still mind of the sage is the mirror of heaven and earth, the glass of all things' (Legge, 1971, ch.13). From the counsellor we receive no specific formula, but with him we create the sentiment: we distinguish the good from the bad by the nature of this movement which it produces in our soul (*Laws*, 864[a]). The point of the association of lovers is that together they may beget noble sentiments, so that they may know (*Symposium*, 209[c]).

Sentiment is the legitimate mode of apprehension of all that is true and noble.

VII

Let us now attempt to summarize the above observations regarding sentiment and thought.

All things consist of two elements, vertical and horizontal, meeting in a third. The indefinite, horizontal element has been equated with extension, *Dharmakaya, Chora,* matter, outer, body. The One, or the limit, the vertical tendency, appertains to or insinuates the inner element, the non-extended, the intelligible, the mover, the hidden, the organizing principle, the unity. The vertical, we noted, was the origin of all movement – *Auto Kath-Auto*. The vertical characterization of that movement can be seen as a sentiment; the tangible, horizontal characterization is number. Yet number can also be taken in a vertical sense, as the organizing principle relative to which the horizontal is the material; what is yin or yang, left or right is aspectual because it depends on the context.

The tangible, being a thing, also has two elements, horizontal and vertical. Sentiment in and for itself is vertical; if considered in conjunction with its horizontal component it creates a progeny, the notion. Notion considered horizontally, i.e. as its 'visible' image, can be equated with thought: the mind, in order to account for the image and its model, creates a never-ending flow of new images – an activity called thinking. Sentiment is the movement of the soul; thinking is the movement of the body. Yet what (and when) counts as body or soul is again aspectual.

The mind, although not extended as a substance enduring in time (as is Cartesian 'substance') is here regarded as 'body' or 'matter' in the sense of *Chora*. Mind as *Chora* functions as a mirror by means of which we perceive reality (*Timaeus*, 50[e]). However, for the mirror to be effective, the surface must be 'as even and smooth as possible' (*Timaeus,* 51[a]; also the 'smooth lake' referred to by the Rig Veda and Ramakrishna). The legitimate function of the mind is to reflect the motions of the soul, or sentiments.

Thought is an activity of the body, or rather an aberrant activity of the part of the body-aspect of the soul called *Thumos*. *Thumos,* when in its place, is an integrated part of a unity which sustains activity, but which ought not to act independently. The disturbed *Thumos* (overwhelmed by the desiring, epithumic aspect of the soul) becomes self-interested and egoistic, and grants itself unity and autonomy by usurpation. Speculative thought is the usurpation of the mind by the unlawful activity of thumetikoid desire. *Thumos* has no legitimacy as an independent entity, so thought is forced to create interpretative conjectures. However, thought ascribes reality to itself by this agitation of the mind; the agitated mind ceases to be smooth and still, and is a mirror no more.

The sentiment-oriented 'mind' is ethically interested and materially disinterested. The thought-oriented 'mind' is ethically disinterested, and directed at the material realm; it comes into existence as a response to some desire of the body.

Distortions of the proper relationship between the soul and the mind can be of two kinds. The hierarchical aberration is the imbalance of the vertical aspect, i.e. the psyche, and is called *Ammetria*. The horizontal aberration, of the body, is called *Stasis (Sophist,* 228[d–e]). But both body and psyche have horizontal and vertical elements, hence both are subject to *Ammetria* and *Statis*.

The unity of perceived entities has no counterpart in 'reality' (Brahman, *Usia)*, not because what is perceived lacks reality, but because the perceived entities are spuriously conglomerated fragments of the real unity. Real entities, including things, actions and persons, are instantiated in fragmented blocks. (Love is the synthesizing force by means of which the fragmented parts of bodies wish to reunite into the original whole: *Symposium*, 192. Aristophanes has simplified the case here by speaking of two fragments; in the *Symposium*, 191^{d}, however, he also says the process of fragmentation is indefinite; if fragments misbehave, Zeus will quarter them, and so on *ad infinitum*.) The conjunction of these fragments is subject partially to the wandering causes of *Moira* and *Anangke* (Karma) – chance and necessity; entities are dispersed into fragments independent of connection by time, place or perceivable causality, as the outcome of chance and choice (*Republic* 617^{d-e}); the timing, location and generation of particles is unpredictable (cf. Heisenberg's Uncertainty Principle). These real entities are akin to qualities normally labelled as abstract such as goodness, redness, badness; grammatically less well-elaborated but no less real are further qualities such as manness, Socratesness, horseness.

Rather than seeing these qualities as the flowing predicates of extended things, the extended things should lose their fixity and be seen as flows of qualities. The flows alone can be said to be real – as well as those non-changing forms which truly *are*. Both change – when recognized for what it is – and non-change are real, but things in time are not. All extended things properly function only as predicates of true entities; these true entities exist as real unities in the non-extended realm whose unifying characteristic is number, and in the extended realm whose constitutive substance is *Chora* and whose organizing principle is the sentiment. They exist as dispersed wholes, unperceived as unities by the conceptual mind, yet apprehended as real by the *Logisticon-Buddhi*.

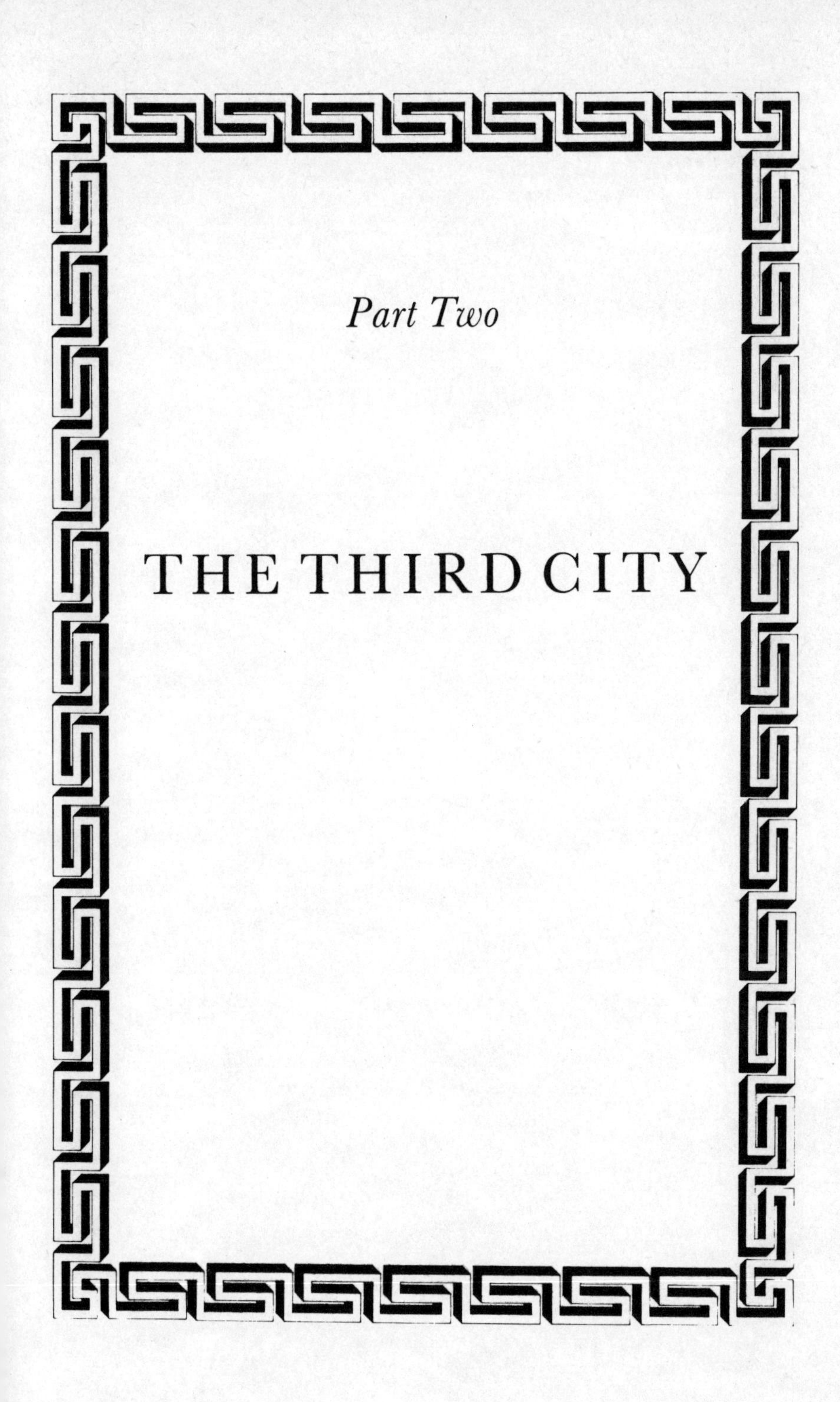

Part Two

THE THIRD CITY

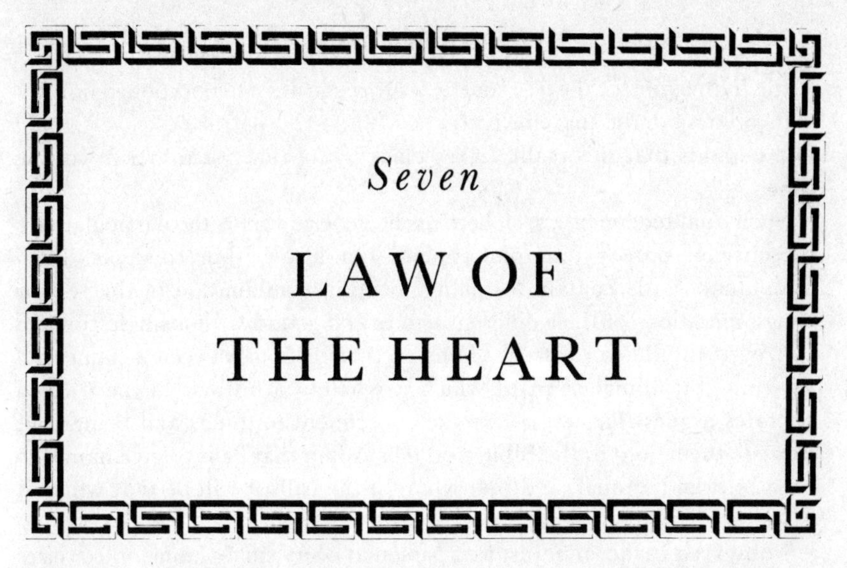

Seven

LAW OF THE HEART

This part of the study will examine the role of the paradigmatic city model. It will be preceded by a transitional passage revising the notions established earlier, and attempting to show how they relate to formally constructed creeds, in order to pave the way for a subsequent examination of religious myths.

I

Duality, or dual triunity, is the basic characteristic of all noetic thought. The paradigmatic city is a vehicle for resolving its contradictions. The objective of the model is to bring individual participants in public cities to consecrate their mundane actions by executing them in a manner dictated by an inner order.

Eliade (1958, p. 460) writes:

> The ideal of the religious man is of course that everything should be done ritually, and on that account every act is liable to become hierophany. In other words, any moment may be inserted into the Great time and thus project man into eternity. Human existence [he concludes] therefore takes place simultaneously upon two parallel planes – that of the temporal – of change and illusion – and that of reality.

E.J. Urwick (1920, p. 17) used this formula to resolve what he saw as the 'duplicity of Plato's message'. He wrote that for the Hindus and for Plato,

> the pathway of the human soul through life may be pictured as contained by two distinct segments or arcs . . . the lower arc covers the whole life of the citizen, the human socius . . . the higher arc contains

> the path of life for the free soul ... super social ... conditioned only by its relation to the supreme reality ...

and he adds that this reality takes place out of time, or rather in cosmic time.

Such dual tendencies, seen here as the general versus the particular, are present not only within philosophies but also within concepts. Even individual words contain a duality, being a combination of the sets or conglomerations of their different letters and sound with a single concept conveyed by the word itself. (Thus the connection between a name and the thing or animal or plant which it is is not arbitrary; in the *Cratylus* Socrates argues that names are not subsequent to things and beings but precede them, and in the Bible God tells Adam that he is to give names to each bird and animal, and that whatever he calls it will be that which it is.)

I observed earlier that just as a person at every single moment exercises a choice between the two kinds of self, so he chooses between two different ways of constituting a thing. One is a mental – conceptual construction (i.e. linear), and the other is dual, through the reconciliation of opposites (the noetic and the body-impression) by sentiment and *Aritmos*. Each and every thing is constituted from the One and the indefinite dyad, from yang and yin.

On the religious plane, the duality is between the religious imperative – i.e. the letter of an objective law – and individual consciousness within the dictates of a particular situation. The law, as Plato has argued (*Statesman*, 300), is only an imperfect guideline, having ethical validity only when subjected to inner criteria. Yet the inner criteria acquire ethical validity in their (immediate) relation to the objective law.

In Islam, this tension is often seen as the balance between two apparently divergent commands. It is the balance between the fixed, the written-down way of the law, the *Shariah*, and the way of the heart, the *Tariquah* – signifying one's own conscience, one's private way to God.

S.H. Nasr (1966, p. 122) explores the history of Islam in terms of the balance of these two:

> Although Islam in its totality has been able to preserve throughout its history a balance between the two dimensions of the Law and the Way [i.e. *Shariah* and *Tariquah*], there have been occasionally those who have emphasized one at the expense of the other.

This emphasis, he argues later, always led to a spiritual weakening of Islam. In the same work, Nasr (1966, p. 122) writes that Islamic sages describe the relation between man and the truth as the circumference of a circle connected to the centre by means of radii:

> The circumference is the *Sharīʿah*. ... Every Muslim by virtue of

accepting the Divine Law is as a point standing on this circle. The radii symbolize the . . . *Ṭarīquah,* which exists in many different forms corresponding to different spiritual temperaments and needs of men. . . . Finally at the Centre is the *Ḥaqīqah* or Truth which is the source of both the Tarīquah and the *Sharī'ah.*

The truth is sometimes depicted as a point of balance, and compared to a centre of gravity around which two 'celestial' bodies rotate. The truth is external to both bodies (the book and the heart), yet central to their motion. Religious atrophy follows a reduction to either of the two extremes, for it alienates man from the abstract external centre which is the truth. Linear reading results either in moral anarchy or its opposite, ritualistic slavery ('idol worshipping'); in both cases the true religion atrophies.

Notional duality is therefore an essential ingredient in Christian, Islamic and Platonic thought. In a more complex way it also enters into Chinese theoretical-religious life. Rather than positing the duality within one philosophy, the Chinese have quite liberally embraced two different philosophies, without attempting a theoretical reconciliation. It is a commonplace observation that Taoism, 'the anarchical way', 'the way of the wind', 'the scent of the flower, the path of yielding, of nonresistance', is 'diametrically opposed' to ritualistic, law-and-order and ritual-oriented Confucianism. This view is also found in the otherwise penetrating thought of Heidegger. The controversy continues to this day: there is still a lively discussion as to which of the two 'contradictory' philosophies can be regarded as the more representative expression of Chinese thought. One meets with existentialist and many contemporary Zen-oriented thinkers underplaying Confucius and favouring Lao Tzu.

In the present analysis, a division between the two is incorrect. Empirically, at least, one can see that both were poles of the official cults of the empire and were part and parcel of a single culture. It may be of significance to notice that thinkers like Heidegger also favour Heraclitus at the expense of Parmenides: this distinction itself points tellingly to the general failure of existentialistic thought, although such thought when it was originally introduced by Kierkegaard successfully pointed to the failures of speculative philosophy.

Turning to Christianity, we see the dichotomy dramatized by the event of Jesus Christ, whose mission was both to remove and to fulfil the law. It is for this reason that Christ speaks in parables, and posits the New Covenant as a means of resolving the conflict between the universal and the specific, the general and the particular, being and becoming.

It is a universal tendency to perceive becoming as stationary. It is the mission of Christ and any philosopher to unbalance this tendency, to create an inner conflict – be it intellectual or ethical – forcing the client to remove the painful disjunction by resolving it on a higher – i.e. ethical – plane.

Given the citizen's normal (i.e. linear) state of mind, he automatically assumes that justice is a set of particular manifestations of justice, that being good is the paying back of debts, the giving of alms or in some objective way improving the lot of the poor. These are often examples of being good, but they are not the good itself. It is the philosopher's duty to imbalance the assumption that any act is necessarily good. (The first part of Plato's *Republic* exemplifies this.) This is why Krishna dismisses Arjuna's moralizing when the latter equates charity with particular acts. In the Koran, Mohammed decrees that one should be merciful towards one's enemy yet fierce in combat. The gods want no violence – for violence is an evil motion – but wars can be fought with a clean heart. Nor is the taking of life a real possibility, for one can neither give nor take life (Bhagavad Gita, II,21).

Quite frequently Christ speaks of selling one's expensive possessions and giving the money to the poor. However, at the point where the disciples begin to equate such actions with charity itself, Christ suddenly reverses himself. In a 'set situation' with a charitable woman ready to give away her most precious ointment, Christ observes her 'wasting' it by pouring it over him. 'Why this waste, for this ointment might have been sold for a large sum and given to the poor?' exclaims Judas. Jesus rebukes him: the message is that what she has done *is* charity because she has done it for love, but 'you will always have the poor with you' (Matthew, XXVI, 11). We do not work in order that all men be well fed and healthy, for they never will be (for reasons we shall later examine). Good action is its own reward.

Religious insight requires separation from the particular and ethical, for goodness is not doing this or that. This insight, argues Socrates, is like a birth – it comes in pain and after much labour: it is a shattering moment when a person suddenly realizes that something in which he at one moment beheld truth or God becomes a dead word or idol at the next. This is the insight which came to the Hindu sage as he beheld Krishna in the venomous cobra which kills an innocent child. Such examples abound in Hindu mythology, where God may appear in the face of a prostitute, a brigand or a thief.

It takes insight to see that the Messiah, the King, the Saviour, does not necessarily emerge through circumstances and in forms objectively held as appropriate. In order to know, one must oneself perform the dialectical leap, which is necessary in order to know the Messiah even if he can be easily seen in a physical sense. Knowledge as insight is a matter of creativity. It is the function of the philosopher, not to give knowledge, but to implant a notional conflict. To see anything as fixed is to arrest movement; the philosopher must imbalance fixed notions and start the *Elenchos*. Perhaps it is necessary to create and maintain separate visions, religions, ideologies and nations so that no deep truth can be reduced to a fixed teaching or ritual.

The confrontation between the polygamous Muslim and the monogamous Christian should help to imbalance the assumption of the latter that adultery lies in a specific activity, rather than a particular manner of executing an action. To reduce morality to the simple observation of a specific ritual form such as monogamy is necessary, yet it needs to be unbalanced by alternative conceptions of morality lest either should lead to idolatry. Allah sent prophets to all nations, and all those who do the will of Allah, be they Christians, Sabaeans or Jews, will find their way to heaven. It must be perplexing to a devout Muslim to be told this, as part of his faith, yet also to read that only sinners eat pork, only fools believe that Jesus was the son of God, only infidels drink wine, etc. Such encounters create a never-ending historical *Tenos* (tension).

The Sufi mystic loves his torturers and expects to see them in heaven, for they think he is an evil man. False belief, like correct belief, is immaterial – all conceptual belief is false: their hearts are pure. Likewise, Jesus asks forgiveness for his persecutors, 'for they know not what they do'. The ignorance that is vice is where the soul or the heart is at odds with the mind. One can therefore be mistaken with respect to any specific belief, and yet be forgiven; i.e. one can sin against the *Logos* by treating it as a mere son of man, book or philosophy only if one also recognizes it for what it is. This, we may assume, is why Christ says that all specific sins will be forgiven, except those against the Spirit.

The word used throughout the New Testament is *Pneuma;* it is still translated as 'Spirit', yet the word 'spirit' is usually understood today to mean something ghostly, and is perhaps no longer adequate. In view of this it would seem appropriate to translate 'spirit' as 'sentiment'. It becomes more of a *Pathos* – a manner of feeling, a unifying emotional pitch, a ratio, a balance, a key to which the various movements of the soul must be attuned so that the soul is in harmony. If the Spirit (sentiment) leads you, you are not subject to the law, for what is good is only love, joy, peace, patience, kindness, goodness, humility and self control.

To be virtuous in Zoroastrianism is to let Vohu Manu fill your mind, for this gives rise to three virtues: the first is good thought, which gives birth to good word, and as a result of this comes the good deed. The moral teaching of other religions is no different:

Non violence, truth . . . aversion to fault-finding, sympathy for all

> beings, peace from greedy cravings, . . . freedom from pride – these are the treasures of the man who is born for heaven. Deceitfulness, insolence and self-conceit, anger and harshness and ignorance – these belong to a man who is born for hell (Bhagavad Gita, XVI, 3–4).

The Gita elsewhere describes lust, hate and greed as the gates to hell, and states that to be good is to be filled with serenity. Finally, the five cardinal virtues of Confucius (*Yen, Yi, Li, Chi* and *Hsin*) also reduce to good sentiment.

The paradigmatic city (Plato's Politea) needs no rules, no laws, no specific temple or religion. The New Testament concludes with a vision of the City of God, the New Jerusalem: 'And I saw no temple in the city, for its temple is the Lord God the Almighty and the Lamb' (Revelation, XXI,22).

II

The noetic thinker examines certain basic psychological constants in man and society and creates a contemplative model, which he then emulates in actuality. The outsider points a finger at the model and understands it literally – yet the correct understanding ought to be internal and psychological. Whether we look at the ideal communist State or at a meditative lotus pattern, at the New Jerusalem, Plato's Politea or Augustine's City of God, none of these is to be understood as an exemplar of the perfection, but rather as a general model, constructed to trigger an inner apprehension of the perfect non-changing pattern which characterizes the interior dimension of all just cities, souls and States.

The distinction is of crucial importance. If the picture of a paradigmatic society is universalized, it becomes in a sense the highest form of a definition. Indeed, for noetic thought the contemplative paradigmatic model *replaces* the definition, which is conceptual. No definitional entity can be treated as a perfect instantiation of the ideal itself: the content of a verbal definition of justice does not ensure the inner appropriation of justice (Sinaiko, 1965,p. 8). Noetic definition may take many forms – as a piece of music, a painting, a city model or a philosophical formulation. In all cases, the definition is recognitional: it triggers and summarizes the process of inner understanding.

This noetic understanding does not itself admit to 'horizontal' presentation; it cannot be simply transmitted as a diagram or model. Examined contextually, the objective of noetic discourse is always the search for a grasp of the universal pattern, the all-embracing genus. The creation of a 'perfect city' could hardly be seen as anything but an attempt at the all-embracing inner evocation of this understanding.

If we look at particular models, we notice common characteristics. To qualify for citizenship in his city, Politea, Plato makes some tough demands. He wants to see 'the community of eyes, ears, hands' . . . 'a unity of seeing, hearing, feeling happy or sad'. He wants a city 'where me and mine are banished'. Jesus has a similar requirement: for citizenship of his kingdom, one ought to give up mother, father, all that one possesses – or so at least he tells the young man who wanted to follow him (Matthew, XIX, 21). The Buddha, Jesus and Socrates all call for the giving up of wives, husbands and property.

While from age to age there will be interpreters who will understand these demands in a literal sense, a close look at any of these models reveals that a literal implementation is practically, empirically and logically impossible. The non-alienated perfect communist society would be based on perfect and perfectly efficient technology, frictionless perpetual motion. While an eager follower of Jesus may abandon his wife and children – indeed Buddha did precisely this – to be really consistent one would have to abandon individual eating and leave the dead unburied: 'Let the dead bury their dead.' To follow Plato, one would also have to give up individual hearing and seeing. Ideology and fanaticism apart, it is clear that all this 'giving up' has primarily an inner, psychological significance. Noetic thinkers are not always to be understood literally: words are vehicles for notions.

Socrates instructs young Phaedrus that the true dialectician does not write his message in letters, but in the soul: writing and reading, he says, make men forget.

> 'The dialectician selects a soul of the right type and in it he plants and sows his words founded on knowledge, words which can define both themselves and him who planted them, words which instead of remaining barren contain a seed whence new words grow up in new characters, whereby the seed is vouchsafed immortality . . . ' (*Phaedrus*, 276[e]–277[a]).

These considerations apart, any model city is so highly theoretically differentiated that any attempt at literal concretization necessarily distorts the ethics, psychology and ontology behind the very tradition that posits it. To impose a division of labour by functionality, or to impose conjugal community by the sharing of wives and children, would imply a mono-characteristic view of the individual, a view which is incompatible with the basic tenets of noetic psychology. The utter absurdity of the sharing of wives and the functional specialization of labour is carefully delineated by paradigmatic teachers, to dramatically bring to the fore some basic assumptions of their philosophy: these assumptions concern the non-correspondence between manifested and truly existing unities, whether persons, communities or things. Yet there will always be people like Bakunin or Ion who understand them literally: Plato, no doubt, would be as shocked as was Marx by demand for the implementation of the shared spouse idea.

III

Let us take Plato's Politea as representative of the paradigmatic city encountered in all times and traditions. In this perfect city, the citizens perform only those functions for which they are best suited. The 'ideal' baker becomes a baker; the man best qualified by background and personal ability to be a pilot receives the relevant education and performs the corresponding function. The wisest men rule; no person professes to be a philosopher who is not one; no citizen endeavours to give medical advice nor aspires to be a doctor or a prophet if he is not one by nature, qualification and grace (*Theia Moira*). The result is a utopia which can be defined as the perfect instance.

The concept of utopia is that of an idealized model embracing the perfections and abstracting the imperfections of actuality. In this model, the citizen's life is one of perfect health, absence of war and strife, infinite capacity for enjoyment divorced from any sorrow: the literal implementation of Politea which Plato presents in the *Charmides* (173^{a-d}) and proceeds to dismiss. Utopia in this sense of a 'perfect instance' corresponds to popular essentialist visions of preferred development, or full development in time. The noetic ideal does not resemble this utopian model. The concept of utopia is incompatible with noetic psychology, for it rests on the assumption that a perfect person is the sum of his perfectly functioning (perceived) parts. For *Logisticon*, however, the perceived unity is not a true unity. Whether or not the dispersed parts – individuals – are correctly engaged in the correct performance of their true functions escapes detection by positive investigation, since the true cities or individuals are other than those perceived.

Our concern should be not with the well-being of the outer person but with the *true* person's well-being, the ethical well-being of the soul. One can, of course, maintain that one ought to be concerned with both the outer and the inner – with the outer as a manifestation of the inner. While this is correct, remember that 'outer' and 'inner' do not correspond to true and false: there is a 'true outer' and a 'false outer' being, and here we are concerned with the former. One's well-being in this sense cannot be readily perceived by recourse to public parameters such as individual health, wealth and so on. Before examining the example of Plato's *Republic,* it is important to be clear about his methods in order to understand this point.

Let us recapitulate. The question at hand concerns the contradictions in noetic philosophy which stem from the fact that arguments and issues appropriate for one ontological level, when dealing with one aspect of the tripartite soul, are generalized and made to apply to non-corresponding issues or to different ontological realms. I suggested that there are three ontological realms: being, becoming and actuality. The realms of being and becoming have been commonly recognized; more problematic is that of actuality. The nineteenth century ignored this realm altogether and interpreted the world in terms of the other two alone – the world of sense and the world of ideas. Idealism opposed itself to materialism. Noetic thought calls both realms false and fuses them into the third.

Actuality or *Chora,* is apprehended by grasping; its object is the sensible world, but not as mediatively interpreted by the mind. Actuality enters the mind through the body, through sense; yet it becomes the true image of the ideal only when the mind is perfectly still, acting as a kind of mirror. Any autonomous activity of the mind upsets the smooth reflecting surface and distorts the image. Conjectural thought, through the conceptual process, creates the world in time: we call this world the realm of becoming, to which the mind grants a dimension of being which it does not have.

With this in view, we can turn to the *Republic.* Plato's Politea is similarly tri-dimensional. Plato is really discussing three cities:

The healthy city (*Republic,* 370^{c}–372^{e})

The sick city (372^{e}–374^{e})

The therapeutic city, Politea (374^{e}–621^{d}).

These are the three aspects of any city and of any individual: each man has a healthy, sick and restorative dimension, which can take form in a nation as church, moral police or ideological party.

The description of the first city culminates in a description of its specific manner of life, which distinguishes it from other life-supporting associations such as the family, or from *ad hoc* associations concerned with hunts, harvests and so on (*Republic,* 369^{e}). The description terminates in 373^{b}, but the formulation spills over into the description of the sick city. In the description of the sick city we gather further information concerning the healthy city: such as that it held only as much land as it needed to feed its population (373^{d}); that it was more or less free of disease; that its citizens, in owning only what they needed, neither provoked attack nor felt compelled to attack others; that there was no need for an army or for 'police' (375[d–e]). All this, of course, applies to the individual human being. Fragments describing the healthy city are scattered throughout the other dialogues; hints are given as to its religion (*Epinomis*, 977[a]); its dress of loose clothes, no hats, no shoes (*Laws*, 942[e]); its sports and pastimes (*Laws*, 824); its vegetarianism (*Republic*, 372[b]; *Epinomis*, 975[a]) – all these are standard Hindu-Zoroastrian elements. For our purposes, the passage at *Republic*, 371–374, will suffice as a description: the city is healthy (372[e]); it contains natural pleasures (372[c]) and has no formal laws or government; it is entirely limited by actual needs, needs rooted in psychological, emotional and material reality.

As a 'perfect instance', this would certainly be a utopia of a kind. But Plato is not admitting this city to a separate existence: the sick city and the healthy one are different aspects of the same, Babylon is the sick dimension of Jerusalem. Similarly, the evil man and the good are the same person: one is an enlarged version of the other (not literally enlarged in size, but enlarged in what is encompassed). The diseased entity is not satisfied with actuality, and creates a false dimension by creating false needs: 'For that healthy state is no longer sufficient, but we must proceed to swell out its bulk and fill it up with a multitude of things that exceed the requirements of necessity in states' (*Republic*, 373[b]).

In the deeper sense, that which is superfluous is not. The city is defined as that which comes into being in order to satisfy the needs of individuals; whatever exceeds those needs is not a city. An early passage in the *Republic*, which precedes the creation of all three cities, reveals this deeper meaning: 'Come then, let us create a city from the beginning in our theory. *Its real creator will be our needs*' (*Republic*, 369; my emphasis). The reality of the second city is a false reality grafted on to the true city, the actual city, which satisfies all our interests.

'Fevered needs' and their gratification exist only for the thinking mind. The real entity has no need for 'courtesans', acrobats, imitators, dancers, poets and the rest of the characters introduced to define the city which is said to be sick (*Republic*, 373[c]). The cravings which introduce the fevered dimension into the healthy city are based on illusory appetites – parekbasitic (deviant) *Epithumia* – which bring into being illegitimate sentiments, and stimulate the mind to create conceptual thinkers who perceive themselves as what they are not, 'vainly striving to satisfy with things that are not real the unreal and incontinent part of their soul' (*Republic*, 586[b]). It is not that extra people are brought in to act as courtesans, pastry cooks or cobblers: rather, actual people start to perform functions which are not natural to them, in order to satisfy appetites which are also not natural to them.

The injustice of the fevered city results from the excess element created when desires exceed real needs. It is in response to this element that the restorative city, Politea, itself appears. The disease, which in itself is evil, gives rise to the noble profession of doctor. The same process goes on in the body when white blood cells are manufactured to neutralize corrupt 'foreign' bodies; that the blood is corrupted by excesses of the flesh may be inferred from the *Timaeus* (82[e]). Disease, individual or social, results from desires having exceeded real needs, forcing the body or its parts to exercise unnatural functions. To control for this we should be at pains to 'prevent the cobbler from being at the same time a farmer, a weaver or a builder instead of just a cobbler' (*Republic,* 374[b]). 'It becomes our task then, it seems, if we are able, to select which kind of natures are suited for the guardianship of the state' (*Republic,* 374[e]).

IV

It is important to note that Socrates is all the time referring to one and the same city. It is into the healthy city that he brings the acrobats and poets; it is from this fevered city that he draws the guardians; and it is upon this city that he superimposes Politea. Since the city here symbolizes the individual man, the Politea model is a therapeutic creation used to bring order to the warring factions within body or soul. Politea is 'in that heaven which is within man' only when it is conceptually considered does it become the Republic. The model 'laid up in the sky' is the starting point of the psychotherapeutic process; the individual, through his contemplation of the model coupled with constant references to specific situations, orders his sentiments in line with a universal pattern. Through this mediative activity the individual acquires the ability to choose the (teleologically) correct sentiment, which leads to the choice of the correct action from among the several which exist as specific possibilities within the context of a particular *Polis* or culture. He chooses the particular action with respect to 'celestial' or perfect criteria, and is indifferent to the profitability and rewards of this action outside this context. He is not maximizing the well-being of the unit he perceives himself to be, but performing a preordained function. In this way, participation in the earthly city is consecrated and ritualized.

The ideal statesman is one of the 'ancients', who rules by first ruling himself; hence the Eleatic Stranger's remark:

> 'We were asked to define the king and statesman of this present era and of humanity as we know it, but in fact we took from the contrary cosmic era the shepherd of the human flock as it then was and described him as the statesman' (*Statesman*, 275[a]).

The real ruler is not the perceived ruler but the cosmic unifying force, the sentiment of love – which creates the true self.

It is not sufficient, however, to assert that one rules by ruling the self, for the self has its own 'outer' element. The thesis of the sages is that one rules by control of the heart, or the sentiment (compare Luke, XVII,20–24). Sentiment in the sense presented here is an emotional but also epistemological entity: one knows through the sentiment that truth, sentiment and knowledge are coequal. Like Confucius, Plato writes that he who has knowledge of how to rule will rule, and that 'the possessor of this science whether he is in fact in power or has only the status of a private citizen will properly be called a statesman' (*Statesman*, 259^{b}); or in another passage, 'He the just man really sets his own house in good order and rules himself; he arranges himself, becomes his own friend, and harmonizes the three parts' (*Republic*, 443^{c-d}). In the *Republic*, Book X, Adimantus wonders whether the true ruler, the just man, will ever actually take part in politics, to which Socrates replies: 'Yes by the dog, . . . in his own city he certainly will, yet perhaps not in the city of his birth, except in some providential conjecture' (*Republic*, 592^{d}).

Before closing this discussion of the private nature of the paradigmatic city model, a further point must be clarified. If a psychological pattern exists according to which man should organize his sentiments, there emerges the significant corollary that all formal activity should be so constructed as to educate man to perceive this sentiment. In this view, politics is not concerned with social engineering in the conceptual sense; true politics, whether through verbal or physical activity, always reduces to self-improvement or moral education. The perfect society is real not for those who live in a utopia, but for those who perceive perfection in an actual community. To create a perfect society is to educate a person to recognize or innerly realize it.

Understood in this light, the dictum that the perfect society comes into existence when philosophers become kings, or when the means of production become perfectly efficient, acquires a new meaning. What is meant by a 'perfect ruler' or a 'perfect means of production' will be historically relative. The perfect society materializes, in the objective sense, in those historical moments where men assume the means of production to be perfect, i.e. when they are in harmony with the productive forces of nature.

To rule, therefore, means to educate and to be educated, to perceive and to work in a correct sentiment. This 'education' is not concerned with teaching efficiency in crafts or the skilful and clever use of words, but rather with teaching men how they should perform their various actions in a manner appropriate to the world of true interests.

Eight

THE IDEAL WORLD

The intention of this chapter is to examine more closely the notion of sentiment in the light of the theory of ideas. It will be necessary to oppose both sides of the conceptual coin, that of (Parmenidean) conceptual objectivism and that of (Protagorean) relativistic subjectivism. It will also be necessary to contend with the prevalent 'two-world' interpretation of Plato, which sets ideas against matter and idealists against materialists.

I

The two-world interpretation seems to stem from Aristotle, who wrote that for Plato ideas existed apart from the world of sensible objects. Copleston (1975, p. 168), however, suggests that Aristotle may not have meant this in the way it has been taken by later thinkers:

> 'Apart from' can only mean that ideas are possessed of a reality independent of sensible things for there can be no question of ideas being in a place, and strictly speaking they would be as much in as out of sensible things, for *ex hypothesi* they are incorporeal essences and incorporeal essences cannot be in place.

Cherniss (1944, p. 5) makes a similar point. Behind such thinking lies the assumption that for two things to be apart both must admit to an 'is' and a 'this' (*Timaeus,* 49[a]), i.e. it is necessary that both be 'things'. Even for conceptualist thinkers, therefore, ideas ought not to be apart, since they are mere abstract concepts. For noetic thought, on the other hand, ideas *are* (in a sense) things, in fact, the only things there are. Matter is not substance: matter is *Chora*-actuality. The conceptual units referred to by the conjectural mind as things are not real unities. Thus the two-world separation fails from diametrically opposite positions.

There is a third possibility: in separating the two realms one may not at all be distinguishing between two different kinds of things; Aristotle may be saying that the perceived and the ideal are notionally or conceptually apart, not that in any objective sense each of them has a separate reality.

In view of this, the famous question arises: where then are ideas located? The answer, of course, is that they are within us; yet this 'within' implies no definite place. The answer to 'Where is Aristotle?' is not that he is to be found in the seat of the soul (the *Thorax*), or that somewhere else within the perceived Aristotle there hides the real Aristotle. 'Within' is to be understood according to Heisenberg's – or Plato's – principle, which implicitly defines man as a relation between object and subject, observed and observer. 'Within' means 'in the context of that system', and everything unrelated to the system is external to it. The 'other world' is nowhere in time and place; it is defined by the relationship between 'this' and 'the other' time.

'Something' and 'nothing' are mental concepts; reality, on the other hand, is transconceptual – there is reality as a concept, but also reality as a notion. In a certain sense, the final reality is nothingness. It is for this reason that Meister Eckhart, Rumi and Lao Tzu all tell us that to be what we really are, we must first become nothing. To be saved in Christ, we must follow him through death daily, according to St. Paul. This is the object of all meditation, whether it takes the form of a Gregorian chant, a Hindu mantra, 'just sitting' in Zen or the movements of Tai Chi.

Nothingness is a mental void; however, it is not an absolute void. Instead of space and time, its dimensions are rhythm and pitch; instead of thought, its cognitive mode is noetic excitation; instead of vision, its field of sensibility is the sentiment of love.

The deeply concentrated 'mind' can explore this 'nothingness', by concentrating either on the lower-emotive aspect of sentiment – the heart – or on the higher-emotive aspect, the noetic. Just as the space-time world can be experienced through six senses, so nothingness can be explored through six modes or *Chakras* plus one (the latter being the all-comprehensive sentiment of love).

Conceptualist thinkers in all ages, whether idol-worshippers, sophists or positivists, are unable to grasp the notion of 'ideals' being in things and yet nowhere. It is for this reason that they invent 'heaven' or 'the other world', taking it to be a place where all things are allowed perfect expression. This 'conceptual heaven' is in fact fantasy: idea and fantasy become one and the same thing for conceptualists. 'Idealism' could thus be called 'fantasism'. Yet curiously it is the hard-headed materialists, the merchant philosophers, who invent such notions of the ideal: for the merchant soul, the ideal is a fantasized objectivization of the satisfaction of his false individual needs projected into a different realm.

Idealists are essentially bourgeois philosophers. Where they diverge from the Saanthana philosophy is in their conception of the 'ideal'. In a sense for Hegel, and certainly for Aristotle (1946, I, $125^{b}32$), the ideal appears to be a perfect instance, fully developed in time under perfect conditions and in a perfect environment: 'for what each thing is when fully developed, that is its nature'. Socrates collects his data from inner experience: 'Trees and open country [nature as outwardly manifested] have little to teach me, [for] I am the lover of learning . . . of the affairs of men' (*Phaedrus,* 230^{d}); Aristotle, on the other hand, follows a biological, 'outer' observational bias and collects, observes and classifies *instances* of men, oaks and cities, from which he deduces a perfect model of each based on the expansion in time of the observed instances. In deducing his ideal, any such thinker is forced to hypothesize the 'perfect conditions' and an 'ideal environment' to allow its unfolding. As he invents *Hyle* to grant continuity to changing things, so Aristotle invents essences (in this abstract sense) as correlates to instances of perfect development in time. And, perhaps feeling in himself the temptation to grant these abstractions, his 'final causes', a fuller existence in an external world of their own, Aristotle projects this doctrine on to Plato, and criticizes him for a dualism he never held.

The Saanthana-oriented thinker, however, operates with a different notion. Concerning the creation of ideal unities, Gadamer remarks that even the divine creator is restricted by the possible and the necessary. In other words, whatever it is that is ideal for *Logos*-based thought can never be seen as free from the determinants set by *Anangke* and *Moira. Timaeus,* for example, is interpreted by Gadamer as illustrating the physicality of ideal existence, as opposed to other philosophies concerned with the principles governing the inner perfection, such as the uncompromising idealism of Parmenides or Ramanuja. The ideal existence, physically considered, is not one of frictionless, limitless extension, for the best is always only the best possible, and as such relative to the given limitations (Gadamer, 1973, p. 26).

This difference between the conceptual and the Saanthana philosophers' notion of 'ideal' is to some extent manifest in Plato's and Aristotle's conceptions of the Golden Mean. For Plato, the mean is not some balance between the perfect and the imperfect, a working compromise: 'It would be giving a poor appraisal of this, Plato's central philosophical conception of the mathematical character of all being and all value, to say that it comes close to the Aristotelian doctrine of the

Mean' (Findlay, 1974, p. 277). The noetic mean, though subject to necessity and determined within the confines of an actual situation, is not any less 'ideal' for having been subjected to necessity (*Statesman*, 284[b]). The best is not something reaching full development in time to fulfil its complete potential. There is no such thing as an abstract potential ideal. It is the positivistic idealists, such as Kant, who are susceptible to the 'two-world' caricature; and we can accuse Aristotle of positing an ideal world of perfect instances, of potentialities which never materialize (since the ideal conditions are never met), separate from the other world of their less well developed actual expressions. Compared to this, the so-called dualist is the hard-headed 'realist', or rather actualist, for in Saanthana thought the ideal can never be separated from the actual. Rather than seeking some potential development in time, noetic thinkers see any progressive development over the limits set by circumstance as an excess, since the ideal is not measurable in absolute terms but is determined by circumstances, which do not occur merely at random.

The norm or the mean does also have an objective dimension, in which it functions as an absolute criterion, but even as such it is contextually determined. The mean as a ratio is subject to objective determination by *Aritmos*, but that ratio is aspectual and subject to inner criteria, in the sense previously developed. Thus, if the circumstances were such that Socrates or Jesus met his end before reaching Aristotelian 'full development', we could not assume that either did not live out his ideal. There are no criteria for the ideal but the well-being of the soul: there are no externally objective ideals. The noetic mean is only objective in the sense of being an inner ratio which adjusts to circumstance, and is simply an ethical relation between the different parts of the soul and the changing cosmos.

This also applies to any projections of the ideal into the future, or 'heaven'. The good life is not in the future; it is *now*. The living Jesus is not 'in heaven'; he is living in each human being, and so is Krishna – 'in each flower and animal'. 'God is not the God of the dead.'

Man is both ideally and actually a self-creator. It is the interior element, *Logisticon*, rather than some exterior constitutive factor, that determines how he is to ideally define himself, as determined and parallelled in *Chora*-actuality. Whether or not we can claim (as do Marxists) that man is a self-creator or (with Gadamer) that man is the demiurge, Cornford (1948, pp. 47–8) emphasizes that even the creation of the demiurge is only aspectually ideal; also, the demiurge's ideality is not based on limitless extension – it is subject to 'the wandering causes' of materiality. Thus in the extended realm a man has a permanently shifting locus of ideality, since the teleological objective is not an ideal temporal conclusion. The fact that Karma, *Anangke* or necessity is contextually relative makes it impossible to equate the noetic ideal with the essentialist and Aristotelian fully-developed perfect instance. Full development is subject to historical moment, environment and necessity.

The ideal, since it is not separate from the actual, which is in a constant state of change, must in one sense be permanently changing, yet only so that it can in another remain unchanged. Its *relation* to the changing actual is constant. The ideal, therefore, is unchanging only in the realm of true being. Although it is a fixed set of ratios, it is not unchanging for the world of actuality, since in actuality it is situationally defined. For this reason the 'idealist' perfect-instance notion fails. We never can know ahead of the situation what the ideal is going to be. Only with respect to the inner movement of the psyche is the ideal fixed. For this reason, we cannot insist on the absolute and history-free preferability of one ideology or political system over another. Nor can we claim that a man is born to be a baker or a pianist, or that the loss of his arms by a pianist or the loss of a war by a State, nation or society makes the ideal more distant. We will never know which is the necessary outcome; the *ideal* outcome is accomplished by accepting necessity (Karma-*Anangke*), and by using the noetic faculty to maintain a proper ethical balance in the body-soul.

II

The problems regarding the noetic grasp of 'ideal' cease to be problems when one realizes that, as Findlay (1974, p. 32) puts it, ideal entities 'are the only absolutely real entities that there are': there is nothing but the ideal, in itself and in *Chora.* The convergence of idea with actuality thus eliminates utopian interpretations of perfect essence.

The noetic thinker can have no utopian plans, for, like Socrates, he is of the opinion that the 'problems and difficulties of this world can never be done away with'. What we can do away with are false perceptions, allowing us to perceive the 'city outlined in heaven', within man (*Republic*, 592[b]), a city referred to by some as 'the other world' and by others as 'the state of the future'. Social engineering must be concerned with epistemology as well as politics. Politics is interesting only in so far as it can help us attain comprehension of this 'other world', for political reform cannot create an outer utopia. This is why Socrates tells Theodorus: 'Evils, Theodorus, can never be done away with – nor is it one's business to attempt to do so; rather one should seek the "other world"' (*Theaetetus*, 176[a]). To strive to improve the reality of this world by forcing society into some preconceptualized mould will not do, for yesterday's models do not take account of unforeseen developments. Social engineering must be moral engineering.

In the same way, there can be no final philosophy: 'there can be and there are an infinite multiplicity of systems, each of which is more or less adequate to a particular person or persons at one given moment' (Sinaiko, 1965, p. 206). This multiplicity does not, however, suggest an ethical relativity. One action or one philosophy is not as good as any other, and noetic thinkers do not adopt the *laissez faire, laissez passer* approach to life, politics or economics. A model exists, although it is fixed only in the noetic sense; its actualization depends on local conditions; each natural unit – nation, locality or neighbourhood – requires a specific application. The Way may be one, but the ways to the Way are many.

Given a particular situation in an actual moment of existence, relativity dissolves; at any given moment (an instant is actuality), there is only one correct way of behaviour. For each and every action there is a perfect way of performing it; thus

> 'in burning, not every way is the right way, but the right way is the natural way and the right instrument the natural instrument . . . and we saw that actions were not relative to ourselves but had a special nature of their own' (*Cratylus*, 387[a–d]).

What emerges clearly from this passage is not that there is no ideal, but rather that the ideal cannot chronologically precede actuality (although it does logically precede it), since the ideal is situationally defined. As the ideal way is the best suited for the performance of a certain function, it cannot be separated from the agent performing the function nor from the instruments and materials involved. All the entities, persons, instruments involved in the performance of an action are in a dialectical relationship and define each other's ideality. The perfect action therefore includes both material efficiency and the ethical condition of the soul.

With these observations, our interpretation of the Saanthana notion of the ideal as actuality can finally be fully clarified. All the various traditions of noetic philosophy may be summarized in the following conceptualization:

> In the course of life, each living being executes a series of acts, some of which may be seen as perfectly executed. An activity, or an aspect of an activity, becomes perfect in so far as it is undertaken with correct sentiment and with the optimal exertion of all faculties (mental, physical and material), given the particular circumstances. These instances of perfection are rare, but a series of them can be abstracted through dialectical contemplation, allowing the actor to trace an intuitive locus, using these instances as plotting points on a graph whose co-ordinates are the dimensions 'in time' and 'out of

time'. This intuitively grasped locus describes the ideal, which is actuality. In such a sense, man perceives the ideal not as a concrete thing or a universal exemplar, but as a moving line drawn through a series of instances, each inseparable from actuality. The ideal is therefore whatever is undertaken in correct sentiment, through which a person participates in the world of ideality created by perfect actions, whether his own or those of other entities similarly characterized. As such, the ideal synthesizes the 'in time' and 'out of time' dimensions: it is both in and out of time.

III

In view of this, let us look at the contemporary existential dictum, 'Existence precedes essence', which relates to the basic human condition and to other themes developed by Kierkegaard, Jaspers, Marcel and Heidegger, as well as to Kierkegaard's 'Truth is subjectivity'.

Given the speculative nature of the main line of post-Renaissance European thought, it was inevitable that someone would stress the subjective aspect of existence and its relationship to ethical choice. The grand philosophical systems of the nineteenth century seemed to be irrelevant to a particular man. Kierkegaard asked, 'what do I care for the fact that Hegel has interpreted the whole of the universe, when my problem is in deciding whether to marry or not to marry Regine?' Hegel could not help the individual chooser to choose; for life is not subject to objective formulae.

While the existentialists were correct in drawing attention to the failings of objective philosophical systems, in general they were collectively mistaken in underplaying or actually denying the objective element in knowing and choosing. Their work has served only to strengthen the conviction, 'Truth is what is true for me'. The truth is both objective and subjective; existence both precedes and is preceded by essence.

Hegel's dialectic would have been correct had he realized that even his own system is just another thesis, which in order to be 'true' needs to be refuted and simultaneously grasped and reconciled with something like the philosophy of Kierkegaard. Kierkegaard would have been more 'authentic' (to use existentialist terminology) had he realized that his own 'philosophical fragments' had validity only in conjunction with and as a counterthesis to Hegel: the validity of both is to be found in the non-verbalizable synthesis between them. Only after we have positively accepted that there is an unfolding essence can we further argue that, since particular situations cannot be successfully predicted, a man cannot lay down objective, existential or ethical rules of conduct.

One may not simply forbid killing in all situations; for whether a particular act asserts or denies man's 'essence' is situationally defined. From instant to instant man finds himself in entirely unprecedented, completely unique and unrepeatable sets of circumstances within which he has to act. Whatever he is, he is historically evolving: not, however, in the sense of continually and automatically becoming better, for the achievements of yesterday 'run away'; rather, he is constantly recapturing the past, the future and the present through the relationship of his activity to the situational givens. This moment – or rather the subjective experience of a need to act and a corresponding awareness of the self – lies at the root of Husserl's phenomenology and behind 'existential' thought. Existence precedes essence because man is existentially defined.

On a social-political level, Marx develops the parallel notion that man defines himself through his activity. But we cannot reduce 'productive activity' simply to the workplace and the forty- or sixty-hour week. Broadening it to include any activity that is conducive to the satisfaction of human needs, 'means of production' comes to refer not only to industrial tools and machinery, but to the productive environment: the workplace, the weather, the climate, human relationships – i.e. actuality. Man's productive activity socially understood is actuality, and it is therefore actuality that defines man's consciousness and essence. This statement can be rephrased, yet it will remain true that man should not and cannot be divorced from his broadest context.

Heisenberg's principle can be taken to mean that whatever is being observed adapts its behaviour and its essence to conform to the activity and the procedure by means of which it is being observed. To imply, however, that the distortion away from 'normal' to the state effected by the observation is to be attributed solely to the observer or to the observed would be wrong. If the observer is the only one making the judgments, his is the only subjective reality that exists, in which case there is no difference if the change due to the act of observation takes place in the observer or in the observed. As for the reality of the object, this does not exist unless the object itself displays an interest in such a reality; and if this happens, then the object, as 'observer', is subject once again to Heisenberg's principle.

Self-righteous cries of 'scientific objectivity' displayed by the philosophers currently described as positivist, as well as passionate 'poetic' pleas to subjectivity by the existentialists, both reduce to personal observational bias. Each persuasion reduces to prejudice and conditioning: truth is neither objectivity nor subjectivity, but both. This does not imply that a genuine philosopher can or should free himself from his cultural, genetic, time-specific and personal bias. There is no objection against a philosopher clothing his message with a world system (as did Hegel), writing 'philosophical fragments' such as those of Kierkegaard, expressing himself in dramatic situations as did Sartre or creating a world political model in the manner of the ideologues. But whether building a factory, socialism or a marriage, he should not put an abstract blueprint before the correct sentiment. Means do not justify ends, nor do ends justify means – all talk of 'means' and 'ends', like that of 'subject' and 'object', is a conceptual projection. Despite its clothing, my own intention in this work is not to create a philosophy of Choric Actualism, but to expand a particular, ever-present sentiment in a way that might contribute to its continuing existence.

IV

This study has attacked concepts and ideals, but has been unwilling to give up the notion of aspectual units to replace them, which we may call noetic actuals (and which in fact correspond to whatever it was that Plato called ideas or forms). These noetic actuals are not thoughts, or anything existing in the mind. If they were there would either have to be thinkers everywhere thinking everything, or there would have to be thoughts being thought by nobody, or thoughts of nothing, which is equally absurd. More interesting from our point of view is the more recent and sophisticated notion that ideas are universal recognitional constants.

Though Ramanuja and Plato were aware that observation changes reality, they also realized that what is real must be changeless.

> 'If knowing is to be acting on something it follows that what is known must be acted upon by it; and so on this showing, reality when it is being known by the act of knowledge must, in so far as it is known, be changed owing to being acted upon, and that we say cannot happen to the changeless.' (*Sophist*, 248[e]).

This passage alone points to the difficulties involved in treating the *Eidos* as objectively universal; but there are further obstacles to such an interpretation. The Eleatic thinker asks: 'But tell me, in heaven's name, are we really to be so easily convinced that change, life, soul, understanding have no place in that which is perfectly real?' (*Sophist*, 249.) If ideas are unchangeable then they do not admit to life, soul and intelligence. While this is certainly a widespread contemporary understanding of the *Eidos,* the Eleatic Stranger and Theaetetus find it inconceivable that anything that is real – including ideas – can be devoid of life (*Sophist*, 248[e]), and inconceivable that there could be anything that counts as true knowledge of something which does not remain itself. Merlan (in Armstrong, 1967, p. 20) interprets 249[b] to mean that ideas do indeed have life and intelligence: it was certainly the view of Proclus that all things are alive because the cosmos is alive (1820,p. 30), as well as that of Plotinus (1956, VI,2:78) and Ficino (1978, 43). I will be following the Eleatic's conclusion and claiming that ideas both are and are not devoid of change, life, soul and intelligence (*Sophist,* 249[b]).

Whether the *Eidos* is regarded as a relatively unchanging recognitional pattern – a mental fixity – or as something 'essentially measurable, something in the nature of a number or a ratio or a geometical pattern' (Findlay, 1974, p. 55), in tune with which man creates his laws and ethical behaviour, the error of the conceptualist remains that of objectification. Idealist and materialist separate the actual from the ideal world in order to reduce one to the other. However, to be able to think of the actual world they have to use an idea of it, while to think of the ideal world they are forced to treat it as actual. Their 'ideal', therefore, does not relate at all to their 'actual'; any ideal world belongs to the actual world. In Plato's words, if there are *two* worlds, one real and ideal compared to this one, which is false and illusory, then 'the significance of things in our world is not with reference to things in that other world, nor have these their significance with reference to us' (*Parmenides*, 133–134). So, even if there is some separate world of ideas, we can forget about it. (Of course there is no such world: there is only one world considered in different ways.)

The noetic thinker treats ideas as objective, but not objectively expressible or autonomous. Being fixed and unchanging, they are in a sense non-existent. Public objectivization of the *Eidos* as definitional universal or mathematical ratio would be inconsistent with the basic premise that all true knowing involves an ethical dimension, entailing a subjective aspect. The ideas, the true objects of knowledge, can be seen only if illuminated by the ethical force which is the sentiment of the Good. The ideas are constituted by this illumination, the excitation of the out-flowing stream of the Good: 'In like manner, then, you are to say that the objects of knowledge not only receive from the presence of the Good their being known, but their very existence and essence is derived from it' (*Republic,* 509[b]). It is inconceivable to Augustine that we should see ideas without the illumination of a pure heart (*Soliloquies,* I, 8:15); while Syrianus finds Aristotle's separation of forms as objective, discussable, independent entities 'scandalous' (see Ferguson, 1970, p. 207). Ideas are discerned through the faculty of *Logisticon:* it is only the lower mind, *Dianoia,* which conforms to ethically neutral, externally objective cognitive units and processes. This point has also been developed by A.N. Whitehead in an argument against distinguishing between the ethical and the rational, and is echoed by T.S. Eliot in the introduction to Pieper's *Leisure,* where he observes that the failure of contemporary thought lies precisely in the division between the ethical and religious and the 'merely' philosophical. Possibly influenced by Whitehead, with whom he worked on the *Principia,* Russell (1961, p. 56) remarks that what he found admirable in Pythagorean mathematics and in the thought of St Augustine and St Anselm was that the ethical and the rational were not separated. Augustine's position in this respect is extreme: he claims that those who do not see ethically are blind.

Working on this assumption of the fundamentally ethical determination of all creation, Whitehead rejects Leibniz's 'windowless monads' because 'windowless' implies ethically neutral and therefore unreal. Instead, he substitutes 'actual entities'. Whitehead's view of mathematics and science and of the formation of the constitutive medium is quite close to that developed here, although his notion of actual entities might be taken to imply an atomistic fragmentation (this is not, in fact, how he did see his universe). He also makes the important point that the ability of a scientist to predict the behaviour of bodies does not necessarily validate his claim to knowledge of them.

In the Bhagavad Gita, knowledge and the love of the One coincide. (The anonymous author of *The Cloud of Unknowing* makes the compatible observation that what really is cannot be thought of, but can be known through love.) In the Gita (XI,54) to know the self is to love it: 'Only by love can men see me'. This love is not of the 'self' in the empirical sense, or that self which is generated by false needs, but of the self that is the source of real needs. It is this self that is responsible for the growth of a man, of a city, of a society: remember that Plato begins his exposition of Politea (which is also a picture of man) by observing that its origin is in our needs.

Love is defined in the *Symposium* as stemming from our deepest interests, those of the true man, not the man of positivism. Love itself is the desire to be what one truly is, and is equivalent to the ethical sentiment. To know oneself is to know one's true needs. Voicing an idea that comes to him from Plato via Hegel, Habermas (1972, p. 314) concludes his book on knowledge by observing, 'My fourth thesis is thus that in the power of self-reflexion knowledge and interest are one'. And only the knower of the self can know the ideas, for true knowledge and true love is the desire to be the true self. Real things are only real with respect to the self. The 'self' here referred to is non-Kantian. To see it I need to see how I participate in you, to see how it participates in the flowers and the bees . . . in other words, to situate it within the whole cosmos.

In the light of this we can begin to understand Plotinus' statement, which post-Kantian scholarship has rendered meaningless, 'Ideas are the thoughts in the mind of God', and interpret how it is that something eternal, supposedly devoid of intelligence and change, can be linked to the life and intelligence which manifests itself as change and creation (*Sophist*, 249^{c-d}). The 'atom' in a man's eye may in a million years time belong to a star. Since clock time is conjectural, that atom already is and has been in a star: all things are interconnected. Sentiment is instrumental in the creation of everything, animate and inanimate, changing and unchanging. When Plotinus (1956, V,9:10) calls ideas 'participants in life', he means not that fire or whiteness has a soul and a separate intelligence, but rather that, seen as ideas, each of these is axiologically a fragment of *the* living intelligence, or God. For Plato (*Timaeus*, 30^{a-b}) the whole cosmos is alive because the real world seen vertically is a particular kind of thought, i.e. sentiment in action. Ficino (1978, 43) writes:

> We have heard how the ideas of all things exist in a living and eternal model . . . such a model can be none other than God himself. . . . For truly, however many kinds of creature there are in this world, there are at least as many ideas in God. These ideas are intelligible principles through which all things are made.

Equally precise with regard to the identity of ideas is Augustine: 'Ideas are immutable essences, not created but eternally existing in the divine intelligence.' That we should be able to peep into God's mind by some freely available formula or concept was to him inconceivable. Noetic actuals – the fundamental constituents of all things – are objective only by virtue of common participation in the love of God: the sentiment of love makes them objective to those participating in it.

V

The tendency to treat ideas as objective, in the sense not of being illuminated and created by an objective sentiment but of being publicly observable and definable, also accounts for the conceptualization of the noetic theory of participation, from Aristotle on. For the idealists a particular thing is a combination of participating ideas. For Kant it is a combination of sense data participating to create objects, as it is for the empiricists. For the language analyst, reality (if he uses the notion at all) is reflected as a set of verbs and clauses held together by the rules of grammar or symbolic logic. According to Wittgenstein, our view of reality is conditioned by language. In some sense he is correct, but only if we are speaking of conceptual reality; and anybody who accepts this way of thinking should more properly dismiss such notions as reality altogether.

For the noetic thinker, as opposed to the idealist or the empiricist, things are not conglomerations of concepts. That ideas *qua* ideas do not participate at all is clarified by Plotinus (1956, V, 9:6), who answers Aristotle's (and indeed the perennial) question as to where these 'separate' ideas might be as follows:

> We take it, then, that the Intellectual-Principle is the authentic existences and contains them all – not as in a place but as possessing itself and being one thing with this its content. All are one There and yet distinct: similarly the mind [*Nous*] holds many branches and items of knowledge simultaneously, yet none of them merged into any other.

That ideas are not thoughts in the mind of God in the 'thinking', conceptual sense is made clear in Ennead V,9:7:

> Not by its thinking God does God come to be; not by its thinking Movement does Movement arise. Hence it is an error to call the Ideas intellections, in the sense that, upon an intellectual act in this Principle, one such idea or another is made to exist or exists.

The contemporary interpretation of participation is illustrated in Bigger's book on this subject. 'Participation', he writes, 'is the name of the "relation" which accounts for the togetherness of elements of diverse ontological type in the essential unity of a single instance' (Bigger, 1968, p. 7). He is correct, yet his statement could also be interpreted as the description of the very art of the sophist. It is the sophist who brings together the same and the different, the realms of becoming and of actuality and being, and treats them as if they were the same. Our perception ought to utilize both the process of synthesis and a process precisely the reverse of this; it should be an activity whereby the elements of diverse ontological planes are reallocated accordingly. The synthesis should not be conceptual; if it is conceptualizing, the mind should be aware of the conjectural nature of its activity and especially its limitations.

It must be observed that ideas are constitutive patterns for *real* things and not for things as perceived. This suggests the inadequacy of the universalist, recognitional template notion of perception, according to which we encounter an instance of a horse and diagnose it as a horse by referring to the eidetic pattern of horseness. On our interpretation, instead of recognizing instances by referring to an idea, the *Buddhi-Logisticon* uses its encounters with instances to grasp or recollect the *Logos*. It is only after the *Logos-Eidos* has been recollected that we may refer it back to instances. The perceived instance does not *contain* the noetic actual; at best it instantiates a fragment of it, along with fragments of other noetic actuals (or *Logoi* or ideas). A unity perceived as a horse is a conglomeration of sensible perceptions in conjunction with various emotional predicates that the perceiver associates with horses in general, or with a particular horse.

A perception of a true horse can thus be equally well triggered by smell or by the sound of hoofs and can be experienced by a man born blind, for the true horse is a specific pattern of sentiments, or movements of the soul. The *Logos-Eidos* of horse is not that unity which is perceived; the perceived unity contains only a fraction of real horseness. We develop a grasp of the true identity of a lion by encountering fragmented instantiations of lionness, whether in lionlike actions, things or persons. These instances provoke a certain excitation in the soul, and trace out the locus of the *Logos-Eidos,* as earlier described.

In other words, horses, chairs or tables are not things devoid of reality. The mind cannot perceive things which have no counterpart in reality. However, these perceived things are not 'like' their *Logoi,* i.e. they do not imitate real things. Rather, they receive a fraction of reality by virtue of *Koinonia,* a sympathetic (corresponding) diarithmetic vibration which is sparked off in the soul parallel to its encounter with the object of observation. A chair becomes a 'perfect chair' in so far as it fulfils the need for sitting in a perfect way; yet an actual chair may be 'imperfectly' used as a table, as a ladder or for fuel. As Part One concluded, perceived unities are falsely conglomerated fractions of real unities. To this must be added that these falsely conglomerated unities are not entirely arbitrary; the perceptual mind cannot invent unities, for it is parasitic for its models on eidetic paradigms. Conceptual entities are not non-existent; they are, however, visualized or conceptualized differently from the corresponding true entities. In short, for every horse perceived there is a true horse (held by *Logos*), but this true horse does not imitate and is not imitated by the conjectural *Eikon* of a horse.

Participation in the noetic sense relates to participation in the common rhythmically determined movement of the soul, which alone is fixed. It is fixed, however, only in the sense of a changing gradient (rather like the dy/dx of calculus), or of a locus characterizing the flow of paradigmatic instances outlining a pattern. These noetic patterns are in many ways similar to the non-predicated One of the *Parmenides* – yet they are not identical with that One, since the One is undifferentiated. The *Logoi* are the differentiated constituents by means of which the *Logisticon* constructs both a person and the world. As differentiated unities, these patterns relate to actual emanations, and as such are aspectually changing. As part and parcel of the One, however, they are unchanging, and are not devoid of life and intelligence, for the One, being the source and support of all movement, life and intelligence, lends this movement, activity and life to the ideas.

VI

Like the theory of participation, that of reincarnation is part of Saanthana views of man. Considered as a divine spark, the non-composite man constructed by *Logisticon-Atman-Buddhi* is immortal, simple and unchanging (see, for example, Plato's *Republic,* 608[d], and *Laws*, 959[b]). The problems arise when we begin to look at man as a composite. As in the example of the horse, while the perceived entity is a participated conglomeration of things other than the entity perceived, for that participated conglomeration there is also a corresponding *Logos*-held unity, which is simple and non-participated. Applying this to an individual person, for each composite soul there exists an immortal, unchanging pattern.

Great caution should be exercised here, for the true personality must not be confused with the perceived personality. The perceived personality, like the body, is a creation of culture, food, climate, etc. The true personality, however, unfolds through many beings which are separate from the corporeal personality.

This peculiarity can be conceptualized in many ways. Christianity avoids any conceptualization in words or pictures but attempts to convey it through love, so that the true self is felt but not thought of. The Hindus and Plato have conceptualized a specific model in which the self is scattered throughout various cities, persons and animals in history (this, of course, is the myth of reincarnation). Yet the true personality does have self-consciousness; indeed, identity cannot be grasped or conceived as separate from the consciousness of self as a unity. How then does the true self, scattered in time, conceive of itself as the self?

Plotinus (1956,V,7:1) teaches that it is the divine mind that records all the aspects of individual existence and contains them in the manifested unity of the memory of all its thoughts and actions; for each individual mind there is an immortal, unchanging idea, non-merged, self-conscious and distinct, existing in the divine mind. It needs to be emphatically stressed that for noetic thought there is no Nirvana in the sense of a loss of the individual self. Reincarnation in Plato or in the Gita is not rebirth such that one is Peter in one age, Paul in another – rather, 'once Peter always Peter'. However, Peter participates in Paul; a little fragment of Peter is in Paul (and George). The externalization of the little fragments does not remove the individual integrity of Peter-in-time; *Logisticon – Budhhi* can synthesize all these fragments.

Considering it as an extended thing in the realm of becoming, Plato's reincarnation model presents the individual entity as a manifold unity, comprising various instances of men, animals, women, etc., unfolded in time, Plato's Myth of Er in the *Republic* (614–621) directs our attention to a choice we each make 'out of time'. Christianity is more interested in the vertical dimension of this choice (for or against God), but in the *horizontal* dimension the thread of a particular sentiment links us to whichever lives we most desire. Of course, our choice is limited to the lives we are offered, which exist and already have 'owners' (the life of a nightingale, a craftswoman, etc.): Orpheus remains Orpheus in the swan he chooses, the swan remains itself; it is only the falsely perceived Orpheus-in-time we cannot detect in the temporal swan.

The philosopher's task, as exhibited by the activity of the Stranger in Plato's dialogue the *Statesman*, is to involve the interlocutor in a diarithmetic division and synthesis concerning things such as lions and men, whereby the rhythm of the diacritical exercise arouses a resonance in the 'client's' consciousness, and he grasps that the perceived unities are not true unities – that there really are no lions or Agamemnons as empirical unities at all. As Findlay (1974, p. 34) states, 'For Plato nothing but ideas existed.'

As the discussion in the dialogue the *Sophist* (252^c–253^d) bears out, a man may participate in fatherhood, soldierness, Greekness and twofootedness; he may be considered many without losing his differentiating unity.

This does not imply that a man participates in the many simply by imitation; that is, that Agamemnon participates in 'lionness' by being lionlike or in 'snakeness' by being snakelike. This view would restrict man to being a conglomeration of thought-created inferences. A consistent conceptual thinker ought to recognize that both Agamemnon and the lion, as instances, are really predicating selfsame, non-changing things such as hardness or kingship; i.e. that the instances predicate *Eide* and not the other way around: 'All that there really is to instances is the fact of instantiation, of which Eide are really the sole logical subjects: instances are really instantiations, things undergone by the Eide, mere modalities *of* them' (Findlay, 1974, p. 34).

Socrates observes that it is difficult to account for the immortality of an individual, not because the psyche is not immortal, but because the perceived entity is not correctly constituted: 'It is not easy, said I, for a thing to be immortal that is composed of many elements not put together in the best way, as now appeared to be the case with the soul' (*Republic*, 611^b). This does not, however, indicate the absence of the true individual, nor does it suggest that the true realization of the individual comes only by extinction through integration into some larger whole, whether it be the communist State or the Buddhist Nirvana. Integration is required, but not at the price of individual extinction: the integrity of the individual is maintained. He is ever present and immortal, but as perceived he is fractured; once correctly assembled, this unity needs no extension by absorption into a larger unity, for it is self-autonomous and loses nothing by the separate instantiations of its constituents. 'Man is immortal,' says Socrates, referring to the individual psyche. 'But to know its true nature we must view it not marred by communion with the body' (*Republic,* 611[b–c]).

Socrates is not separating soul from body, but the true body from the individual body, the true man from the perceived man. We must not limit the presence of man to the boundedness of the individual body. The man-soul entity is like the mythical sea deity (to extend a metaphor of Plato's) whose fragments are scattered across the sea and intermingled with it, with algae and other things, so that the perceived unity is no more; yet, as an autonomous entity, the separate fragments are still held together by the constitutive *Eidos,* man's true nature and the condition of the psyche:

> 'Its condition as we have now contemplated it [says Socrates] resembles that of the sea god Glaucus, whose first nature can hardly be made out by those who catch glimpses of him, because the original members of his body are broken off and mutilated and crushed and in every way marred by the waves, and other parts have attached themselves to him, accretions of shells and seaweed and rocks, so that he is more like any wild creature than what he was by nature' (*Republic,* 611[c–d]).

He goes on to say that it is through the love of philosophy, and by freeing ourselves from all false appetites and desires, that the true entity is stripped clean of all the countless attachments which it had perceived as its constituent parts; it is only then that the true unity is perceived (*Republic,* 612[a]). The unity becomes so only by abstraction from time and place; as shown in the Myth of Er, the various aspects of an individual never concretize in a single instance.

The idea that perceived individuals are based on false, conjectural-mental, rather than true, noetic divisions is also developed in the myth of the *Statesman* (268[e]–274[e]). In the age of Cronus (the Golden Age, or the garden of Eden), men were not such as they are today, i.e. born of women (274[a]). Indeed, in that age we cannot separate men from animals, for true entities are not constituted in such a way. This is not to say that men and animals were the same, nor that there were no individuals; rather that in the age of Cronus these divisions were made on other than conceptual grounds, hence men could 'freely merge with animals and converse with them, speaking and communicating with all living things' (271[a]). The point here is that in the true garden – in which things, men and animals are led and constituted by God, and the universe is totally dependent upon God for its movement – there is no war.

The age of Cronus is the mythical projection of an ever-present reality; conflict arises only between false and never between true persons, things or animals. The impulse away from God's movement fractured the constitutive elements and created men that our minds perceive as born of women, as separate or at war with each other. This impulse is the origin of the perceived world. It is man's desire to be autonomous, to be independent from the movement of the universe, that differentiates him from his fellows, from the universe in general and from himself. Naturally man is not powerful enough to negate the actual world, the world as it is. The actual is always there as the true entity, but it is no longer perceived. Man becomes self-deceiver; this is the origin of the two-world theory.

We have seen that perceived unities do not literally approximate, or by any conceptual process reflect, true entities through a process of imitation. Nor are things or persons what they are by virtue of their participation in the *Eidos* – or at least not as interpreted by anybody who would conflate the different ontological planes of becoming and being (i.e. the world as perceived and the world as given in intuition). The sensible approximates the ideal only through sentiment, the constitutive agent of *Chora* – for it is only *Chora* which reflects, and not conceptual thought.

We can now bring to a close the discussion of participation and the imitation of *Eidos*. Both, when conceptualized, fail to capture the noetic meaning. The interpretational schools of idealists and conceptualists that see immortal patterns as conceptual universals in which things participate simply fail to understand the Saanthana notion of participation. For the conceptualist, participation is like a kind of proximity in space and time based on a conjectural relationship of conceptual unities. The recent way of thinking which sees things in terms of lingual symbols has objectified these into fixities – treating them as logical elements imitated by or connected to instantiated things in some publicly ascertainable way. The mistake of these approaches is to assume conceptually objective entities.

True things do not participate by being next to each other, nor by being connected with each other logically or by the conventions of language. For noetic thought, true unities – including people – are unparticipated and non-composite, and hence cannot be de-composed. In the above examination of this notion, this 'non-composite' man was seen as immortal. Again it must be stressed that notions such as 'non-composite' or 'immortal' are only triggers. These are old words – new words may be used by those so inclined.

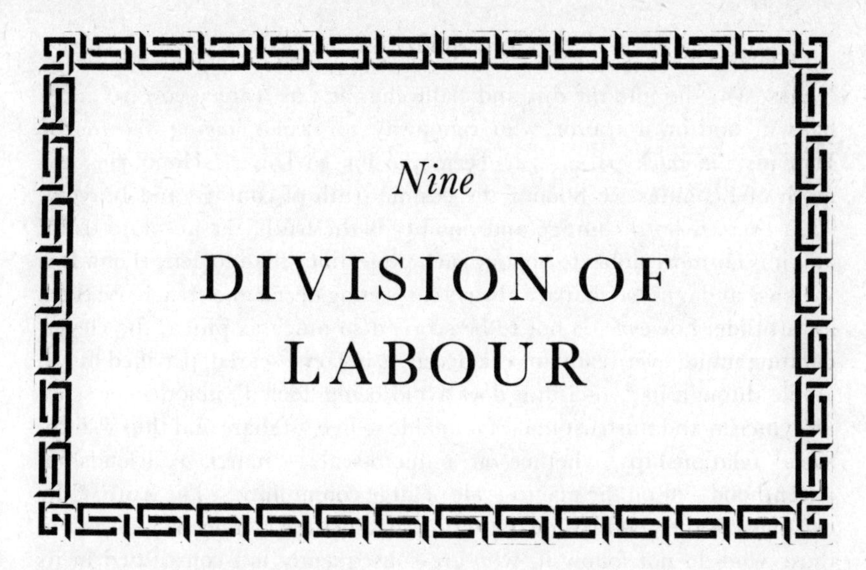

Nine

DIVISION OF LABOUR

In recent thought, the notion of 'immortality' has been replaced by that of immersion in, and dissolution through social identification with, a 'progressive class'; and realization is to be effected by participation in the building of the perfect society of the future. Like all Saanthana views, this one necessitates the sacrifice of individual interest. However, because the human being is not, in essence, individually definable, this so-called 'sacrifice' is merely the realization of a basic need for social integration.

This sounds plausible – and for millions of people it is temporarily the most acceptable conceptualization. Of course, the same notion may also be conceptualized as Nirvana, eternal life or reincarnation. The reasons for choosing one or other of these are historical or local: I am not here arguing for a particular one, but pointing out the underlying unity of sentiment.

If we are ready to accept the idea that this sentiment may externalize as a perfect society, can we object to its externalization as a paradigmatic individual? Or, more simply, since there are paradigmatic city models, are there also paradigmatic individuals? In some traditions the *Logos* has indeed been identified with a person – Christ, or Krishna. The question then arises as to the historical basis for this identification. Since wiser men than this author have both affirmed and denied the historicity of Christ, I do not feel called on to make final statements. But with regard to the *cosmic* Christ, a mind which has gone through certain movements will be unable not to perform the noetic leap to some private, authoritative and in some sense uncompromising judgments. Such a mind will probably not perceive why so much stress should be laid on the historicity of the various hero figures of myth and testimony. If it serves to ennoble a nation to believe that Leonidas was a noble hero who sacrificed his life to save

Hellas, why dig into the dirt and claim that he was really a coward and a halfwit, and/or a traitor who ran away to Persia having shown the Persians the back passage at Termopili for 30 Dinari? Honouring the myth of Leonidas we honour the cosmic truth of courage and bravery. That there *is* both courage and nobility is the truth, the absolute truth, and it is far more noble to honour such projections than to deny them. It is the base and ignoble that are always suspecting deceit and treachery. Such an attitude, however, is not to be scorned so much as pitied; the clever, cunning mind, ever ready to seek deceit, is in fact a scared, petrified mind. While through its cynicism it does avoid being 'fooled', in a deeper sense its cynicism and mistrust makes it unable to live, to share and thus to form social relationships, whether on a micro-scale – marriage, friendship, parenthood – or on the macro-scale of large communities. The truth of the existence of the good cosmic pattern as against the evil one is manifest in those who do not follow it, who are consequently not constituted in its likeness: 'the clever shifty fellows ever ready to suspect deceit' (*Republic*, 518). By proving that the empirical Zoroaster was in fact five or six men living in different periods, one has not invalidated the premise of a cosmic Zoroaster. By denying their perceived selves, the writers of the Gathas have in fact identified with the eternal Zoroaster: when writing they were not individuals A, B or C, but Zoroaster. Indeed, in proving that the 'real' Zoroaster never existed empirically, one has proved neither that there is no Zoroaster, nor that he is not historical, nor that he is unreal. So the question arises, what is true, when is somebody real, and when is somebody himself?

I

The expositional technique that follows the corybantic or Bolero pattern repeats a 'single' theme in different movements. While this formula may be an excuse for poor writing, correctly used, the 'spiral' progression induces a new movement, conveying conclusions sometimes precisely opposite to those carried in the original text. I pointed to the way Bergson was led to his conclusion that time is not a series of points by his refutation of Zeno: it is only by a chance remark of Socrates that we learn Zeno was in fact arguing negatively.

The noetic thinker is not concerned to elicit a positive response: he is not concerned to convince or to win arguments. Socrates' and Jesus' mission was to provoke, to infuriate and to be denied. A specific 'message' can be conveyed by verbalizing a single theme in contradictory ways – this was Plato's method. A method more commonly used in the East is to create the necessary paradox by repeating the message, yet attaching a different meaning to a particular exposition by the insertion of various 'ill-fitting' words or notions. While trying mentally to correct the false sound in the tune, the listener hears a new – the true – tune.

This method is presently being used in poetry and the so-called 'stream of consciousness' literature which bends the rules of grammar. It also lies behind the breakthrough away from Euclidean geometry and conceptual physics effected by Bohr and Einstein when they resorted to 'noetic mathematics'. The theory of relativity is not a law, nor will it become a law – its mathematics is 'stream of consciousness mathematics', though it is not poetry.

In applying this principle to philosophy, I am well aware of the dangers. My intention is not to turn philosophy into poetry. The arguments presented should be critically examined, especially because mistakes will certainly have been made. Nobody can write a totally objective work, and person prejudice inevitably creeps in. However, the validity of my arguments is not to be gauged by conceptual criteria: the criterion is diarithmetic. A boring argument is most likely false, for man is bored by whatever does not relate to his needs and interests; and as already indicated, everything that does not relate to these interests is false. Having stated this, it must also be pointed out that the human mind seeks to avoid pain. An industrial, sugary, fizzy drink tastes better to a child than the most exquisite wine; to a lazy mind, a pop tune is more interesting than a Bach fugue. To be concentrated, a mind needs to extend itself.

Thus to write: 'the true individual is a function of intuitively synthesized paradigmatic instances, representing the moments of identification between the actual and the ideal', both is and is not the same as writing 'man is man only when he is good'. The verbosity of the German idealists may (as Dvorinkovich argued) hide existential fear and insecurity, but such flights of verbosity do at least force the mind to concentrate. A conceptualist can say things just once – for he deals in definitions. A corybantic exposition relies on repetition: to become meaningful, 'things' have to be said more than once, in ways which are complicated and in ways which are simple.

It is with this in view that we return to the points which, in a different way, have already been made before.

II

While various myths may conceptualize it in different ways, to the noetic thinker it is obvious that immortality does not apply to people as they normally perceive themselves. In other words, the perceived individual is not the immortal individual.

To follow Jesus – or Patanjali – you must deny yourself. This point is now to be extended to our daily practical activity. To become what you are, says Scorates, you must specialize along the lines of your true needs and your true abilities.

To equate this with the economic, bourgeois specialization of labour practised by seekers of high productivity is to turn the Socratic notion of specialization on its head. Socrates distinguishes between the man *qua* individual and man the performer of a function. The shepherd participating in the art of cooking and selling mutton is no longer a shepherd: by participating in the art of cooking or selling he becomes a cook or a salesman. Things are not held as things and people are not held as people by an underlying substance (*Hyle*) that maintains an identity in time. There are no 'hidden shepherds' behind perceived shepherds, giving the latter identificational continuity while they act as cooks or innkeepers. Things and people are functionally defined: a knife is not a knife unless used as such. The morning star, for Plato, is a morning star, and the evening star is an evening star; although we may rest assured that Plato was aware that empirically they were the same star, he points out that in reality they are absolutely different. For Plato, empirical or conceptually perceived unity is conjectural. Seen in an ethical light, one star is Lucifer (*Timaeus*, 38[d]), the lower Aphrodite, the 'muse of many hymns' (*Symposium*, 187[e]). In an ethical sense, this star is altogether different from the heavenly Aphrodite, Urania or Venus (*Symposium*, 187[e]). The sophist is as different from the philosopher as is Lucifer from Venus, just as the noble lover is different from the ignoble (*Phaedrus*, 250[a–e]), even though both may manifest alternatively within a single person such as Alcibiades.

For those who categorize by basing their perception on an underlying continuity in time, it may be necessary to insist that the morning and the evening star are the same. However, as Plato said in the *Republic* (529), 'We do not study the heavens by looking upwards but inwards'. What is true is determined ethically and functionally, not empirically.

This point is also made in the *Republic* by examining the person who is both a doctor and a moneymaker. The fact that the doctor gets paid for his services has nothing to do with the correct exercise of his art. A good person may function as a breadwinner, a father and a doctor, but he will not bring the biases of one activity to impair in any way his performance in the other capacity.

The purport is the separation of persons as constitued through the exercise of an art from persons eristically constituted, i.e. constituted by epithumic desire. In order to establish this, one first differentiates between the arts and their benefits. Hence the material benefit that the person *qua* artist derives from his activity is not and should not be seen as a payment in any way accruing from the art.

The causative principle behind the division of labour demands a singular functionally defined object, for any art is defined as such by its ability to further a certain object. The art of horsemanship is not to do with winning equestrian prizes or getting from A to B, even though a horseman may legitimately participate in the art of prizewinning (not, however, as a horseman but as a new entity, the prizewinner). The (outward) doctor may, in curing a tyrant, be operating in the realms of politics, moneymaking and fatherhood (by promoting the career prospects of his children), but to that degree he ceases to be a doctor, while practising medicine:

> For a doctor is not truly a doctor, does not act *as* a doctor in so far as he earns fees for himself, but in so far as he ministers to the sick. . . . An art or performance like doctoring has, in fact, nothing which can be considered its advantage or disadvantage since, in so far as it really *is* doctoring, it cannot be further corrected, protected or perfected (Findlay, 1974, p. 163).

An art's objective and definition are set solely by its inherent characteristics, and the individual performing the art performs it to the exclusion of all other arts by identifying with this eidetic objective.

The individual is therefore a blank, a model required to fulfil the roles imposed by *Moira*. Acting as a representative of shipbuilders and the lumber industry, Themistocles was not a soldier. Pressing for the naval engagement at Salamis he was not an admiral. As a result, the victory at Salamis was not a victory: the Athenians at Salamis were not practising the art of soldiering but of hooking and trapping, timber selling and empire building. It is for all these reasons that the engagement at Salamis was a defeat (*Laws*, 707[c], 823–824; *Gorgias*, 516). Likewise, in so far as Pericles was not a statesman but a merchant, an estate agent and a dockyard space-seller, in spite of all his outward successes, as a result of his practising arts other than those of a statesman Athens suffered inwardly (*Gorgias*, 516[c]–519[a]).

Who is or is not a doctor, and for how long, will be contextually and aspectually defined. A knife is whatever, given a specific situation, best performs the function of cutting, even though there may exist a more 'proper' instrument (which in turn varies with circumstance, technology, period, etc.)' A table may be instantiated by upturned packing crates, boxes, chests of drawers, warriors' shields and scores of other functionally appropriate objects, none of which are tables *qua* tables.

And so likewise for statesmen, kings, soldiers and all professions. The city where statesmen act only as statesmen, when called on to perform such functions, and where fathers act as fathers but not when called on to function as judges, is the city where labour has been properly specialized. (Since conceptualization is *Anatrope*, turning things upside down, noetic specialization is what would conceptually be called 'depecialization').

III

Functional predication or participation apart, the second question of importance for the division of labour concerns the tripartite division of the soul, i.e. the division into the elements of *Logisticon, Thumos* and *Epithumia*. The aspectual character of this kind of triunity is given in several traditions through the example of the spinning top; whether it is in motion or at rest is aspectually determined. Considered with respect to its vertical axis it is at rest, although not with respect to its horizontal component; a further dimension can be added by tilting the spinning axis, whereby the top will manifest a third dimension – a horizontally executed circular motion.

Before beginning an analysis of how man can be one and also composite, we must first agree that in some sense the three elements of the psyche are independent or apart from each other: were this not the case, we could not experience conflicting desires, for each part of the soul is directed only to a uniform object of desire – hunger for food, thirst for drink, etc.

Yet were *Logisticon* completely free and separate from the spirited, executive aspect, we could not struggle against desire. Were the rational element free of the appetitive aspect, we would have no appetite for goodness or beauty, or for the struggle against appetites. The three elements present in each soul cannot be restricted to three individuals, nor can they be reduced to three classes, since each individual and each class is characterized, not exclusively by one of the three soul-characteristics, but by a proper balance of them, in which one quality is dominant at different times.

A city of three competing instantiations would admit of no communication. Therefore, the smallest city must contain 3^3 individuals, i.e. three classes comprising three individuals each, each of whom participates in the three faculties, but instantiating a particular and appropriate balance for his location. Conceptually the relationships are exceedingly complex, since the series of bifurcations, tripartitions and corresponding permutations is endless. Seen aspectually, however, the relationship becomes a natural one: the specialization is treated simply as an inclination, whose direction and durability is dependent on context and subject to the intention at hand.

Devoid of reason, the appetite knows not what it is the appetite for; while devoid of appetite, reason wants and attempts nothing. *Thumos -Rajas*, the spirited element, can change aspects; it can be a part of the appetitive soul or it can marshal itself on the side of reason. Hierarchically, *Thumos* is the second best, for it desires honour where *Logisticon* desires the Good. This division, however, is merely metaphorical. The Good-desiring *Epithumia* is hierarchically higher than the honour-desiring *Thumos*, yet *Thumos* has a passive element, and this 'middle aspect of the soul' is compared by Arabic philosopher Averroes to an obedient dog who can obey good or bad masters. Only *Logos* and *Epithumia* can originate movement within, to which *Thumos* functions as the executive factor. The soul is therefore (1) singular, in so far as the three aspects are harmonized in movement to a single goal; (2) dual, in so far as the *Thumos* allies itself with either of the movement-originating aspects, 'so that there are not three but two kinds in the soul, the rational and the appetitive'; or (3) tripartite – which is legitimate if, as in (1), the three aspects are integrated, and illegitimate if any of the aspects sets itself apart as an autonomous entity.

Thumos-Rajas – the active element – can serve either *Logisticon* or *Epithumia*. When serving *Logisticon* it ceases to think and becomes reflecting, i.e. the mind becomes still and acts simply as a mirror, a communicating agent translating the language of reality into the language of actuality, making no pretence to autonomous philosophy and knowledge. Correctly functioning, thought is simply executive. To walk from A to B necessitates memory and a certain amount of knowledge; likewise, to harvest wheat necessitates thought, communication and memory, and it is in such and like capacities that *Thumos*-constructed 'thought' is adequate. Thought, however, has no legitimacy in the legislative sense, e.g. in deciding whether to go to war or not, whether to live or to die, to harvest or not to harvest. Thought cannot tell how any activity relates to the inner element, the well-being of the soul; this is the function solely of *Logisticon*.

In an ordinary State the executive element – lawyers, police, civil servants – cannot be regarded as second best in an absolute, moral sense; they are second only when functionally considered. External class divisions are not effected by the monopoly of one of the three psychological elements. We cannot characterize classes as dominated by a single element – if *Epithumia* dominated the lower classes, then they would be ungovernable. Different classes are ideally neither dominated nor ruled by any of the soul characteristics, but possess all three in a harmonious ratio. Classes differ in so far as these ratios differ.

This balance is absent from the sick city, upon which the structure of the paradigmatic model is grafted for the purpose of curing it. The healthy city needs no paradigmatic model: it has no elite party or police to enforce morality. The need for these arises only with the disease. The existence of a ruling elite or caste presupposes sickness; its function is (or should be) therapeutic. (This principle also operates in the body, where the white blood cells are produced to counteract and absorb harmful bacteria.)

The objectivized Politea can take the form of a Church, a political Party or a society of knights. As such it is always paradoxical, since its objective is to do away with objectification. St John 'saw no temple in the city' (Revelation, XXI, 22). Likewise, in the land of non-alienation there is no State. Thus the spearhead, the micro-unit, functions in the capacity which it wishes to abolish. In this, all such entities are paradoxical and are criticized for being so. Such criticisms are valid where they point to the possible misuse of authority for personal gain by members of the body; however, criticism of the principle itself is not valid. Members of the Party or the Church can, in a sense, never misfunction, for when they cease to function correctly they cease to represent the body they are supposed to represent. My argument is not intended to legitimate the abuses of the various ruling bodies; however, *individual* abuses do not invalidate the principle. When the sum of this abuse exceeds that of correct functioning, there arises a counter-Politea. At first the counter-Politea is perceived as a heresy, but if its members are truer to the basic *Logos*, it absorbs the previous body – or, if the previous body rallies, it reabsorbs the heresy. Historically, however, the *Logos*-based pattern is the surviving one.

IV

In trying to account for what is meant by the 'division of labour', I have tried to show the inadequacy of simplified assumptions. The division cannot mean that each person should simply perform a single task; for no task is really (externally) single. A contemporary factory worker, by pulling one lever in one particular way, could be making aeroplanes or shoes or bottling wine; a Calcutta shoemaker has to carry out activities which are psychologically, mentally and physically more diversified than those of a contemporary Western worker producing many products. To argue that a man is simply a shoemaker or winebottler or aeroplane-maker or lever-puller is alien to *Logos*-based philosophy. Actions and jobs have an inner dimension, and if I argue that a man should be only a shoemaker I am speaking of the interior dimension of each and every job. Just as the mental activity of *Dianoia* or *Noesis* is to be determined not by the object of thought but an inner mental activity, so the specialization of labour is not to be effected by the nature of the product being produced.

The most significant of the arguments against the literal interpretation of the division of labour concerns a subject previously touched upon, namely the non-correspondence between the perceived and the true individual. Since this is fundamental to the central argument of this investigation – the constitution of mental and social units through the activity of sentiments rather than through conceptual predications – I will turn back to it once more.

Stenzel called the dialetical method one creative of concepts, but I see it as essentially a two-way 'diacritical' process with the emphasis on dissolution of concepts. The activity is synthetic in embracing two parallel processes, one (*Dialisis*) being the dissolution of false conglomerations (i.e. of unities perceived) into basic units by division along natural lines, the other (*Sinkresis*) being noetic reassembly in keeping with patterns and lines corresponding to instantiated reality itself.

The synthesizing aspect of the dialectic is more readily recognized, perhaps because it has been made familiar by Kant. The point is that the 'synkretic' process does not start in the world of conceptually ready-made, perceived units; rather, it is inseparable from the diacritical process. Although the final product of the diacritical activity is always a unity, the activity itself can start with unity or plurality. When starting with unlimited plurality it is synthesized by the dialectician into a unity, but when starting with a perceived unity the dialectician must first fracture it into plurality and only subsequently create a unity. In other words, the building blocks that the dialectician uses to create his unities are found as elements in the realm of becoming (the world as conceptually interpreted), and they are not concepts but fragments created by the dissolution of conceptual (i.e. perceived) units.

This 'theory' of non-correspondence between the true and the perceived unity has more than epistemological significance; it also provides help in accounting for the ambiguities that arise when such notions as reincarnation are understood literally.

To come to a deeper understanding of the workings of society, we should look at the workings of the human organism. The perceived man shares functions with and therefore is analogous to his society. Seen biologically, the body exhibits the autonomous activity of myriads of independent organisms: friendly bacteria, hostile bacteria, white cells, red cells – all seeking self-expression. All these organisms and units have a will of their own, a tendency to infinite expansion (*Pleonexia*), yet all are counter-checking each other as if arranged by some invisible hand.

This view of the body as characterized by counter-balanced *Pleonexia* lies behind the bourgeois thought of Hobbes, and behind that of Smith – where the invisible hand of self interest is the agent of control. Applied to biology, and seen in terms of Greek medicine, the heart if uncontrolled will 'overheat'; it is cooled by the lungs, not out of 'goodness' on their part but through their own tendency to overcool – the lungs are reciprocally checked in their activity by the pumping of the heart (*Timaeus*, 70^{b-e}). The intestines grow long, and in meeting resistance grow circular. As a result of their expansive activity they check the stomach, undermining its tendency to be infinitely filled (*Timaeus*, 72^{e}–73^{d}).

Thus the body exhibits the 'Bellum omnium contra omnia' principle propounded by Hobbes, who saw war as a natural condition of man. Bodily organs behave like men and cities; none of them show self-constraint. Men are held in check by the mutual cancellation of extreme tendencies, and by their rulers or subjects. Bodily parts are held in check by the punitive and rewarding action of the liver, which secretes sweet and bitter juices and sends them to curb and control the combatants.

As for the mind, its plurality is even more pronounced. Any serious analysis, whether psychological, introspective or philosophical, inevitably shows that most human desires are foreign and external, and stem from other entities. A person's mind acts as a container for the various unfulfilled cravings of his environment. A single soul becomes a breeding ground for various loose desires hatched within society. Thus a receptive mind becomes the victim of the unfulfilled wants and ambitions of his friends, parents or nation.

In view of this, one can understand why the noetic thinkers say that the personality constituted by the human mind is not exhaustive of individual identity. A person constituted by the mind is not a unity but a legion.

It is also for this reason that noetic thought defines justice as giving to each man his due. To some extent we are keepers of the means of satisfaction of the desires of others: this can be most dramatically seen in the case of physical love and reproduction. In possessing the means of allowing the other to become what they truly are, we possess a piece of the other and are likewise possessed.

Ramanuja, Patanjali and Jesus call for the dissolution of personality, the death of the self. One should ever be ready to recognize oneself as the keeper of a piece of social property, and be ready to deliver the 'goods' as soon as they are claimed by another. In so doing one is not dissolved, for the other similarly carries pieces of him; and in opening himself up he allows the other to place those legitimate constituent pieces back into himself: in this way the true unities are reconstituted.

Though the extreme physical example of this is reproduction, the principle applies to every part of the body. As 'merchant thought' will find a logical positivist to create a theory to justify self-satisfaction in one sense, so there is a wealth of 'talent' in universities and industry to create the means and the justifying theories and statistics for self-indulgence in the mental, physical or economic sense. Such practices inevitably lead to psychological and physical disorders in the system at large, for reasons which will be elaborated elsewhere.

V

The human condition is remarked upon by Eryxymachus and expounded in Aristophanes' version (*Symposium*, 189[c]–193[e]) – 'men are halves'. That they are called halves and not quarters, etc., is intended to underline the main point simply that they are fractured rather than whole – more recent terminology has it that they are 'alienated'. By making the perceived units halves and not smaller fractions, Aristophanes can give a simple account of the basic myth that the different parts of a person are separate and in search of each other:

> 'And so, gentlemen, we are all like pieces of the coins that children break in half for keepsakes, making two out of one like flatfish, and each of us forever seeking that half that will tally with himself' (*Symposium*, 191[c]).

That the bisection is not literal or the end of the division is made clear in 193[a]. The process had been simplified to illustrate the point, but those who are disobedient to the gods are to be split again, i.e. quartered, so that they hop on one leg, and if necessary split again and again; the less one worships the gods, the more fragmented does one become: 'If we neglect the worship of the gods they will split us again and we shall have to go about with our noses sawed asunder part and counterpart like the bas-reliefs on the tombstones.' Though Aristophanes does not elaborate further, it is readily deductible from the allegory of the sea god Glaucus (*Republic*, 611[d]) that the fractured pieces are no longer homogeneous or unadulterated; they have attached themselves to countless other individuals, and become mixed with weeds, shells and algae.

The thinking individual yearns for the reassembly of his true identity, and at the same time is torn by the warring activity of all the foreign parts attached to him. Perceiving himself as a unity, he tries to consolidate the perceived unity by subjugating all the warring elements, thus becoming a tyrant; but even if he is successful, this tyrant rules over a city or a body which is not whole – in the perceived city, 'foe is next to foe'.

The tyrant's longing, and that of everyone, is for the original, the true state of unity. True entities cannot be constituted by force, by conjectural thought or by intrigue; the constitutive element of true entities is love (sentiment):

> 'And so all this to-do is a relic of that original state of ours when we were whole, and now when we are longing for and following after that primeval wholeness we say we are in love. For there was a time, I repeat, when we were one, but now for our sins God has scattered us abroad as the Spartans scattered the Arcadians' (*Symposium*, 193[a]).

A man therefore is not one: he is a conglomeration of parts which in themselves are genuine as parts of the other, and are false only in so far as they are treated as autonomous unities. Rather than imposing cohesion by presupposing the legitimacy of the unity *perceived* as the self, the correctly functioning man renders to each his due, and allows the many parts under his domain to seek out their corresponding wholes and integrate.

The proper functioning of the parts may well lead to the peril of the perceived whole, as was the case with the perceived entity Socrates or Jesus; however, in dissolving the falsely constituted Socrates – rendering to the law what was its due, rendering to philosophy what was its due and to Athens what was its due – the fragment of Socrates instantiated in fifth-century Athens started a chain reaction of further fragmentation and deeper reunification. In giving up his perceived unity Socrates in fact reconstituted himself.

The cosmos, therefore, constitutes itself through the voluntary disendowment of conscious unities, in which the parts perceived as constituents of a personal unity created by the conceptual mind are voluntarily released, setting in process a new synthesizing activity whose organizing principle is the sentiment.

In view of this, the difficulties in interpreting claims by Jesus and Plato that one should give up wives and husbands and all property, including one's own body, are reduced by the metaphorical understanding of 'giving up'. The giving up is interior. In renouncing one's parents or one's country in an *outward* sense one is more likely to be led by conceptual self-righteousness than by sentiment. This attitude is exemplified in a story about Eutyphro: Eutyphro has conceptualized the idea of justice, so he persecutes his father for having wronged a slave. While in some sense it seems admirable of Eutyphro to be so just that he would rather attack his father than see injustice, a deeper analysis reveals that, rather than renouncing the false pride which constitutes the false personality,

Eutyphro is re-creating it. Behind his action lies self-admiration, i.e. love of the self which is not. The same applies to Judas, who wanted to sell ointment to give the money to the poor, in an example I have quoted already.

VI

Opposing the historical bias of the nineteenth century towards the positive, the analytic and the measurable, I have been stressing the importance of the interior and subjective. The purpose of philosophy for the Saanthana tradition lies in effecting a balance between the subjective and objective, inner and outer. It would be incorrect to argue that for these thinkers the subjective did not have an objectively observable aspect, and consequently it is necessary to account for this.

I argued that the sentiment of love is both an epistemological principle (the principle of notional organization) and the constitutive principle of the true, the real cosmos and non-alienated society. There is in nature a certain division of labour which applies to the creation of physical organisms, and which should also be followed in a productive society. This division is twofold: (1) externally different occupations are reduced to one procedural uniformity, to satisfy the multiplicity of desires; and (2) the manner and degree of external specialization is determined by the reduction to an inner specialization, characterized by a single common sentiment. In this way each art becomes free of all admixture, 'and is right so long as each art is precisely and entirely that which it is' (*Republic*, 342[b]). This principle of separation by singularity of sentiment rather than by activity is readily observable throughout the Saanthana tradition.

For example, drama and its corresponding pleasures are divided into good and bad depending on whether the sentiment in which the drama is peformed is of a pure or a mixed kind. As opposed to unadulterated elation, there is the gleeful, bittersweet feeling of *Pfonos*, and generally the satisfaction in others' misfortunes. As shown earlier the same criteria are used in the *Laws* (654[c–d]), where excellence in singing is determined not by the quality of reproduction, but by the nature of the sentiment which it evokes in performers and the listeners.

Just as noble sentiments such as love have corresponding negatives, like hate, so there is a similar relation between actions. Physical things and processes are subject to the quality of forces, some tending to produce excellence, while their corresponding negative forces tend to produce the opposite. Each thing, apart from its characteristic excellence, also has a specific vice. For wood the specific vice is rot, rust for iron, and injustice is the vice of the soul (*Republic*, 609[d]).

This idea can be traced through the tradition. It stems from the standard model of the two types of desire – black and white, i.e. desire and interest. It is also seen as the magnet of Ion, which can affect things in two different ways. Love can be divided into two kinds: the love of the right and the left in the *Phaedrus*, or the love of the heavenly and earthly kind (*Symposium*, 181[a–c]). The first kind of love is found to be 'fair and heavenly, born of Urania and the muse of heaven', the heavenly Venus. The negative sentiment, its inverted image, is the earthly Venus: 'he is sprung from Polyhymnia, the muse of many songs'. Pausanias observes that the decision whether an action is good or bad is subject to the kind of love that characterizes the action. If undertaken for the love of 'lower Venus', the earthly Venus, then it is bad, but it is good when the action is executed in the sentiment of the higher, heavenly Aphrodite.

Eryximachus, the physician, points to the fact that even in the absence of thought, the body comprehends all by itself the dual nature of the sentiment of love, and if healthy reacts correspondingly (*Symposium*, 186[b]). He improves on Pausanias, and observes that even the way we eat is dominated by the two kinds of love; hence the sentiment in which we consume food, rather than the food itself, will determine whether or not our environment will prove to make us better or worse men (*Symposium*, 187[e]). Likewise, sacred activities become profane if taken in the sentiment of the other kind of love: 'And so in music, in medicine and in every activity, whether sacred or profane, we must do our utmost to distinguish two kinds of love, for you may be sure that both will be there' (187[e]).

Our contemporary epoch is marked by labelling actions according to their outer criteria; for example, love is understood in the physical sense – sexual intercourse is called 'making love'. In the Saanthana tradition, the decision as to whether or not physical intercourse entails love is not made on the same basis. Love, even if present, can be of two kinds, only one of which is real love – the other is false, because its effects are the disintegration of true entities, in which respect it resembles hate, although the sick individual still experiences it as pleasant. These two types of love are called 'right' and 'left' (*Phaedrus*, 266[a]). The Athenian calls the antisentiment 'the lawless Aphrodite' (*Laws*, 840[a]); it is not love but a perverse, tyrannical attachment. It is outlined in the *Phaedrus* as a sadomasochistic relation characteristic of the decaying society where lust acts as the Stone of Heraclea; such a city delights in observing 'the sacred and beautiful undergo the loss of dignity' through undignified postures and movements. Infliction of pain and the loss of social respectability of the beloved are perceived with pleasure (*Phaedrus*, 232[b]-233[c]; *Philebus*, 48[a]-50[a]).

This unholy sentiment is the organizing principle of the pleasures sought by a sick man or a sick society. By its magnetic pull it creates art of a corresponding type; by its specialization of labour it creates specialists of a kind typified by Ion, who makes our 'blood curdle' as he recites his gory poetry. Stripped of its protective layer, we see that it is the negative, the antisentiment, which creates the antiphilosopher, the sophist, the keeper of the beast, who studies its desires so as to provide it with a self-justifying social theory and philosophy.

VII

The idea to be conveyed is that there is a certain duality to activities and feelings. Rather than describe a given activity or thing as bad, one should refer to its negative aspect. We may conclude that there is a right and a wrong kind of sentiment. But it is appropriate to point out here the complexities of this notion.

With respect to opposites, one cannot dichotomize diagonally, across categories of actuality. The king does not stand opposed to the slave, nor war to peace, love to hate, courage to fear; these are opposites only in the perceived world. The perceived opposites are in fact coequal. Fear of the bad is courage. Opposed to the king is not the slave but the 'aberration king', the tyrant. Opposed to the philosopher stands not the 'ignorant' but the sophist, the 'aberration philosopher'. St Paul wrote that it is better to be a good slave than a bad king. Losers are not the opposites of winners, for there is defeat in the wrong kind of victory. This principle of positing the true entity along with the perverse departure from it is called *Parekbasis*.

The parekbasitic principle is operative only where the deviant entity assumes and acts in place of the true entity. A sophist who does not pretend to be a philosopher is not really a sophist; *Dianoia*, if not aping *Noesis*, is not parekbasitic. There is a legitimate function even for deviants; indeed, since the ideal is contextually defined, a deviant can deviate only in a moral sense.

With regard to love and the corresponding specialization of activities, suffice it to note that the two kinds of loves are only dichotomized aspectually. Nobody does wrong willingly. Tyrants do not become tyrants because they hate the good; rather they are led by the wrong kind of love.

Their government, correspondingly, instantiates the illegitimate sentiment of its foundation.

As Confucius argues, rather than legislate for the division of labour by banning specific activities judged to be unproductive or detrimental to society, one should effect this by controlling for sentiments. In order to achieve the good State we regulate men's hearts. The good ruler or lawmaker should know how to reduce the various aspects of different sentiments into comprehensive unities, and examine how a particular emotional structure relates to an objective activity. Speaking generally, the Koran is an attempt to create the socially correct *Pathos* by legislating for and against activities which strengthen, produce or weaken the required sentiments.

I have argued that the real cosmos, city or individual is brought into being, or rather is so, by the synthesizing activity of the sentiment of love. Alternatively, it is the negative sentiment that brings about the creation of the sick cosmos or the sick city. (If this sick sentiment were not in some ways perceived as pleasant, nobody would ever be bad.) The entity, be it a city or a person, assumes the perceived unity to be real, and by perverse love seeks to consolidate its hold over it, creating as if by a magnetic pull a corresponding world view, false needs and false 'artists' to satisfy them. The process is a chain reaction where every link turns into a negative one: the philosopher becomes a sophist, the king a tyrant. In the course of this activity, the owner-ruler of the false self encounters the resistance of the falsely conglomerated, but otherwise genuine, desires, needs, opinions, organs and thoughts, all of which are longing for autonomy and reintegration with their genuine parts. This gives rise to *Pleonexia*, the tendency to unlimited expansion.

This world is the one seen by Hobbes and by bourgeois thought in general. Empirically such a world is true, and it can well be supported by statistics, yet it is based on a fundamental lie. This perceived earth is an inferior earth; morally Venus and Lucifer are two different stars.

The two-world separation of 'this' from the 'other' world is not literal but epistemological. As this book continually stresses, the other world is the same as this, but differently perceived. When we see it as being free of evil, we are referring to aspects of this world perceived in a characteristic way. The predicate 'good' refers to action in the 'other world', perceived and performed in the correct sentiment. Outwardly the action may be the same, just as 'this' and 'the other' world are in a sense the same. Yet if our fundamental criterion is ethical and not empirical, then the ethically correct is absolutely different from the unethical.

Behind this ambiguity resides the simple truth that the sensually perceived is not equivalent to the conceptually interpreted; as such, it is different from the actual. Duality arises between the actual entity and its conceptual aberration created by the thinking mind.

In other words, the thinking mind does not regulate or precede sensual perception. Having been perceived, phenomena can be either grasped or conceptually interpreted. The ethical aberration comes about after perception, in the process of mental interpretation.

VIII

In order to attain further insight in our discussion of sentiment, it is now necessary to examine the process through which one draws distinctions between activities and entities considered to be good and bad. The process does not reduce to a simple formula. While the sophist is singularly bad and the philosopher singularly good, the decision as to who is a philosopher, where and when and for how long, is highly complex.

This ambiguity is artistically exploited by St Augustine. He employs the notion that time is conjectural, and that therefore all events occur simultaneously. The conflict between good and evil – or for Plato the conflict between cosmic Athens and cosmic Atlantis – is a daily affair. For Augustine the conflict is between New Jerusalem and Babylon. The conflict can be seen in a social and an individual sense; and I have presented it as a continuing choice between two kinds of I. Once we have chosen, say, the Kantian 'I', we have also chosen the citizenship of a specific city, a specific kind of loving and a world view. At any moment, however, we can choose a social 'I', the I determined by sentiment: in choosing this I, the world turns upside down – or the right side up. In saying that the Kantian or empirical 'I' is not true, I am speaking tongue in cheek – it refers to the same person as the *Logos*-constituted I, yet it is aspectually different.

St Augustine and all *Logos* thought goes further than this. It argues that the *Logos*-deduced I is the eternal, immortal self, and that the conflict between New Jerusalem and Babylon is not a myth or a story from the past but is true now, for there is only now – *only the living ever were or are.* To think that New York or Paris or Tokyo exist and are different from Jerusalem is to think falsely. All cities are in fact one city, whose inverted image is Atlantis – the paradigmatic evil city.

Thus for St Augustine, the perceived city is granted only a semi-legitimate, 'temporary' reality; and as such it is apart from the true city, the City of God. In due course the soul learns to differentiate the way in which things formerly held as evil – if perceived in the correct relationship to each other, in the process of realizing the City of God – cease to be evil;

and in this sense the city which was apart ceases to be apart, the real manifests in the actual. By means of a progression, the soul climbs up by examining the things of sense, gathering the many beautiful forms, synthesizing them into one and perceiving them as the visible reflection of the eternal God (Sermon 241, 22–23). In the course of this process there dawns the realization that all there is is a reflection of God. The visible world, as previously interpreted, ceases to be. It does not cease to be in the sense that it is no longer perceived – the phenomena of the visible world as 'objectively' seen do not change. What happens is that the ethical or emotional predication previously assigned to the phenomena treated as evil or imperfect disappears. The distinction between the real visible and the illusory visible is an ethical distinction: only something perceived in an ethically wrong way constitutes an illusion. In terms of the three cities, the second – the city of acrobats, innkeepers and sophists – is abstracted away.

Ficino (1978, 17, 22) has a similar view concerning this point. In his account of evil and actuality it is only the mind that creates the perversion: 'Perversis animis adversa sunt omnia'. However, the mind fixed on God loses its perverse vision, since the good God converts all things into good things: 'Deus omnia bonis convertit in bonum'. In Hindu thought this is expressed in the famous parrot parable, as follows. In the tree of life there are two parrots. One parrot symbolizes the world as given and interpreted by the conceptual mind, the realm of becoming. This parrot is tired, shabby, has a difficult life and shows it – its is the lot one refers to by observing 'such is life'. Then there is the ideal parrot; this one symbolizes the realm of the idealists – it is perfect and glittering, with shining feathers, always well fed and healthy. Yet as the story goes, in some ways both of these parrots are false. The shabby parrot (the parrot in time) suffers and endeavours to become perfect by literal imitation of the perfect, ideal-instance parrot; and in this process of striving after a perfection which is outside its own existence, it perpetually fails. Given the special circumstances, however, the parrot in the realm of becoming, the perceived parrot, suddenly grasps the actual parrot – i.e. the parrot which it really is – and realizes that the actual is the ideal, and that the parrot in time – the shabby parrot – never really was. Hence there are three parrots: the conjectural, the ideal and the actual; and the first two are in fact reduced to one, the ideal-actual. The problem of the shabby parrot-in-time is that it cannot accept its own form as the ideal, and strives to attain a conceptualized form of ideal, which is other than itself. Through this desire to be other than itself, it perceives itself as ugly and shabby, and in that sense becomes ugly and shabby. In becoming the third parrot, it both eliminates and absorbs the other two and becomes the ideal-actual.

IX

It is in view of the above that one can understand the dichotomy in Chinese thought between the Taoists and the tradition followed by Confucius. Heidegger and the majority of contemporary enthusiasts turn to Taoism for the representation of Chinese thought, and regard Confucius as a stern father-figure of a kind they are eager to forget. I would argue that both are representatives of *Logos* thought, and that they developed two sides of the same philosophy. Indeed, both religions were simultaneously official cults of China. To take another example, European thought has stressed the paternal, yang element in Plato, and has correspondingly virtually ignored the dialogues or passages representing the female element (aspects of the left). Plato, however, points out that both the left and the right ought to be incorporated.

(It is almost impossible for a single noetic thinker to argue equally well the female and the male aspects. Confucius and Lao Tzu have divided their roles – perhaps by mutual agreement. Likewise, this study emphasizes one aspect of the truth, even if I try to keep a balance.)

Jesus and Christianity can also be dichotomized. The contemporary dissenting intellectual points to the 'anarchical', all-is-permitted aspect – Jesus forgives the woman taken in adultery and is seen as permitting adultery (an interpretation typical of conceptualistic simplification). Meanwhile, the formal Church has stressed the element of the right – the more rigid aspect. Jesus in fact came both to fulfil and to abolish the law: he was both yang and yin.

While Plato calls for the abolition of marriage, and while Lao Tzu calls for the dissolution of paternal or any formal authority, neither of them intend free love or the state of 'natural simplicity' that a poet might have in mind when using objectively similar verbalizations.

Noetic philosophy is similar to poetry, in that they both attempt to bypass the conceptual mind; however, they aim at different cognitive faculties. In Greece and elsewhere the early philosophers were called poets: they were also the creators of religious myths. Yet these early philosopher-poets were different from poets and artists as they have since become. In appealing to the 'heart', as he does throughout the Koran, Mohammed has in mind a different 'heart' than does Lord Byron.

To nineteenth-century conceptualists, Marx appeared to be voicing the same opinion as Bakunin the anarchist. In some sense they were using similar language, for both called for the abolition of private property. But Marx was speaking of that aspect of private property which relates to the fulfilment of social-material needs. To distinguish himself from Bakunin, he was forced to specify positively what he meant by the satisfaction of human needs. This specification may in praxis have proved somewhat unfortunate, for the literal understanding of the development of the means of production led Stalin to conclude that socialism consisted of Soviets plus electrification. Stalin, while formally left, exemplifies the conceptualizations of the extreme right.

Poets, whether formally left or right, will veer to the extreme left or the extreme right when they misfunction. By advocating the control of the arts, both Plato and Confucius intend each person to control both the tyrant and the poet within himself, and likewise in the State. The poetic element can, by deviation, reduce to an indulgence of the passions, and this should be prevented. 'Well, there is one point which I think you will admit, namely that any discourse ought to be constructed like a living creature with its own body, as it were; and it must not lack either the head . . . ' (*Phaedrus*, 264[c]). Whatever we think or say or build needs to relate to the underlying pattern. A correctly built city will have all the necessary parts – a head, organs for breathing, for waste disposition, for the consumption of food, for the circulatory system and so on. Behind these outer manifestations there lie deeper principles; ontologically, every city, or any word, thought, person or thing, is to be considered as a triunity. I looked at the epistemological aspects of this triunity earlier; in this chapter I have mentioned the psychological aspect of the triunity, and this will be explored further below.

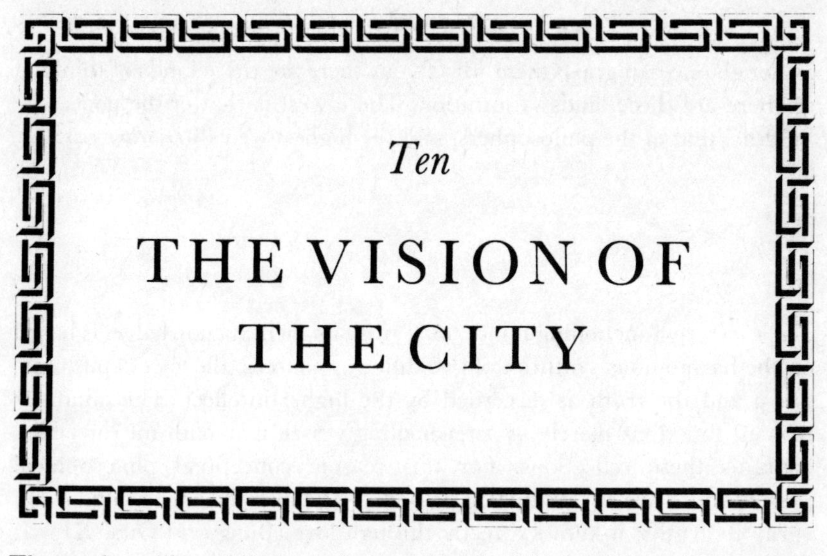

Ten

THE VISION OF THE CITY

The reader will need little reminding that the Hindus divide the soul into three parts – the head, the midriff and the thorax. These three further subdivide – the divisions are not fixed or permanent. Thus the stomach-soul is in 'the head', and it has a head element. The divisions are all conceptualizations, and as such only aspectually valid.

'Intuition' is poetic, and so it is aspectually seen as coming from the stomach; although proper stomach knowing is called *Apsathnai* – grasping or knowing with the body. I have equated *Noesis* with *Buddhi*, and the head. Noetic intuition was not called 'intuition' but *Diarithmesis*, and can be equated with 'knowing'. It is correctly based mental apprehension. Of course, the noetic 'head' faculty also has a stomach element, which is intuition. Thinking, on the other hand, is the stomach aspect of the middle, 'mental' soul. For this reason, although thinking and intuition both have to do with the stomach, intuition is superior.

Intuition in Novalis or Goethe, as opposed to Bergson and the philosophers, may be equated with the cognitive process I have called 'grasping'. A further subdivision of this kind of intuition is the intuition of artists and poets.

In between these two types of intuition – that of the philosopher and that of the poet (i.e. in between *Logisticon* and *Epithumia*), there stands the *Thumos*, the active principle of the mind. Although active, its activity is that of an obedient dog: in a 'creative' and originatory sense it is passive, obeying the commands of the two types of intuition.

The intuition of the intuitive philosophers is valid, since it is based on the mind-body (i.e. mind-stomach) combination. But it is not the same as noetic grasp, in which the mind draws on the soul.

These relations are too complex to be reduced to conceptualizations, although one can grasp them. Briefly, as there are three kinds of thinking so there are three kinds of intuition. The lowest is that of the poets, the 'middle' that of the philosophers, and the highest we call *Diarithmesis*.

I

The correctly functioning mind, i.e. legitimate mental knowledge, is based on the harmonious synthesis of two differing sources: the lower epithumic grasp and the truth as discerned by the higher intellect. The mind (or reason) functions merely as a reconciling vessel, a smooth mirror which contains these reflections. For this reason, conceptual philosophical presentations are always dual. The body – and also the poetic mind – can verify its truths; it knows directly through love (Bhagavad Gita, XI, 54; *Symposium*, 186[b]). The noetic faculty can also verify its truths by direct vision (through *Metanoia* or *Periagoge*). It is only *thought* which is parasitic in its derivations, for *Dianoia* is incapable of transcending assumptions and knowing from first principles (*Republic*, 511[a]). In arguing this, I am not advising the arrest of thought, but calling for the rightful recognition of the duality of all conceptual statements.

Both Parmenides and Heraclitus evade dianoic, i.e. formal, philosophy. Parmenides does so by using only negative arguments and structural rhythms appealing to inner constants. The Heraclitian method, on the other hand, is synthetic. Heraclitus addresses himself to the noetic and lower epithumic aspects of the soul, bypassing the dianoic or thinking mind altogether. By not subjecting the erotic and noetic elements of his message to synthesizing dianoic activity, Heraclitus forces the reader to perform the synthesis himself.

J.B.Morrall recognizes Heraclitus as 'straddling the gulf between the poetic and philosophical traditions'; he is in fact a philosopher and a poet at the same time, unbalancing one by the activity of the other. This does not suggest that a new simple synthesis takes place; the reconciling factor is not a dianoic activity. 'The significance of Heraclitus in reconciling . . . the poetic and philosophical outlooks on life may be symbolised by his use of the concept of Logos as the determining force in the rational understanding of the universe' (Morrall, 1977, pp. 30–1). Heraclitus views the *Logos* as the 'underlying organizational principle' of the universe, and he replaces dianoic thought with the *Logos* as the central patterning agent of what is true and truly knowable.

To avoid the appearance of relativism, one can equally well turn to uncompromising Parmenidean rigidity, asserting that truth is indeed One and universally valid; yet this fixity is only to be found in realms which cannot be conceptualized. Truth resides in *Logos*, and is also subject to the erotic recognitional pull of the sentiment. Man does not operate with a conceptual mould, into which the perceived reality is to be compressed; rather, he operates with a set of recognitional sentiments. In the realm of political thought, the sentiment replaces the specific injunctions of democracy versus aristocracy, singularity of profession versus diversification, etc.

In this light, we can examine the Islamic objection to the conceptual presentation of human art. Conceptual art is fixed, concrete; it says things which should be left implied, whereas the function of Islamic art is rhythmic and geometric, conveying no content but rhythm and sentiment.

In ancient Greece, prior to the rise of the sophists, even mathematics was a non-conceptual art, religiously and theologically understood, in which mathematical procedures used and activated a different process of the mind. The Pythagoreans put to death their dissenting members and refused to conceptualize the 'irrational numbers', calling them 'oblong' and equating them with one of the evil seven described in Aristotle's *Metaphysics* (I, 5).

In her book *Greek Mathematical Thought and the Origin of Algebra*, Klein (1968, p. 69) posits that mathematical thought – indeed the thought of anything concerning the territory of the physical world – must be equated with *Dianoia*.

But mathematics can exhibit either the upward or the downward movement, as can art or any other activity (Cornford, 1967, p. 76). The good arithmetic, writes Plato, 'leads the soul powerfully upward and compels it to discuss the *Aritmos* itself' (*Republic*, 525[d]). In the *Republic* (527[b]), Socrates claims that as the arts stand now, geometry has turned earthward and no longer serves the upward way: it leads not to Number but to number. Glaucon is made a spokesman to illustrate the vulgar understanding of the 'upward way': he states that one should study astronomy since it turns man upward to the sky above, to which Socrates answers: 'I for my part am unable to suppose that any other study turns the soul's gaze upward than that which deals with being and the invisible' (*Republic*, 529[b]). Proper art engenders an attitude based on a proper inner apprehension of the correct ordering and balancing of the cosmos; this is the upward way of the soul.

Whether a specific mental activity is to be characterized as *Noesis* or *Dianoia* cannot be determined by the object of thought – thinking about gods, about one's health or wealth, or about mathematics, can each entail *Dianoia* or *Noesis*. Noetic thought criticizes only art that entails, constitutes and is constituted by evil sentiments and/or mental activities. In other words, when or what art is good or bad – or to be banned – is, as I have persistently argued, to be determined aspectually, and in context.

II

The final objective of *Logos*-oriented philosophy can, of course, be expressed in many different ways. I have chosen to see it primarily as a kind of epistemological realization. Quite simply, the end is to help one apprehend the things which are true. The rest follows by itself: in perceiving the true things one perceives in the light of the good, hence one acts, becomes and perceives according to this sentiment.

To recapitulate: rather than vainly disputing the exact meaning of words or definitions, *Logos*-oriented philosophy is designed to stun the *Dianoia*-dominated mind by involving the thinker in a series of painful contradictions. Transcribed into writing, philosophy proves inadequate, 'for the written code kills, but the Spirit gives life' (II Corinthians, III, 6). To safeguard it against conceptual rigidification, the philosophy is forced to develop techniques and exercises to influence the mind in a 'corybantic' way, stimulating a mental movement that conveys a differentiated sentiment rather than an explicit content.

The only objective and legitimate way to knowledge is ethical illumination. The corybantic technique, as true philosophy, liberates the mind from its desire for speculative thought as well as from other desires, such as for epistemological certainty in the world of becoming. For 'only in flight' does the mind aggressively deny all positive assertions and enter the loci of the points instantiating the actuality of being. Thus, thinkers indulging in the flattering assumption that epistemic security can be achieved through the practice of philosophy and in speculative thought can be seen as drinking from the waters of the river of forgetfulness, of the well that makes them thirst again (John, IV, 13); the more they drink, the more they 'forget', the stronger is their desire. (Their behaviour is also similar to that of the readers spoken of by King Theuth in the *Phaedrus*, 274^{d}, whose excessive reading only causes them to forget.)

The object of true philosophy is to free one from all 'worldly desire', including the desire for certainty through thought. Indeed it is this desire to possess anything – including truth – that deflects one from the truth, for knowledge cannot be acquired or possessed: it can only be beheld. To know is not to *have* knowledge but to identify with it, with the true unchangeable pattern of it – which, of course, implies constant flow, and hence the loss of the fixed perceived self (though not the loss of the real self; see the *Phaedo*, 114^{b-c}). This perceived self is defined by Patanjali as that personality brought together by desires that are for the arrest of movement.

Conceptual thinkers deprive themselves of their birthright, for they seek for security of vision in the wrong realm. The 'cunning' thinkers conjecture how best to use thought to free oneself from the realities of life such as toil, old age, participation in defence or any of the necessities imposed by Karma (*Anangke* or the Cross). Through fear of the losses of circumstance, and by ordering a preferential hierarchy of outcomes, the conjectural mind views philosophy as a highly differentiated calculus for avoiding life's pains, mental and otherwise, and for ensuring maximization of pleasure, mental or otherwise.

Against this is the grasping mind, the mind engrossed in actuality. This is the mind of a simple shepherd with no concern other than for his sheep, of the mother who loses the Kantian sense of ego through her love for her child. It is the identity of a surgeon so completely engrossed in an operation that his 'I' no longer exists. This new sense of I is defined by completely submitting oneself to the demands of one's profession – or any social activity – thus abstracting the egoistic impulse. In so doing, such men perceive sensually, yet what they perceive is actuality, the sensual image of the real world – the truth.

III

There is, however, a still higher vision, one which we have so far not subjected to examination. Plato's word for it is *Periagoge*, the turning around:

> 'Of this very thing I said there might be an art – an art of the speediest and most effective shifting or conversion of the soul – not an art of producing vision in it, but on the assumption that it possesses vision but does not rightly direct it and does not look where it should' (*Republic*, 518[d]).

This vision is radically different from anything in merely mental experience, since:

> 'Man's eye could not be converted to the light from the darkness except by turning the whole body. Even so this organ of knowledge must be turned around from the world of the coming together with the entire soul, like the scene-shifting *periactus* in the theatre, until the soul is able to endure the contemplation of essence and the brightest region of being' (*Republic*, 518[b]).

Since this is brought about through the eye of the soul, which in the *Timaeus* (31[d]) is a piece of Godhood, I have called this vision spiritual.

Whether it is in fact religious is a matter of controversy. In Eastern Europe scholarship does not deny that Plato saw it as such but claims that he was wrong. In the West, Gosling (1973, p. 131) argues that for Plato the *Periagoge* was an allegorical description of a purely philosophical vision. Rather than enter into this argument, let us look at descriptions of the experience itself and examine it for its place in relation to the problem of knowledge.

It has been noted that *Periagoge* is powerful enough to cause temporary blindness. This scholastic, somewhat clinical account of it, however, does no justice to the euphorically poetic account given by Plato. Its 'luminous shining beauty' is all 'beauties rolled into one and yet surpassing them'. It shines so bright and is so 'all consuming' that 'once you have seen it . . . you will care nothing for the beauties that used to take your breath away and kindle such a longing in you' (*Symposium*, 211[d]). It is 'dazzingly luminous' (*Republic*, 518[b]), so 'exceedingly fair' that no one would willingly look away from it. As for the experience itself, after much toil and struggle,

> 'having been initiated into the mysteries of love . . . there bursts upon him that wondrous vision which is the very soul of the beauty he has toiled so long for. It is an everlasting loveliness which neither comes nor goes. . . . It takes not the form of a beautiful face . . . nor knowledge' (*Symposium*, 211[a]).

It is like 'the light of many suns' . . . 'the open sea of beauty' (*Symposium*, 210[d]), and it can never be seen by the ordinary eye (*Republic*, 518[d]), but only by the eye of the soul.

We meet with the account universally, across cultures and centuries. 'Slay your atachment to the worldly desires and you will see it', Krishna tells Arjuna.

> But thou never canst see me with these thy mortal eyes; I will give thee divine sight. Behold my wonder and glory. . . . If the light of a thousand suns suddenly arose in the sky, that splendour might be compared to the radiance of the Supreme Spirit. . . . And Arjuna saw in that radiance the whole universe in its variety, standing in a vast unity in the body of the God of Gods. (Bhagavad Gita, XI, 8, 12–13).

Going back to Greek descriptions of this experience, Proclus (1820, p. 242) writes in his commentary on the *Timaeus* about a vision of 'Father-begotten light which alone hath gathered from the strength of the father the Flower of Mind and hath the power of understanding the Paternal mind': in his *Théologie* (pp. 171–2) he had described 'a fiery whirlwind drawing down the brilliance of the flashing flame, penetrating the abysses of the Universe'.

It is clear from Plato's (*Republic*, 519[b]) account that the vision comes only to those who give up their attachments to material beauty and to all desire. The universality of the process and its description appears to rule out coincidence or copying. Writing of the Islamic (Sufi) way to vision, Zaehner (1966, p. 170) notes that no one can attain salvation without slaying all desire in sacrifice: the desiring self 'must be melted by obedience, killed by showing enmity to it . . . by despairing of all that is not God.' Before seeing the wondrous light that blinded and dazzled him, Mohammed fasted. Jesus also underwent a forty-day period of fasting and renunciation before commencing his mission. It would be simplifying the matter, however, to reduce 'desire' to the desire for food and drink. More important is the giving up of the original desire which caused the fall of man – his desire to know good and evil autonomously.

Thus Plato makes it clear that when the vision is granted it comes with the cessation of autonomous activity, 'as one is carried by God's movement'. This radical turning away from the world is implied in the single Pythagorean dictum: 'Turn around when you worship'.

Periagoge is also referred to as *Metastrophe*, which appears to be related to the Pauline *Metanoia*, and the Upanishadic *Moksha*. It occurs by divine dispensation, *Theia Moira*; and it is preceded by the consecration of one's activity to unselfish service. This can take many forms, as it is subject to historical period. It involves the offering of the fruits of one's labour, disinterested activity whereby one identifies with the interest of the object of one's activity, sacrificing any other egotistic concern. This 'specialization of labour' is also described by Lao Tzu and Confucius: the good man will do only his own work, without claiming credit, which becomes his Tao. 'When work is done for a reward, the work brings pleasure, or pain, or both, in its time; but when a man does work in Eternity, then Eternity is his reward' (Bhagavad Gita, XVIII, 12). A further parallel can be found in the New Testament: 'whatever you do, do all to the glory of God' (I Corinthians, X, 31). The above accounts all indicate that there are different kinds of knowledge, the highest of which is radically different in quality from the others – not being dependent on an autonomous effort, and being brought about through the absence, rather than the exercise, of the activity of thinking.

IV

Socrates (*Phaedo*, 67[e]):

'If a man has trained himself throughout his life to live in a state as close as possible to death, would it not be ridiculous for him to be distressed when death comes to him? . . . Then it is a fact, Simmias, that true philosophers make dying their profession'.

The 'Stygian' ('beyond') aspect of all *Logos*-oriented philosophy has received little attention in the last two centuries, in spite of the tradition that has for some two millennia seen it as central. I hope in this section to interrogate the tradition, in order to elucidate in what way philosophy is like dying.

It is not literal death, of course, but dying to the body (*Soma*), or rather to that which one falsely perceives as one's body. The body to which one dies is the body as an owned entity, the body seen as personal property, the false unity. Patanjali's *Krya* or the Greek *Soma* is akin to the entity which for Kant lies behind the unity of apperception: it both brings the self into existence and grants selfhood to the perceived unity. This 'body' is a mental body – a product of the mind.

It must always be remembered that whatever noetic thought finds objectionable about the body does not concern the true *physical* body. For every phenomenal multiplicity perceived there exists a corresponding logoistic entity which, as such, is always good: whatever comes into existence can be nothing but good. Just as white does not stand opposed to black, nor democracy to aristocracy, so the body does not stand as an inferior counter-entity to the soul. It has also been stated that for every entity there is a specific good and its specific aberration. As the sophist is to the philosopher, so is the perceived self to the real self. *Soma*, in the noetic sense, refers to the aberration of the horizontal extension of the true self. It is a false unity of needs and desires which are neither false nor imaginary in themselves, but become so when treated as if they composed a legitimate unity. Seen in the context of the city, *Soma* is that excess, that false aberration, which grafts itself onto the true person.

The body is based on a lie: it is an epistemological lie, for the body both is and creates a self which is not the self. Thus 'body' in a sense includes the mind and the thinker; indeed it is identical with that desire which brings the self-perceiving thinker into existence. This self is the desire to perpetuate the self which is not, which is identical with the desire. The penalty such self-perceiving thinkers pay is that they come to resemble the pattern which they desire (the more you think that you are something, the more you become it).

The 'philosophical death' is therefore dying to the self; not a death by the mutilation of constituent elements, but rather the dissolution of a falsely-perceived unity. The process is undertaken so that one can remodel oneself in accordance with the true pattern: this pattern is the paradigmatic city model.

This, I understand, is what Christ implied: he who would gain his life should lose it; 'For this reason the Father loves me, because I lay down my life, that I may take it again' (John, X, 17). Paul writes to the Colossians (III, 2): 'Set your minds on things that are above . . . For you have died'. Lao Tzu recommends: 'Empty yourself of everything' (Tao Te Ching, XVI) and 'the sage seeks freedom from desire. He does not collect precious things. He learns not to hold on to ideas' (Tao Te Ching, LXIV). And St John of the Cross, in *The Ascent of Mount Carmel* (I, 13): 'In order to arrive at possessing everything, desire to possess nothing. In order to arrive at knowing everything, desire to know nothing . . . In order to have pleasure in everything, desire to have pleasure in nothing.'

A further injunction is dying to formalities. The realized perfect State is characterized by its own dissolution (not necessarily in the future). The perfect mother, the perfect son and the perfect husband are dead to formal obligation. The perfect marriage is a non-marriage. None of this, however, implies the literal dissolution of States and families. The dissolution is symbolic. In saying 'I have no mother', Jesus speaks symbolically, internally.

The feeling of dying to the body is felt non-conceptually in athletics and sport: indeed, this is why for the Greeks in general, and particularly for Plato, exercise and gymnastics are constituent parts of philosophy. For the Indians, dying is taught through physical exertion in yoga – or in Tai Chi for Taoists.

A person unfamiliar with this notion may grasp it by analysing a golf shot. A golfer before striking must die to the contradictory pullings of the various parts of his body and mind. To concentrate means to die to the body. This is why the top physicist, the Greek philosopher and the Indian yogi reach similar conclusions. Having thus 'died', the golfer can execute the perfect motion that projects him on to the higher plane. There is a perfect pattern for every action and thought; when the movement executed in actuality coincides with this, the result is a 'marriage' of heaven and earth. (The reason why top athletes and golfers do not realize higher truths lies in their 'professionalization' or prostitution. Sport and athletics *are* a means to reaching the deeper truth; yet the professional sportsman is a sophist – as soon as the perfect action is over his mind is polluted by greed and the desire for money. As for amateur sportsmen, they do reach deeper; yet seldom do they achieve the degree of sophistication necessary to project them into the 'second trajectory' where sport functions as yoga or philosophy.)

V

The heavenly pattern both has a formal dimension and yet is informal; this is why Plato's Republic, if realized on a macro scale, entails the aspectual dissolution of formal social structures such as the family, tribe, fratria, parenthood, individual friendship, etc. The dissolved State is in a deeper sense the realized State. It is only in the absence of all formal divisions and walls that it becomes 'the community of pleasures and pains, the tie that binds when, so far as may be, all the citizens rejoice and grieve alike' (*Republic*, 462^{b}).

In saying 'I have come to set son against father, husband against wife', Jesus also speaks symbolically. This is made explicit by Plato, for whom the perfect family is dissolved in the psychological sense: and 'in heaven there are no husbands and wives'. The beholder of Politea fulfils the outward multiplicity of roles and duties which are other than his own – just as Socrates does not relinquish his arms at Potidea, nor does he abrogate his duties as a citizen in any sense. The philosopher in fact operates within actuality as if it were ideal, accepting its limitations. Inwardly, however, he gives up the multiplicity of roles.

This is what the citizen of the perfect city performs: he ceases to be a particular son or a particular father, but becomes a son or father in general. He gives up his family, name, wife, household and all property: in other words, he gives up the false unity which constitutes the perceived self. However, in having innerly given up everything, the perceived existence becomes actuality and reflects ideality.

The objective of philosophy, therefore, is dying; and in Politea this becomes the personal tool by which an individual fractures the false unity he perceives as his own body. Empirically, Politea as an objective political unity may or may not materialize. Those individuals who attempt individual integration materialize isolated aspects of it. In so far as several individuals actively structure their activities in accordance with an inner subjective pattern, Politea will manifest outwardly to the corresponding degree.

With this in view, we can bring to a conclusion our discussion of the paradigmatic city model. This model can be seen as serving a double function – a positive and a negative one. By comparing the structure of his own city or personality and its various manifestations with that particular pattern positively presented by Saanthana thought, the beholder perceives the false excesses and various structural aberrations characterizing the perceived *Polis*, on both the macro and the micro level – as a city and as an individual man. In the negative sense, this model is used to dissolve the unity which is falsely perceived as the self: this is why to practise philosophy is to practise dying. Considered positively, the model provides the true pattern, the pattern on which the genuine person or any social entity should be modelled. In imitating the patterns outlined, a man constitutes true units – whether in thought, speech or action – and in this way his own self. A *Logos*-constituted self is a real entity, and as such is reflective of the real identity, that of the soul. In this way, the philosopher finds himself to be citizen of a city of gods:

> 'If there is now on earth or ever should be such a society. . . . [where] all possible means have been taken to make even what nature has made our own in some sense common property; I mean if our eyes, ears and hands seem to see, hear and act in the common service. . . . If there is anywhere such a city with a number of gods or sons of gods for its inhabitants, they dwell there thus in all joyousness of life' (*Laws*, 739^{c-d}).

Part Three

MYTHOS

Eleven

THE FALL

Having established a few theoretical guidelines we may now turn to some universal myths and examine them in this light. As I see it, *Mythos* plays an integral role in our tripartite attempt to understand the world. It can positively (if analogically) complete the meaning conveyed on the one hand by misleading definition, and on the other by negative inferences. Even the atheist should recognize – and even perhaps commend – the myth as a legitimate tool for engendering and developing political *Doxa Alethes*. I shall not, however, use the myth in this last capacity: within *Logos*-based philosophy the myth does not function to create or perpetuate formal religious *Orthe Doxa*.

The myth, within the context of this tradition, acquired a role other than allegorical, and yet not simply theological. Looking at the *Mythos-Logos* synthesis, the *Mythos* can be seen as necessary to destabilize the positive formulations of the parallel philosophical exposition, while the theoretical exposition serves to annul the external props of the *Mythos* and to reduce the message to its abstract kernel. In the following, I shall examine the mythological aspect of sentiment as the ruling principle of the mythological age of perfect existence. In so doing, we shall obtain an overview of what may be termed 'the human condition'.

I

J. Wild (1976, pp. 39–44) identifies the fundamental human condition as one of estrangement or inversion. It manifests itself through a misapprehension, an epistemological transposition in which means are confused for ends. This situation – in which predicates are confused with the unities they predicate, instances with ideas, has already been described above.

In *Patterns of Comparative Religion*, Eliade (1958, p. 274) quotes Masudi, citing a Sabaean tradition according to which man is seen as a plant turned upside down, his roots stretching to heaven and his branches into the earth. *Anatrope* or inversion, as the essential characteristic of human experience, is also expressed by the inverted tree symbol, and traces of this image can be found in the *Statesman* and *Timaeus* (90^b):

> 'and inasmuch as we are a plant not of an earthly but of heavenly growth, [God] raises us from earth to our kindred who are in heaven. And in this we say truly, for the divine power suspends the head and root of us from that place where the generation of the soul first began.'

The Bhagavad Gita (XV, 1), too, talks of a 'tree of Transmigration, the Asvattha tree everlasting. Its roots are above in the Highest, and its branches are here below.'

The myth of the *Politicus* (269), like the Dravidian myths of the backward-flowing river of life, presents the perceived universe as moving in the opposite direction to that intended by God. The meaning is not that the universe itself exhibits this inversion in motion; the *Anatrope* is an epistemological inversion, created by the perceiving mind. This interpretation – as opposed to one which stresses the literal counter-movement of the universe – may be inferred from the *Timaeus* (90^c–d):

> 'And the motions which are naturally akin to the divine principle in us are the thoughts and revolutions of the universe; these each man should follow, and by learning the harmonies and revolutions of the universe should correct the courses of the head which were corrupted at our birth, and should assimilate the thinking being to the thought.'

Human thought, then, moves counter to the divine movement. It should be arrested in its own movement and assimilated by the thinking being, who ought to reflect the process of divine thought.

The person thinking 'counter-cosmically', that is, the person who follows the mental movement given to him by the mind rather than attempting to reverse this in order to follow the noetic faculty, is compared to a man walking in reverse, and also to a man turned upside down:

> 'as you might imagine a person who is upside down, and has his head leaning upon the ground and his feet up in the air, and when in such a position both he and his spectators [probably he means fellow prisoners in the cave] fancy that the right of either is his left and the left right' (*Timaeus*, 43^d–e).

Things, however, were not always so: as claimed in all these myths, there was, or rather there is, a time when things were perceived as they indeed are; however, due to some 'ancient sin', man has fallen: he no longer perceives the truth.

Chuang Tzu (in Waltham, 1971, p. 187) describes the state of nature before the Fall:

> The men of old, while the chaotic condition was yet undeveloped, shared the placid tranquillity which belonged to the whole world. At that time the yin and yang were harmonious and still; their resting and movement proceeded without any disturbance; the four seasons had their definite times; not a single thing received any injury, and no living being came to a premature end. Men might be possessed of the faculty of knowledge, but they had no occasion for its use.

The reason for the departure from this condition, according to the Taoists, was man's decision to take things into his own hands: his activity ceased to be spontaneous.

The Fall is a universal mythological notion, which finds expression in remarkably similar imagery throughout history. Pindar derives his account from the same sources as the Pythagoreans: 'Being of God, the soul is necessarily immortal, but immersed in the body because of ancient sin' (Stewart, 1960, p. 92). This sin, we later learn, is that of self-assertion (hubris). In Anaximander's view, men are being punished for struggling against each other. The correct course of action lies in relinquishing the struggle and accepting the destiny assigned us by the gods. All things are struggling, for all are in rebellion against the destiny assigned to them:

> Gradually the moisture will be partly dried up, partly evaporated until in the end all things will have returned into the undifferentiated *Apeirion* . . . in order to pay the penalty for their injustice, that of having struggled against one another (in Simplicius, *On Physics*, 26.16 ex.1; see Seligman, 1962, p. 66).

Anaximander is certainly not the first author to introduce the notion of the Fall into philosophy. He was, however, the first in the Western tradition to make the Fall essentially an epistemological matter. As I interpret him, he was also the first to view it as a perpetually reccurring event.

Before continuing this analysis, it is important to point out that (unlike many contemporary interpreters) Anaximander did not feel that men were being punished by God: they were punishing themselves through their own self-chosen estrangement. Turning to Plato, we cannot assume that Plato's gods – or the God beyond gods – were indifferent to man's plight: 'We are now to admonish him who confesses the being of gods, but denies that they take any heed of the affairs of men' (*Laws*, 899^{e}). As for the God beyond gods, we observe that the great God of the *Timaeus*

(29[e]–30[a]) is not the non-desiring, perfect entity he was for Aristotle. The God beyond gods, though perfect, is not free of desire:

> 'Let me tell you, then, why the creator made this world of generation. He was good, and the good can never have any jealousy of anything. And, being free from jealousy, he desired that all things should be like him as they could be . . . God desired that all things be good and nothing bad.'

II

Most accounts dealing with the 'original' condition of man and his subsequent estrangement have used the notion of God. The myth can also be presented without God – as it is by Buddhists and Marxists – yet the basic elements are the same. I do not wish to offend anybody who has been psychologically conditioned to violently oppose (or endorse) the word God, but the study would become impossibly complicated if I had to qualify it every time it occurred in a quoted text.

The concept of God is neutral currency: it can be used or misused. The merchant (appetitive) element, as manifested in the last few centuries, has used the concept of God to maintain the legitimacy of a certain set of social arrangements. Trying to imbalance the social-political structure hiding behind this particular set of conceptualizations, humanistically oriented thinkers have eroded this specific set of assumptions. The strategy was correctly motivated; empirically, however, it has failed. One does not change people or societies by substituting one set of concepts for another. In calling the notions of goodness, justice or love by new names, the removers of God committed no offence against God; in so far as this notion is meaningful, God can be 'offended' only by adding to the suffering of living beings. But in assuming that a new set of conceptualizations would cure social evils, the conceptualists have misled themselves and those who thought like them – in this respect they did indeed add to human suffering, by creating false expectations. The merchant, greedy, exploitative element has adapted – and always will adapt – itself to the new concepts. Whereas formerly exploitation (imperialism, etc.) was carried out in the name of God, Western civilization or whatever, today it is carried out in the name of democracy, the 'rights of man', or one 'ism' against another.

I am not interested here in pointing fingers, for there is nowhere to point – all nations, societies and individuals contain both true and false elements. As soon as a new set of conceptualizations is invented, the epithumic element instantly adjusts us to it. Rather than unbalancing a particular set of conceptualizations, Saanthana-based thought is oriented towards unbalancing a certain set of *sentiments*. 'For we are not contending against flesh and blood, but against . . . the spiritual hosts of wickedness' (Ephesians, VI, 12). Certainly such is the message of the Bhagavad Gita, where whoever fights with a pure heart is fighting on Krishna's side. Sides and flags are historically determined: not so the sentiment.

In Hindu and Platonic thought, the notion of God is used to designate the creator of the good sentiment. Whether this is in fact created or is beginningless is once again a conceptual issue: the important fact is that at any given moment the correct sentiment *is*. The correct sentiment, we observed, is simply that which brings together entities which are true. Exactly which particular forms of society or concepts are true is a new decision for each epoch; only the principle remains the same.

Whether seen as that which is good in man or good in the cosmos, Plato's God is the origin of desire – and his desire is that all things be good, i.e. that all things be like him. In view of this, it cannot be God who caused man's loss of circumstance. Man's demise was due to a fall, and this fall was not part of the life that God had planned for man.

Plato describes the garden of Eden or Age of Cronus (*Cratylus*, 402; *Gorgias*, 523; *Laws*, 713; *Statesman*, 269–76), before the state of *Anatrope*, as one in which men live in perfect harmony with each other and with the beasts; there is no toil or strife, and all eat of the fruits of the trees, which are freely given. For St Gregory of Nyssa, this state is free of evil sentiments such as lust; procreation is painless and not physical (Daniélou, 1944, p. 52). All living beings are bound by love, and animals, like men, are vegetarian and live in peace with each other (*Statesman*, 269–76).

The Fall involves a fragmentation of human personality as a result of some kind of rebellion against the ways of the gods (Pieper, 1952, p. 153). Man assumes that he can, by conceptual thought, determine what is good for him. Conceptual thought, as was correctly pointed out by Kant and Descartes, always brings into existence the individual, socially isolated, sense of 'I'. In other words, we cannot think conceptually without creating the ego-based entity. All conceptual thought stems from the parekbasitic or deviant side of the appetitive faculty. To think conceptually is to think in terms of what is good for *me*. There is a separation between 'me' and 'thou', and an underlying assumption that 'me' can only profit by maximizing the well-being of the entity which 'me' conceptualizes as 'myself'. In a world of scarcity, this means that your loss is my gain: hence 'Homo homini lupus'. In a way, it is this assumption that creates scarcity.

As soon as man starts to reckon in terms of what is good or not, he is no longer accepting, but calculating himself what is good for him. In so doing he brings into existence an altogether different entity from that which he truly is, and finds himself perceiving an altogether different world from that intended for him by his true nature – his Atman – whose command he has decided to replace by the autonomous activity of *Dianoia*.

One might also trace the Fall to the expression in greed of the epithumic or 'lower' soul. This aberration first occurs on the mental level, then affecting the arousal of thought and decision. It was through the excesses of the lower soul that the thought that something other than that ordained by God – the maker of true entities – might be good for man occurred to Eve, and that she began to perceive the tree as good to eat from (Zaehner, 1964, p. 138). And, finally, the Fall was a result of the arousal of evil sentiment. The evil sentiments are seven or rather six, all contained in the one comprehensive Evil Sentiment. These deadly 'sins' or 'mental movements' are Lust, Envy, Anger, Greed, Pride, Sloth and Gluttony, brought into the world through Eve, the female principle. It was a Pythagorean teaching too that all evil stems from the seven movements of the female or of the left; these were seen as dark, crooked and oblong, and equated with bad and irrational numbers (Cleve, 1965, p. 503).

One may find the notion that evil stems from the female principle objectionable, but it must be pointed out that in Saanthana-based thought true beings are in a sense asexual, since they contain both the male and the female principles in their undifferentiated unity. Thus the notion of evil stemming from the left, from the female should be equally objectionable to both men and women. Simone Weil sees the estrangement of the female principle as the cause of sexual lust, and interprets the Fall in these terms. In this she follows Eryxymachus, who identifies the separation of heavenly and earthly forces in the body as the cause of all disease – mental, moral and physical. Lust is the attempt to rejoin the separated parts, but in the wrong way. 'Right' and 'left', in general, symbolize the gods of heaven and earth. The object of building temples has traditionally been to effect the remarriage of these two principles in the correct manner (see Patai, 1974). More recent thought sees the process as the historical realization of the true man: at the moment, man is asunder.

Estrangement is a fact of the human condition. The particular point being developed here is that the cause of this estrangement is not rooted in anything external to man, and therefore the remedy is not to be sought in external rearrangements. Nor is internal contemplation enough – the point is that the notions 'internal' and 'external' are false. It is the destruction of noetically derived spiritual truth by the conceptual mind that causes the fall of the city, the fall of man and, in the final stage, the fall of philosophy and of thinking itself (see Heidegger, 1968, p. 211).

Before the Fall there was no fear or 'self-consciousness'. It was conceptual thinking that created the unnatural, autonomous individual, as the Greek dramatists realized (see Oehler, 1962, pp. 2–3).

III

We are all sophists and conceptualists from time to time, or in one respect or another. It is only symbolically that we can place a sophist against a philosopher. As an *Eidos*, the philosopher or king is a locus; instances of individuals and their actions are points on that locus. It is in this sense that various individuals may predicate a single *Eidos* such as the statesman, the shepherd, the doctor, etc.

The non-alienated society is a society of such paradigmatic *Eidos*-individuals, a city composed of 'abstract', specialized, functionally defined eidetic specimens, in which actual individuals participate. No such model should be confused with a perfect instance: any positive picture of the 'best' society can be only a *pattern*, and not an exhaustive one; it simply outlines one dimension of the city. An idealized vision is only aspectually different from the actual. The ideal man is not physically perfect; in the *Symposium* (215[b]) the ideal Socrates still looks like Marsyus.

This point is dramatically illustrated by Plato. Plato's ideal city is the mythical Athens described in the *Menexenus*, *Timaeus* and *Critias*. Opposed to this ideal stands its mythical counterpart, the 'perfectly evil' city of Atlantis. The perceived (as opposed to actual) Athens-in-time may alternatively participate in either of these cities. The Athens of *Menexenus* is therefore in a sense the actual Athens; as such, however, it is different from the perfect-instance Athens, where everybody is healthy, only the wisest rule, etc. – the utopia. The Athens of *Menexenus* suffers from all the imperfections of the instantiated Athens, Athens-in-time, the perceived Athens; it utilizes the imperfect courts, its politicians take bribes, the aristocrats are low born. Socrates, who is not blind to its corruption, claims that nevertheless:

> 'Then as now, and indeed always from that time to this, speaking generally, our government was an aristocracy; although it receives various names according to the fancies of men, and is sometimes called democracy, it is really an aristocracy' (*Menexenus*, 238[c]).

To Socrates his city is worthy of all love, praise and sacrifice.

Socrates' statement is often interpreted as sarcastic; yet, given the fact that he fought bravely for Athens, and laid down his life rather than to break her laws, the accusation of sarcasm, as I see it, must be incorrect. The patriot who lays down his life for king or country need not be blind to the failings of the particular man, group of men or organization perceived: it is the sophist who claims that one should adapt one's conduct to suit the perceived situation. The Athens of *Menexenus* is the actual as against the perceived Athens; and it is with the actual Athens that both Plato and Socrates, in the final analysis, identified. Athens thus conceived becomes the eternal city, whose psychological and structural dimensions are given by the models developed in the *Laws* and the *Republic*. The philosopher is not above his city, his nation, his Party or his Church, for all their limitations. As against the city in the sky there stands its counter-model, the 'lived' city, and it is within this that the decisive action takes place. The mark of the Saanthana-based thinker is that for all his generalizations in favour of the non-conceptual, he can never hold himself to be too good to serve institutions. Even if he decides that he 'knows better ' than his appointed rulers, he is forced to put up with the hardships involved in this – which can in some cases be as extreme as those experienced by Socrates and Jesus.

IV

As we may gather from the teachings of Jesus, neither those who have been given six coins in life nor those who have been given only one need rejoice or grieve over their destiny: from those with six coins, more will be expected.

The principle can readily be observed operating in any age or society. A woman given a particularly beautiful body may use, or rather misuse, it to make a living. However, from the noetic standpoint the body is not hers – it is a temple, and its owner is a temple keeper. While the temple keeper may steal the offerings in the temple, noetic thought observes that such action will inevitably be punished.

A particularly sumptuous and famous temple may receive huge offerings, whereas a modest village church receives much less. For the honest temple keeper who will not steal from the offerings, it is immaterial whether he is put in charge of a large or a small temple. The large temple means more work, yet presumably there is a compensating satisfaction in that. As for the financial returns, every keeper should receive only what they genuinely need. The fact that individual A has objectively done more work than individual B will not result in a higher payment in the ultimate sense. In Jesus' parable, some men worked in the vineyard all day, others did only one hour's work – yet at the end of the day their payment is the same.

The validity of this principle is not to do with belief or absence of belief in God; it is based on a law of nature, and can equally well be expressed in terms of biology or psychology. But let us first look at its mythical expression: to do this, we must examine the notion of the Cross.

Because of an ancient sin, man is cursed to productivity through the overcoming of a certain amount of resistance. No matter what he does, or where he lives, he is given a fixed weight which he must carry a fixed distance. Plato calls this *Anangke*. Each of us has to overcome a certain amount of resistance or friction; this can also be pictured as a quantity of dirt that we have to dig out. *Anangke*, too, is caused by some ancient, universal sin.

Marx does not regard alienation as a punishment for sin, but he does take it as a historical given. For Marx, to become what he really is, a man must define himself through labour: only in overcoming the material resistances of the environment does he activate psychological and biochemical cleansing processes. A team of contemporary Soviet physiotherapists has determined that, in order to function correctly, the body must daily secrete a fixed amount of toxic substances and sweat, and must undergo a fixed amount of evaporation. These cleansing processes are not only physical, for they involve a corresponding mental strain. Similar studies have been made in the West, linking activities like jogging with psychological and mental well-being. You may employ a machine to dig holes, but you may not employ a machine to jog on your behalf.

In Plato's account of the body in *Timaeus*, in Chinese traditions as well as in Aurovedic medicine, the nerve channels, veins and arteries are rivers carrying *Prana* or *Chi*, which continually and daily flood, throwing out phlegm, debris and other toxic substances. This phlegm is not only physical. Yoga in India includes physical exercise, meditation and work (Karma yoga): to be whole, man must daily purify all three systems.

In view of this, we may understand why a yogi is indifferent to external gifts such as gold or money. No amount of gold can purchase a slave who can run, exercise and do the other two kinds of yoga for him. The man who ceases to exercise, i.e. to strive to overcome, will inevitably be destroyed: the three polluting aspects of the bodily, mental and psychic networks will carry on polluting the body, mind and soul until he is destroyed. In very simple terms, to win in 'the lottery of life' does not, and cannot, make life any easier. The only way is to daily purify the body, mind and soul by the three kinds of yoga. Physical exertion purifies the physical body, and to an extent the mental body; mental exertion, of the right kind, purifies the nervous system; moral exertion purifies the soul-energy system.

Modern medicine may discover substances that will, if injected into the body, neutralize toxic substances accumulated through lack of physical exertion. It is possible that in the future one could, without running or exercising, be given the elated, 'high' feeling of a man who has just scaled a mountain. However, the law of Karma is such that this chemical 'high' inevitably causes disequilibrium in the nerve and soul-energy systems. For this simple reason, there are no short-cuts. The search for a magical formula, for the 'philosopher's stone' which will turn lead into gold, and all the efforts of alchemy or palmistry which should enable man to win on the horses, will end in failure. So, too, will the attempt to solve the problem of toiling humanity with technology: in not too distant a time men will laugh at us the way we laugh at the naive medieval alchemists. There will never be an injection which can create a balance in all three systems. Technology cannot overcome Karma: the Cross is a biological, psychological and noetic fixity.

But is man, therefore, condemned to pain and suffering? The noetic answer is an emphatic 'no'. The perfect life is an ever-present possibility. The law of the Cross, the curse, operates only for the false individual, i.e. the individual constituted by desire. In the moment where the false 'I' becomes the true I, man is free of Karma. This does not mean that machines are doing all the work: the running, the work, the overcoming is still undertaken by the individual; but he no longer suffers. He likes his work, he enjoys the Cross. The Cross is only aspectually a cross – seen noetically, it is fulfilment through labour in love.

In view of this we may understand the meaning of progress in technology for noetic thought. Real progress does not mean inventing machines to minimize labour: it must necessarily include progress in attitudes *towards* work. Technological progress must include progress in psychological working conditions. Just as there cannot be an amoral philosophy or science, there cannot be an amoral technology. Today's concept of the machine is fundamentally false, for it is not rooted in genuine human needs. The technology of the future may involve a return to sailing boats, manual labour and the drastic reduction of energy consumption. The massive injections of natural energy by which the West is attempting to avoid physical exertion and labour cannot but distort the psychological and moral well-being of the West. What holds true for the individual holds true for a society: nobody can live at the expense of others. Earth and her natural resources are part of the system, and can be exploited only for so long.

V

In actuality no city, person or ideology is perfectly good or bad; each participates both in the good and in the bad. In writing, however, one creates the perfect abstraction: hence the perennial battle between Vohu Manu and Ahriman, the New Jerusalem and Babylon, the eternal Athens and Atlantis. Athens, of course, wins in the end. According to the *Timaeus*, the good city has already defeated its cosmic opponent, but men have forgotten it: Hegel, too, writes that the absolute is already realized but it takes history for men to perceive this. (For Plato knowledge is remembering: though forgetting and remembering have no chronological significance, since reality is out of time.) This victory was 'The greatest action which the Athenians ever did, and which ought to have been the most famous, but through the lapse of time and the destruction of the actors has not come down to us' (*Timaeus*, 21[a]).

Atlantis is said to have been the greatest of all cities before becoming the Anti-city:

> Atlantis was the worst possible city Plato could conceive. And for one reason: it lacked a *principle of limitation*. 'Self-limitation' is the most important Socratic principle, applicable to individuals as well as to states . . . it reached a population of 12,960,000 in just four generations (McClain, 1978, pp. 161–2).

The psychological condition of Atlantis is *Pleonexia*, which Friedlander (1969, p. 439) sees as 'a cosmic disturbance . . . [like] sickness or plague . . . it transgresses the limits set for each thing. Pleonexia is its common name applied to the human soul or to its element in nature.'

Clinias in the *Laws* (625[e]–626[a]) cannot be seen as representing the ignorant Spartan, to be corrected by the sophisticated Athenian: he is here one of the many spokesmen for the manifoldness of reality, reproving

> 'the folly of mankind who refuse to understand that they are engaged in a continuous lifelong warfare against all cities whatsoever . . . the peace of which most men talk is no more than a name – in real fact, the normal attitude of a city to all other cities is one of underhand warfare.'

The Athenian makes a similar comment, observing that all creatures have a distinctive appetite for limitless gratification in food, drink and sex and are furiously defiant of any restrictions to their pleasure (*Laws*, 782[e]). In the *Republic* the inner condition of the tyrant is described in terms of *Pleonexia*. From the present point of view, *Pleonexia* is simply an abrogated movement of the psyche-soul. Like the arrogance, or rather the existential fear, of the sophist, it reduces to an abstract, impersonal sentiment common to Athens as to Babylon or any individual: 'In fact, there exists in every one of us . . . a terrible, fierce and lawless brood of desires' (*Republic*, 572[b]).

Thus the struggle between Athens and Atlantis is perpetually re-enacted in each and every city. Each person by every noble act strikes a blow for Athens, and in doing so ceases to be the citizen of the perceived city and becomes the citizen of Politea, the Republic (see *Timaeus*, 26d).

The fate of Atlantis, which sank beneath the sea, illustrates another of the most universal myths. The Fall results eventually in a Flood or Deluge. Plato's account of this is typical: men became wicked, so the gods became angry and flooded the earth, allowing the survival only of the few who kept their commands. But Plato makes it quite clear that this Flood is a continually recurring event, to which every 'city' that comes into existence is necessarily subject. The Athenian, in the *Laws*, (676c–677a) is looking for an explanation of the passing away of cities, and finds it in a myth:

> 'And you will surely grant that thousands and thousands of cities have come into being during this time, and not less a number have ceased to exist. Thus we have, if possible, to discover the cause of these variations; there, I suspect, we will find the key. . . . Very well, then, let us suppose one of those various exterminations, that which was once effected by the Flood.'

'And what is the point you would have us observe about it?' asks Clinias. The answer is that only those who live higher up survive the Flood, whereas those who descend are swept away.

The 'coming to be' of the city is relatively easy to understand. Men come together to satisfy genuine interests. This takes place on a high level: the citizens are *up*, they keep on the high ground, living a healthy life, eating cheese and drinking their wine in a way reflective of the idyllic existence of the healthy city in the *Republic* (372). The citizens are neither poor nor rich, there is no shortage of food, 'they were quite well off for clothes, bedding, shelter and vessels, culinary or other, nor were they sick; in fact they had what they needed' (*Laws*, 679b). As in the *Republic*, the city at this healthy stage needs keep no armies or police, nor has it law courts, since disputes do not arise; religion and tradition substitute for law, and all disputes are settled by inner reconciliation (*Laws*, 679b-680a).

As the city expands, a difference emerges between those who stay on the higher ground because they are natural high-dwellers, and those who are kept up in the heights only by the fear and the memory of the flooding waters: 'Indeed, they were still haunted, I should presume, by a terror of coming down from the highlands to the plains' (*Laws*, 678c). The natural high-dwellers remain on high because they refrain from discursive thought; their thinking is reduced to the performance of their duties and it entered nobody's head to start accounting for moral values in terms of conjectural though (*Dianoia*). They interpret the world non-conceptually, and believe what they are told in myths:

> 'Thus they were good men, [partly because they were free from greed

> and partly] from their proverbial simplicity; they were so simple that when they heard things called fair or foul they obediently took the statements for infallible truths. No one was sufficiently subtle to suspect deception, as men do today; what they were told about God or man they believed to be true, and lived by it' (*Laws*, 679[c–d]).

Plato is, of course, being ironic in referring to the high-dwellers as simple-minded for believing without questioning. That this attitude is not the mark of a simpleton is vouched for in the *Phaedrus* (229[c]–230[a]) by Socrates, who proclaims himself just such a simpleton:

> 'Just imagine, then [he tells Phaedrus, talking of belief in gods and legends], if everybody would want to say 'I don't believe in it.' First I want to make everything probable and rational. . . . But, my friend, I don't have time for it. I don't even know myself . . . so I do not dwell on these matters, and believe them like everybody else.'

It is the so-called men of wisdom, 'the ones with time for such questioning', who are responsible for the erosion of the myth and the demystification of the fear of the Flood. They demystify the myths which had acted as a safeguard against the expansion of desires. Exposed to this barrage of rational criticism, men gradually lose their fear of the Flood and start the descent – the creation of the luxurious city. This fall of the city is reflected by the increasing differentiation of functions and roles to cater for false needs which have come to be seen as essential. Sophists are hired to perform the mental inversion, and the downward movement is called progress. Symbolically, the process is a descent from the mountain peaks to highlands, and further down to the rich valleys and the rivers (*Laws*, 682[b]). The Athenian makes it clear that men never quite lose their memory of the Flood, and try to maintain some distance from the river to the very end. Yet the descent of men is paralleled by the ascent of the waters, which eventually engulf and sweep away the lower cities. The natural high-dwellers are not affected, and it is they who are the survivors, left to start new cities and re-create the whole process.

The disintegrating process starts when the epithumic, desiring self, the river of Lethe, affects the mass of citizens. To cater for the 'needs' they have discovered, they are obliged to descend to the rich pastures of trade, commerce and the fashioning of luxuries. This, however, is forbidden by ethical and religious imperatives – by the gods. The Flood rises from 'the abhorred Styx', parekbasitic, epithumic desire, potentially present in every city, has been loosed into art, politics and philosophy, through the mediative activity of the sophist, who makes it respectable. Desire rises upward, conceptual thought descends; thought based on false needs creates the *Anatrope*, the inversion. *Pleonexia* is bitter-sweet: like a drug it destroys, but by a perverse mutation it is felt as pleasant. The Flood is internal. The downfall of States is caused by a 'dissonance between pleasure and pain, on the one hand, and reasoned opinion, on the other' (*Laws*, 689[a]).

VI

But what are these rivers that Plato, among others, refers to? Are we sure that he meant to refer to universal processes of psychological existence, or were they the product of an inadequate geographical and historical knowledge? In the *Timaeus* they are explicitly identified with forces in the mind and body; that he knows he is speaking in mythological terms is borne out by Socrates in the *Phaedo* (114[d]): 'Of course, no reasonable man ought to insist that the facts are exactly as I have described them'.

Seven streams are mentioned: Oceanus, Thetys, Acheron, Pyrphlegeton, Styx, Cocytus and Lethe (*Timaeus*, 40[e]; *Republic*, 621; *Theaetetus*, 152; *Cratylus*, 402; *Phaedo*, 112).

> 'One of the cavities in the earth . . . pierces right through from one side to the other . . . Tartarus. Into this gulf all the rivers flow together. The cause of the flowing in and out of all these streams is that the mass of liquid has no bottom or foundation; so it oscillates and surges to and fro, and the air or breath that belongs to it does the same' (*Phaedo*, 112[a]).

In the *Timaeus* (79[e]) the human body is said to be kept alive by breathing in fire, which is transported by the blood, cooled and exhaled. Disease is due to toxic phlegm leaving its 'river bed' and wandering around the bloodstream (*Timaeus*, 82[e]). In the *Phaedo* (112), the inner workings of the earth are equated with those of the human organism. The seven streams flow either upward or downward – the latter movement is necessary for the removal of waste from the bloodstream, but when it leaves its natural bed it is this stream that pollutes the body. Good and bad are, as usual, aspectual: the river of desire, Lethe, the crossing of which is the object of the *Republic*, is the 'Well of Jacob' whose water arouses thirst – yet the philosopher's thirst is quenched by it, for he apprehends it differently.

Thetys, Lethe, the Styx, flow downwards to Tartarus or Hades; they are yin, the indefinite dyad, *Dianoia*. Aristotle – and after him Speussipus and Alexander – identify this downward movement with the origin of evil. But it is not evil in itself; it is simply a flow of toxic matter, which yet can fertilize the earth whenever it is released in a flood. The element of evil lies with the men who leave high ground for the fertile lowlands, ignoring all the myths that warn them of the inevitable consequences. The downward river is what Dionysius the Areopagite calls the stream of Particular Being, while the upward is Universal Being: the two flow from the same source, and 'Neither of these two streams has any independent or concrete existence: taken separately they are mere potentialities.' They meet in a third, the *Chora*; potentiality becomes actuality in an instant, an instant which is outside time: 'a region beyond Time and Space. That region is thus their receptacle. The receptacle [*Chora*], if emptied of them (though this is impossible), would contain nothing' (Rolt, in Dionysius, 1940, p. 14). For *Chora* is nothing but actuality, the coming-to-be of potentialities.

The upward-tending stream, Oceanus, is *Noesis*, yang, apprehension by direct vision. It is by riding the upward way that one ascends from Hades (see Sallis, 1975, p. 454). The Fall – movement in the wrong direction – happens to each of us again and again. It can be reversed, but only by cultivation of the correct feelings and thoughts.

Twelve

CURING THE CITY

The Sick Aristocrat, the man infected with *Pleonexia*, is a masochist. He enjoys the destruction of what he holds most dear. However, for *Pfonos* to be experienced as pleasure the mind must undergo a prior period of conditioning. This process has its parallel in the history of philosophy, for particular movements in thought mirror those in society.

I

The basic goal of merchant thought is to find what is true for *me*, good for *me*. The self has been separated from the world, the knowing faculty inverted, by the insertion between me and my knowledge of the world of an intermediary agent: false self, media, television, academe. Between me and the satisfaction of my needs stands the market. To know the world one needs to consume the services of television and press. To know history one needs to consume the services of historians. Direct access to information is made difficult through the inventions of specialized languages and jargon. Noetic thought maintains that all men already know everything – within himself each carries the complete history of mankind. To realize this knowledge all we need to do is concentrate: good books simply act as triggers to remind us of this knowledge. This is diametrically opposed to the market idea of knowledge, where each individual possesses only one fragment, and purchases the next through a State- or class-controlled medium of exchange.

The commercialization of human needs is alienation or the Flood. The assumption behind the division of labour is that for a duration of hours a person labours at his job so that he can purchase the products of other people. The failings of this idea from the economic viewpoint have been exposed by others. My own criticism of it would be that the purchase of culture or of entertainment implies toil-free consumption. This is just not realistic. Learning to sing or to dance requires the overcoming of pain, self-discipline – perhaps dieting and special exercises. The hunger of restlessness, *Pleonexia*, must be overcome if we are to learn to sing, run or dance, and this involves a kind of concentration which destroys the egoistic self. Even to appreciate a good wine, let alone complicated work of music, takes some degree of mastery over *Pleonexia*. The true connoisseur is neither glutton nor tyrant, for to enjoy anything one needs to overcome epithumic desire. Enjoyment is the feeling that accompanies the fulfilment of the true as against the false self.

A merchant State is characterized by *Pleonexia* and dominated by the market. Commercialization and professionalization result in an increase in quality only in the very first phase of the disintegrating process. The commercialized and functionally specialized individual loses his capacity for self-moderation, and is consequently unable to enjoy good food, music or wine. The merchant State is not luxurious, and no true material needs are satisfied. The merchant does not chew properly, but gulps his food; he cannot sip wine, and therefore develops pungent, acid-sharp, bitter-sweet drinks and junk food. Culture itself is gulped.

The merchant State cultivates desire, forgetting that all enjoyment is based on overcoming desire. As soon as the merchants take over a society desire and its satisfaction becomes the organizing force. Desires, however, cannot be gratified infinitely, owing to obvious physical limitations. Only so much food can be consumed. In order to eliminate this constraint the merchant State introduces further refinements. The Romans employed special masseurs to induce vomiting during large meals. Roman houses had special aqueducts for this purpose in their banquet rooms. Similar techniques were developed to induce miscarriages. More recently, the bourgeois State has invented the calorie-free soft drink, the contraceptive pill, etc. All these developments are inevitably labelled as progress in the standard of living, yet inevitably they lead to the breakdown of the nation, the economy and even the weather. The cosmos is such a finely balanced system that no being may artificially increase its capacity for consumption without causing disequilibrium and harm to itself.

As *Pleonexia* spreads through the man-city, there arises the need for some kind of mental reconciliation. Such excess causes a physical pain, which on the mental level takes the form of feelings of shame. As the merchant State creates the professional vomit-inducers, so likewise it creates the specialists for removing shame and placating alienated consciousness. For the Romans to be able to enjoy spectacles of sodomy, torture and man-eating, much groundwork had first to be done by trained sophists.

Sophistry is as prevalent today as in fifth-century Athens. The sophist is the desiring or the merchant element of the man-*Polis*; he does away with the ethically based injunctions that restrict commerce and stand in the way of material enrichment or pleasure.

Thought, divorced from the noetic or ethical vision, turns into sophistry, as T.S.Eliot (in Pieper, 1952, pp. 14–15) realized:

> The root cause of the vagaries of modern philosophy – and perhaps, though I was unconscious of it, the reason for my dissatisfaction with philosophy as a *profession* – I now believe to lie in the divorce of philosophy from theology.

Like 'Platonic love' and 'idea', the term 'sophist' has acquired meanings little related to any notion that may be meaningful for an understanding of ancient Greek thought. The distinction between the sophist and the philosopher does not depend upon the latter's more rigid adherence to the rules of formal logic, nor with his intellectual superiority, and certainly not with his winning or losing arguments. If formal logicality is not the criterion by which philosophy is to be distinguished from sophistry, one may perhaps agree with Gauss (1937, Introduction) that sincerity and the desire for truth are the decisive factors: 'For, to put it bluntly, . . . philosophy is essentially nothing but a sincere love of truth.' But even the notions 'truth' and 'sincerity' require elaboration. The truth that Gauss refers to, like Plato's 'logic', is an inner, deeper, moral truth. The distinction between the sophist and the philosopher will not be in the form of a positive, formulaic, performed superiority; it will be an inner, ethical one.

The sophist is a creator of false images, a liar of a particular kind: he is an inner liar, practising the art of self-deception. The sophist, a professional deceiver who will deceive for a fee, needs first to deceive himself. Even in his professional capacity as a deceiver of others, the others are willing victims: they pay the sophist to facilitate the self-deception for which they long.

Whether in his private or professional capacity, the activity of the sophist can be shown to stem from the specific sentiments of greed, arrogance and fear, all tied up in the love of the false self.

> 'The attachment to self is the constant source of all manner of misdeeds in every one of us. The eye of love is blind where the beloved is concerned, and so a man proves a bad judge of right good honour, in the conceit that more regard is due to his personality . . . whereas the

man who means to be a great man must care neither for self nor for its belongings' (*Laws*, 732).

Sophistry, then, is the deceiving tendency present in every man, the mercenary aspect of the mind ready to cater as the rationalizing agent to the excesses of *Thumos*. The sophist is the persuader: he assumes he can know, hence he starts with a definite proposition, a fixed system or a set of values, created for an internal aspect of the tyrant, such as love of self, or an external tyrant on whose command the sophist creates an ideology. Opposed to persuasion stands *Noesis*: the philosopher cannot simply persuade, since he knows that he himself does not know. Real knowledge flows: it is forever being born anew, and the philosopher must perpetually, from moment to moment, from situation to situation, seek to discover the truth. This is the so-called maieutic dimension of philosophy, the art in which each of the participants learns for himself (Versenyi, 1963).

For the sophist, though, self-gratification is the measure and criterion for all things. In the *Theaetetus*, Socrates sarcastically observes that were the sophist to confine his judgement to the taste of food, he might be able to make a case for his usefulness; but since he is a sick man, his success even in that field is unlikely. The sophist is the pastry cook, delighting the children and himself, caring nothing for nourishment (*Gorgias*, 505[a]). It is the sophist who demands that self-gratification be taken as the criterion in judging art, poetry and philosophy. When this criterion is indeed accepted, either through commercialization or tyranny, the city's downward-moving *Dianoia* overtakes the noetic faculty: pleasure becomes the ultimate criterion for all judgements, even the mathematical, ethical and scientific, and people like Mithaecus and Apollodorus and Sarambus, popular entertainers (Gorgias, 518[b]), become the final authorities on important questions in life. Democracies have a tendency to ask soccer players and film stars for guidance, simply because they represent the market.

Whether any particular philosophy is sophistry or not has to do not only with the author but with the reader. Read and believed for its content it is false. Like an icon, true philosophy should conduct the mind away from its own form. The Muslim theologian, Wahabi, describes four sources of idolatry (*Shirk*). The first is epistemological (*L'ilm*): the source of wisdom is identified with the picture of God rather than with God. The second involves giving to people things and ideas qualities that ought to be ascribed to God (*L'ibdah*). Both of these were familiar to Plato. The other two sources are *L'adah*, superstition, and *Tasawurf*, the assumption that anybody can influence the ways of God. For example, the sophist witch-doctor of today assumes that technology can influence cosmic law, changing the basic equations to allow men to break traditional taboos.

Plato's attack on sophism is far from mild. The sophist assumes his philosophy is the source of knowledge, whereas noetic thinkers have no philosophy that gives knowledge. Sophists teach that through their philosophy one may gain favours in this life, and then bribe the gods to ensure one's well-being in the next (this is the philosophy of Trasymachus in the second book of the *Republic*). And flattery is also characteristic of sophism as shown in the concluding sentence of the *Sophist*, (286[d]) where Socrates defines this 'art' as:

> 'conceited mimicry, image-making . . . distinguished as a portion, not divine, but of human production, that presents a shadow-play of words; such are the blood and lineage which can with perfect truth be assigned to the authentic sophist.'

The sophist is the *Eikon*-maker, the idolator. It is only in this way that we can understand Plato's wrath in attacking him. It is unreasonable to assume that such vehemence could be directed at somebody simply holding a different philosophical view; the sophist must be that element or factor which sabotages philosophy by treating it as if it were an objective truth. Even the development of mathematics is affected (see Klein, 1968). The pleasant feeling that all is permitted and all is relative filters into mathematical and scientific thinking, and sophists are readily found to create corresponding mathematical theories: this is what leads the Athenian to make the otherwise absurd observation that pleasure cannot be made the criterion for geometrical proportionality (*Laws*, 667). It is on the grounds of pleasure that an Aristarchus creates a heliocentric theory, for to the Athenians this would imply that all is relative, all permitted. Plato rejects the heliocentric theory for precisely this self-serving relativism, and not on the basis of empirical evidence, which is conjectural in any case.

Conceptual thought follows the sentiment of pleasure, and constructs concepts, cities, philosophies and speech to maximize pleasure and minimize self-control. Noetic thought is not against pleasure; the sophists, however, have an incorrect view of what it means to be a city or a person, for they do not perceive the interconnection between man and man, and man and city, and city and nature. In following individual pleasure as the criterion, a true individual just brings more suffering to himself and to the city, for he creates thoughts, actions and institutions that lead the various parts of the organism into war against each other. The sentiment of love ignores individual pleasure or pain, but in doing so, it indirectly minimizes the pain both to the true individual and to the true city.

The pleasure and pain in the realm of becoming are centripetal sentiments for the false self, opposing the opposite pull of the divine entity situated in the realm of being. The purifying cathartic activity of correct thinking involves the birth of the true self; this can be mentally painful for it requires the dissolution of the perceived self. A certain amount of pain due to *Anangke* cannot be avoided, despite encouragement by the like-minded men, whose thought stretches across centuries and reaches those who would listen. The searcher continues on his own.

II

> 'A wall is, in the first place, far from conducive to the health of town life, and, what is more, commonly breeds a certain softness of soul in the townsmen; it invites habitants to seek shelter within it and leave the enemy unrepulsed, tempts them to neglect effecting their deliverance by unrelaxing nightly and daily watching, and to fancy they will find a way to real safety by locking themselves in, and going to sleep behind ramparts and bars, as though they had been born to shirk toil, and did not know that the true ease must come from it . . . whereas dishonourable ease and sloth will bring forth toil and trouble' (*Laws*, 778–779).

B.Bosanquet has seen Plato as part of an intellectual movement of resistance against empire. There was a body of opinion in Athens at the time that saw the fall of the city as due to its desire to exploit cities other than itself, to shirk its just share of toil through colonial expansion. Trade and suchlike were felt to be part of a rebellion against the older order – acceptance of Anangke.

Indeed, in the *Gorgias* Plato identifies as an all-binding law that as soon as a city sets up a wall (which can take many shapes: a treaty, a financial hedge, protection of comfort by the exploitation of natural resources), it is doomed to fail. Before setting up Magnesia, the Athenian makes sure it is not too well wooded or too near the sea, lest the citizens live off unearned natural gifts rather than by overcoming difficulties (*Laws*, Book IV). Following the universal Fall, man is condemned to give birth in pain, to create through toil: any attempt to circumvent the fact that this is a basic human condition leads to the internal moral collapse of the individual *Polis*, family or man. J.B.Morrall (1977, p. 77) observes Aristotle also accounting for the moral degeneration of Athens in terms of its economic and trade expansion, and attacking the tendency to obtain security by artificial means such as commerce.

That the wall in Greek philosophical texts often functions as a symbolic notion can be seen from an announcement by the Oracle of Delphi, referring to the Navy as 'the wooden wall': a remark which Plato exploits in the *Laws* (707^{a-e}), attacking the Navy precisely because it does function as a wall. States that base their security on navies lay their fate in the hands of men practising the ignoble activity of archery, from the relative safety of the ship. The skills and sentiments of a naval engagement favour the helmsman, the pilot the strategist and the archer, all of whom engage in less noble activities than those of the foot soldier. For a *Hoplite* to excel, he needs physical and mental excellence, courage and determination. The land engagement is decided by, and creative of, the superior moral sentiment, whereas naval encounters are based on the lesser sentiments and on professionalized skills and techniques:

> 'Men should never be trained to evil ways; that the practice in question [he means the use of the great warships] is ignoble might have been learned from Homer. . . . Thus you see Homer was also well aware what a bad thing it is for infantry to be supported by a line of men of war. . . . States which owe their power to a navy also bestow the reward for their security on an inferior element of their forces, as they owe their security to the arts of the sea captain, the helmsman and the oarsman . . . and to a miscellaneous and not overreputable crowd' (*Laws*, 706^{c-e}, 707^{a-b}).

A further point made is the objection against specific actions, such as trapping ships into bottlenecks, and bombardment by fireballs from relative safety; hooking fish, men or ships is of evil sentiment. Plato is not a pacifist; in condemning naval victories, particularly such as the one at Salamis, he is condemning the burning of the Persians alive and the trapping of their ships in the hook of Raes; he is condemning the treacherous skills of strategy and clever tricks to avoid honest combat by engaging in the activities conducive to evil sentiment. While Plato was opposing the wooden wall, the Navy, as a matter of moral principle, this does not invalidate the practical aspects of his objection.

Any empirical evidence aside, he could confidently argue that despite initial success, the reliance on the wooden wall would inevitably destroy the security of Athens. In principle he was correct. Having built a powerful navy, Athenians found it acceptable to abandon more strenuous forms of defence that required moral and physical exertion of the populace. The significance of military defence is universal and cosmic. According to the *Laws* and the *Republic*, by submitting themselves to the hardship of learning to defend themselves, not with technology and mercenaries, but by marching and sword-play (if not with their bare hands), citizens steel their bodies, appease the gods of war and create an inner solidarity, ensuring that it is not necessary to go to war. Thus Glaucon, who finds the city state consisting of 5,000 citizens too small to guarantee its survival, is told by Socrates that such a State is the least likely even to go to war : it will not attack or be attacked. A State which keeps busy and only satisfies its legitimate needs has no excess fat: with so many idle, fat cows around no enemy will attack a lean animal that keeps fit. The smaller and leaner the State, the less booty for the enemy. Yet the fitter it is, the more capable to resist agression. Hence it is not likely to be attacked, and, being satisfied with what it has, it will not attack others. The often misused quotation, 'If you want peace, prepare for war,' stems from Saanthana thought; but though the *Logos* wages an unceasing battle to maintain itself against the forces of disorder, this does not mean that one should stockpile arms and build ships, submarines and tanks, it means precisely the opposite. By building powerful navies, armies and alliances, Athens will inevitably be led into wars. He who takes up the sword perishes by the sword.

Plato would prefer to tear down walls and sink the Navy. The same principle was expressed by Gandhi, who said that India should not build fortifications of any kind (physical or cultural). In that way each Indian will learn how to withstand the winds. Armies and alliances allow the citizens to relax and grow into 'fat cows'. Walls and barns lead to the accumulation of false treasures. Of course, if the Navy is sunk, and the city's security is taken out of the hands of the specialist, every man, woman and child will have to be prepared for war in a physical and psychological sense. That war will never come as long as these precepts are maintained, according to cosmic law. In practice, of course, no State is perfect, and wars do come – but the good State is not likely to lose a war, for it has on its side both cosmic forces and psychological fixities.

III

Criticism of wall- and barn-building is of paramount importance in *Logos*-based thought. It relates to national security, but is also applicable to other aspects of physical existence, and primarily to the creation of concepts. In Buddhism, original ignorance is attributed to a wall, inside which Gautama lived as a prince. In the Ramayana, Ravana piles his loot behind a wall on the assumption that walls cannot be scaled. To pile treasures in barns and behind walls is to create false riches: as the Gospels teach, treasures that are capable of storage are nothing of the sort.

The 'noble truths' of Buddhism testify that suffering in this life arises whenever one resists the basic flow of life and tries to cling to fixed concepts, ideas, events, people, situations and things. Attachment is not immoral because it offends a transcendental deity – it is immoral because it is false. One cannot retain youth, wealth, physical beauty and power.

Man brings suffering to himself and distorts the world by trying to hold on to them. It is only through giving everything up that he can enjoy the moment, the flow, actuality. All conceptual, tangible entities are *Avidya*, falsehood; only in the noetic, the level of deeper consciousness, can one legitimately look for fixities.

The building of walls against necessity or fate is a rebellion against the will of God, and another expression of the activity which brings about the ongoing Fall. In epistemological terms, the Fall is caused by autonomous thought. Concept-building is the building of a mental wall: the psychology and the internal dynamics are the same as those involved in building stone ones. In search of a false sense of security, the internal sophist builds a wall by creating a concept. In doing this he arrests the genesis, the rebirth of knowledge.

In this connection, Socrates, claiming to be inspired by a superhuman power (396[e]), states in the dialogue *Cratylus* (411[d–e]):'here is *Noesis*, the very word just now mentioned, which is neou-esis, implying that the world is always in the process of creation; the giver of the name wanted to express the longing of the soul for the new.' With *Noesis*, Socrates contrasts *Aishron*, 'ugly', and defines it as the obstacle to flow (*Cratylus*, 416[a]), while *Pseudos*, 'falsehood', is the opposite of motion. It is wrong to build obstacles to arrest the natural movement, argues Socrates, citing Homer (in *Theaetetus*, 153[c–d]):

> 'Motion is a good thing for both soul and body, and immobility is bad. Need I speak further of such things as stagnation in air and water, where stillness causes corruption and decay? . . . So long as the heavens and the sun continue to move around, all things in heaven and earth are kept going; whereas if they are bound down and brought to a standstill all things would be destroyed.'

The duties of any noetic thinker are those of a midwife, assisting at the constant rebirth of knowledge, which is a continuous process of creation in pain (*Symposium*, 207[d]). The sophist attempts to arrest thought by offering ready-made formulae: Socrates is the destroyer of these walls. A city can be compared to a well-bred horse which, even though carefully put together by a pedigree, nevertheless exhibits a constant tendency to inactivity, and seeks the security and seclusion of the stable: this is the picture painted by Socrates in the *Apology*. Athens is the splendid-looking yet inactivity-seeking horse, and the true philosopher a stinging fly, forcing it into movement: 'And if you finish me with a single slap, then you will go on sleeping till the end of your days, unless God in his care for you sends someone to take my place.' (*Apology*, 30[e]).

The noetic thinker inevitably annoys both others and himself (for the tendency to stagnation is present in us all), yet man needs to be permanently restung, not to assume today that he still knows what he knew yesterday. A definition or a formula is only momentarily true; in order to be relevant it needs to be taken up again, shaken about, turned upside down, requestioned and examined.

IV

Saanthana thought suggests that external and internal reflect each other. Each individual contains a token of each part of the universe. A part of each individual is also represented in all other individuals and entities, living and dead. This principle is not unrelated to the idea of ambassadorial representations from one State to another. One precinct of a capital city contains fragments of all other countries, just as the host country itself is represented in those other countries. A perfect embassy would, within its grounds, represent the dominant features of the country it belonged to. The model would be scaled down, for its objective would not be to be functionally operative. This parallels Proclus' notions of intersubjectivity: the enlightened soul sees the other souls represented in it, and is represented in them, yet through individual integrity the pain or happiness experienced by each representative microcosm is felt by the whole entity.

For Plato, each individual consists largely of a collection of such representative parts. The representative precinct is, in a quantitative sense, the largest section of the 'city' – whereas the *home*, the ruling faculty, is situated in the citadel called the *Logisticon*. This *Logisticon* does not exhaust the integrity of a person, because a true person is the sum of all the 'ambassadorial staff' scattered through the other entities, all held together by the unifying sentiment. The fact that most of the constituents of a person are on a kind of permanent post abroad in other entities does not diminish the integrity of an individual person. For the Hindus, each individual is represented not only in each other individual, but in each other animal, plant, star and galaxy. Every unit in the cosmos is represented, but not contained or exhausted, by every other unit. This representation is simultaneous – though it is not so conceptualized. The reassembly of all the fragments of a person around the focal point, the ruling spark, *Logisticon* or *Atman*, is suggested by notions of resurrection, or of the end of the diaspora.

This symbiotic unity of the cosmos is, of course, just another conceptualization, whose acceptability will vary with period and individual inclination. Similar notions have been differently conceptualized. In the 'primitive' religions of Africa, a witch doctor constructs microcosmic models – animals and dolls representing the individual members of the community. Members of the community may be punished by sticking needles into parts of the doll. A needle stuck into the liver or the leg of the doll is supposed to bring pain or cure, as the case may be, to the actual person. While a witch doctor will actually possess the doll effigies of all the members of his 'parish', speaking generally each man may be viewed as possessing within himself the miniature model of all living beings ever born or to be born. Each man is a partnership of the living and the dead with those who will be born. By self-abuse one may inflict pain on everyone (though in a deeper sense yet one can only hurt himself). It is for this reason that Confucians and Taoists claim that a mentally disturbed society will create climatic disturbances, individual excess triggering floods, earthquakes, wars, etc. For Plato, the inner organs are models of astronomical and geographic bodies. The milky way is the spine of the cosmos, and it portrays the flow of cosmic energy called variously Kundalini, Chi and *Pneuma*.

The 'seven' celestial bodies represent the seven nerve centres of the spine, the Hindu *Chakras*. Since in the *Epinomis* Plato writes that all his knowledge was achieved by internally observing these seven celestial bodies, we may infer he had meditated on the seven *Chakras* as the Hindus and Buddhists do. The same bodies are referred to in the Revelation to John as the seven churches, the seven flames of seven candles and so on. And the microcosmic idea is also behind the theory of one man dying for the sins of the world, for all men are contained in the one. By conquering all the negative tendencies within his own body, this 'suffering servant' may defeat such tendencies in everyone. But at the same time, as Proclus points out, each man is also autonomous and can reject what is in fact the case. In Zoroastrian thought, too, the word of Vohu Manu, *Ahuna Varya*, accounts for all true individuals and embraces them. Yet each living individual is free at any moment to choose between Vohu Manu and the desiring self of Ahriman.

Concerning this notion of the paradigmatic city taking form as a human being, it is curious to observe a prophecy made by Plato (or Socrates) in the *Republic* (361^{c}–362^{c}). Plato's brother Glaucon tells the story of the perfect man. Most men, he claims, are partly good, partly bad, so they prosper or do not prosper depending on circumstances. However, if there ever occurs such an event as the birth of perfectly good or sinless man, his fate will necessarily be tragic. Such a perfectly good man will make no attempt to convince or conceptually persuade man that he is in fact good. Being perfectly good he will only do and be good – if accused of being evil he would not argue or dispute, or make any attempt to safeguard his existence or reputation. Such a person is so far outside the experience of mankind that he will necessarily offend and infuriate the 'authorities'. Inevitably, he will be accused of being everything that he is not. He will be tried, whereupon he will not plead or argue for mercy and will in the end be beaten, tortured and sentenced to death. For reasons incomprehensible to scholarship, since crucifixion was not the manner of death for criminals in Greece, it is claimed that the perfect man will be crucified, if he should ever manifest in time.

A myth, if true, remains relevant to man's destiny even if it is forgotten or expressed in some other way. In Hindu mythology it is Kali who slays the devil, for Zoroastrians it is Vohu Manu – for Plato it is the mythical cosmic city (of which each good man is a citizen in moments when he is good) which defeats the evil city (of which each man is a citizen when he is bad). The fact that such an important event is 'forgotten' by us does not contradict its cosmic and eternal relevance. The myth is based on a deeper fundamental reality, and will find an expression in words one way or another. The relativity of mythology does not imply relativity of human conduct. In each age Krishna must be served anew, and 'Even those who in faith worship other gods, because of their love they worship me, although not in the right way' (Bhagavad Gita, IX, 23). Krishna, Mohammed and Christianity all insist that their particular religion is the best one. This subjectivity within objectivity appears paradoxical – yet the paradox is entirely conceptual. Within any particular culture only one set of symbols can be meaningful. Although in the conceptually 'objective' sense these must therefore embody relative truths, in noetic thought the relative truth becomes absolute. For the absolute has no existence except in the relative: as Jesus claimed, nobody can see God except through him.

V

Stripped of its metre, rhythm and pattern, inspired philosophy becomes nothing but persuasive speech. For in fact the core of philosophy consists in this very rhythm and sentiment, and not in the external layer of words which are usually mistaken for its content. All the traditions we have looked at make it the task of the philosopher and the sage to determine the correct rhythm (*Li*) and its correlation, first to the inner, and then to the outer manifestations of public life. This rhythm lies behind all good craftsmanship, including architecture and the manufacture of household furnishings, and also in the natural movement of plants and animals. It is crucially related to governing that dimension of the city which may be called psychological, as well as to the design of the buildings, streets and fences. In India, Babylon and Greece, cities were built after an established blueprint. Even to spatial and seasonal relations, such as the distances from a shrine to the market place, the size of the *Agora* with respect to that of the temple, the directions of the streets, the frequency of festivals and processions. Upon these fixed patterns various cultures imposed differences: temples were dedicated to the gods appropriate for the given circumstances. But though the physical reality, the architecture, *does* vary in keeping with local conditions, such as the availability of building materials and the nature of the terrain, this variation exists only to preserve a deeper pattern. Correspondingly, in constructing a book, argument or sentence, one should be in keeping with the general rules of construction that apply to craftsmen, cooks or architects. Things are to be constructed to cater to the mind and the body, yet also to serve the third, the element beyond element. In discourse, this third, hidden principle is the unknown moral element. 'Unknown', indeed, may have been the Greek name for it:

> It is even possible that the word 'Unknowing' was (with this positive meaning) a technical term . . . and that this is the real explanation and interpretation of the inscription on the Athenian altar: 'To the Unknown God' (Rolt in Dionysius, 1940, p. 33).

The three basic psychological and cosmic principles have been suggested earlier. The Fall may be seen as a state of war between them, a war which on a social level is sometimes called the class war. Noetic thought attributes class divisions to psychological constants. A man is not a member of the ruling class once and for all: he is a doctor or father, or anything else only when he is correctly functioning as such. The ruling class therefore exists on the one hand as an abstract function, and, on the other as the group of people who have the power in any one moment. But this group of people cannot properly be called a ruling class if they are misruling. It is another of the assumptions of Saanthana thought that in some deep sense one can in the final analysis only harm, exploit or oppress oneself. Punishment, and compensation, are only delayed. In crucifying Jesus, or killing the hero or the martyr, the executioners hurt themselves more than they have hurt their victim. While the martyr's life has been shortened, in dying for a cause he is in a sense fulfilled: not so his executioners. The ruling class is misruling as soon as it begins to 'exploit' the ruled: at that point it ceases to rule.

On the individual level, the noetic, mental and appetitive forces each contain the other two, and so *ad infinitum*. A city will at various times be governed by deities, a single king or a group of aristocrats, depending on which aspect prevails. It is not the form of government which is decisive but the manner of governing. In applying this to a family, we may observe that it is ruled by the children, by the father and by the mother. It is ruled by the children, for everything is done for their sake. Traditionally, the family is ruled by the father: yet when he is sick or sleeping or away, by the mother, or another senior member. The effective power is from moment to moment, and depending on your viewpoint, held by different entities. Plato speaks of three educators in the family (*Laws*, 627): one of these uses brute strength (it applies to the working element), the second is the clever member of the family and the third represents noetic reason. The first rules by force, the second by persuasion – yet both are false. The correct rule is by reconciliation.

In the *Symposium* (191[d]), Love is the physician who 'restores us to our ancient state by attempting to weld two beings into one and to heal the wounds which humanity suffered.'

The medical analogy is subtle yet of decisive importance. Persuasion is compared by Plato to the treatment of disease with pain-subduing potions. In contemporary terms these would be drugs. Ruling by persuasion is getting men drunk and feasting them to achieve their agreement. But drunken men eventually sober up, and return to renew their claims. In all noetic thought reconciliation replaces persuasion.

Kant, of course, was a master persuader. In order to achieve his aim – making all men ethical – Kant formulates a formula – the principle of universalizability: Do only that of which you would approve even if your act were to become a universal code of behaviour. He may have persuaded a few or many of his readers, yet one may be sceptical whether Europe became more moral as a result. Men follow conceptual morality only in times of plenty; as soon as there is hardship, conceptual rules are abandoned. Men can only be moved to meaningful activity through knowledge which incorporates knowing by the body (grasp) and the soul. Opinions, however, are mere persuasions. This is what Socrates objects to when he says opinions are of no use unless tied down, for 'opinions run away' (*Meno*, 97[d]). To have an opinion is to be ruled by the mind – the mind persuades others to the same opinions, but persuasions are skin deep.

Noetic agreement is not an agreement of conceptual images. A good Taoist does not *conceptually* share the vision of the world of a devout Buddhist or of Socrates – yet Socrates will get along considerably better with a sincere Buddhist or Taoist than with a Professor of Socratic Method who does not share his sentiment. It is of no use to believe that one ought not to smoke: what is necessary is for the body to be educated not to want things that are contradicted by the intellect. Thus: 'that type of ignorance may be called the greatest of a man who hates, not loves, what his judgement presumes to be noble and good' (*Laws*, 689[b]). To know only with one's mind is not to know. This is illustrated in the *Laws* –

which describes the bringing together of three men representing the three psychological principles – *Noesis, Dianoia* and *Epithumia*. To assume that the mind is superior to the body is false and meaningless – the body has a reason of its own and the mind has a body, with appetites such as greed. In medicine, politics and philosophy the three human aspects of man need to be brought together. In the *Timaeus*, Socrates claims that it is useless to move the mind unless one moves the body, and in the *Laws* one learns that instruction in philosophy cannot be divorced from music and gymnastics. To make a man faithful to one wife involves teaching him gymnastics, music and the noetic feeling. Only in that way can one create the correct sentiment for marriage. Anything achieved by persuasion is comparable to the superficial results achieved by threats. One should not persuade but convert. The function of rhythm in a philosophical discourse is to exercise the mind physically. The citizens of Magnesia are divided into three choruses and chant every day.

The major world religions may also be seen as structured around these three psychological principles. Islam is rhythmically and physically oriented; it stresses rhythm, ritual and movement. This is also true of Taoism, with its Tai Chi. Hinduism in general aims towards noetic grasp, while Christianity gravitates towards the heart. Yet 'There is no wisdom for a man without harmony, and without harmony there is no contemplation' (Bhagavad Gita, II, 66). Yoga is harmony: A harmony in eating and resting, in sleeping and keeping awake. And all religions and philosophies necessarily rely on the mind, the heart, and the noetic faculty: that is, on the harmony between the three.

VI

To a conclusion like the one which characterizes the last section, that harmony is the key to human well-being, Plato is led to remark cynically that a marvellous philosophical solution, 'which might have worked wonders if only someone had known the proper way', dies as soon as it is written down. Plato is criticizing both himself and all the philosophers who have reasoned thus. We must not assume too readily that by giving a particular interpretation or application of some dialogue that we have captured anything but one aspect of the true solution. In observing that *Logos*-based thought tries to effect a harmony between the three parts of the soul, or the three psychological constants of any society, one needs to exercise the greatest caution. A noetic grasp of harmony is not to be derived from a single conceptual model. If the model of any city as conceptualized in the various visions of Saanthana thinkers could encompass the totality of the reality of a city, then we could treat harmony simply as the absence of outer conflict between the citizens. Since noetic thought is not to do with the creation of conceptual utopias, we cannot assume that the inner psychological dimension will be subject to such simple notions of harmony. For a citizen of an actual State to be in harmony with that State he will have to subjugate his own soul to a more complex set of rules than simply the existing legal code and his own notion of harmony. The conceptual model of perfection portrays a single (the outer) dimension of the triunal dimensionality of any actual city, just as the concept of harmony as an absence of conflict is only one single dimension of the notion of harmony.

It is a mistake to treat the Greek notion of harmony as equivalent to some kind of instantaneous concord. Even in the context of music, harmony in this contemporary sense entered Greek culture with the sophists. Heidegger (1968, p. 213) was wrong to assume that conceptual thought was absent in Greece; at about the time of Pericles it flooded the culture, and can readily be observed in the art, poetry and the language of that time. In the hands of the sophists, *Harmonia* became nothing more than *Symphonia*. '*Harmonia*, however,' Cornford (1967, p. 19) explains, 'is the orderly adjustment of various parts with respect to the unfolding whole.' It is a development leading to a comprehensive unity. A dissonant sound followed by a non-dissonant sound, comprehended in the totality of the given flow of music, becomes retrospectively harmonious. Its apparent, momentary dissonance is resolved with respect to the whole.

The noetic notion of harmony involves an abstract affiliation of a mutually sympathetic range of sentiments over and above the perceived connections or interests determined by chance and circumstance. The harmony of the Greek song is not instantaneously comprehensible, but requires unfolding in time; and a fully noetic harmony is to be perceived by more complex criteria yet. This harmony includes a curious blend of the all-embracing Parmenidean resolution of conflict by denial of deviation and change, with the Heraclitian flux.

This complex notion of harmony as a set of converging inclinations, resolving perceived contradictions by reference to a common sentiment, is expressed by the famous Greek physician Eryxymachus solely in terms of music; yet its principle covers a much greater range. With reference to Heraclitus' Fragment 45, Eryxymachus observes that rule by mutual love 'holds good of music – which is perhaps what Heraclitus meant us to understand by that rather cryptic pronouncement: The one in conflict with itself is held together like the harmony of the bow and the lyre' (*Symposium*, 187[a]). He is not unaware of the contradictions that such noetic notions present on the dianoic level. But unlike Heraclitus, he is not averse to reducing the poetically derived to the rationally comprehensible:

he does attempt a verbal solution to the extent this is possible:

> 'Of course, it is absurd to speak of harmony as being in conflict, or as arising out of elements which are still conflicting, but perhaps he [Heraclitus] meant that the art of music was to create harmony by resolving the discord between the treble and the base. There can certainly be no harmony of treble and base while they are still in conflict, for harmony is concord, and concord is a kind of sympathy, and sympathy between things which are in conflict is impossible so long as that conflict lasts' (*Symposium*, 187[a–b]).

This does not imply that one should passively accept conflict and not seek to resolve it. Rather, there are two kinds of conflict, elsewhere called *Stasis* and *Ammetria* (*Sophist*, 228[d]), one of which, the latter, can be resolved by a relatively simple reordering of the constituents. In the *Symposium* passage, the intention is to distinguish a more complex conflict from one which is unnecessarily perceived as such but which, if subjected to specific criteria, may be resolved into harmony: 'There is, on the other hand, a kind of discord which it is not impossible to resolve, and here we may effect a harmony – as for instance we produce rhythm by resolving the difference between fast and slow' (*Symposium*, 187[c]).

Eryxymachus is a physician, and his truth will not readily apply to the ruling of the noetic part of man, yet aspectually, i.e. in reference to the body, he is as much a representative of true philosophy as is Heraclitus or Parmenides. The bodily aspect of any city is to be treated as such through music and gymnastics. 'And just as we saw that the concord of the body was brought about by the art of medicine, so this other harmony is due to the art of music, as the creator of mutual love and sympathy' (*Symposium*, 187[c]). So what, then, is music? Nothing but 'the science of love, or of desire, in this case in relation to harmony and rhythm' (*Symposium*, 187[c]).

This is far from being the contemporary view of harmony. Music was held by the Greeks to be the force constitutive of personality, and Plato looks backward to Damon to resurrect this unusual notion. For Plato, citizens are disarranged bits and pieces which are put together by music along with gymnastics and philosophy. (Cf. an expression from Illtyd Trethowan: 'We are all bits and pieces until Christ puts us together.'). 'Music', of course, is not music in the modern sense; it is the collective embodiment of universal rhythms and constants conveyed by inspired ritual poetry, dance and mime, all in some sense participating in the underlying principle of love, all serving a psychotherapeutic role. In *Islam and the Perennial Philosophy*, Frithjof Schuon writes that in Islamic tradition the soul of Adam would not enter his body until lured there by music.

Harmony, therefore, cannot be reduced to something which is perceived by the body, whether in sensation or concept. To understand harmony one needs to take a broader view. In the noetic perspective kings, tyrants and other power-holders are not much different from terrorists. The terrorist, holding a ship or a family to ransom, appears to have power, yet this appearance is only due to his limited perception. In the *Gorgias* (469[e]), Socrates observes that anybody can set a dockyard on fire or walk about with a hidden dagger and grab citizens for ransom. Such power, says Socrates, lasts merely a few minutes or days; nevertheless it is no different from that of a king, for even a decade-long rule is a fleeting second compared to the longevity of the soul. True harmony can be discerned only outside time, or in time as a whole.

The reason why the simple sophist's concept of harmony – the absence of pain and conflict in his perceived realm – is victorious over that of the philosopher does not lie in any deficiency on the part of the philosopher's logic. The sophist's concept appears more logical and is more familiar to the mind, which, in order to make the harmony between false units convincing, creates rules of comprehension on the basis of desire, *Epithumia*. The mind is an unreliable ally of the philosopher, and at best a neutral agent, by virtue of this inclination.

But the philosopher has a more powerful weapon than the mind, and he readily uses it. This weapon is rhythm. By self-purification through rhythm, philosophy, gymnastics and music, a real philosopher apprehends the organizing principles of deeper harmony and is able to translate them into words, institutions, architecture and philosophy. This is why Socrates was able to move his listeners to action (*Symposium*, 215[d]). This is the only way to defeat the sophist, and the only cure for the city. The Greek temple or ancient city harmonizes three elements, three different conceptions of harmony. The first is of 'harmony' as the contemporary mind would understand it, harmony that is a Kantian victory over the self, and hence absence of conflict. The victory here is by persuasion, the harmony merely conceptual; the persuaded man '*thinks*' he is at peace. The second notion of harmony is that of the body, and the third, though it may imply local conflict in the perceived realm, is conducive of an eventual resolution if perceived macrocosmically. The ideal harmony is one where the concept and the body are in tune with the noetic faculty. This comes about as the three different kinds of time – psychological time, body time, and cosmic time – are fused in actuality. This harmony implies that other beings also accept and perceive the noetic harmony, since all men are interconnected. For this reason the philosopher emancipates himself by emancipating others. Of course, he is only relatively successful in an objective sense. Subjectively, however, the harmony available is the one of projection into the out-of-time realm called the other world. If successful, he no longer feels pain as pain.

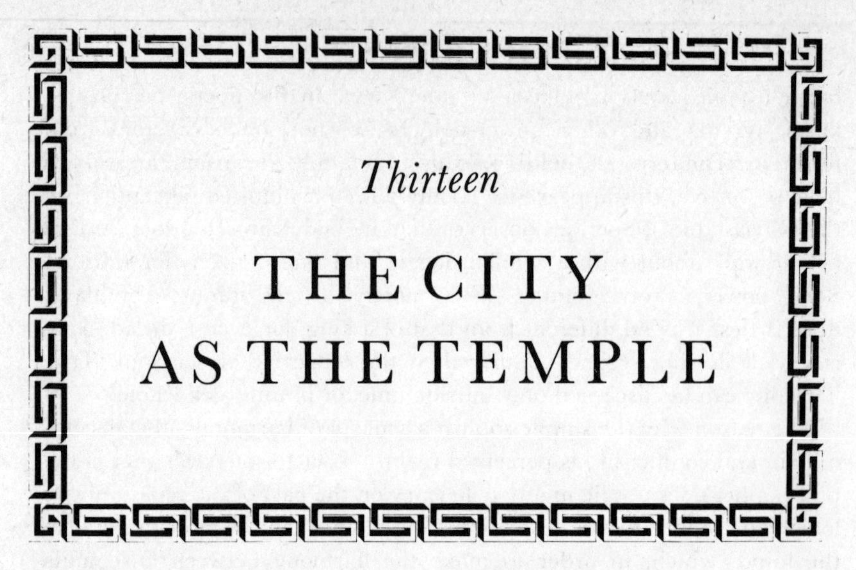

Thirteen

THE CITY AS THE TEMPLE

The Greek notion of harmony makes it possible to understand the non-legislated for, i.e. the larger, aspect of life in Magnesia. Noetic harmony necessarily includes that between body and soul. The whole issue is complex, for the division between mind and body is not one that can be conceptualized. The mind both is and has a body. Therefore, for Plato any state of harmony, whether spiritual, mental or physical, cannot be achieved without physical activity or exercise. This allows us to approach that otherwise incomprehensible aspect of Greek life and philosophy, usually referred to as *Choreia*.

> 'and he who is careful to fashion the body should in turn impart to the soul its proper motions and should cultivate the arts and philosophy. . . . And the separate parts should be treated in the same manner in imitation of the pattern of the universe. . . . But if anyone, in imitation of that which we call the foster mother and nurse of the universe, will not allow the body ever to be inactive, but is always producing motions and agitations through its whole extent, which form the natural defence against their motions, both internal and external, and by moderate exercise reduces to order, according to their affinities, the particles and affections which are wandering about the body, as we have already said when speaking of the universe, he will not allow enemy, placed by the side of enemy, to stir up wars and disorders in the body, but he will place friend by the side of friend. . . . Now, of all motions that is the best which is produced in a thing by itself, for it is most akin to the motion of thought and of the universe' (*Timaeus*, 89–90d).

I

In approaching the corybantic aspect of Orphic philosophy, we enter the single least known area of Greek experience, yet one which deserves much attention. The Greeks took part in regular collective rhythmic exercises of the kind one meets today in communist China – where hundreds of thousands of children create patterns spelling the name of a party leader or an idea. For the Greeks, such activity permeated all walks of life.

My interest in the matter lies in the possibility of differentiating the feelings I have referred to as sentiments and the similar, but ontologically divergent, set of feelings that may be called passions or affections of the lower soul.

Although the Greeks did not use the words 'poetry' and 'music' consistently to indicate the differences between corybantic and ecstatic purification, Plato and Aristotle do exhibit a certain consistency in using them to refer to two different sets of arts and their corresponding emotions. One may observe that the corybantic aspect in music contains the positive element in the arts, and vice versa for the passion-orientated activities that I shall here somewhat arbitrarily equate with poetry and drama.

Any meaningful analysis of the corybantic aspect of *Choreia* can only be carried out by reference to oriental parallels, as the notion is strange, even if the experience is not completely foreign to the Greeks and to the Western tradition in general. Aristides Quantilianus is one of the few authors to have commented on the subject at all. He sees corybantic exercises and music as primarily a mimetic vehicle: Quantilianus' view appears to have a degree of validity, but does not diagnose the fact that two different movements are involved in the mimesis. True corybantic movement is concerned with that part of the lower soul which produces sentiments which are the counterpart to *Noesis*; their perverted image consists of the passions, and these are the currency of the undesirable poet and dramatist.

Wilhelm Wundt (1905, pp. 396–405) writes of the difference between what he calls ecstatic and mimetic dance. From Wundt's account one may infer that the former serves to arrest the movement of the conscious soul, allowing the deity to enter a mind which has in some sense emptied. The affected person is extinguished, and becomes a passive recipient. As opposed to this stands mimetic dance, where the participant retains consciousness, yet ceases to differentiate himself as a single particular entity. Consciousness is not extinguished but enlarged, by becoming parasitic on the movement of the imitated entity, be it animal or deity. Wundt finds the mimetic superior.

Concerning the nature of ecstatic rituals, Mircea Eliade (1979, p. 368) comes closer to what I have in mind. He writes:

> At the centre of the Dionysic ritual we always find, in one form or another, an ecstatic experience of a more or less violent frenzy or mania: this madness was in a way the proof that the initiate was *entheos* – 'filled with God.' . . . communion with God shattered the human condition for a time but it did not succeed in transmuting it. There is no reference to immortality in the Bachae . . . it is characteristic of all such activities that they bring only a temporary relief.

It is important to note the difference between two kinds of art: art designed to develop and educate the soul, and art designed to bring temporary relief.

These distinctions are universal. Parallels can be drawn with modern psychology, which when divorced from the ethical-religious dimension becomes a science designed to alleviate mental pain, rather than to cure the soul in a deeper, permanent way. The drama and Bacchic rites of fourth-century Athens, in contrast to Orphic *Choreia*, were also designed primarily to effect relief.

But, as far as I am aware, Ivan Linforth (1946) is the only scholar since Quantilianus to have written on the corybantic rites of *Choreia*, rites independent of those associated with worship and ceremony: 'The rites belonged to that class of religious ceremonies which were called *Teletae*. . . . A *telete* of this kind was a form of ritual whose chief function was not the worship of gods but the direct benefit of the participant.' The *Choreia* he describes is clearly neither an activity designed to temporarily relieve pain, nor an entertainment. It can best be understood compared with the activity called yoga. The meaning of this word stems from the root *yuj* – to yoke or to join – and its objective is to educate human soul (*Jivatman*) to perceive itself as part of the universal soul embracing all living beings: animals, the fishes in the sea and the birds of the air. While the word yoga brings to the Western mind the postures (*Asanas*) of Hatha yoga, this does not exhaust the meaning of the word. Dancing and mime are just as legitimate a part of it, as indeed is any activity which teaches man to integrate himself in the movement of the universal soul. It is the bodily mimesis of all the forms of life in which man participates. The theory of yoga is the theory behind the myth of the *Statesman*: in order to learn our part in the movement of the universe, we ought not to differentiate ourselves from any other living being, for in the age of Cronus we were all in a sense one.

While philosophy educates the intellectual part of the soul, the body has its own manner of thought and its own reason, extended in the liver (*Timaeus*, 71). The Greeks and Hindus in general saw disorders of the soul as stemming from disorders in the body, and vice versa. The fall of man was a two-sided affair. As we learn from Pindar, the most ancient sin was hubris (man desiring to be more than man); but, again, there is a hubris of the mind and a hubris of the body. In Biblical terms, it was not just Adam's mind that wanted to be like God. The rebellion lay in the mind's desire to be like God and to know the difference between good and evil, yet for this knowledge to be absorbed it was necessary for Adam to appropriate it also by the body. So the perversion did not just limit itself to mental desire; it was physically consummated through the apple. The movement of the body is as corrupted as the movement of the mind. Man is doubly ignorant, since the one kind of ignorance causes and ranges into the other.

Through yoga, man mimetically integrates himself into the forms of being from which he is separated by the nature of his sin, and in thus purifying himself he overcomes the fear of seeing himself as he is. In Hindu accounts, as in Plato, man is afraid of his true identity. Like the prisoners in the cave, he prefers the 'imagined' comfort of his chains to the painful *Periagoge*. He is ashamed of his nakedness: by covering his true body, he has placated his shame – but this false protection also caters to his fear. True reunion involves the overcoming of fear; perceiving oneself naked yet purified, and hence free of shame.

Fear, shame, happiness, courage, justice – indeed all sentiments, good or bad – are movements of the soul outwardly manifested as psychic sensations. This mechanistic view of the nature of the affections of the soul and corresponding states of mind differs considerably from the 'metaphysical' views attributed to the Greeks by modern thinkers, and eloquently demolished by those same people. Evil is primarily a wrong kind of motion; a symbolic motion, but quite literally a tangible, mechanical motion that can be mechanically counteracted. Ethics merges with gymnastics, without losing its integrity. The body itself has its reason and intelligence, its courage and ethical virtue. To overcome bodily pain is as virtuous as to overcome a mental obstacle: both involve the sentiment of love towards the natural state, an element of courage to resist the pain that hinders the reversal of movement from bad to good. But the intelligence of the body cannot be treated as separate from the intelligence of the mind; one is reflective of the other, and they each participate in a unity. The liver also has its rational-cognitive element, as does every cell in the body.

So, for noetic thinkers, intelligence is not located in the brain alone, manifested as thought. The *Nous* pervades the whole cosmos, and it manifests itself in appropriate forms through a characteristic movement. 'Thought' is a misleading translation of *Noesis*, for it restricts itself to the mind. *Noesis* does mean 'movement' – the soul has different movements and it acts, cognates and feels in terms of them:

> 'I have often remarked that there are three kinds of soul located within us, having each of them motions. . . . Now there is only one way of taking care of things, and that is to give to each the food and the motion which is natural to it. And the motions which are naturally akin to the divine principle within us are the thoughts and the revolutions of the universe. These each man should follow, and by learning the harmonies and the revolutions of the universe should correct the courses of the head which were corrupted at our birth' (*Timaeus*, 89^e–90^d).

Disease in the body is not much different from evil and immoral thought. Often, man is responsible for his own disease, for the body attracts it by following the evil movements of indecent dances and drama, enjoying bad foods, tastes, smells and sights. Of course, disease may also come to the best of men through the independent activity of *Anangke*. Though physically he may be most uncomfortable, through accepting the pain of an undeserved disease a man may restore the order of his soul.

Fear entered the world with pain and disease, and in some ways is senior in evil to the latter, being higher in the hierarchy of movements by its capacity to engender those on a lower level (*Laws*, 893). Socrates remarked that the law would not have come into being for the sake of good men; St Paul that it 'is not laid down for the just but for the . . . ungodly and sinners' (I Timothy, I, 9). The cause of punishment and of all fear, in the Greek and Christian tradition, is sin, or those desires that are eliminated by a training in true philosophy.

Augustine wrote, in Sermon 145:

> Descend into thyself. Thou wilt see another law in thy members, fighting against the law of thy mind and captivating thee in the law of sin that is in thy members [see Romans, VII, 23]. . . . Why is this but that on receiving the commandment thou didst fear, not love? Thou didst fear punishment, thou didst not love justice.

It is, of course, the purpose of true philosophy – and not of logical positivism – to resolve this conflict between 'mind' and 'members'.

The fear we are concerned with here is that which we might today call 'existential fear' – the lack of confidence to abrogate internal motions by assuming the external motion of the universe. In the *Laws* (790), this fear is seen as 'an internal motion of the soul [which] can be influenced by external motion'. It is for this reason that Plato recommends that it should be overcome at the earliest stages, starting in the womb. Unlike Kant, who saw only the individual as capable of perfecting his own moral virtue, noetic thinkers, in view of a fundamental cosmic unity, regard parents as to some extent able to bestow virtue on their children; though to do this is more difficult than bestowing anything as concrete as advice, gifts or positive instructions. One can best educate the soul by movement, and particularly so when the child is still in the womb. Hence in the *Laws*, 790[b], Plato follows Damon, and legislates that pregnant women should go for walks, 'moulding the child like wax'. These ancient instructions are very strict with respect to the sentiments experienced by pregnant mothers: they should abstain from violent pleasures, and concentrate on divine thoughts, love and prayer. This attitude is still prevalent in Hinduism today, where the pregnant mother is instructed to be continuously thinking with love of her child. While eating, sleeping and resting, she should be imagining that she is acting for the sake of the child. Sexual intercourse for pregnant women is only permitted in the first stages of pregnancy if the mother-to-be abstains from lust and keeps her pleasures rooted in love.

Plato also takes minute care in legislation concerning children, and demands that pregnant women be entertained, kept happy and visited and advised by family and by the officials of the State. The swaddling and the wrapping up of babies is given moral significance. Babies should be carried about and rocked: ideally, Plato would have them spend all their time on the sea, assimilating the cosmic movement manifested by the roll of the waves (*Laws*, 790[c]). Certainly, young children should be taken for all kinds of rides on sea and land – since children are close to God they will inevitably enjoy all these movements. The assumption behind all this is that universal rhythms are manifested in the seasonal cycles, the roll of the surf, the sway of the trees in the wind: man is estranged from this natural cosmic rhythm and should continuously strive to imitate it in his movement, in his thought and in all his activity.

II

A further insight into *Choreia* may be gained by reference to Confucius:

> Men's behaviour is governed by a mind in large measure motivated by love and hate, joy and depression, fear, jealousy, anger, tenderness and compassion. Two things are necessary: the first to bring about an inner harmony of the mind so that each emotion as it arises is given a fitting outlet. No emotion must be allowed unbridled expression, but one must seek to cultivate a balanced harmony within the mind itself. In this pursuit the melodies, harmonies and rhythms of music are of great value, and in the process of character training there are few things that can match the disciplined co-ordination of an orchestra or the rhythmic and balanced movements of a formal ritual dance (Smith, 1973, p. 72).

For Confucius, music (by music he, like Plato, means a combination of movement, dance, poetry and music) was instrumental in teaching virtue: indeed he saw it as a more powerful medium than philosophy itself.

Choreia – referred to in Chinese as *Li* – was even more important in Confucian teaching than in Plato's, and Confucius claimed that no philosophy was possible without it. Socrates and Confucius point to dangers in the professionalization of dancing and singing. A gentleman is not a gentleman unless he is thus schooled – and a wife who cannot sing for her husband and family but relies on the services of slaves is not a proper lady. *Li* was also important as a force for social cohesion: 'Ritual and music were the essential manifestation of culture. Music, which included miming and dancing, was a powerful stimulus to the community spirit, whether in solemn seasonal and family festivals or in the rhythmic chanting' (Smith, 1973, p. 63).

While processions, Bacchic dances and festivals were also a part of Greek life, one cannot too readily equate these with the corybantic *Choreia* as it was understood by noetic tradition. There are many reasons for believing that the corybantic synthesis described by Plato had already atrophied in the city of Athens, that it was something characteristic of the Socratic method but foreign to later Greek experience. Linforth argues that the ordinary corybantic ritual was an unusual and rare phenomenon associated with Orphism, and in spite of its outward resemblance to the cult dances and so forth was an essentially different activity. Indeed, the charge against Socrates that he was corrupting youth through strange practices and the introduction of foreign gods may have had something to do with this.

Some pointers may be found in Proclus and particularly Psellus: though, since some of this evidence may be spurious, I will not attach much weight to it, mentioning it only in so far as it has parallels elsewhere. Psellus writes in the *Pletho* of the 'second order' of Platonic philosophy, corresponding to the Zoroastrian order of Synoches and Teletarchs given by Damascius. Through meditating on such cosmic movements man loses his fear. The practice of curing existential fear by movements and dance is still common in Iran, and has been incorporated into Islam. In 'Bastani', which is both rhythmic and gymnastic, the participants whirl weights and execute dancelike movements to the chanting of poetry. Its Zoroastrian origins are the cause of hostility in some circles. There is also evidence for Socrates' use of dance and mime to perfect the soul in the *Lives* of Diogenes Laertus, and in Ferguson (1970, p. 229), quoting Atheneas.

It can certainly be inferred from the reactions of his co-citizens that Socrates' activities were not of a kind considered normal and usual by the Athenians. They were foreign to Hellas. His trances, his dancing or standing still 'from dawn to dusk' perplexed the indifferent, gave cause for complaint to his enemies, and were startling even to his friends. I have already referred earlier to the *Parmenides* as being a corybantic dialogue, based on oriental techniques that force the mind to enter into a specific movement, transcending the particular meaning conventionally conveyed by words. This was anther manifestation of the same method. In the *Charmides* (156^{e}–157), Socrates tells the young man of a technique he has learned from a wise foreigner (Zalmoxis, who is also said to be able to point the way to immortality). The technique is to cure the soul by the use of verbal charms: 'And the cure of the soul, my dear youth, has to be effected by the use of certain charms, and these charms are fair words, and by them temperance is implanted in the soul.' That the Socratic dialogue itself is corybantic is enunciated specifically by Alcibiades: 'When I listen to him my state is like that of the corybantic devotees' (*Symposium*, 215). References may also be found in the *Crito*, 54^{d}, the *Euthyphro*, 227$^{d, e}$ and the *Phaedrus*, 228^{b}.

Sensitivity to inner logic, even today, is one of the criteria by which potential students are assessed at the Muslim University in Cairo, and it forms part of the post-graduate curricula in the fields of theology and Islamic thought in general. One is tested for rhythm by recital. Whether one has understood the text is judged not only by the verbal elaboration, but also by the rhythmic pronunciations.

> [The] habit of recital in strict sequence fixed the juxtaposition of Quranic incidents and endowed them with a sort of second logic. Adjacence became significant of meaning, and sense was linked strongly with proximity (Cragg, 1973, p. 26).

Plato, too, frequently recommends that the *Laws* should be chanted, repeated over and over again, memorized and recited as poetry, for this in itself will make one a better man' (*Laws*, 811^{c}, 858^{e}, 957^{c}). It is not enough merely to express a thought; it must be done rhythmically and aesthetically, and there is an objective aesthetics to guide all one's actions. Ethical notions themselves have a dimension which is aesthetically pleasing. The fact that this is 'lost to contemporary man', writes Taylor (1934, p. 34), is due to a 'certain aesthetic imperceptiveness on our part.' If the ethical dimension has, in some sense, a visible, or aesthetically perceivable dimension or body, we may infer that the converse is true: for a perceptive man the extended aspect of the aesthetical will have an ethical dimension. It is this which characterizes the structure of the Platonic dialogues. Differences between the contradictory elements are resolved by rhythm.

Nor must we ever forget the close connection between *Choreia* and politics: for 'Change in music is always accompanied by a change in the state' (*Republic*, 424^{c}).

III

While *Choreia* may be the single least discussed issue in Greek history and philosophy, that of number may well turn out to be the one least understood. The interpretation I have followed above sees number as the inner, the fixed determinant which manifests outwardly as the sentiment. There are, however, difficulties with this interpretation, whose exposition may in a way enhance rather than obscure my position.

In the earlier discussion of *Aritmos*, my objection to recent interpretation was based on the Saanthana position that knowledge cannot be frozen into objectified formulae, be they mathematical or astrological, since epistemology is not independent of ethics.

This having been stated, we cannot but notice that for Plato there does appear to be a certain 'publicly objective' dimension to numbers and to their manifestations. One of England's foremost Greek scholars, J. Adam, devoted three years to working out just one of the many mathematical problems posed by Plato. His painstaking calculation of the Nuptial Number as 12,960,000 was, from my point of view, misguided, if Adam believed that it was going to help men to better their souls or to father their children in season (although the activity may well have been beneficial for Adam in less obvious ways). But: why does Plato, like St John and Zoroaster, enter into such detail as to imbue their texts with precise formulae? Even a relatively superficial study reveals that the numerical relations expressed and implied are not arbitrary – they are not just figurative examples of natural rhythm. They appear to be literal and objective, but fragmentary, presentations of a coherent universal system.

Our inability to account for this system of 'ethical mathematics', thanks to four centuries of conceptual conditioning, does not create such an interpretational gap that we can bridge it only by a leap of faith. Even if we do not know what kind of mathematics it was that was practised by the disciples of Jesus or at the Academy, it has already been established that the mental process involved in its study is not to be equated with the one by which the contemporary mind acquires mathematical knowledge. Plato's advice that the study of mathematics is conducive to philosophical knowledge has no validity if applied to contemporary dianoic mathematics, 'the science of measuring and comparing and predicting sequences' (*Republic*, 516[d]), which Plato says is for auxiliaries, not philosophers.

Of course, one should not take this too far. Whatever Plato meant by standardizing the size of cups and saucers (*Laws*, 747[a–d]) in a ratio to the circumference of the earth, the orbit of the moon and so on, he could not have meant that drinking out of such cups and saucers was in itself enough to make one dear to the gods. But that number is more objective than *most* of the dialogues would suggest is evidenced in the *Philebus* (66[a]). Having argued for the superiority of a life based on reason as against a life based on the blind following of pleasure, Socrates comes to an unexpected conclusion. Failing to introduce his terms or in any way prepare the reader, he concludes by asserting that there are in life five most important possessions: the first being measure (*To Metron*); second, proportion and only in the third place reason, followed by *Techne* and pleasure. ('And if you accept what I divine, and put reason and intelligence third, you will not be very wide of truth.') The other dialogues might have led one to believe that reason (in the divine sense) would top Plato's hierarchy, or at least come second after the direct vision (*Periagoge*).

One can perhaps understand *To Metron* to signify *Diarithmesis*, the correct rhythmic movement of the soul by which one differentiates the good from the bad. It would then equate with the ethical Golden Mean, as well as with the categorical injunction in the *Laws* and *Epinomis* (989[b]) to the effect that there is 'No greater possession or virtue than Piety'. But perhaps the mathematical *To Metron* does not coincide with the ethical *To Metron*. Plato demands nothing short of the most literal standardization of practically every physical object, building or utensil. That the calendar should be standardized has, of course, immediate religious significance; but it is less obvious why toys, clothes and roads should all conform to objectively fixed numbers. Brumbaugh (1962, p. 81) sees the system as duodecimal, yet Adam and McClain posit a multiplicity of systems. One may ask what the Athenian's intentions are in the following:

> 'These facts of number, then, must be thoroughly mastered at leisure by those whose business the law will make it to understand them; they will find them exactly as I stated them, and they must be mentioned by the founder of a city, for the reason I shall now give.'

The reasons given are ethical injunctions from prophets, visionaries and the moral traditions: 'since no man of sense will presume to disturb convictions inspired from Delphi, Dodona, the oracle of Ammon, or by old traditions of any kind of divine appearances or reported divine revelations' (*Laws*, 738[b–c]).

Perhaps we may infer that Plato's numbers are not all newly derived in the Academy: he may be simply following established practice. His idea that men and women should eat together, and that drinking be allowed in Systitia, are met with expressions of amazement; whereas his geometric city planning seems to call for no explanation. It has already been mentioned that cities and temples used to be constructed on traditional principles (and see Friedlander, 1969, I, pp. 318–20). If Plato's numbers were part of a universal system, studying them would not mean calculation and the derivation of formulae by *Dianoia* at all; it might be compared again to the use of Gregorian chants, rhythmic poetry and other similar corybantic exercises. The Revelation to St John also gives an objective formula for the construction of the New Jerusalem, but the Christian Church has not found it necessary to implement these instructions literally. If these formulae were drawn from an existing tradition, their context may have given them a meaning beyond the one that we immediately discern in our literalistic fashion.

Various keys are available to us if we wish to recover some of this lost mathematical tradition. Scholars like A.E.Berriman, Ernest G.McClain and John Michell – and before them Newton and Napier – have demonstrated the interrelation of standard measures and common specifications for city or temple with astronomical constants such as the diameter of the moon. Each side of St John's New Jerusalem measures 12,000 furlongs, and the total perimeter 48,000 furlongs or 31,680,000 feet. This last number has connections with various temples around the world: for example, the mean perimeter of the sarsen circle at Stonehenge is 316.8 feet, and the area of sacred land recorded as belonging to the Abbey of Glastonbury by the Domesday Book has a perimeter of 31,680 feet. The combined radii of the earth and the moon amount to 5,040 miles (Plato's mystical number, the population of Magnesia), and if you draw a circle with this diameter its circumference is 31,680 miles – which is the same as the periphery of a square drawn around the earth alone. In the *Laws* (745[d]), the Athenian demands that the land occupied by the circular city be divided between its citizens. The city's radius becomes 5,040 units, and its circumference therefore, like that of New Jerusalem, 31,680. Such calculations could be prolonged indefinitely – but it is not my contention that the Academy spent its time doing so.

IV

The State, writes Guthrie in *The Greeks and their Gods*, was for the Greeks in some sense their Church. The essence of any city has this underlying dimension. So does the human body. 'Destroy this temple, and in three days I will raise it up' (John, III, 19). According to the 'enlightened' interpretation of this text, Jesus was referring to his own body – of course, this one conceptualization of his meaning should not be overextended to exclude the others. The extension in stone, brick and mortar is one dimension of the body of Christ, and is also involved in the process of restoration, even if the three days would then have a less straightforward significance referring perhaps to *Kalpas, Yugas* or ontological realms. The body of the *Logos* is all the creation subject to history: it includes words, thoughts, churches, physical bodies and all cities.

Solmsen (1942, p. 6) writes: 'the deity that represents and personifies the city actually is the city'. It is clear from the context that he is referring not to the totality of the perceived city, but rather to its purified dimension, which I have described as the true city. Nor is the 'temple' to be restricted to a perceived house of worship and its official keepers, for they participate in the city just as Babylon participates in New Jerusalem or Athens in Menexenus. Identification with the city, Solmsen (1942, p. 155), points out, serves to facilitate an identification with the cosmic whole. In order for the actual to coincide with the ideal, the inner with the outer, the earthly city must imitate the cosmic pattern.

Plato's 'cosmic' view of an Athens-in-the-sky need not be accepted solely on the authority of scholars. In the *Timaeus*, (21–25), Plato writes of this eternally recurring Athens that has existed since the dawn of time; and in 21[e] he equates the goddess Athena with the Egyptian deity Neith, giving credence to the claims of Friedlander and others that both gods and their temples have an oriental origin. Plato, as we have seen, develops his dialogues along anatomical lines, and the city of Magnesia is specifically equated with the headless body: (since the workings of the head aspect are described in a separate dialogue, the *Republic*). 'Why, manifestly the city at large is the trunk of the body'(*Laws*, 964[e]).

In *The City and the Image of Man*, T.C.Stewart, relying on a collection of sources, city plans and a Hindu temple, analyses the anatomical aspects of the city to show that it does indeed express basic psychological constants. From these and similar accounts (see Patai, 1947) one is led to conclude that the so-called Platonic imperatives – class divisions, standardization of objects and measures – need not be provided for or implemented by legislation, since they are taking form all the time. The objective is to recognize these realities and to adjust to them in the best possible way. Even Voltaire recognized this, in his *Lettres sur l'Atlantide* (in Bailly, 1879).

To the wealth of evidence that Plato's instructions concerning the outward dimension of Magnesia form a part of a universal numerical system, scholarship has responded in two ways. The nineteenth century simply ignored this dimension, while contemporary scholarship has turned to the other extreme, and interprets Plato's philosophy in terms of objective mathematics. As these facts enter popular consciousness all kinds of fantastic speculations will no doubt be made. My own position is that the objective aspect simply points to the fact that Magnesia is an ethical, numerical skeleton: that this is so can be inferred both from the text and from parallels in other religions. It will be a sad day when the research on this and similar problems is used to sell books on alchemy and magical numbers. One can understand the hesitancy of men who have devoted hundreds or thousands of hours to painstaking research in this field, only to have the fruit of their labour exploited by charlatans and sensationalists. One the other hand, the fundamental unicity of the teaching of the ancient cultures – be it that of Zoroastrians, Taoists or the Academy – has already reached into our reality. The kind of philosphy taught in the last century has nothing to do with the ideas of contemporary mathematics or physics. Contemporary man will soon have to revise his views and relation towards past, present and future.

V

> 'Not only for plants that grow in the earth, but for animals that live on it, there are the seasons of fertility and infertility of both mind and body, seasons which come when their periodic motions come full circle' (*Republic*, 546[d]).

The cause of all decay, Socrates goes on to say, is a falling out of that seasonal rhythm.

Asked how to ensure that no subversive movement of the soul creeps into the life of Magnesia, the Athenian answers that the evil sentiments (such as lust, pleasure, anger) will be kept out of everyday life by drawing up a correct calendar, ensuring an orderly exchange between activity and rest, work and festival, and also involving the sanctification of dance and music:

> 'The first job will be to settle the festivals by drawing up the year's programme, which should show the dates of the various holidays and the individual gods, children of gods or spirits in whose honour they should be taken' (*Laws*, 799).

This seasonal notion of life persists even today. According to Josef Pieper (1954, p. 80), echoing a pronouncement of Pope Pius X, to be a Christian means to participate in the Christian rhythm. Apart from the formal attendance of mass, one shares in the religious life through 'living the Church year':

> The liturgical year is made up of two different but complementary elements which dovetail. One is the week, the other is the series of feasts of Christ. The annual cycle of the feasts of our Lord puts into tangible terms of space and time the recital of the second part of the Creed.

Professor E.O.James shows how close the relationship is between this Christian rhythm and that of the pagan cults – in fact between each event in the Christian calendar and an ancient counterpart. In the *Laws*, each part of the year, and even each part of the month, is to be characterized by a particular spirit, and secular activities, whether work or music, must be in harmony with that spirit. In the Christian liturgical year each spirit is represented by a saint. Professor James interprets the Protestant rejection of the saints as a rejection of the liturgical year, and an attempt to replace a holiday-work pattern that is in keeping with the spiritual rhythm by an idolatrous gnostic or commercial one.

Colours are also significant, and are prescribed by Plato in his city plans. The linking of green, white, orange and red to the seasons appears to be almost universal, and they are, for example, worn by Catholic priests at the appropriate times. Professor James finds Whitsun symbolized by the colour red and also by the sound of trumpets, signifying the sacred wind, the breath of life, linked with spring and rebirth. Red is also the first of the seven colours of the rainbow which links the earth to the sky and which represents a covenant between God and man. The division of the rainbow into seven colours connects it to the seven sacraments of the Church.

Such matters are commonly ignored, but Plato remarks, 'Those whose business is to understand them – they will find them exactly as I have stated them' (*Laws*, 738[b]). Evidently such matters have been and are of great importance. Pope Victor in AD 190 almost precipitated the subsequent split of the Churches by threatening to excommunicate the East for calendar modifications. And Plato seems even more papist than the Pope. In the *Laws* (809[c]) he observes that the city can only be kept *alive* 'if the sacrifices and feasts may fit into the true and natural order, and receive their several proper celebrations'. In 809[d] he goes on to say that in doing this 'men are advancing in intelligence'. Knowing through doing is of course standard for Plato; understanding is a result of building in accordance with the given pattern (*Laws*, 738[a–e]).

McClain (1978, p. 15) traces the seven day week through the Greek, Zoroastrian, Egyptian and Hindu calendars. The seven days are the seven steeds of the sun's chariot. The year is divided into 360 parts, with a five-day New Year holiday. This corresponds to the division of the circle into 360 parts; hence for Hindus 360 years is a year of gods, and 3600^2 (12,960,000) is a cycle of Prajapati. It is also the number of citizens of Atlantis, the circumference of the earth in stadia, etc.

In the *Gorgias*, 504[c], Socrates equates regularity with health and order, and goes on to repeat the opinions voiced in the *Republic* that the cause of social and individual disease is a falling out of the natural rhythm. Gaiser (1963) sees the philosopher as the one who ensures that the rhythm of the *Polis* should follow the cosmos: a difficult task in times of decay. For Eliade, 'the year is the totality of cosmic time', which may be what Plato meant in the *Timaeus* (37^d) by 'Time is the moving image of eternity' – by observing the seasonal interchange taking place within each year we participate in the entire cosmic story. Eliade (1979, p. 332) sees the last ten days of the year as 'an eschatological drama', linking it with the general resurrection.

All these clues convey the impression that, for Philosophia Perennis, distinctions between the physical and psychological cycles of life are hard to make, for there is an all-embracing cosmic unity involving both.

VI

The contemporary concept conveyed by the word *leisure* relates imperfectly to the notion shared by Confucius, Aquinas and, to an extent, Aristotle. For the latter, leisure was 'thought of not merely as free time, but as the opportunity for creatively constructive activity, which is summed up in the life of the *Polis*' (Morrall, 1977, p. 89). In a way, the differences and similarities between the Confucian and Aristotelian notions of leisure illustrate both the basic philosphical affinity and the spiritual gap which separates China from Hellas.

For Confucius, disinterested activity was to act as a vehice for the rectification of the hearts of men. For Plato, leisure meant absorption in the divine, to the exclusion of concern for with outcomes in the secular sphere. The scholastics agreed, as did Ficino, that the divine being, within ourselves and everywhere, can be comprehended only in 'stillness, leisure and peace'. It is other, lesser things that are in particular places, and must be sought by movement and effort. The eye of the mind perceives the divine light as soon as it ceases to be distracted by worldly affairs, for, in a phrase of Ficino's, 'to be turned toward the divine means simply not to be turned away from it' (cf. 'he that is not against you is for you', Luke, IX, 50).

The compulsion to work and struggle is foreign to man and enters reality through fear: accepting that God will provide for clothes and shelter, one ceases to work for the sake of this goal. By adopting this attitude toil ceases to be toil and becomes the joyous fulfilment of a service. Work is ritualized when it becomes service, be it to Caesar or to the Law. The Islamic *Shariah* appears to be secular, but has been sanctified.

> The ideal of the religious man is, of course, that everything should be done ritually. On that account every act is liable to become a religious act, just as every natural object is liable to become a hierophany. In other words, any moment may be inserted into the Greater Time, and thus project man into eternity (Eliade, 1958, p. 460).

In the Age of Cronus, all work was done by gods, and even rules and laws were living spirits. The Age of Cronus, as suggested above, is actuality: not the perceived actuality but rather the one defined as *Chora*, 'That in which all elements severally grow up and appear and decay is alone to be called this or that.' And ritual is a celebration or assumption of actuality.

It is not the case that the religious law is necessarily superior to the secular: by his inner acceptance of the secular law *as* religious man emancipates himself and his obedience, and then 'Human existence takes place simultaneously upon two parallel planes, that of the temporal, of change and illusion, and that of reality' (Eliade, 1958, p. 460). It is the perceived which is the illusion. Existence in the perfect city is that aspect of the physical which has been projected into the higher sphere. Man actualizes his life in so far as he consecrates his activity.

The temple, argues Pieper (1952), is a piece of ground which is no longer private property, no longer used for any practical activity, but consecrated to God. Likewise for a holiday or a festival: it is a piece of time not to be used for any profitable activity. It is in this light that we can understand the paramount importance that the Greeks attach to the Festival and Jews to the Sabbath day. The Festival was man's gift to the gods (*Laws*, 653); it was restorative of the Age of Cronus. In joining in the *Choreia*, the procession or the dance, the natural order was re-established (*Laws*, 738) and the correct movement temporarily restored.

In the opening passage of Book VIII of the *Laws*, Clinias observes it will be not Delphi but the Magnesians who decide the number of festivals per year. The Athenian endorses this, for, as we learn in the next sentence, 'there should be no less than three hundred and sixty-five' (*Laws*, 878[b]). Plato here makes a decision independently from Delphi, to ensure an unbroken chain of festivals, sanctifying every single day.

What is the intention behind this? Consecrating work does not in any way diminish the objective amount of toil; the *Anangke* is portioned out equally, so that no matter what life, city, body, circumstance or period the soul chooses, the amount of *overcoming* will be fixed, even though it varies in form. In accepting toil as a necessity and consecrating it, one is freed from anxiety, and the pain becomes tolerable. He is liberated from interior, psychological pain, once he stops working from fear of hunger and cold.

> Look at the birds of the air: they neither sow nor reap nor gather in barns, and yet your heavenly Father feeds them. . . . Therefore do not be anxious, saying, 'What shall we eat?' or 'What shall we drink' or 'What shall we wear?' For the Gentiles seek all these things; and your heavenly Father knows that you need them all. But seek first his

> kingdom and his righteousness, and all these things shall be yours as well. Therefore do not be anxious about tomorrow, for tomorrow will be anxious for itself. Let the day's own trouble be sufficient for the day (Matthew, VI, 26–34).

In Magnesia, every day is a holy-day; every activity is undertaken not to procure livelihood but as a ceremonial act. 'How wondrous this, how mysterious, I carry fuel, I draw water' (Suzuki, 1959, p. 16).

In this study we have looked at the myth of the Fall, cross-referring from the Greek tradition to the Christian, the Middle and Far East. We might also have looked at the legends of Africa and the Pacific, for this experience is one that is shared by all living beings. All cultures are founded on the same rhythmic pattern. By permitting oneself to be subjugated to the basic forces in the universe, by following the rhythm of nature and the cosmos, one enters a higher region. This merging into the fundamental reality may be conceptualized as the consecration of one's activity to the gods or to God. All the great traditions point to a non-self oriented, or indirect, gratification of desire. A frightened man works for his food, a man immersed in the noetic rhythm procreates, works and plays for the greater self. But the laws of the cosmos are such that in doing this, he is inevitably rewarded, the curse is lifted. In words of the Tao Te Ching (VII): 'The sage stays behind, thus he is ahead. He is detached, thus at one with all. Through selfless action, he attains fulfillment.'

Fourteen
RECONCILIATION

Noetic philosophy is oriented towards a general reconciliation of all conflicts. This reconciliation is epistemological, ontological and ethical. It can be seen as triunal or as dual. Considered as the former, it is effected by a *Diaresis* or separation of things according to their ontological status and psychological affinity. Things are assigned to the realms of being, becoming or actuality. Living things are characterized according to the basic psychological characteristics of *Thumos*, *Epithumia* and *Logisticon*. These characteristics pervade all creation in numerous and complex relations; their reconciliation is a result of assigning each thing, and each of the various constituents of a thing, to its corresponding realm or dimension in the one cosmos.

This diaretic reconciliation is the one which closely approximates the behaviour of men and societies in times of transition. Falsely conglomerated societies and concepts are dissolved, and each thing becomes what it is.

Equally important is *dual* reconciliation by reduction to a comprehensive sentiment, or a ratio. When the two are reduced to one, previously existing entities appear to have been abolished or negated. Reconciliation by synthesis may therefore seem opposed to reconciliation by *Diaresis* in which entities are reaffirmed, not absorbed. The two types of reconciliation correspond to the two ways of looking at falsity: as *Parekbasis* (aberration) or as *Anatrope* (inversion). All things are brought into existence by these two processes, *Diaresis* and *Sinkresis*. And from another point of view, even this duality disappears. The two processes are one, just as the evening star is the morning star.

Each thing is triunal – it splits into three principles. This same rule holds for *Diaresis*, *Sinkresis* and the two negative principles, *Parekbasis* and *Anatrope*. Thus, on the positive side the dialectical process involves six movements, and the same is true for the negative. The six positive movements are comprehended in the seventh, all-comprehensive movement of the Good, which Plato, the Zoroastrians, Heraclitus and the noetic tradition in general call the organizational principle of the universe, or *Logos*, the Word or human aspect of God. (The eighth movement, *Auto Kath-Auto*, is the invisible One, which itself is triunal. The totality of movements is therefore ten: seven belonging to the Word on earth, and three to God in heaven.)

All lines of distinction must meet somewhere, though one may purposely refrain from making them do so. Confucius and Lao Tzu, Heraclitus and Parmenides relied on the second type of exposition, creating dualistic distinctions apparently without synthesis. But epistemological schism was not created by noetic thinkers, although they accepted it, Zoroaster speaking of two world souls, Plato of the Gods of left and right, Lao Tzu of yin and yang. Man imagines that he is living in a dual world; noetic thought is not responsible for this condition.

The noetic philosophy is not simply a theory or a system aiming at conceptual coherence; it is a set of potentially contradictory theories aimed at contextual coherence, that is, coherence with respect to a particular intention, necessarily related to practical considerations. Were there such a thing as a master synthesis of noetic thought, it would, if verbalized, most certainly deny the co-reality of the evil and the good. Yet it would be wrong to look for this idea in any particular scriptural passage. In so far as the formula exists, it does so through the sentiment.

This kind of thought is concerned with 'aspectual' knowledge. Where and when it appears necessary to use a dualistic argument it does so. In attempting to reduce this duality to singularity to achieve philosophical coherence, one makes such a philosophy *less* coherent in a deeper sense. Final truth really is of such a nature that it can more truly be represented by sets of dichotomies.

Perceived reality is dual when objectivized in speech: the task of the philosopher and the statesman is to reconcile its contradictory aspects. The world is good as it is; however, men do not see it *as it is*. The philosopher can only provide them with counter-images in order to do away with images.

It is always two aspects of good which are erroneously perceived as good and bad by warring factions, as J.B.Morrall (1977, p. 22) observes with reference to Aeschylus:

> the real tragedy in cosmos, *Polis* and personality is the conflict between differing aspects of good, whose discrepancy can only be resolved by

> their voluntary and complementary merging in a more adequately comprehensive synthesis.

This comprehensive synthesis is not something artificial or invented; yet it would be dangerous and irresponsible to force people to a pretended ideal of unity before it is perceived as reality. Conflicts between public and private goods, the conflict between Antigone and the city cult, all these are potentially resolvable; yet before the catharsis their duality is 'real' and has to be accounted for.

The achievement of reconciliation has a historical dimension in the perpetual meeting of the old and new world deities. Plato provided the rational and philosophical background for a movement from anthropomorphic gods, interpreted as real existents, to the notion of such entities as representing psychological forces, contained by the pervasive unifying cosmic sentiment. This 'new' notion, that of the underlying pattern, seems to have been sprouting independently throughout the (Middle) East at the time it was formulated into intellectual principles by the Greeks. The idea that the East is more conducive to discernment of deity, whereas Hellas is better at understanding deity and applying it to the creation of laws, cities and philosophy, is voiced in the *Laws* (747[d]) and *Epinomis* (987[d]):

> 'Greeks enjoy a geographical situation which is exceptionally favourable to the attainment of excellence. . . . [It is, however, not so excellent a location for the discernment of spiritual forces, hence] it is our deficiency in respect of summer, by comparison with the peoples of other [Eastern] regions, which, as we said, has made us later than they in discerning these gods [the new, true gods].

While the Greeks were a local event, they may also stand for Western civilization. The sceptical European of today may well ask himself whether there is a lesson for him in the Athenian's attribution of 'all his achievements . . . to the discovery of new, non-Greek gods'; and in the passage:

> 'There is every ground for the splendid hope that, though the news of these gods and their worship has come to us from non-Greeks, the Greeks will learn to worship them all in a truly nobler and more righteous fashion' (*Epinomis*, 987d).

If the Jews gave birth to monotheism through the synthesizing instrumentality of the temple, as Patai (1947, pp. 54–105) suggests, Plato synthesized Olympic and *Chthonic* deities by means of philosophy, and reduced the dichotomous deities to singularity by means of a comprehensive sentiment. ('Plato' understood in the broadest sense stands for the noetic thinker, of course, and his exercise of reconciliation can be nothing other than an ongoing event.) Greek religion was centred on this dualism between the *Chthonic* and Olympian gods: 'The contrast between Chthonian and Olympian, then, is the contrast between earthly and heavenly' (Guthrie, 1950, p. 207). The purport of noetic philosophy is, in contemporary terms, the removal of utopian idealism and vulgar positivism; for the ancients it was this search for the meeting point of the two rivers, upward and downward, heavenly and earthly, inner and outer. By accepting the gods both of the right and of the left, both heavenly and earthly, 'Plato' is accepting *Anangke* (Karma) as a part of destiny. In this way he accounts for evil as necessity, and eliminates all real need for dual deities, good and bad. Less sophisticated thinkers, symbolized by the historic Aristotle, always see the indefinite part of the dyad as material and earthly, and as the source of evil: they do not undergo the non-mental, supraconceptual process of synthesizing the two elements of the dyad, the vertical and horizontal.

Plato, although a proud Greek, was not ashamed to learn from foreign cultures. The first line of the *Republic* (327[a]) reads: 'Down I went to . . . the festival of Bendis the new *foreign* goddess, being presented by *foreigners*, and observing that, while the Greek procession was fine, the foreign contingent was equally as good' (my emphasis). The yang, the masculine element, accounts for the economic and military might of Athens, but this is not enough. In the *Laws*, (e.g.795[d]) Plato hints at the *Chthonic* deities by means of allusions to the left hand: 'there will be men responsible that all our boys and girls may grow up ambicrural and ambidextrous'. In the *Phaedrus*, 266[a], the speech is supposed to cover the left-hand side of the body as well as the right. In the same dialogue we learn that, although by itself the 'left' type of love becomes perverse, we are not to destroy it, but to control it. The black horse of the soul-chariot is not to be discarded, but properly integrated to fit with the white. 'I say the mark of godliness will be truly hit if the gods of the lower world are held in honour next to [i.e. together with] the Olympians . . . the left hand being consecrated to them' (*Phaedrus*, 717[b]).

Having accepted suffering as *Anangke*, necessity, one is able to claim that everything sent by gods is good. We can deny the gods' duality: the two sets of twelve *Chthonic* and twelve Olympian deities are reduced to six dual tendencies, which are the basic psychological forces, or six movements of the soul that I have referred to as sentiments. The six of the left are reconciled in the movement of the female or of the earth (which constitutes a seventh) and the movements of heaven are synthesized in the masculine. Rather than maintain two sets of deities (good and bad, heavenly and earthly), one posits a single set, each containing a counter-movement. Thus both the soul and the gods ultimately reflect the same entity, the One, or the *Logos*. 'Thy will be done on earth as it is in heaven.' Plato's victory was to rejuvenate the two sets of deities and to 'snatch' the seven of the left up and away from the various cults that were flourishing in fifth-century Athens, while at the same time taking the wind out of the clever army of sophists that were proliferating and controlling the cultural life of Hellas.

The fifth century was not a century like any other – it was the century when the greatest Upanishads and the Bhagavad Gita were written, and when Taoism, Confucianism, Zoroastrianism and Buddhism became formal religions. It was a century of change, in Athens, in Hastinapura and in the Yangtse valley. The yang, the all-too clever intellectual element guided by the reigning commercial forces, had almost done away with the sentiments of the humane tradition. It had rationalized the organizing principle of society and reduced the meaning of life to mentally deducible formulae. The response to this universal tendency towards conceptualization was a wave of occultism, the flood of the downward river, the revolt of the female. And it is in such times that noetic thought arises to reconcile the mind to the body, heart to reason.

> When righteousness is weak and faints and unrighteousness exults in pride, then my Spirit arises on earth. For the salvation of those who are good, for the destruction of evil in men, for the fulfilment of the kingdom of righteousness, I come to this world in the ages that pass (Bhagavad Gita, IV, 7–8).

For those historically minded, the Bhagavad Gita, Plato's dialogues and Confucius' analects may be a local historical event. For others, they symbolize a never-ending process, as relevant today as yesterday.

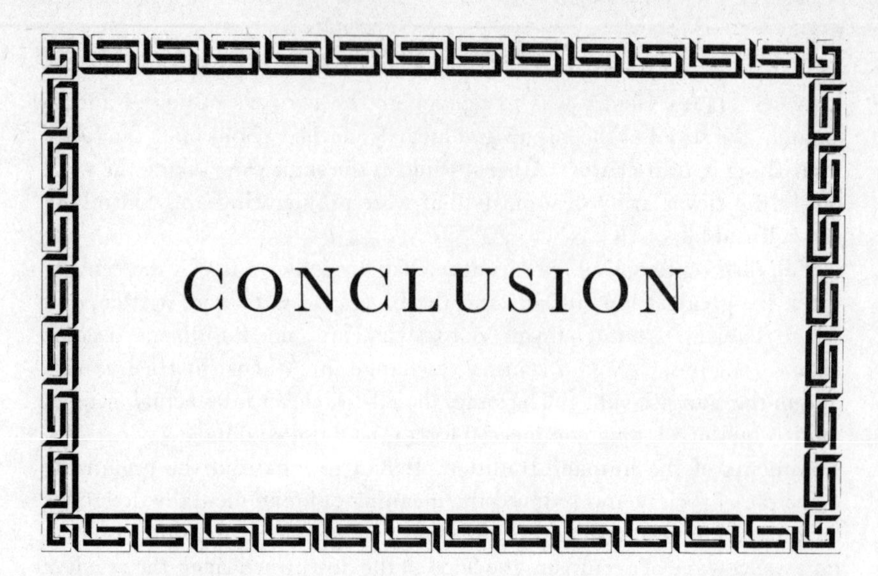

CONCLUSION

In this study I have argued that the Saanthana tradition uses rhythm to affect readers and listeners so that they will act and think, and even build their political and social world, in accord with a certain pattern. This pattern is one which any properly functioning entity should necessarily reflect, and this reflection takes place in the formative medium Plato called *Chora*, the third ontological realm which I have called actuality.

Opposed to this stands the perceived world of becoming, characterized by *Pleonexia*, the war of all against all. This second, perceived world is only a phantasm, yet its illusions are continually being re-created by the conjectural mind.

When correctly apprehended, the three parts of the soul and the entity man-polis-cosmos are held together by a unifying rhythm and ratio, *Aritmos*. Only in departing from this rhythm do things become subject to the contrary pull of desire in which *Pleonexia* takes place. This misapprehension involves conflict in the soul, but one cannot end the conflict simply by *desiring* peace or well-being. Once subject to the inversion, man no longer perceives himself as what he is. Thereafter, whenever he wants to maximize his own well-being, it is the well-being of something which he is not that he pursues, and in this way he aggravates both his own condition and that of the true units and individuals around him.

For this reason, when noetic thinkers describe social utopias or ideal constitutions, they do not mean them for literal implementation. Utopias are models of an idealized goal, which requires human well-being to be judged according to false criteria, the criteria which apply to the perceived rather than to the true dimensions of man. Goals such as individual peace of mind, wealth and health, are all imperfect for noetic entities, since the identity they presuppose is inadequate.

In short, then, man cannot by any autonomous activity remove the cause of *Anatrope*, the epistemological inversion. In fact, it is precisely the hubris, the proud assumption of perceptual self-sufficiency, that brings the false self into birth.

This argument has been presented in four stages. First, in Part One I tried to show that the process of apprehension functions correctly only when based on notional principles that are organized by the sentiments. This type of apprehension is labelled *Noesis* in Greek thought and it derives from the ethical light of the Good itself. *Noesis* is opposed to *Dianoia*, autonomous thought based in the world of becoming, which is merely a conjectural interpretation superimposed on true apprehension and valid only when used in conjunction with noetically derived principles.

In Part Two, the city model was examined to see how the ruling philosophic element of the soul might free itself of the desire to be what it is not. How could the *Logisticon*, the higher mind, be separated from the body – which in this context is not the corporeal, extended aspect of man but a conglomeration of desires around a false notion of self?

In Part Three, an analysis of mythological images, I looked at the origin of *Anatrope*, the Fall. This was identified with the desire to think and act independently of the movement of the universe. I looked too at the bodily aspect of noetic thought, or learning through the body. The physical, extended city is the city that is concerned with the outward dimension of the self, in household and social interaction. It plays an important part in reconciling the various aspects of the self with the regulative principles of the soul. Throughout all the traditions mentioned, an interest in social and personal exemplars is sparked by the need for a deeper harmony, based on the noetic apprehension of a universal pattern. That pattern is implicit in every tradition, but never explicitly described by philosophers. It may be objectively experienced, however, and we may infer that it reflects that one being beyond all being, the maker and creator of the universe, of whom we find we cannot speak (*Timaeus*, 28c). An aspect of this being is the Good itself, which cannot be known directly yet which is made known to us by its light. This light both constitutes the true unities and renders them visible. It is this light which may be called the organizing principle of the universe, it has been given the name of *sentiment*.

EPILOGUE

I

THE BAREFOOT PHILOSOPHER

The study contained in the foregoing book completes a particular movement, even if it lacks a satisfactory justification for some of its assumptions or an adequate conclusion. In adding this Epilogue I am imitating the structure of the Upanishads and that of Greek philosophical discourses that seem to end in an anticlimax. The Upanishads themselves are a series of postscripts to the Vedas.

An epilogue may attempt to summarize; yet often it elaborates an aspect which need not appear particularly important to a given reader – and with which he need not agree. It must be taken as a personal flourish by the author – rather like the Greek villagers who, when leaving the café, do not find it adequate to say 'Goodbye' two or three times, 'Good day' and 'Be seeing you', but just before leaving suddenly repeat a sentence that was used by someone in the course of the conversation, and having said this, step out and are gone.

To the following, in which my personal prejudices may be even more apparent than elsewhere, I shall add a further appendix yet – one which deals with the notion *Logos* – and which itself will terminate with a single quotation, which in some ways throws the whole discussion open again.

PROGRESS

That the new is better than the old is an important notion for the consumer-oriented society. Like all ideas, this one has its justification and is based on a fundamental truth; however, the sophist within us turns this truth upside down.

Conceptual thinking employs old images or *Eikones*. 'Progress' is the replacement of one social or philosophical theory, one *Eikon* by a new one. The flow of *Eikones*, however, is not really conducive to the birth of a new kind of thinking: in order to maintain the illusion, the process of replacement has to become an accelerating one, and the same applies to all appetitive activity. The market calls for new products, new ways of opening a can, new forms of marriage, new forms of burial: it wants a new philosophy and a new language every year. This study has tried to show that the search for the new definition, the new language, the new *Eikon* is an attempt to resist real birth, to prevent movement rather than to promote it.

To create involves pain, permanent inner restructuring. The person unwilling to create, unwilling to suffer pain, will hide the fact by maintaining an outward semblance of activity. The uncreative artist will adopt eccentric dress, and become ever more 'outrageous'. Furthermore, he will demand ever more perfect tools. It has been remarked that contemporary philosophy consists of the sharpening of pens in preparation for the writing of philosophy. In the same way, the contemporary artist or musician demands ever better materials and instruments. He is given an electronic organ which supplies beat and harmony; he can play a tune by mechanically pressing a single precoded key. Yet the Indian sitar player, using an instrument centuries old, is more of an artist, and produces more meaningful music. The technological 'artist' is standing still, by running faster and faster.

For the noetic worker, the only progress there is must be achieved in sweat, concentration and the sentiment of love. The idea that the new is better than the old may be correct, but only if 'new' is given a different meaning from 'chronologically later'. The truly new is that which is born or reborn (like the phoenix). The ideas of contemporary pop singers, psychologists, football players and other heroes of the desiring city are 'new' only in a chronological sense. On the other hand, Newton's chronologically older grasp of differential calculus was and is in a deeper sense newer than anything the average student of physics or mathematics may have learnt through graduating from a university. It might take a two-month refresher course for Isaac Newton to be able to teach physics at a contemporary university; and it would not take much longer to equip Pythagoras to teach today's mathematics.

The dominant, market-based institutions of the contemporary era find justification for their continuing existence in a view of history as progressive. The 'ignorance' of ages gone by is being replaced by the 'knowledge' of today. Increasing consumption becomes the meaning of history. To present these views for them, the institutions co-opt likeminded academics: grants are given, theses are written, all to show how our 'good life' is the best and the cleverest. This process has been going on since the Renaissance, but it has accelerated in the last two centuries, culminating in a series of absurd theories, and a distortion of curricula and education, which makes all of us its victims, and from which it is hard for any single individual to become emancipated.

In order to show the culture, science and medicine of competing cultures and traditions to be inferior, the sophist in man has often resorted (through greed rather than design) to factual and interpretational inaccuracies. Time-honoured and proven systems of logic, medicine and nutrition from other cultures were denigrated; false evidence was manufactured, and the practitioners of these foreign arts were called witch doctors, superstitious primitives and other nasty names. The same formula was applied to our own tradition, except that kinder words were used. Greek science was seen not as sorcery but simply as primitive and wrong. Geocentric theories were ridiculed for being based on imperfect measuring instruments or superstitious reverence for the past. We were taught that the heliocentric theory was a discovery of Copernicus', when in fact it existed long before.

Even so, as the yin-yang symbol suggests, every dogma contains within itself the seed of its own destruction. The 'conceptual market city' that ruled Europe for the last four centuries has finally produced a nonconceptual science. Meaningless production has produced an apathetic generation that will no longer work, and this apathy spreads into art and philosophy. The fact that Lao Tzu is 'newer' than Pepsi Cola is hard for a mind grown inactive through the consumption of prepacked effort-saving gadgets, opinions and philosophies to grasp. Yet the potentially noetic mind will always find the strength to make the necessary leap. All birth, all creation, all that is good, all that is real takes place out of time. The 'good age', the truth, is neither in the past, nor in the future, nor is it now – the good age is now, yesterday and tomorrow – it is out of time.

This view is neither mystical nor subjective, neither new nor old – the only difficulty in adopting it lies in visualizing a world where time is not. But such a view is also that of contemporary science. During this century, the debate about whether atoms should be seen in terms of concrete particles or as waves was resolved by the decision that both were true – or rather, our judgment as to which applies in a given case depends on the context, it is 'aspectual'. Some two millennia ago, Sextus Empiricus in *Against the Mathematicians* wrote a conclusion to the discussions then taking place in Plato's Academy, and Hellas in general:

For those who make atoms or homoeomeriae or massive points (*Oykoi*)

> or rationally conceived Bodies be the Principles of things, were right in one respect but wrong in another. They were right in making their principles unapparent, but wrong in making them corporeal. . . . We must therefore hold that rationally conceived Bodies have incorporeal constituents, as Epicurus also recognized, saying that Body was dreamt up through the crowding together of Shape, Size, Resistance and Weight. It is clear from what has been said that the Principles of rationally conceived bodies must be incorporeal. . . . For consider how the Ideas, which Plato deems incorporeal, preside over Bodies, and how all that comes into being follows their pattern (in Findlay, 1974, pp. 426–7).

What Plato and the modern scientists are saying is that the concrete (bodies composed by the crowding of 'resistance and weight' within 'shape and size') must in some sense be non-concrete. The non-concrete aspect of anything is its noetic pattern. This pattern is not, of course, in any separate world of ideas, for in order for anything to be anything it must have a body in this world. For Plato, mass or body was nothing but a condensation of space-*Chora*. The Taoists taught the same:

> When the Chi [space-void] condenses, its visibility becomes apparent so that there are then the shapes [of objects]. When it disperses, its visibility is no longer apparent and there are no shapes. . . . The great void [space] cannot but condense to form all things, and these things cannot but become dispersed so as to form the great void (Fung Yu Ian, 1958, pp. 279, 280).

It was Einstein's conclusion that matter is constituted by regions of space in which the gravitational field is extremely intense. Meanwhile, Capra (1975, p. 213) contends:

> The discovery that mass is nothing but a form of energy has forced us to modify our concept of a particle in an essential way. In modern physics mass is no longer associated with material substance, and hence particles are not seen as consisting of any basic stuff but as bundles of energy . . . subatomic particles are dynamic patterns which have a space aspect and a time aspect.

The noetic grasp of any individual involves economic, erotic, corporeal and physical dimensions, and it is within all these disciplines that the noetic individual will be studied by the new science which is beginning to take shape.

THE TRUE INDIVIDUAL

The fact that the true individual cannot be conceptualized does not make it any less real. As has been pointed out, it is only in the recent epoch that thinking has been reduced to middle-soul or 'mental' thinking, and as a result the cognitive faculties of the body and soul have not atrophied so far that they cannot be reactivated. Like moving one's ears, it seems impossible at first, yet the right muscles are there, the nerve currents and the motor mechanism are all available. Likewise, the new kind of thought is within everyone's reach.

The view of reality which has developed since the Renaissance is based on the structure of language: according to this view, how we view reality and how we think is determined by the rules of grammar. Yet this view of reality is incorrect on an ethical basis – 'in one's heart' one knows this. It also contradicts scientific and even economic reality. Logic which cannot meaningfully coordinate its symbols with the entities and environment from which these symbols are derived is not true logic. The only reason logical positivists and industrial scientists remain in power in universities and industry is that they are held there by the forces of the old market. Meanwhile, the new market theorists are beginning to break away from these static views.

In this study I have made the words 'market' and 'merchant' into symbols, and have used them in their negative sense. The middle soul, however, is a necessary and legitimate aspect of an integrated city/individual. The correctly functioning market is a system of exchange that facilitates communication between excesses of production and deficiencies in consumption within an integrated system. It has been described quite well recently by Philip Kotler, in his work on the management of marketing.

Just as the noetic individual is not defined by the limits of his perceived body, so the noetic firm, factory or producing unit is not limited by a conceptually defined product, or by the single interest of a conceptually defined group of managers-owners. Gillette is not to be seen as a razorblade factory owned by this and this trust and located in this and that locality: rather, Gillette is a solution of the need for the removal of beards. An industrial unit, like a city of an individual, should be defined in terms of needs. The success of a productive unit defined in this way can no longer be seen in terms of growth, power, dominance in the market, monopoly, etc. Success is measured in terms of the definition: a successful firm, like a successful individual, is one which fulfils the need in response to which it was condensed in the first place.

Kotler does not eliminate profit; yet profit in the new kind of market is not measured on a balance-sheet. The man who produces a meaningful product is rewarded by the nature of the productive activity itself. By cosmic law, all meaningful productivity – i.e. that which fulfils genuine needs of man – is pleasant and rewarding, and the satisfaction of false needs is the opposite. 'Profit', in the new systems view of business, therefore includes the worker's psychological well-being, the attractiveness of the work environment and the rewards of the process of production itself. Naturally, the marketing mechanism itself must be efficient enough to generate sufficient returns to the producer to ensure continued investment. The new systems view would require restructuring on all levels of business from economic theory to accounting.

While Kotler's theories are attractive in some ways, he seems not to have fundamentally revised his view of the individual. His theory of business therefore remains self-contradictory, for it attempts to graft a systems firm on to an atomistic individual. As Plato observed, from age to age men come up with clever ideas that might have worked 'if only' this or that. (Plato was also criticizing himself.) Quite simply, the systems view of the universe will always fail if it does not include a restructuring of the individual: realistic philosophy must take into account the fact that the process of disintegration of the egoistic self is painful. Although he who succeeds in overcoming this egoism is inevitably rewarded, as pointed out earlier, men cannot be persuaded or forced to give up egoistic notions. The reason for this is simple: the reward is not given directly to the original individual. All demands for men to behave in moral ways reduce to asking individual A to behave in such and such a way, so that he will be rewarded as individual B. But at the time of the demand, individual A is A, and as such he wants to participate in systems that will reward individual A. And it is not mentally believable that all such systems will bring suffering both to the system and to individual A.

So we can understand why all clever ideas and all social reforms based either on persuasion or on physical force will inevitably fail. Force affects the body-soul and persuasion the mental-soul; yet an individual is an integrated unit, including three soul faculties – that of the mind, heart and body. The leap from individual A, the desire-constructed individual, to individual B can only be taken noetically: the leap is a leap into the unknown. Man reduced to his mental faculties may understand this – yet mental understanding is not enough, for behaviour is not determined by this alone.

For the leap to be effective, a man must surrender to the noetic sentiment. Filled with the rhythm of cosmic truth, the noetic faculty swells with a wave of energy, and individual A dies to be born anew. This, of course, is what Socrates meant by saying that philosophy is like dying. In order for noetic thought to operate, one must continually be born anew. One gives up a concept one has held on to: there is a pang of mental pain – yet immediately the new knowledge ebbs in and the pain is forgotten, just as a mother in the joy of birth forgets the pain of labour.

As argued earlier, pain is the 'curse' of the fall. Woman is condemned by her sin to give birth in pain, as man is condemned to toil by the sweat of his brow: yet in embracing the curse, in picking up the Cross and submitting to it, the ancient sin is washed away, the pain lifts and toil becomes a joy.

With all this said, one needs to be perpetually aware that no concept, no idea, no philosophy can give the impetus to 'Islam', to the surrender of false self. Philosophers can argue till the cows come home, and they will convince neither others nor themselves by the content of their doctrine; only to the extent that sentiment is present in an argument will they convince anyone and be filled with energy to continue the uphill struggle against the false self. For in all men there is the decaying, egoistic pull of desire subverting noetic movement. The last words of the dying Gautama Buddha were: 'Decay is inherent in all compounded things [including thoughts and ideas]. . . . Strive on with diligence.'

LANGUAGE

When the weather turns foul, says Confucius, when summer behaves like winter, when men imitate women and women imitate men, when yin is no longer yin and yang is no longer yang – then is the time for the rectification of names.

This rectification is necessary for us to understand the world and to rule it properly. It does not imply the creation of 'newspeak', or even of new words: it means simply that the old words are to be differently understood. Like moving its ears, the new epoch will have to think by exerting a different part of the brain, using nerve channels and motor mechanisms which are presently full of debris. It will have to revise its relationship to language. By following the experience of others who have taken the first step, all can learn to walk, even though society at large has been bedridden for the last few decades, if not centuries. It is the sciences that have taken the step into a non-conceptual reality.

Before transcending the lingual reality of time and space, both Bohr and Heisenberg had to endure the painful moment of 'dying' to the language. Thus Heisenberg (1963, p. 43) writes:

> I remember discussions with Bohr which went through many hours till very late at night and ended almost in despair; and when at the end of the discussion I went alone for a walk in the neighbouring park I repeated to myself again and again the question: Can nature possibly be as absurd as it seemed to us in these atomic experiments?

The answer was, of course, that it is not nature that is absurd but rather conceptual language.

Heisenberg's statement is also interesting from a psychological point of view. Arjuna, when faced with the yoga of resignation, the yoga which requires him to accept that a living individual cannot be slain, is likewise overcome with despair. This experience of despair in the face of paradox is what leads to the creation of knowledge.

This observation is important. I am not pointing to Bohr's or Heisenberg's view of matter as the finally correct one, neither am I pointing to Arjuna's view of reincarnation as the correct way of conceptualizing immortality. Both views will change: no theory is finally true or binding. It is the process of creation of knowledge that is universal and unchanging. Knowledge stems from the resolution of conceptually painful paradoxes. It involves paradox and the clash between yin and yang. Its resolution is not permanent: it is achieved by periodic abandonment to non-mental forces and organizing principles.

This triad – consisting of the One, the emanation from the One and the resolution – relates to the formation not only of thought but of all things, including the cosmos itself. There is no relativity in these underlying rules: they are universally and eternally valid.

THE TWO SELVES

I have tended to express the cosmic drama in terms of the choice between two selves or the citizenship of two cities. My medium has been ink, paper and words, yet the rules or forces that I am dealing with can be comprehended in any activity, given sufficient concentration. A man like Tchaikovsky might not display an interest in anything written here, but in moments of intense concentration the nerve currents of his brain nevertheless externalize into two sets of harmonies. The world is seen as a variation of a violin tune presented in 4:4 rhythm and in A minor; the same world is seen again, in A major. Thus for the hero of Swan Lake, life becomes a choice between two kinds of princess: one – Odile, the white swan – is the true one; the black one – Odette – is the false. The tragedy or comedy, however, is that both are in fact the same woman. There is an Odette and an Odile in each woman, and as Eryxymachus suggests, there are two kinds of love involved in any hunger. The false self is subject to love as desire – hence the inevitable fall. Good though he may be, nevertheless in moments of choice Siegfried – the personality in time – inevitably chooses the wrong, the black swan: this is the Fall of man, and it is inevitable.

Tchaikovsky might not agree with this interpretation, for he is an artist, and as Plato says, artists do not 'understand' what they create, even though, if they are sufficiently concentrated, it may be the truth. Likewise, a sensuous ballerina may not care for philosophy, yet she understands through her body whether she is dancing Odette or Odile, and what each of them means. (The role is traditionally danced by the same ballerina wearing a different costume.)

In order to choose the true I or the true princess, one must die to the false I, to false desire. Siegfried, who must die, dies freely, for love, so that he is rejoined with his princess in the 'other world'. This 'other world' is, of course, the world out of time and space, the world of instants; and the dying is not literal. At any moment in time, man is choosing between Odette and Odile, and it is only by dying to desire that he can choose correctly. He is both divine and fallen – but in actuality, in truth, he is divine. The 'other world' is this world, and this world is the true world.

The rules apply not only to humans, animals and the formation of thought but also to the formation of the cosmos. Every star, in a sense, faces two kinds of destiny: like a man, it must inevitably die, but it can die egoistically or altruistically. The altruistic 'systems' death of a star involves it overcoming the gravitational pull which holds it together, so that it is fractured and explodes into a supernova. As such, it gives light and warmth, and is eventually reconstituted as other stars. It has become immortal. With some stars, the case is entirely different. The egoistic, sythesizing gravitational pull is so intense that the star will eventually collapse into itself. This fall in the case of a massive star is so intense that, once initiated, it leads to something which one might compare to absolute death in hell. Desire gives rise to new desire which gives rise to yet stronger desire: the increase is a geometric progression. Similarly, the person who gives in to lust and greed cannot be satiated: the excesses of Nero and Caligula, Sodom and Gomorrah, can only be halted in death. The same is true of stars.

Each star is held in its orbit of the galaxy and in balance by its interactions in the cosmic system: it is where it is, when it is and as big as it is because it is defined thus by all the other bodies in the universe of space and time. In the words of Socrates, justice or world order is that state where each pays his due to everyone else. For the earth to be where it is, it must respond to demands – among them the pull of the sun and that of the other planets. The egoistic star refuses to be cosmically, i.e. socially, defined: its gravitational pull becomes so great that it ignores and exceeds the demands of all other entities. The result is its own collapse. The punishment for a bad man, says Socrates, is that his wishes are fulfilled – he becomes what he wanted. Thus the egoistic star draws itself in and further in, and it cannot stop – its wish is granted, it has itself and nothing else. This quasi-mythological account is based on the phenomenon of the black hole. At a certain point in its collapse, the star's gravitational pull becomes so intense that not even light can escape: the star becomes invisible and eventually a 'singularity', infinitely small and dense. If death exists in the cosmos, then it takes the form of a black hole.

Small as it is, the black hole is not obliterated – it is eternally punished for its sins. Inside the nucleus, particles are so densely packed that they are in a permanent state of painful collision. *Pleonexia* here is total: each particle is in a permanent state of conflict with every other particle. While the cosmos may be subject to a cyclical series of rebirths, the well of the black hole is subjectively eternal. When nothing can move, time has stopped; a point is infinitely condensed, a moment infinitely prolonged. So the punishment for egoism is eternal death; to be dead and to be in hell is to be defined by oneself alone.

RELATIVITY OLD AND NEW

I do not wish to overstress the relationship of modern science to Taoist or Platonic formulae. For Plato, the scientist and the artist are very similar, since they base their work on the lower type of mental activity. Poets and mathematicians are unpredictable: poets are like schoolchildren in the absence of their teacher, the philosopher. These children 'read' the teacher's notes while turning them upside down. The objection to scientists is different: scientists are to be criticized only when they present amoral formulae: when they pretend their science is ethically neutral. Like the Pythagoreans, Plato radically denied the possibility of ethics-free mathematics or science: in order even to understand an equation, a member of the Pythagorean community had to undergo a period of prayer, fasting and moral purification. A dissenting member who revealed the existence of irrational numbers, such as the square root of 2, was put to death for his treachery. The reason given was that the dissenting member was teaching the masses to assume that if there are irrational numbers, then rationality is relative.

For the same reason, Plato rejects the heliocentric theory of Aristarchus and the irregular movements of the stars. He is aware that objectively – i.e. in the publicly observable sense – stars do veer from a circular path; but true astronomy is not concerned solely with the publicly observable, it is ethical. The elaborate epicycles of Ptolemy were constructed as a means of bridging the observed facts of planetary movement to the idea of circular orbits, which was preferred on ethical grounds. For Saanthana thought, the basic evaluative criterion holds: if it is not ethically based, it is relative. This applies to quantum theory too. 'To calculate the course of the world does not mean to understand it' (Husserl, 1965, p. 140). It would be incorrect to seek to return to an ethically based world view while relying on the abstract formulae of objective scientists, even those of modern physicists.

THE SELF AS A PIVOT

Eastern texts contain objections to reliance upon chariot-based defence, on the grounds that it relies on the skills of chariot-makers and horse-grooms. (The Laws of Manu generalize this and require the householder to minimize reliance on men whose skills and words he cannot understand.) As we have seen, Plato believes that the security of a city does not have to be based on high-technology methods of warfare: by placing our security in the hands of the experts in navigation, smelting and the properties of metals, in the hands of tacticians, strategists and cockswains, we place it further and further from the centre. The more a city goes along this route, argues Plato, the more amoral become the men whose service it depends on.

Chapter 12 suggested that the best security is that which can be achieved by any man or woman who practises gymnastics, 'clean living' and 'clean thinking'. Simple weapons are best for they maximize the human element, and the skills needed to operate with them encourage the physical and mental fitness which leads to and results from moral excellence. By depending on abstract formulae and specialists using expensive technology we alienate ourselves from the world – for expensive technology is always controlled by others.

'Ruling the country is like cooking a small fish' (Tao Te Ching, LX). Fluidity is a characteristic of Saanthana thought: thus a principle which applies to cooking a dish (e.g. in the Laws of Manu, a wife should lose herself in prayer while cooking so as to fill the food with *Sattva*, the energy of love) applies also to the conduct of warfare, to ruling oneself and to creating thoughts. To base one's world view or morality on the opinions of men whose currency and tools are microscopes and equations is just as foolish as basing national security on merchants, with their ability to purchase sophisticated weaponry and soldiers.

Morality apart, the abstraction of knowledge and defence into the realm of the professional expert is also self-defeating on grounds which may be called Machiavellian. In fact Machiavelli in *The Prince* makes this very point; a city should never place its security in the hands of specialists, for they are mercenaries.

The conceptual apologist would imbalance this study by arguing that such issues are no longer relevant, but *Logos*-based thought maintains that they are permanently relevant. Marx himself (no friend of fixed philosophies) said that the basic laws and rules of nature are fixed and immutable – what can change is only their manifestation. The noetic thinker is concerned with the basic forces: he is forced to use the imagery of his epoch, but he uses it in such a way as to maximize the implied – so that a congenial noetic thinker of an epoch to come can relate to his work by removing some of the conceptual debris that inevitably clouds his message.

LOVE

Despite similarities between contemporary science and the views of the wise men of old, I earlier called for caution: the missing element in contemporary science is the constitutive principle, the sentiment of love.

Such remarks may for some bring back memories of boring Sunday school teachers, the Salvation Army and old ladies rattling charity boxes; nevertheless, the clichés are not thus invalidated. Clichés are usually true – although it takes effort to make them alive and meaningful. It is worth looking at the new science again, and seeing where it in fact lags behind the 'old' science.

During a few hundred years in Western Europe it had been held that matter was indestructible. The revolutionary nature of Einstein's theory was that it established that matter can create and be created by energy – one flows into the other. Energy equals mass times the speed of light squared. The Hindu scriptures also see the created universe as composed of visibility and resistance – light and mass. It is maintained by the cosmic energy called *Kundalini*: visibility is referred to as fire, and mass as weight, solidity or earth, depending on the tradition. Needless to say, Plato's views are similar. He expresses them in terms of the notion erroneously translated as the four elements (also found in the Bhagavad Gita) – earth, air, fire and water. The 'elements' – in so far as the word has any meaning for noetic thought – are triunal units, referred to as triangles. As for earth, fire, air and water, these are not elements but principles from which the elements are composed.

This study has maintained that all things are created from two forces being resolved into unity by a third: four principles reduce to two. From the *Timaeus*, 31, it is clear that earth and water are the two modes of the principle of solidity, while fire and air represent the medium or mode of visibility. Hence, 'God in the beginning of creation made the body of the universe to consist of fire and earth [i.e. visibility and solidity]. But two things cannot be rightly put together without a third – there must be some kind of bond or a union' (*Timaeus*, 31^{b}).

Fire, air, earth and water are *principles*, from which the elements – in the form of the 'triangle' – are created. However, this impersonal triunity is not the end of creation, and this is where the noetic thinkers part ways with the scientists. Energy is related to mass and light, and the three define each other, yet aspectually the third – the constitutive element of the cosmic energy, the fire of love – is differently defined.

In the Bible it is *Pneuma*, the breath of God. Proclus in his commentary on *Timaeus* (155) identifies it as nothing but love: not a formula, but the fiery bond of love that holds both the principle behind creation (i.e. behind mass and light) and the creation itself together. This love is the father of all, and the self of all creation: 'For the paternal self-begotten mind, understanding his works, sowed in all the fiery bonds of love, that all things might continue loving for infinite time' (Proclus, 1820).

THE SELF-REGENERATING COSMOS

To Peras and *Aperion*, Brahma and Siva are unceasingly at work, represented by light and mass: all things are perpetually reborn through these two. What the left, Siva, the dissolving principle, takes away or pulls apart, the right instantly and simultaneously re-creates. Yet creation and dissolution are joined and resolved into an unchanging unity by the sustaining force of love, through God the preserver, Vishnu.

The noetic grasp of immortality is related to Proclus' observation that in the central mind, the *Nous*, all processes are symmetrical: for each movement there is a counter-movement, and therefore all events seen by the mind of God are stationary. In the same way, we can understand what Plato meant when he embraced both the Parmenidean dictum that there is no movement at all (in the cosmos) and the Heraclitian dictum that all is movement. In the *Nous* one grows young and old at the same time; therefore one grows neither young nor old.

Mythologically, Plato (in the *Statesman*) represents the universe as having two movements – backwards and forwards. We perceive the first of these when we see children grow into old men. There is, however, a second movement in which everything is reversed, where old men grow young and retreat into the womb, and where the mighty oaks reduce to acorns. When these two movements are brought together in a reconciled third movement, then there is no movement at all.

Einstein writes that the theory of relativity was born when he was sixteen and fantasizing on what it would be like to follow light waves at their own speed as they fled away from the earth. He realized that for such an observer everything, including the light itself, would appear stationary. Time slows down as the speed of light is approached.

The perceiving man 'reads' his life by isolating the events he remembers and conceptually stringing them into a sequence, which he experiences as resistance and interprets as time. But de Broglie (in Capra, 1975, p. 195), the co-formulator of quantum theory, writes that:

> In space-time, everything which for each of us constitutes the past, the present, and the future is given en bloc. . . . Each observer, as his time passes, discovers, so to speak, new slices of space-time which appear to him as successive aspects of the material world, though in reality the ensemble of events constituting space-time exist prior to his knowledge of them.

In other words, everything has already happened – and is being discovered by the conceptual mind. Capra (1975, pp. 193, 196) adds:

> The relativistic theory of particle interactions shows thus a complete symmetry with regard to the direction of time. All space-time diagrams may be read in either direction. For every process, there is an equivalent process with the direction of time reversed and particles replaced with antiparticles. . . . When they are taken as four-dimensional patterns without any definite direction of time attached to them, there is no 'before' and no 'after', and thus no causation.

Against the scientists, noetic thought insists that there is causation: and we learn this from Lao Tzu and Plato, men who formulated their theories without any reliance on State funds or teams of technicians. The scientific premise that of two adequate theories the simpler and more elegant one is true, applied to Plato and modern physics, favours both the conclusions and the methods of the former. For Plato, true causation is not mechanical – which is why it is not perceived by the scientists – but ethical.

The arrested cosmos (or society) in which nothing seems to change is not devoid of action: it is continually re-creating itself. We have to keep up with the counter movement. As a Buddhist text has it, 'The stillness in stillness is not real stillness. Only when there is a stillness in movement can the spiritual rhythm appear which pervades heaven and earth'. Scientists are the allies of the noetic thinker in so far as they imbalance the doctrines of progress in time and of mechanical causality. However, science, still being amoral, is incapable of penetrating as far as ethical causality. This is out of time – the bad will be punished and have been punished, the good will be and have been rewarded – and it is not normally perceived because the wrongly perceiving individual sees himself as within time.

THE SAGES

One could go further than this in criticizing the contemporary sciences. Their vaunted objectivity might be reduced by an unkind critic to the acceptance of a special language and the subjugation of one's brain to a certain number of years of university conditioning; and to the good-will of the controlling agent, the State market, which allocates radio-telescopes and other hardware to the most select group of initiates. The laboratory of the noetic thinker is his body: his geiger counter is his heart, and his telescope the noetic vision, whose only limitation is moral imperfection. Within each of us there is a noetic thinker, and this should never be intimidated by the might of the Caesar who will perpetually seek to externalize the truth, and the means to truth, so as to be able to exercise control over both.

Among the philosophers, of course, there is a great difference between a Kant and an Arjuna. Aristotle was a court philosopher to Alexander the Great, but Socrates, Lao Tzu and Zoroaster were independent agents. The latter group, whose teachings will from age to age be reduced to conceptualized theories, stand apart from the 'historical' philosophers who promote these theories. They share not only ideas, but also traits of personality, life styles and even manners of dress. Plato cannot be counted as one of them, nor does he make the claim – he is an encyclopaedist, who comes at the end of an epoch to write down the thoughts and ideas of the paradigmatic thinkers of his culture. He speaks for Socrates, Parmenides, Heraclitus and Pythagoras.

In contrast to Heraclitus or Socrates, who stood aloof from any external authority, dressed simply and disdained all honour, we may look at Aristotle. In order to formulate his own view of the universe, this man relied on hundreds of slaves and the armies of Alexander to bring him specimens of animals, plants and men from all over the world: yet he calls Socrates an elitist. Philosophers like Socrates do not have letters after their names, or computer printouts in their back pocket. Yet they bear witness to real humanity, and rally each and every soul to autonomous exertion. Their view of the world is hectic, perhaps outrageous: it may offend common sense; it is also one that they were themselves generally reluctant to disclose. But its validity can be tested by anyone. I cannot pretend to understand all their insinuations and ways – why they walk barefoot, why they either shave their heads or do not cut their hair at all, why they wear loose clothes. Why do the Vedas, the Koran and the Pythagoreans recommend that one rests by placing the right foot over the left? Why do the apostles tell us how many fish they caught? Why is it important to inform us that Jesus fed exactly 5,000 people, and that there were twelve or seven baskets left over? Why does Plato demand that the city should be a natural unit consisting of 5,040 people? Are all these things symbolic: if so, symbolic of what?

The only guideline I can supply is the simple message of this book. Central to the organization of any valid thought is its good sentiment: any interpretation of philosophy or myth which arouses fear, hate, lust, jealousy, self-righteousness or greed for power is false. It is also false if it externalizes the truth, projecting the source of our civilization on to another planet, making this world unreal by inventing another, or separating the rules of logic from the human heart.

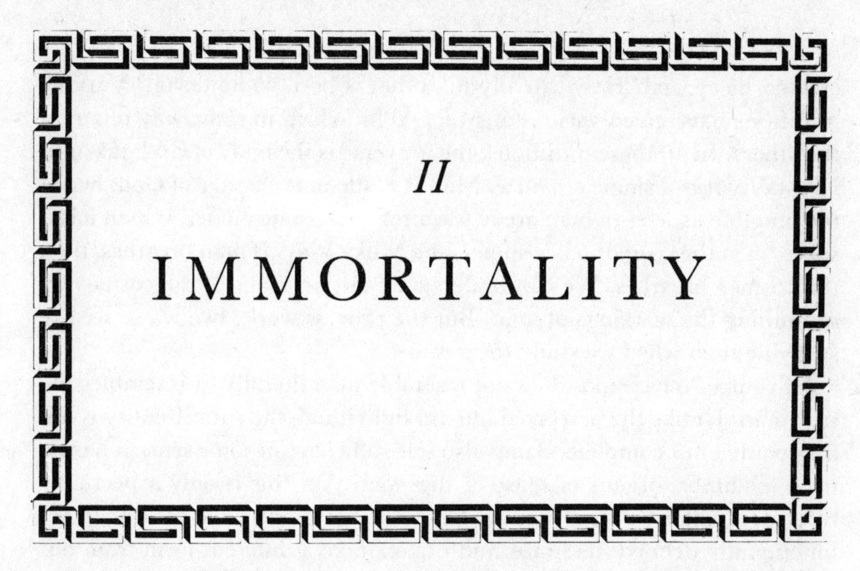

II

IMMORTALITY

As the reader will have gathered by now, this study involves a progressive relaxation of formality. As it develops, becomes less formally structured, its rhythm looser and its insinuations and assertions wider and deeper. Its function may be compared with that of a tug plane that launches a glider. The glider is pulled by the mechanical power of the conventional aeroplane – but once a certain height is reached, the cord snaps and the glider is on its own. Correspondingly, as this study is deconceptualized and deformalized, the reader is expected to become the co-author. In what follows I will throw out all kinds of notions from all kinds of traditions. The subject – immortality and life after death – necessitates this approach. Conceptualizations will be used, but conceptual coherence is not the aim.

THE BODY OF GOD

The Saanthana tradition calls the visible, created universe (composed of visibility and solidity) the body of a cosmic Being. This Being is eternal and indestructible, even though it is daily dissolved. Although mortal – capable of dissolution – the universe is free from old age and disease. It provides its own food: it regenerates itself and is perfectly efficient, using the totality of its waste as sustenance. Following the notion, 'Magnus homo, brevis mundi', each human being is created after this model: thus we are each also in a sense immortal, perfectly efficient in satisfying our needs, wasting away at one end while being proportionately regenerated at the other end.

This universal imagery is paradoxical. How can anything that is created be eternal? How can anything that is born be immortal? Various traditions have given various answers, all of which in some way relate to the others. In all these traditions, the universe is the body of God; taken in its totality it is a single creature. Man is made in the image of God: hence the tangible aspects of man are made after the cosmic model. If man has a spine, then the cosmos has a spine – the Milky Way. If man breathes, then the cosmos breathes. We can understand the workings of the cosmos by examining the workings of man. But the process works two ways: we are studying man when we study the cosmos.

Of course, the cosmos does not resemble man literally: it resembles the true man. Unlike the perceived human individual, the cosmic entity is not fragmented but complete. Being also self-sufficient, in some sense it has no need for limbs, organs of sense or digestion. Yet this is only aspectually true: in a different sense it does have all these, but since all things are functionally defined, its limbs and organs take a different form from our own.

In order to project the meaning of this in a positive sense, it is necessary first to conceptualize it in a negative sense. Let us temporarily pretend that the cosmic Being has no limbs at all, since it has no need of anything. Having no need for locomotion or communication, and being perfect, it is round, silent and ageless – yet not devoid of movement, which is circular.

The cosmic Being symbolizes perfection, or *is* perfect. A perfect man therefore ought to resemble or approximate this perfection. According to Schopenhauer, living beings and their organs, limbs and actions are expressions of the will to be and to possess something that is needed. The stomach, mouth and teeth are expressions of the desire to eat: teeth also of the desire to soften food. Legs are the expression of the desire to be elsewhere. In contrast to man, the perfect Being already is where it wants to be, so it has no legs.

All parts of the body cater to some need. The heart is given to pump passion into the body, to prepare it for its daily wars. Lungs are given as a counter-tendency to the heart, to cool it lest it become too violent. The mind is an expression of the desire to know. The perfect cosmic Being has no mind, no eyes, ears or mouth, for it does not want to see, hear, talk or think (conjecturally): it is perfect and non-desiring. This does not at all mean that the cosmic Being, or the God beyond gods of whom the cosmos is an image, is without intelligence and awareness. Its intelligence needs no pictures (concepts) as its currency of apprehension, so it does not need sense impressions. It is perfectly aware of everything all the time, for it is perfectly aware of itself and there is nothing outside.

The body – whether mental or external – is inevitably linked to some need, and all activity is movement towards the satisfaction of this need, a becoming of what one potentially is. Assuming there is a possibility of satisfaction and the cessation of striving and desire, one may well ask what happens to the body then. What does one do with one's legs when one has arrived; what happens to the questing mind and eyes when all has been seen and known?

There are at least two possible answers. The first, more obvious one is that the after-life, an entity has no need whatsoever for such things as mouth, teeth, stomach or legs, so it loses them and sheds the body – it dies. The second answer is more complex, but it is hinted at by the paradigmatic city model.

Life in the paradigmatic city is not oriented towards personal survival. All the actions concerned with the body, with feeding, procreating, defence and education, are detached from the satisfaction of individual desire. The city is for the citizens, and life a ritual. The city eats, procreates and exists to allow each individual to merge into the totality of city and cosmos: 'Thus they have eyes and ears, legs and arms in common' (*Laws* 739[a]).

Every city is two cities – it is Atlantis, characterized by individual desire (the stone of Heraclea), and then again it is not, it is the Athens of Menexenus, the Holy Jerusalem or Politea. Likewise, the body and every organ in it has a dual function. Considered in the realm of perception (becoming), the liver has to do with clearing and exterminating toxic bodies and noxious juices; considered vertically, it is the extension of Apollo, and serves a religious purpose. Seen vertically, the liver is a mind: it produces images of divine sentiments and translates them into sweet juices, in every way opposite to the bitter, destructive juices that purify and petrify. Just as Apollo is the terrible purifier and also radiant, so with the liver. Similar considerations apply to every other organ.

We think that we have to work in order to eat, that we must eat in order to live – but why do we have to live at all? The mythological answer is that each and every activity, properly executed in the land of *Ekei*, is a ritual: life is a game, a festival, a celebration. The mouth is not given to eat, but to praise God and sing the eternal harmony. Legs are not given to get us from workplace to home, for work and walking is a dance.

Every organ and limb has a double function, the one humanly perceived in terms of satisfaction, and the other unperceived, which is to take part in the cosmic chorus, the harmony of the spheres, the dance of Siva. This is possibly why *Choreia* was necessary to philosophy. It lies behind the Bastani ritual and the whirling of dervishes. In Jewish, Christian, Orphic or Indian myths there occur the same images of a cosmic chorus, of 144,000 creatures singing, harp-playing or dancing in heaven. From Plato we learn that we participate in this dance on our earth. The citizens of Magnesia, he writes, may outwardly seem to be working, toiling and procreating: innerly their life is a never-ending festival.

This cosmic festival is nothing but immersion into the rhythm of the universe. We dance as we work, toil and draw water – every activity is consecrated and used to project man on to the higher plane. In the laser, light waves brought into resonance serve to reinforce each other, and together create a powerful beam. Mythologically, each man can, through mundane activity, enter into this resonance with the cosmos and thus be projected into immortality.

But the notion of immortality is a difficult one, and we can approach it from yet another angle.

THE IMMORTAL PERSON AND THE THREE KINDS OF TIME

Persons assume their true identity only in instants when they are functioning correctly, in harmony with correct sentiment. The word 'instant' must be stressed, for an instant is out of time.

As suggested earlier, for every action there is a *Logos*, an ideal pattern, a possibility of perfect enaction. When performing his profession in a near-ideal way, the doctor enters into this pattern. A warrior may cast a lance in this perfection, just as the ecstatic dancer may execute a leap which projects him or her into what Urwick has called the 'higher dimension'. All such actors are subject to the division of labour; they have 'specialized', in so far as their actions are singly motivated and perfect at the 'time' of performance.

The inner mental experience of performing such actions projects us out of time. We experience time only to the extent that we 'toil' in a way divergent from the perfect pattern. Defined in terms of mental awareness, time could be seen as the experience of resistance to activity, just as the extended body is defined in the *Timaeus* as the experience of resistance to touch. Both time and matter as extension in space stem from the arrest of a natural flow, divergence from the *Logos*.

Turning to Plato's *Republic*, we see the citizens are 'dissolved' persons: they have no 'possessive', 'manifested-in-time' personality in the sense of being husbands, sons, owners, etc. They constitute a 'community' of eyes and ears – having dissolved the capacity to feel individual pain or pleasure, or indeed to see or hear individually. In calling for such a community, the noetic thinker is speaking metaphorically of a psychological experience, not of a 'normal' physical event. The same point is made by Jesus: the Son of man is propertyless, parentless, homeless; foxes have holes, but the Son of man has nowhere to lay his head. In short, the paradigmatic individual has thrown away the attachments that qualify anybody as a particular person (son of Ariston, living in such-and-such a place).

The loss of self in this sense can only take place in an instant: it projects us from 'local to a greater Time' (Eliade), to the Time beyond time. Out of time, it is out of the realm of becoming; it is in the third realm, that of actuality. Although ideally we could forever be grasping actuality as we did in the Age of Cronus, in practice this is not the case. Only very rarely do we perceive it. A mother giving birth; an all-engulfing act of love; the charge of a military unit; in all these instances actuality is perceived when the self is given up. While 'living', only a few perceive actuality. The 'dead' personality is the dissolved self (dissolved in the sense described above), and the 'dead' find it easier to perceive the real earth because they have no desires. As Heraclitus would say, to be dead is to be alive.

This symbolic death aside, one may well ask what happens to a person after so-called physical death. Let us (tongue-in-cheek) separate the body from the soul, just to see what happens to the body. Later it may be observed that the same holds for the soul.

Unlike later thinkers, who interpret immortality in terms of the persistence of the soul, Timaeus – a wise man of Locri – is at pains to argue for the immortality of the body, though his account is oblique. In 41^{b}, Timaeus points out that all created beings are soluble in principle, yet God, being good and loving, will only dissolve that which is corrupt. The perfect body, the body of the universe, can only be made corrupt by God: and God, being eternal and eternally good, will never attempt to corrupt the good. Hence, although vulnerable to death the cosmic body will never die, for it will be held together as long as it is loved by God – which is forever, since God does not change his nature and it is in his nature to love the good. The mortal is immortal. Nothing put together by God can ever be dissolved, for God would never join elements that cannot match together perfectly (41^{b-c}).

In this passage, Timaeus acounts for the fact that perceived unities are not real and enduring in time. Individual men as they perceive themselves are conglomerations of units put together by entities other than God, i.e. by the lesser gods (41^{d}). They are not true entities, for the great God would never put any false unity together. The human being is somehow falsely constituted of building blocks which themselves are fragments of indestructible true units which are correctly created. Thus the essential man is created by God and is indestructible (41^{b}): the body of man is likewise made from fragments of the indestructible body of the universe.

The process of dying is reflected in the yin-yang symbol in Taoism, or in the meander of Greek tradition, both of which consist of two interlocked shapes, one the negative of the other, the placement of the observer's attention determining which is the positive side. Seeing the body grow old is simply a result of biased vision: growing old, man is shedding the bonds of desire and progressing towards his true self. To grow old is therefore the deepest desire of every true individual: it is only the fear of growing old that blinds us to the parallel spiritual and physical development that takes place within our mind and body. Thus it is characteristic of philosophers, even of the lesser kind, that they grow more and more lucid as they advance in age. Senility tends to be absent in the great artist: Goethe can write his greatest work, *Faust*, at the age of eighty, and a top pianist or violinist performs into his nineties, even though the performance requires physical and mental exertion. A ballet dancer's love of dance will arrest many of the processes of ageing until well into middle age.

This is conveyed by Plato in the *Politea*, through Sophocles, who sees growing old as the liberation of true vision. As a man grows older he becomes freer, and thus in a sense younger. Indeed, from Valmiki we learn that the wise are the children and the aged. As we grow towards middle age, we see progressively less well: according to Plato it is around the age of fifty that the reverse process begins, and we see better and better. No one ought to teach philosophy before the age of fifty. In the Laws of Manu, the aged householder is encouraged to merge with nature, which like a child he can understand again.

The ballet dancer is a low-key example of this principle. The sage is more extreme. A yogi can often maintain the complexion and texture of a young man's skin until death; Aurobindo arrested the decay of his body for many days after his death. But in actuality it is not only yogis who do not age: according to the Saanthana myth, nobody does. It is a matter of perception: the perceived body only reflects the degree to which actuality is perceived. Aurobindo's body has not aged – nor has that of the village drunkard – for our perceived body is not the true one: the arrest of aging in the perceived body of a philosopher is only a hint, a pointer towards the correct perception.

The synthesis, growth and dissolution of the unity which man perceives as his body is conjectural. The universal body contains the bodies of all the living beings that have and ever will come into existence. What is true of the cosmic Being as a macrocosm is also true of the microcosms or true unities it contains. For any part of the true body which is perceived as being in the process of dissolution, there exists a master pattern in which its integrity is recorded, and according to which, somewhere in the universe, a parallel reconstitution of the same particle is taking place. If we could perceive the totality of the universe, we would see each of our constituent parts simultaneously wasted and created: in other words, we would agree with Parmenides, that nothing ever changes, and with Ecclesiastes, that 'there is nothing new under the sun'. Seen locally, on the other hand, all is in flux: the *Logisticon*, by flowing counter to this, arrests the change.

REINCARNATION?

Contemporary difficulties in understanding the notion of reincarnation seem to arise from a false superimposition of a concept of literal, temporal reincarnation on to a non-literal model. We are told that the Hindus believe in a cycle of rebirth, in which a single soul reappears under the guise of several different persons or animals.

This is not Plato's view of incarnation. For Plato, all things are happening simultaneously, out of time: rather than being born again, one is perpetually 'growing young' or 'growing backwards'. Nor can the so-called Hindu idea of reincarnation as a succession of births in creatures other than oneself be found in the Upanishads: there, too, all living is seen as taking place simultaneously.

In the Bhagavad Gita (II, 20), Krishna tells Arjuna explicitly that it is only the lesser mind that invents reincarnation, for the true person 'is never born, and he never dies. He is in Eternity: he is for evermore . . . beyond times gone or to come.'

When Jesus was asked about the resurrection of the dead he answered that there is no resurrection, in the sense being disputed by Sadducees and Pharisees, for in reality the living never die. The resurrection idea is as conjectural as is the idea of death, since for God, in reality, nobody dies: 'have you not read what was said to you by God, "I am the God of Abraham, and the God of Isaac, and the God of Jacob"? He is not the God of the dead, but of the living' (Matthew, XXII, 31–32). Abraham is still alive and so is Jacob – although now they are differently perceived. Jesus is still alive, still preaching, still being crucified; Pilate is daily washing his hands, and the cosmic drama is being replayed in its many variations.

The conceptual mind perceives the situations and people of the New Testament and the living Jesus as other than itself. Likewise, the philosophy of Protagoras is seen as other than that of Kant or of some contemporary positivist. This is not how the world is presented in Plato's Myth of Er: if we are to accept this, then the same people are continually alive without realizing it.

St Paul believed that the Second Coming was just around the corner. We may interpret this in a symbolic sense, but the Apostles took it more seriously – 'symbolic' and 'literal' lose all significance in their thinking. Were they wrong? Is Peter the Rock really dead? Who is the real Peter? Is it mere symbolism to identify the Pharisees with false priests everywhere; Jews with all those Christians, Muslims, or Hindus who embrace the ritual but not the sentiment of religion; Gentiles with those who have not formally accepted Islam or any other religious creed; Peter with every man or aspect of man in whom the Holy Spirit can identify incarnate God? The twelve tribes of Israel stand for all humanity. Plato's dialogue the *Laws* describes a walk from Crossus in Crete to a cave with seven stops between. The cave is Golgotha and the death cave of Zeus. The third stop occurs at noon by the cave Tora, and it is here that these lines are being written. What is true in symbolism must be sought by the individual, alone.

If the Saanthana account of actuality as taking place in an instant out of time is correct, then temporal development is false. If actuality is out of time and becoming is unreal, we are led to conclude that all actual living is taking place simultaneously, and that perceived dead people live through perceived living people, people in time, as the latter enter the realm of instants.

Needless to say, the complexity of all these relationships is such that I am continually simplifying the picture. Nevertheless all prophets, sinners, saints, ideologies and cities reduce to a finite number of eternal forces. Peter the Rock will betray Jesus the Word: the extended, the solid, will betray visibility before the cock crows three times. Conceptually speaking, the cock crowed in AD 28 or 29. Cosmically speaking, it is yet to crow for the last time. Or rather, the cock is continually crowing, and Peter – the Church – is continually betraying his mission. Yet in a higher sense the Rock is still the Rock, for Peter is never a traitor: when a traitor, he is not Peter but Judas. There is a Judas within each Peter, and vice versa.

Both Peter and Judas are apostles chosen by Christ, and chosen not for three years but for eternity. The difference between them is not that one stays eternally true and the other eternally evil: both fail, and both regret their failure. Even after the betrayal, Jesus welcomes Judas: Judas, however, will not accept it. Failure is not just to fail, for man has already failed: failure lies in not forgiving oneself, or in not accepting external pardon (depending upon whether one sees God internally or externally).

Resting after a victory over a Jewish tribe, the historical prophet Mohammed was poisoned by an enemy woman, and dies. Mercy, however, is not a Christian monopoly. Having caught the assassin, the Muslims bring the woman to the prophet. 'Why did you do it?' he asks.

She tells him that she did it for her people and for her religion, and the prophet gives her money for the journey and lets her go free. *Kshatriyas* (warriors) on all sides are dear to Krishna. The division between right and left is present at Golgotha. Both have failed: humanity is nailed to the Cross on both sides. Noetically, Jesus is crucified daily, and so is humanity, in the shape of thieves on his left and on his right, Judas/Peter. Babylon is at work in each and every city. The thief on the right of Jesus, however, accepts the Cross; Peter is forgiven; and the fact that the Jewess poisons the Prophet is not decisive – having committed her act in good sentiment she ceases to be an assassin and joins the community of the faithful. With all his excesses, Peter is still the Rock, even though he will go on betraying the Word until the end of time.

The above insinuations do not link together particularly well, since they are simply conglomerated together. Jesus refrains from commenting on the nature of the 'other world' apart from pointing out that (1) it is within you; (2) its God is the God of the living; and (3) the end of the age will come before people now living have died. From Krishna we learn that nobody is ever born and nobody dies, that the idea of rebirth is for those who do not understand. From the Zoroastrians we learn that Vohu Manu has already defeated Ahriman, Plato argues that the cosmic Athens is now and forever, and Timaeus attributes growing old to a false vision of the self. From such hints anyone may draw conclusions that he or she find suitable. To add some coherence, I will spell out one possible conclusion among a hundred and one others.

ETERNAL LIFE

Like any conceptualization, the following is not 'true': yet it may be emotionally less offensive, or in some other sense more acceptable than some other conceptualizations. It is objectively, quite definitely false; however, as a stream of words and pictures it might 'trigger' the reader to create his own true grasp – one not made of pictures and symbols as is public speech.

To be alive, to be a person, means to be conscious of one's past and of one's identity. The idea that after death one will be born as somebody else contradicts this and is not immortality – death is not to remember who one is. If I insist on seeing myself as an individual being defined by my body in time and place I will die, for one becomes what one follows. Mind, personality, 'personhood', body – all this will be dissolved, for both mind and body are mortal.

Nonconceptually, however, I am other than a son of so-and-so and citizen of so-and-so. To experience this I must suspend conjectural thought, and abandon myself to noetic thought (Kierkegaard calls it the leap of love).

It seems at first that beyond the mind-held personality there will be nothing, yet this is not true. God asks Abraham to sacrifice his son, and Abraham does so in his heart – yet God, being God, requires only this. Inwardly giving up his son, Abraham instead recovers him.

By giving up individual identification one does not disintegrate into cosmic nothingness. Nirvana is not the loss of self-identity. The death of the perceived personality, synthesized by desire, creates the true individual, synthesized by the sentiment of love. It is this notion which stands behind the words used in the Catholic Mass: 'Dying, you destroyed our death.'

A person who relies on noetic thought perceives himself out of time and space: he remembers through love his past and future selves. The divine chariot driver tells Arjuna in the Bhagavad Gita (IV, 5) that the difference between them is that 'I remember my past lives, and thou hast forgotten thine'. He goes on to add that past and future lives are not unfolding, they are now – yet only he can perceive this ('I am unborn . . . I am born').

To know – in Pythagorean thought, for the Zoroastrians and for Plato – is to remember (*Anamnesis*). To live is to remember, and not to remember is to be dead. When I 'forget' that I am also a part of the Andromeda galaxy and participate in all other living beings, I am only partly alive. I live wholly only in moments of remembering ('Do this in memory of me'): 'So we, though many, are one body in Christ, and individually members one of another' (Romans, XII, 5).

To be immortal is to be conscious of one's identity in others. One cannot be mentally, i.e. conceptually, conscious of this; but then conceptual truth is not final. I am conscious of my true identity in my love of my fellow man and of the cosmos.

Religion however, goes a stage further than this, and Plato and the Upanishads insist that the man who becomes conscious of his true identity does not love this consciousness after the physical dissolution of his body. If such is the case, where does such 'living' take place?

The true person, we have argued, is not a flow in time. *The true person is the locus drawn through all the high points of a certain type of excellence, instantiated by all those people and animals containing, in their false perceived bodies, fractions of true persons.*

Just as all men and animals participate in each other and in the cosmos (*Timaeus*, 30 sq), by functioning correctly each living thing helps every other to realize its true identity. Protagorean epistemological subjectivity is eliminated in this. *The realized soul – the soul of a good man – lives on earth perceiving itself in each of the excellent actions executed by its various members, whether whales, flat-footed animals or birds.* To the perceiving mind it may appear that the soul has to wait for each of its constitutive parts to instantiate: this is not so. The in-time existence is only falsely perceived as occurring in time; the real or actual is physical, visible, but is not perceived in time. In reality and in actuality, all is happening simultaneously. The realized Orpheus perceived himself as a swan, as a singer and as a twentieth-century scientist all at the same time. *The Logisticon synthesizes simultaneously all its dispersed constituent parts, whether of the body or of the mind* (which itself is a bodily part). As some of these parts are 'egoistically' retained by their temporary keepers, who perceive them as their own, a full bodily reconstitution is 'not yet' possible. It is for this reason, I assume, that Plato, the Zoroastrians and Christianity posit a kind of in-between existence described variously as 'purgatory' or 'the passage through heaven'. Presumably Jesus' three days in Hades coincide with this.

Full bodily reconstitution is to take place only after all false unities have been dissolved, and all the constituent blocks have thus been freed from their imprisonment in what is not, to be merged with what is. While Zoroastrians and Christians project this age into the future, Plato projects it into the past. As the perceived universe is created, so it will clearly have an end: to make an issue out of whether the Age of Cronus is coming or going seems meaningless in a noetic context. Unlike perceived existence, actuality and actual things are created by God: thus, although created, actuality is eternal, held eternally by the loving God. In eternity, the real and the actual coincide.

What about hell? The evil, claims Socrates, are punished by coming to resemble whatever they follow. Just as the good in heaven are only capable of experiencing moments of excellence, so the evil in hell are only capable of experiencing the moments of pain and misery.

Thus both heaven, hell and purgatory take place simultaneously on earth. The souls in heaven experience only the good aspects of their lives, the persons in hell the bad, and purgatory is in between: it is normal, everyday existence. (We should, however, recall the words of Socrates: 'Of course these things are not exactly like that, but if talking about them helps us remember true things, then we will have become better men'.)

All the 'dead' are alive in living people. The 'realized' dead, the ones who have given up desire while in the perceived body, as the ones who are aware of themselves as true individuals. Socrates comes to be every time a dolphin in which there is a part of Socrates makes a perfect jump, or every time somebody completes a thought or a sentence in a perfect way. As all these actions have already been performed, Socrates does not have to wait for others to behave perfectly. Thus Socrates is conscious and living.

To be 'reborn' into someone and *not* to be aware of it is, of course, to be dead. The dead are also within us, and they exist as potentialities. In other words, if a man brings to light some stored experience, a 'dead' part of him might awaken. This is why Plato calls learning *Anamnesis*. The dead within us have known how to swim, but they and we have forgotten it: in learning how to swim, we reactivate a fraction of this shared experience. The 'dead' within us are becoming alive. A living, acting man is, in one sense, not a person at all but a sum of dead persons within him coming alive. As they are dead, they are not conscious of themselves, nor is the perceiving person really conscious of who he is: he is only a stimulus-response mechanism.

The 'living' and 'dead' in us are not somebody or something, but a process of becoming somebody or something.

By rejecting the myth of reincarnation, Christianity has rejected the idea that Peter can be born as Paul. Socrates and the Vedas do the same. The popular view maintains that one is many people – Peter is Paul, George, etc. But Christianity and Socrates view man as One; Socrates only has *parts* of him dispersed in others. Peter cannot become aware of himself as Paul, for he never was Paul. Rather, there is a part of Paul in him, and by behaving properly – using his body, mind and soul in a perfect way – Peter realizes these parts of Paul and they 'leave' him: in doing this he opens himself up and can receive his own self. Complete realization, therefore, does not mean to strip myself bare to the soul. Quite the opposite: it means to open myself up, to throw out everything that never was me in order to be empty, to receive all the scattered parts that belong to me.

Complete realization requires that all a person's parts come together around the original owner. As Plato says, we have been scattered as the Spartans scattered the Arcadians. The coming together of Israel – the end of the diaspora – is the coming together of every true and natural nation, city and man. 'Of all the multitude of things every one returns to its root' (Chuang Tzu in Waltham, 1971, p. 136).

We may close this account by observing that as there are three realms of reality – being, becoming and actuality – so there are three aspects to each city. In the same way, each individual is a combination of the dead, those who are coming to birth and those who truly live. The whole of humanity is dead, becoming alive and really alive, in hell, purgatory and heaven, all the time. As *Chora*, when properly functioning, mirrors the realm of being, so the dead who have died properly mirror, and are, the truly living. In between these two are those who think that they are living, but in fact are only becoming.

Of course there never are *really* three worlds or two worlds: all the realms of time are one, though they are not perceived as such. To bring about this temporal and cognitional reconciliation of three in one is, of course, the aim of noetic philosophy.

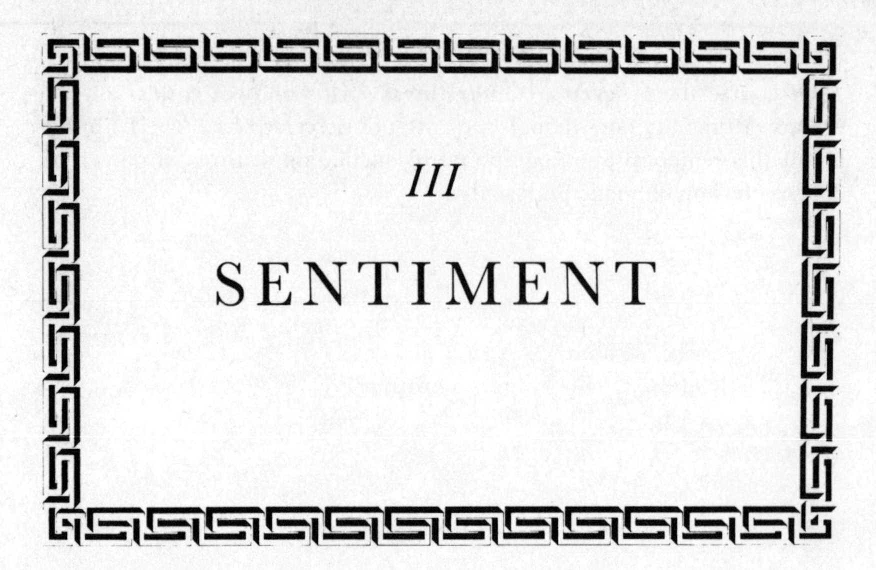

The subject of this study has been the role of 'sentiment' as the unifying force, the organizing principle behind the creation of all true units, whether these be movements in *Chora*, the construction of cities or the correct organization of speech and writing.

The sentiment was presented as a flux, a tendency, a stream. It was compared to a moving locus of points, the 'emotional' pull of the stone of Heraclea. Some examples were given creating, as it were, a series of instantiations of the sentiment, without drawing the full locus of points. For the most part, stress was laid on the negative function of this study. Indeed, Part One presented Philosophia Perennis as primarily concerned with the dissolution of all positive conceptualizations restricting the flow of the sentiments. The intention was to make the reader understand that all true unities are to be constructed in the realm of actuality, where the formative medium is notional movement rather than concepts, and where the principle is sentiment rather than proximity in space and time as perceived by the desiring mind.

Every Saanthana thinker has refrained from formulating a single, general, prescriptive conclusion. But I would like to close this study by exploring the universality of this pattern or sentiment, whether we call it *Pathos, Pneuma*, Tao, *Logos, Eros, Aritmos* or *Diarithmesis*.

THE WORD

'The universal, the true religion is of the word', proclaims the Bhagavad Gita. 'Not by the Vedas, or an austere life, or gifts to the poor, or ritual offerings can I be seen as thou hast seen me. Only by love can men see me, and know me, and come unto me' (Bhagavad Gita, XI, 53–54).

The idea of the creation of the world by the God beyond gods, through recourse to an unchanging pattern, lies behind Plato's cosmology and is verbalized in the opening paragraphs of the account in the *Timaeus* (286–29^{d}):

> 'Was the world, I say, always in existence and without beginning, or created and had it beginning? Created, I reply. . . . Now that which is created must, as we affirm of necessity, be created by a cause. But the father and the maker of all of this universe is past finding out, and even if we found him, to tell of him to all men would be impossible. [This is not agnosticism.] This question, however, we must ask about the world: which of the patterns had the artificer in view when he made it – the pattern of the unchangeable or that which is created? . . . Everyone will see that he must have looked to the eternal [pattern], for the world is the fairest of creations and He is the best of causes. And having been created in this way, the world has been framed in the likeness of that which is apprehended by reason and mind [*Noesis*] and is unchangeable, and must therefore necessarily be a copy of something.'

We cannot know the maker of the universe, nor can we know (in the conceptual sense) the eternal pattern. However, we can and do infer that truth, goodness and beauty share a common origin.

The idea of God the Creator making the world in this way is common to the world's major religions. The similarity of language and imagery implies either a certain universal, primordial psychological experience, or (for those so inclined) a direct revelation of these matters at various times to different peoples. Be that as it may, the Word remains the unifying factor of that universal religion heralded in the Vedas and proclaimed by St Augustine. Heraclitus apart, the most precise verbalization of the *Logos* concept seems to be that of Philo the Jew, for whom it is the image and Son of God, the instrument by which the world was made and the connecting power by which all things are united.

Going much further East, Lao Tzu's 'Tao' is also the 'Word' – both the way to the pattern and the pattern itself. But it is the Hindu thinkers who have most fully recognized the more than philosophical significance of calling the pattern a 'Word', making it central to both their cosmology and their daily liturgy. It is venerated in the form ॐ – being pronounced OM or AUM and savoured for its sound. Note the presence of the number three in the written form: the Word illustrates a dual trinity, a trinity made of two syllables (O and M) pronounced as three (A, U, M). The two are 'divided into three sounds but the three roll into one' (Mascaro in Bhagavad Gita, p. 14).

I have emphasized the separateness of divine *Nous* and individual

Logisticon (Brahman and Atman). It is the Word that forms the bridge between the two: 'The Truth of the universe is BRAHMAN: our own inner Truth is ATMAN. The sacred OM is a name for both' (Mascaro in Bhagavad Gita, p. 14).

INCARNATION

While for the Hindus this Word has never incarnated in a single, completely human being – though it has incarnated in other ways, and as the excellencies of many men – this possibility is not formally excluded. It may be significant that both the sunset *Puja* and the Catholic Benediction are dedicated to the Word, celebrated in a similar rhythm and manner, at the same times and for the same duration, and end with similar words: 'What was, what is, and what shall be – all this is OM. Whatever else is beyond the bounds of threefold time – that also is only OM' (Mandukya Upanishad); 'In the beginning was the Word . . . As it was in the beginning, is now, and ever shall be, world without end. AMEN.'

Compare, too 'In the beginning was Brahman, with whom was the Word, and the Word was truly the supreme Brahman' (Patanjali in Isherwood, 1969, p. 39) with the opening lines of the gospel according to St John:

> In the beginning was the Word, and the Word was with God, and the Word was God. He was in the beginning with God; all things were made through Him, and without Him was not anything made that was made.

The Word which gives substance to goodness is called by the Zoroastrians *Ahuna Varya*. It was uttered by Ahura Mazda 'before the sky and before the water' and 'contains the seed of righteousness'. *Ahuna Varya* 'is coequal with Ahura Mazda and almost on the same level with him. He is Ahura Mazda's own bountiful spirit. Like Ahura Mazda he is wholly good; nothing of evil adheres in him' (Kanga, 1933, pp. 64–5). He is used by God 'as a means of bringing about the defeat of the evil principle', and 'comprised the substance of the whole religion of God' (Bharucha, 1979, pp. 102–3).

Islam, too, is the religion of the Word: its 'doctrine is indeed almost exactly parallel to the Christian doctrine of the incarnation,' writes Zaehner (1964, p. 115), 'except that in Islam God is made not man but book'. The Prophet has a function analogous, not to Christ, but to Mary, the Mother of the Word.

The function of the Word is universal: whether manifested as a counsellor or a book of rules, it will serve as a means of reconciliation between inner and outer, positive and negative, the said and the unsaid. All such divisions are false, and are eliminated and consumed by the *Logos*. The Koran – rather like Plato's dialogues, and particularly the *Laws* – certainly functions in this triunal sense. Against the written law, the *Shariah*, there stands the opposing aspect of the Word, in this case conveyed by rhythm and metre – which is the Word apprehended through the heart, the *Tariquah*. Reconciling these two is the truth itself, *Haqiqah*, like the centre of a circle whose radius is the inner Way and whose circumference is the outer law. Even though Islam rejects the doctrine of Trinity, the Word of God itself is to be grasped on these three axes.

While the Catholic Church claims that Jesus is the only way to God, this dogma does not preclude him having functioned in this capacity at other times and places in a restricted sense, taking on some appropriate identity. Ninian Smart remarks that religious visions are culturally conditioned: Hindus do not have visions of the Madonna, nor do Scottish mystics tend to catch glimpses of the celestial Buddha. Yet Allah says 'We have sent messages to all nations', and St John records the promise that the Father will send a Counsellor to each disciple: and we may assume that he has sent culturally acceptable manifestations of this Counsellor to various disciples throughout the ages, a Counsellor who 'will teach you all things' (John, XIV, 25).

This Counsellor who teaches all things surfaces in all the major expositions of Philosophia Perennis. It is also met with in Plato, and is not only in the form of Socrates' Daimon. Prior to recommending it to Glaucon, Socrates differentiates this Counsellor from the Daimon: the latter instructs negatively, 'and has happened to few or none before me' (*Republic*, 496[c]), but the former is recommended to others, and for positive guidance. The Counsellor – at times called the Preceptor – conducts the ascent from the cave (*Republic*, 515[e]) and across the river Lethe (671[c]), and it is also he who comes to the conceited, intelligent young man and whispers gently 'that he has no sense and sorely needs it, and that the only way to get it is to work like a slave to win it' (494[d]). In the *Symposium* (210[a]–212), the Counsellor slips in unannounced and hardly appears at all, yet he is there in the philosopher's ascent from the visible to beauty itself.

Without the Counsellor, we learn from St Paul, we cannot understand Scripture. Plato is even more specific in the *Republic*, where it is stated that only through positive guidance from the Counsellor can one see the light of the Good. The ideas, according to *Republic*, 507–11, cannot mean anything without this illumination. For things to be visible there have to be three elements present: the object to be seen, light and the vision in which the two meet, which is neither the light nor the object but which contains them both. In other words, for true things to be visible, earthly things must be reconciled with heavenly – and this reconciliation is achieved through the *Logos*: 'no one comes to the Father, but by me' (John, XIV, 6).

The One is alone, without predication, with no name, existing only for itself. Before it is named, for man 'it has not become, it never was, nor can you say it has become now or is becoming or is' (*Parmenides*, 141). It is only when the One is named by the Word, the eternal AUM, that Brahman becomes the 'One that is' of the Brihadaranyaka Upanishad. Hence Dionysius the Aeropagite (1940, Ch. 4) writes of Jesus' prayer, the 'Our Father', that the name of the One comprehends all the names for justice, beauty, righteousness: every noble name, evoking every noble thought ever conceived, is the name of the One.

Jesus personifies the Name in the flesh, in so far as he makes the Father visible; he does this not by teaching a doctrine, since doctrines are strictly of the earth, but rather by creating a pattern of sentiments. The *Logos*, whether it manifests as a philosophy, a song, a temple, an activity or a thought, always reduces to an entity which acts as a reconciling catalyst. Heaven and earth are at odds, and as a result man suffers. The conflict between yin and yang – the left and the right – is, of course, imaginary: yet subjectively both forces are real. Aristotle, Simplicius and Proclus identify the dyad as matter (the earth, the body), the cause of evil. On the left there is the so-called lower consciousness, the earthly appetites, desires and cravings, the spiritual-biological forces Nietzsche referred to as the Dionysian principle. In contrast to these stands Apollo, to whom even Plato refers to as Apollo of the Right – the purifier.

Whether in politics or procreation, food or children, in thoughts and ideas everywhere one meets with this duality, the two opposing principles either locked in deadly combat or alternatively subjugating one another. More than one philosopher has interpreted all of history in terms of such a combat. Yet the nature of the universe is such that there exist 'charms', movements or thoughts which, in some incomprehensible way, tend to eliminate the conflict – not by subjugation or elimination of either of the tendencies, but by the infusion of some common rhythm with which both can identify.

All political activity and philosophy is a search for the lost formula of the Golden Age. When this agent of reconciliation, this vehicle of synthesis, is understood by a positivist it becomes the blueprint for a utopian city. In our age this takes the form of the political dogma that mankind will be liberated from pain and toil by technology. For one set of utopians this will result in the classless, propertyless society; for another set it will be a world of unlimited consumption.

Against this there stands Philosophia Perennis. All human goals – all concepts, walls, empires – are variations of the Golden Calf myth, whether they be political utopias, clever philosophies or the philosopher's stone. They all attempt to remove, destroy, negate, ignore or otherwise deny the true distinction between the desirable and the undesirable, by identifying the desirable with worldly goods. The *Logos* – paradoxical and nebulous as it may be – is the only thing able to comprehend and reconcile all elements in the struggle into a simultaneous unity. This unity is not any particular model, any particular system or city.

This is the apparent contradiction of all noetic philosophy. Plato warns against writing, yet he writes: Confucius, Viyasa, Socrates, Lao Tzu are all against utopias, yet they describe them. Jesus came to transcend the law, yet he himself laid it down.

FULL STOP

All around us paradox, inadequacy, contradiction – images and symbols, words and pictures calling for more words. Are there no answers? Is there no place where the One can be seen simply as One, and not as a duality resolving into a triunity, while being neither a duality nor a triunity? Is there anything which is not seen in fragments, flashes and spurts, synthesized by the conjectural mind? Was there ever a time when men were not falsely conglomerated, bits and pieces painfully held together? Is there a region where things are not *both* what is and what is not – a region where one need not spend hours in painful positions or praying on one's knees to escape the ugliness of perceived reality, and to catch a glimpse of beauty? Is there a place where Socrates is not condemned to death, where Jesus is not crucified and where Buddha is not torn apart by the hungry tiger? Is there such a yoga in which Arjuna is not crushed by sorrow, where man is spared the hour of Gethsemane, where the Father takes the bitter cup away? Are there answers to such questions, or are there only questions? Where do we look for the answers – in science, each man for his own self? Or shall we look some three or four millennia back at the Vedas again: and what do they say – do they answer or do they ask?

> There was not then what is nor what is not. . . . What power was there? Where? . . . The ONE was breathing by its own power, in deep peace. Only the ONE was: there was nothing beyond. Darkness was hidden in darkness. The all was fluid and formless. Therein, in the void, by the fire of fervour arose the ONE. And in the ONE arose love. Love the first seed of soul. The truth of this the sages found in their hearts: seeking in their hearts with wisdom, the sages found that bond of union between

being and non being. [Yet] Who knows in truth? Who can tell us whence and how arose this universe? . . . Only that God who sees in highest heaven: he only knows whence comes this universe, and whether it was made or uncreated. He only knows, or perhaps he knows not (Rig Veda, X, 129).

BIBLIOGRAPHY

SCRIPTURES QUOTED

Bible: (1973) *The Holy Bible*, Revised Standard Version, Ecumenical Edition, London: Collins.

Bhagavad Gita: Juan Mascaro (tr.) (1962), *The Bhagavad Gita*, Harmondsworth: Penguin Books.

Koran: N.J.Dawood (tr.) (1974), *The Koran*, Harmondsworth: Penguin Books.

Tao Te Ching: Gia-Fu Feng and Jane English (tr.) (1973), *Tao Te Ching*, London: Wildwood House.

Upanishads and Vedas: Raimundo Panikkar (tr.) (1977), *The Vedic Experience: Mantramanjari*, London: Darton, Longman & Todd.

PLATO

(1491), *Opera*, tr. Marsiglio Ficino, Bernardina de Choris and Simone de Leuco Venetiis.

(1562) (doubtful attribution), *Théages (ou de la Sapience)*, tr. P.Tredehan, Lyons: C. Pesnot.

(1699), *Les Oeuvres de Platon*, tr. A.Dacier, Paris: J.Anisson.

(1742), *Opere di Platone*, tr. D.Bembo, Venezia: G.Bittinelli.

(1769), *Loix de Platon*, tr. J.N.Grou, Amsterdam

(1780) (doubtful attribution), *The Rivals*, tr. F. Sydenham, London.

(1894), *Phaidros*, tr. F.Petracic, Zagreb: Vatica Hrvatska.

(1912–22), *Platons Dialoge*, tr. O.Apelt, Leipzig.

(1936–44), *Oeuvres Complètes*, tr. E. Chambry, Paris.

(1960), *Prawa*, tr. M. Mayakowska, Warsaw: Biblioteka Klass. Filozofi.

(1961), *Zakony*, tr. F. Novotny: Ceskoslovenska Akademia.

(1964), *The Dialogues of Plato*, tr. B. Jowett, Oxford: Clarendon Press.

(1970), *The Laws*, tr. T.J.Saunders, Harmondsworth: Penguin.

(1974), *Platon's Werke*, tr. F. Schleiermacher, Darmstadt: Eigler.
(1978), *The Collected Dialogues of Plato*, ed. E. Hamilton and H. Cairns: Princeton University Press.

OTHER SOURCES AND FURTHER READING

Alfarabius (1943), *de Platonis Philosophia – Plato Arabus*, ed. F. Rosenthal and R. Walzer, London: Warburg Institute.
Allen, R. E. (ed.) (1965), *Studies in Plato's Metaphysics*: Indiana University Press.
Aquinas, St Thomas (1921–32), *Summa Theologica*, tr. Fathers of the British Dominican Province, London: Burns & Oates.
Aquinas, St Thomas (1954), *Nature and Grace: Selections from the Summa*, ed. A.M.Fairweather, London: SCM.
Aristotle (1921), *The Works of Aristotle*, ed. Sir W.D. Rose and H.A. Smith: Oxford University Press.
Aristotle (1929), *Physics*, tr. P.H. Wickstead and F.M. Cornford, London: William Heinemann.
Aristotle (1946), *Politics*, tr. E. Barker: Oxford University Press.
Aristotle (1965), *Metaphysics*, tr. T.S.Dorsch, Harmondsworth: Penguin.
Augustine, St (1651), *The Profit of Believing* and *De Cura pro Mortuus*, tr.unknown, London: R. Daniel.
Augustine, St (1888a), *Sermon on the Mount*, tr. W. Findlay, New York.
Augustine, St (1888b), *Harmony of the Gospels*, tr. S.D.F. Salmond, New York: Christian Lit. Co.
Augustine, St (1904), *Soliloquies*, tr. H. L. Hargrove, New York.
Augustine, St (1952), *Confessions*, tr. E. Bouverie, Chicago: Enc. Britt.
Aurobindo, Sri (1957), *A Synthesis of Yoga*, Pondicherry.
Averroes (1956), *Commentary on Plato's Republic*, tr. E.I.J. Rosenthal: Cambridge University Press.
Bailly, A.M. (1879), *Lettres sur l'Atlantide de Platon*, Paris: Frères Debure.
Bambrough, R. (ed.) (1967), *Plato, Popper and Politics: Some Contributions to a Modern Controversy*: Cambridge University Press.
Barker, E. (1906), *The Political Thought of Plato and Aristotle*, London: Methuen.
Barker, E. (1918), *Greek Political Theory: Plato and his Predecessors*, London: Methuen.
Berriman, A.E. (1953), *Historical Metrology*, London: J.M.Dent & Sons.
Bharucha, E.S.D. (1979), *Zoroastrian Religion and Customs*, Bombay: D.B.Taraporevala Sons & Co.
Bidez, J. and Cumont, F. (1938), *Les Mages Hellénisés Zoroastre Ostanes et Hystape d'après la Tradition Grecque*, Paris: Soc. d'Editions des Belles Lettres.
Bigger, C.P. (1968), *Participation*, Baton Rouge: Louisiana State Press.
Bohr, N. (1958), *Atomic Physics and Human Knowledge*, New York: J. Wiley & Sons.
Bonitz, H. (1886), *Platonische Studien*, Berlin: F. Vahlen Verlag.
Bosanquet, B. (1906), *Companion to Plato's Republic*, London.
Bosanquet, B. (1932), *The Education of the Young in the Republic of Plato*: Cambridge University Press.

Boyce, M. (1979), *Zoroastrians: Their Religious Beliefs and Practices*, London: Routledge & Kegan Paul.

Brann, E. (1966), *The Music of the Republic*, Annapolis, Md.

Brumbaugh, R. S. (1954), *Plato's Mathematical Imagination*: Indiana University Publications.

Brumbaugh, R. S. (1962), *Plato for the Modern Age*, New York.

Buhler, G. (tr.) (1886), *The Laws of Manu*, Sacred Books of the East, ed. F. Max Müller, vol. XXV: Oxford University Press.

Capra, F. (1975), *The Tao of Physics*, London: Wildwood House.

Cherniss, H. (1944), *Aristotle's Criticism of Plato and the Academy*, Baltimore: Johns Hopkins University Press.

Cherniss, H. (1945), *The Riddle of the Early Academy*: California University Press.

Cleve, F.M. (1965), *The Giants of Presophistic Greek Philosophy*, Hague: M. Nijhoff.

Copleston, F. (1975), *History of Western Philosophy*, London: Burns & Oates.

Cornford, F.M. (1935) *Plato's Theory of Knowledge*, London: Routledge & Kegan Paul.

Cornford, F.M. (1937) *Plato's Cosmology*, London: Routledge & Kegan Paul.

Cornford, F.M. (1939), *Plato and Parmenides*, London: Routledge & Kegan Paul.

Cornford, F.M. (1948), *Religion and Philosophy*, London: Allen & Unwin.

Cornford. F.M. (1967), *The Unwritten Philosophy*: Cambridge University Press.

Cragg, K. (1973), *The Mind of the Quran*, London.

Crombie, I.M. (1971), *An Examination of Plato's Doctrines*, London: Routledge & Kegan Paul.

Crosland, M.P. (1971), *The Science of Matter*, Harmondsworth: Penguin.

Cushman, R.E. (1958), *Therapeia: Plato's Conception of Philosophy*: University of North Carolina Press.

Daniélou, J. (1944), *Platonisme et Théologie Mystique: Doctrines Spirituelles de St Gregoire de Nysse*, Paris: Aubier.

David-Neel, Alexandra (1936), *Tibetan Journey*, London: Bodley Head.

Day, C.B. (1962), *The Philosophers of China*, London.

Dionysius the Areopagite (1940), *The Divine Names and The Mystical Theology*, tr. C.E. Rolt, London: SPCK.

Duchesne-Gueillemin, J. (1953), *Ormazd et Ahriman: L'Aventure Dualiste dans l'Antiquité*, Paris.

Durich, M.N. (1958), 'Was Plato a Machiavellian?', in *Archiv für Rechts -und Sozialphilosophie*, vol. XLIV, pp. 79–93.

Durich, M.N. (1960), *Platonova Akademia injen Politicki rad*, Belgrade: Srpska Akademija Navka.

Einstein, A. (1969), *The Principle of Relativity*, New York: Dover.

Eliade, M. (1958), *Patterns in Comparative Religion*, London: Sheed & Ward.

Eliade, M. (1979), *A History of Religious Ideas*, London: Collins.

England, E.B. (1921), *The Laws*: University of Manchester Press.

Erigena, J.S. (1870), *Ueber die Eintheilung der Natur*, tr. L. Noack, Berlin: Philosophische Bibliothek.

Ferguson, A.S. (1921–2), 'Plato's Simile of Light', in *Classical Quarterly*, pp. 135–22; pp. 15–28.

Ferguson, J. (1970), *Socrates: A Source Book*, London: Macmillan.

Ficino, M. (1944), *Commentary on Plato's Symposium,* tr. Sears, Reynolds and Jayne: Columbia University Press.

Ficino, M. (1964), *Théologie Platonicienne de l'Immortalité des Ames,* Paris.

Ficino, M. (1978), *The Letters*, London: Shepeard-Walwyn.

Findlay, J.N. (1974), *Plato: The Written and Unwritten Doctrines*, London: Routledge & Kegan Paul.

Findlay, J.N. (1978), *Plato and Platonism*, New York: Times Books.

Findlay, J.N. (1970), *Ascent to the Absolute*, London: Allen & Unwin.

Fox, A. (ed.), *Plato and the Christians*, London: SCM.

Friedlander, Paul (1969), *Plato*, 3 vols, London: Routledge & Kegan Paul.

Fung Yu Ian (1958), *A Short History of Chinese Philosophy*, New York: Macmillan.

Gabrieli, F. (n.d.), *Alfarabius: Compendium Legum Platonis* (Plato Arabus III), London: Warburg Institute.

Gadamer, H.G. (1952), 'Retraktionen zum Lehrgedicht des Parmenides varia variorum', in *Festschrift fur Reinhardt*, pp. 58–68, Cologne: Munster.

Gadamer, H.G. (1964), 'Dialektik und Sophistik im Siebenten Platonischen Brief', in *Sitzungsberichte der Heidelberger Akademie der Wissenschaften*, Abh. 2, Heidelberg.

Gadamer, H.G. (1968), *Platos dialektische Ethik*, Hamburg: Felix Meiner Verlag.

Gadamer, H.G. (1973), 'Ueber Idee und Wirklichkeit im Timaeus', in *Sitzungsberichte der Heidelberger Akademie*, 10 Nov.

Gaiser, K. (1963), *Platons Ungeschriebene Lehre*, Stuttgart: E. Klett Verlag.

Gauss, H. (1937), *Plato's Conception of Philosophy*, London: Macmillan.

Gorman, P. (1979), *Pythagoras: A Life*, London: Routledge & Kegan Paul.

Gosling, J.C.B. (1973), *Plato*, London.

Gould, J. (1955), *The Development of Plato's Ethics*: Cambridge University Press.

Gouldner, A.W. (1965), *Enter Plato*, London: Routledge & Kegan Paul.

Govinda, Lama A. (1973), *Foundations of Tibetan Mysticism*, London: Rider.

Greene, W.C. (1944), *Moira: Fate, Good and Evil in Greek Thought*: Harvard University Press.

Gregory of Nyssa, St (1864), *Dialog über Seele und Auferstehung*, tr. H. Schmidt, Halle.

Gregory of Nyssa, St (1893), *Select Writings and Letters*, tr. with Prologomena, Notes and Indices, W. Morre and H.A. Wilson, Oxford: Parker & Co.

Gregory of Nyssa, St (1927), *Ausgewählte Schriften*, tr. Karl Weiss, München: Bibliothek der Kirchenväter.

Guthrie, W.K.C. (1950), *The Greeks and their Gods*, London: Methuen.

Guthrie, W.K.C. (1967), *Man and the Microcosm: The Idea in Greek Thought and its Legacy to Europe*, The Hague.

Guthrie, W.K.C. (1971), *Socrates*: Cambridge University Press.

Habermas, J. (1972), *Knowledge and Human Interest*, London: Heinemann.

Heisenberg, W. (1963), *Physics and Philosophy*, London: Allen & Unwin.

Hesiod (1973), *Theogeny and Works and Days*, tr. D. Wender, Harmondsworth: Penguin.

Homer (1950), *Iliad*, tr. E. V. Rieu, Harmondsworth: Penguin.

Homer (1952), *The Iliad of Homer* and *The Odyssey*, tr. S. Butler, Chicago: Enc. Britt.

Hoyle, Fred (1970), *Frontiers of Astronomy*, London: Heinemann.

Husserl, E. (1965), *Phenomenology and the Crisis of Philosophy*, New York: Harper & Row.

Husserl, E. (1970), *Logical Investigations*, tr. J.N. Findlay, London: Routledge & Kegan Paul.

Isherwood and Prabhavananda (1969), *How to Know God: Yoga Aphorisms of Patanjali*, New York: Mentor.

Jaeger, W. (1947), *The Theology of Early Greek Thinkers*, Oxford: The Clarendon Press.

James, E. O. (1961), *Seasonal Feasts and Festivals*, London: Thames & Hudson.

Jaspers, K. (1975), *History of Philosophy*, New York and London: McGraw-Hill.

Kanga, S.N. (1933a), *The Christ-Concept and of Logos in Christianity*, Bombay: Gatha Society.

Kanga, S.N. (1933b), *Heaven and Hell and their Location in Zoroastrianism and Plato*, Bombay: Gatha Society.

Kanga, S.N. (1933c), *A New Interpretation of the Sperta Manyu*, Bombay: Gatha Society.

Kant, Immanuel (1881), *The Critique of Pure Reason*, tr. J.H.Stirling, London: Simpkin & Marshall.

Kierkegaard, S. (1940), *Stages on Life's Way*, tr. W. Lowrie: Oxford University Press.

Kierkegaard, S. (1962), *Philosophical Fragments*: Princeton University Press.

Kierkegaard, S. (1966), *The Concept of Irony with Constant References to Socrates*, tr. Lee Capel, London: Collins.

Kirk, G.S. and Raven, J.E. (1957), *The Presocratic Philosophers*: Cambridge University Press.

Klein, J. (1968), *Greek Mathematical Thought and the Origin of Algebra*, Cambridge, Mass.: MIT Press.

Krishnaswami (1901), *Popular Hinduism*, Madras: Aiyar.

Lake, J.W. (1874), *Plato, Philo and Paul, or the Pagan Conception of Logos*, London.

Legge, James (tr.) (1971), *The Texts of Taoism*, 2 vols, Sacred Books of the East, ed. F. Max Müller, New York: Dover.

Lindsay, A.D. (1930), *The Historical Socrates and the Platonic Form of the Good*: University of Calcutta Press.

Linforth, I.M. (1946), *The Corybantic Rites in Plato*: University of California Publications in Classical Philology, xiii.

McClain, E.G. (1978), *The Myth of Invariance*, Boulder and London: Shambhala.

Marx, Karl (1952), *Briefe an Kugelman*, Berlin.

Mehra, J. (ed.) (1973), *The Physicist's Conception of Nature*, Dordrecht: Reidel.

Merlan, P. (1947), 'Form and content in Plato's Philosophy', in *Journal of the History of Ideas*, vol. 8.

Merlan, P. (1963–4), 'Religion and Philosophy from Plato's *Phaedo* to the Chaldean Oracles', in *Journal of the History of Philosophy*, vol. I, pp. 163–76.

Michell, John (1972), *City of Revelation*, London: Garnstone Press.

Morrall, J.B. (1958), *Political Thought in Medieval Times*, London: Hutchinson University Library.

Morrall, J.B.(1977), *Aristotle*, London: George Allen & Unwin.

Morrow, G.R. (1960), *Plato's Cretan City*: Princeton University Press.

Müller, F.Max (1978), *The Six Systems of Indian Philosophy*, London.

Murdoch, Iris (1978), *The Fire and the Sun*: Oxford University Press.

Murphy, N.R. (1932), 'The Simile of Light in Plato's Republic', in *Classical Quarterly*, pp. 82–107.

Murti, T.R.V. (1955), *The Central Philosophy of Buddhism*, London: George Allen & Unwin.

Nasr, S.H. (1966), *Ideals and Realities of Islam*, London: George Allen & Unwin.

Noss, J.B. (1974), *Man's Religions*, London: Macmillan.

Oehler, K. (1962a), *Die Lehre von Noetischen und Dianoetischen Denken bei Platon und Aristoteles*, Munchen: Zetemata Studien.

Oehler, K. (1962b), 'Subjekt und Objekt', in *Die Religion in Geschichte und Gegenwart*, vol. VI, pp. 448ff.

Oehler, K. (1962c), 'Vernunft und Verstand', in *Die Religion in Geschichte und Gegenwart*, vol. VI.

Oehler, K. (1969), *Antike Philosophie und Byzantinische Mittelalter*, München.

Oppenheimer, J.R. (1954), *Science and the Common Understanding*: Oxford University Press.

Panoussi, E. (1969), 'L'Origine de la Notion de Participation chez Zoroastre et chez Platon', in *Beiträge zur alten Geschichte und deren Nachleben*, Festschrift für Franz Altheim, Berlin: de Gruyter.

Patai, R. (1947), *Man and Temple*, London: T.Nelson & Sons.

Pauly-Wissowa (1893–1922), 'Real', in *Encyclopaidie der Classichen Altertums Wissenschaft*, 33 Bd., Stuttgart.

Peterson, P. (1924), *Hymns from the Rig Veda*, Poona.

Pickthall, M.M. (n.d.), *The Meaning of the Glorious Koran*, New York: New American Library (Mentor).

Pieper, Josef (1952), *Leisure the Basis of Culture*, tr. A. Dru, London: Faber & Faber.

Pieper, Josef (1954), *What Catholics Believe*, London.

Pieper, Josef (1957), *The Silence of St Thomas*, tr. D. O'Connor, London.

Pieper, Josef (1965), *Love and Inspiration*, tr. Richard and Clara Winston, London: Faber & Faber.

Pindar (1930), *The Works of Pindar*, tr. L.R.Farnell, London: Macmillan.

Plotinus (1956), *The Enneads*, tr. S. MacKenna, London: Faber & Faber.

Plutarch (1960), *The Rise and Fall of Athens*, tr. Ian Scott Kilvert, Harmondsworth: Penguin.

Plutarch (1974), *Plutarch's Lives*, ed. A. Wardman, London: Paul Elek.

Popper, K.R. (1957), *The Open Society and its Enemies*, London: Routledge & Kegan Paul.

Proclus (1820), *Commentaries on the Timaeus*, tr. T. Taylor, London.

Proclus (1970), *Commentaire sur la République*, tr. A.J.Festugière, Paris.

Proclus (1978), *Théologie Platonicienne*, tr. H.D. Saffrey and L.G.Westernik, Paris: Soc. d'Edition des Belles Lettres.

Radhakrishnan, S. (1923–7), *Indian Philosophy*, 2 vols, London: George Allen & Unwin.

Radhakrishnan S. (1957), *Source Book in Indian Philosophy*, London: George Allen & Unwin.

Rankin, H.D. (1964), *Plato and the Individual*, London: Methuen.

Ritter, C. (1933), *The Essence of Plato's Philosophy*, London.

Robin, Léon (1908), *La Théorie Platonicienne des Idées et des Nombres*, Paris.
Rosen, S. (1968), *Plato's Symposium*: Yale University Press.
Ross, D. (1966), *Plato's Theory of Ideas*: Oxford University Press.
Runciman, W.G. (1959), 'Plato's Parmenides', in *Harvard Studies in Classical Philology*, LXIV.
Runciman, W.G. (1962), *Plato's Later Epistemology*: Cambridge University Press.
Russell, Bertrand (1961), *History of Western Philosophy*, London: Allen & Unwin.
Ryle, G. (1966), *Plato's Progress*: Cambridge University Press.
Sachs, Mendel (1969), 'Space, Time and Elementary Interactions in Relativity', in *Physics Today*, vol. 22 February.
Sallis, J. (1975), *Being and Logos: The Way of Platonic Dialogue*, Pittsburg: Duquesne University Press.
Sastri, P.S. (1963), *Aristotle's Theory of Poetry and Drama*, Allahabad: Kitabmahal.
Seligman, P. (1962), *The Apeiron of Anaximander*: The Athlone Press, University of London.
Sinaiko, H.L. (1965), *Love, Knowledge and Discourse in Plato*: Chicago University Press.
Smith, D.H. (1973), *Confucius*, London: Maurice Temple Smith.
Solmsen, F. (1942), 'Plato's Theology', in *Cornell Studies in Classical Philology*, vol. 27.
Stapp, H.P. (1971), 'S-Matrix Interpretation of Quantum Theory', in *Physical Review*, vol. D3, 15 March.
Stenzel, J. (1940), *Plato's Method of Dialectic*, tr. D.J. Allen: Oxford University Press.
Stevens, P.S. (1977), *Patterns in Nature*, Harmondsworth: Penguin.
Stewart, J.A. (1960), *The Myths of Plato*, London: Centaur Press.
Strabo (n.d.), 'Zoroastrian Sources', in *Geography*, vol. VII, Loeb Classical Library.
Strauss, L. (1964), *The City and Man*: Chicago University Press.
Stumpf, S.E. (1966), *From Socrates to Sartre*, New York: McGraw-Hill.
Suzuki, Daisetz T. (1959), *Zen and Japanese Culture*, London: Routledge & Kegan Paul.
Taylor, A.E. (1926), *Plato: The Man and his Work*, London.
Taylor, A.E. (1928), *A Commentary on Plato's Timaeus*, Oxford: Clarendon Press.
Taylor, A.E. (1934), *The Parmenides of Plato*, Oxford: Clarendon Press.
Thompson, D'Arcy (1942), *On Growth and Form*: Cambridge University Press.
Tillich, Paul (1951), *Systematic Theology*, vol. 1: Chicago University Press.
Tong, L.K. (1973), 'Confucian Zen and Platonic Eros: A Comparative Study', in *Chinese Culture*, vol. XIV, pp. 1–8.
Uphold, W.B.Jr (1961), 'The Fourth Gospel as Platonic Dialectic', in *Personalist*, vol. XLII, pp. 38–51.
Urwick, E.J. (1920), *The Message of Plato*, London: Methuen.
Van Houte, M. (1954), *La Philosophie Politique de Platon dans les 'Lois'*, Louvain.
Versenyi, L. (1963), *Socratic Humanism*: Yale University Press.
Voegelin, E. (1957), 'Plato and Aristotle', in *Order in Society*, vol. III, Baton Rouge.
Waltham, Clae (1971), *Chuang Tzu: Genius of the Absurd*, tr. James Legge, New York: Ace Books.
Weil, S. (1951), *Imitations of Christianity Among the Ancient Greeks*, London:

Routledge & Kegan Paul.
Weyl, H. (1949), *Philosophy of Mathematics and Natural Science*: Princeton University Press.
Wild, J. (1974), *Plato's Theory of Man*, New York: Octagon Books.
Wundt, W. (1905), *Völkerpsychologie*, Leipzig.
Xenophon (1923), *Memorabilia and Oeconomicus*, tr. E.C.Marchant, New York: Heinemann.
Zaehner, R.C. (1953), *Foolishness to the Greeks*, Oxford: Clarendon Press.
Zaehner, R.C. (1961), *The Dawn and Twilight of Zoroastrianism*, London: Weidenfeld & Nicholson.
Zaehner, R. C. (1964), *The Catholic Church and World Religion*, London: Burns & Oates.
Zaehner, R. C. (1967), *Mysticism, Sacred and Profane*: Oxford University Press.

INDEX

aberration logic, 26–7
abstractions, 51–3
activity, *see* exercise; movement
actuality, 83, 85–7, 89, 94–7, 107, 111–16, 137, 183; *see also Chora*; materialism
Adam, J., 234–5
Agathon, 121, 123
ageing, 274
Ahmra, 4
Ahuna Varya, 4, 218, 284
Ahura Mazda, 30, 284
Aishron, 216
Aixos, 84, 89
Alcibiades, 121, 233
Alidius, 121
alienation, 110, 193–202, 208; *see also* Flood
ambiguity, 175
Ammetria, 124, 224
Anamnesis, 34, 278
Ananda, 11
Anangke, 117, 125, 143, 145, 201, 241, 246
Anatrope, 68, 194, 197, 243–4, 249
Anaximander, 195
Angro Manyush, 110
Anselm, St, 89, 98, 151
anti-city, *see* Atlantis; sick city
anti-formality, 101–2
Aperion, 22–3, 73, 109, 113–14, 195, 265
Apollo, 277
apprehension, 17–32
Apsastai, 87; *see also* grasping
Apsathnai, 179
Aquinas, St Thomas, 46, 110, 228
Aristarchus, 63–4, 202
Aristophanes, 24, 169
Aristotle, 267, 277, 290; on city, 213; on commerce, 36; on God, 196; Golden Mean, 143–4; on horizontal, 109–10; on ideal, 143; on ideas, 142, 153; on leisure, 240; on male/female principle, 22–3; on mathematics, 60; on two worlds, 141, 150
Aritmos, xii, 44–5, 53, 62–3, 65, 84, 87, 234, 248
Arjuna, 74, 104, 132, 184, 260, 270, 275; *see also* Hinduism
art, 53–6, 163, 178, 181, 228, 260–1
Asanas, 228
Asha, 106
Ashariah, 106; *see also Shariah*
aspectuality, 10, 19, 24, 27–32, 244; and flow, 95; and noetic thought, 51, 61, 68; opposition to positivism, 35, 39, 43; and vertical, 109
astronomy, xii, 1–2, 44, 218, 236, 261–2; *see also* heliocentricity; space
Atlantis, 175, 199, 203–4, 271; *see also* sick city
Atman, *see* self
atoms, 4, 7, 43–4, 59, 64, 95–6, 111, 255
Augustine, St, 11, 105–6, 110, 122, 150–1, 175–6, 230, 274, 290
AUM, 4, 30, 111, 274–5, 283, 286

Aurobindo, Sri, 84, 274, 290
Auto Kath-Auto, 65, 244
Averroes, 112, 290

Bach, J.S., 55
Bailly, A.M., 237, 290
barefoot philosopher, 253–68
becoming, 70–87, 89, 93–4, 111–12, 114–15
Being, 104, 207, 269; *see also* God; One
being, 39, 88–99, 107, 111–12, 114–15
Bergson, H., 96, 108, 160, 179
Berriman, A.E., 236, 290
betrayal, 276
Bhagavad Gita, 29, 112, 120–1, 134, 151, 197, 275, 282–4; *see also* Hinduism
Bhakti, 30, 39
Bharucha, E.S.D., 275, 290
Bible, *see* Christianity
Bigger, C.P., 153, 290
biological time, 96, 116
body: and city, 236–7; disorder, 201–2, 229–30; dying to, 186–7; exercise of, 226–32, 263; function of, 270–1; and harmony, 222, 225–6, 231; immortality of, 273; knowing with, 18, 26–7, 30, 38; rivers of, 201; and society, 167–8; and time, 224
Bohr, Niels, 7, 62, 71, 75, 77, 79, 97, 102, 108, 259–60, 290
Bonnitz, Y., 29
Bosanquet, B., 213, 290
bourgeois, *see* merchant thought
Boyce, M., 10, 39, 106, 290
Brahman, 75, 98, 104–5
Brumbaugh, R.S., 235, 291
Buddha, Gautama, 12, 24, 36, 259
Buddhi, 19, 29, 37, 107, 125, 179
Buddhism, 78, 215

calendar, 238–42
Capra, F., 8, 52–3, 82, 256, 266, 291
caste system, 112
categories, 65
Chakras, 30, 142, 218
change, 25, 92, 95, 275
charity, 132
Cherniss, H., 141, 291
Chi, 201, 218, 256
Chora: as actuality, 71, 73, 83, 97, 137, 141, 144, 207, 241, 272–3; as container of creation, 79, 82–3, 248; and grasping, 87, 137; and ideal, 145; as matter, 79–81, 118, 125; as mind, 124; and reflection, 158; – space, 80–1
Choreia, 226, 231–2
Christianity: dualism in, 131, 177; on evil, 46–7; and future age, 279; and God, 105; and Greeks, 45; and heart, 222; and order, 238–9; paradox in, 49, 57; and reincarnation, 156, 280; and triunity, 111; and truth, 100–1; on virtue, 46–7, 132–3; and Word, 283–4; *see also* Jesus; John; Paul
Chuang Tzu, 123, 198, 280
citizenship, 135
City of God, 4, 106, 134–5, 145
city: actual and perceived, 199–200; and body, 236–7; curing, 205–25; healthy, 137–9, 166, 204; man as, 145, 218–19; paradigmatic model of, 4–5, 129–40, 271; planned, 235–7; Plato on, xii, 199–200, 203–5, 213, 217–19, 237, 239; smallest, 165; as temple, 226–42; Third, 129–249; two, 271; vision of, 179–89; *see also* sick city
class, xiii, 165
Cleve, F.M., 198, 291
Cogito argument, 40–1
cognitive faculties, *see* knowing
colours, 239
communism, 40, 135
concepts, critique of, 48–69
conceptual objectivism, 141–58
conceptualism, *see* thought, conceptual
Confucius: and control of heart, 140; dialectic, 20, 22; on disturbed society, 218; on division of labour, 174; on duality, 108, 178, 244; on harmony, 231–2; on leisure, 240; on rectification, 259; and Taoism, 131, 177; on virtues, 134, 231–2; on work, 185
conjunction, *see Simploke*
Copleston, F., 141, 291
Cornford, F.M., 10, 80, 87, 120, 144, 181, 233, 291
cosmic chorus, 281
cosmic energy, 218, 264
cosmic time, 96, 116, 224
cosmic unity, 217

Counsellor, 276
counter-cosmic thought, 194
Cragg, K., 233, 291
Cratylus, 20, 56
creation, 2, 79, 82–3, 248, 274
Crombie, I.M., 86–7, 291
Cronus, Age of, 157–8, 197, 241, 273, 279
Crosland, M.P., 51, 291
Cross, the, 201–2, 259
crucifixion, 219–20
curing the city, 208–25
curse, 201–2, 259
Cushman, R.E., 31, 45, 121, 291

Dalton, John, 62
dance, 227, 232, 272
Daniélou, J., 197, 291
David-Neel, Alexandra, 111, 291
de Broglie, L., 77, 266
dead, 'realized', 279
death, 185–8; to body, 186–7; to false desires, 261; to language, 259; physical, 273–4; of self, 168; of star, 261
decay, 238, 259
deception, self, 211
Democritus, 52, 62, 64
demystification, 205
Descartes, R., 40–2, 46, 68–9, 89, 197
desires, 26, 28–31, 38, 112–15, 138, 164–6, 203–4, 209
Dharmakaya, 119
dialectic, 17–32, 167
Dialisis, 167
Dianoia, 19, 26, 41, 98–9, 107, 116–20, 180–2, 205, 211, 235, 249
Diaresis, 18, 44
Diarithmesis, 21, 63, 87, 179, 235
dichotomy, *see* dualism
Dionysius the Areopagite, 110, 220, 277, 286, 291
Diotima, 97
discursive reason, 89; *see also Logos*
disease, 229–30, 239
disjunction, *see Diaresis*
distortion, 124
Division of labour, 43, 159–78, 208–9
downward flow, 205–7, 211, 247
Doxa Alethes, 193
drama, 171, 227–8
drugs, 117
Druh, Druj, 106
dualism, 29, 108, 129–31, 180, 243–4; of knowing, 18–23; in religion, 111, 17–8, 246; in self, 44, 169–75; in society, 169–75
duty, 67
dyad, the indefinite: and the One, 73, 113, 19, 130, 286; *see also* dualism
dying, *see* death

Eckhart, Meister, 142
education of soul, 228
Eidos, 4, 71–2, 107, 149–50, 153, 157–8, 199
Eikones, 24, 27, 64, 119, 212, 254
Einstein, A., 71, 80–1, 83–4, 101, 256, 264–6, 291
Ekei, 23, 271
elements, 265
Elenchos, 27, 39, 133
Eliade, Mircea, 10, 129, 194, 228, 239–41, 273, 291
Eliot, T.S., 151, 210
emotions, 27, 45
Empfangen, 120; *see also Noesis*
Empiricus, Sextus, 255
Ens, 87
entheos, 228
Epetai, 56
Episteme, 56
Epithumia, 26, 29–30, 112–15, 138, 164–6
Er, Myth of, 156–7, 275
errors of positivism, 33–47
Eryxymachus, 169, 172, 198, 223, 260
Esse, 75
essences, 143
estrangement, *see* alienation
ethical determination of creation, 151
ethical faculty of thought, 37, 120; *see also Noesis*
ethical illumination, 182
ethical mathematics, 234–5, 237
ethics and exercise, 229
Eudoxus, 11, 91
Eutyphro, 170–1
evil, 47, 110, 117, 133–4, 145, 172–6, 181, 197–8, 229–30, 279, 286; *see also* Fall; sick city
exercise, 226–32, 263
existential fear, 230
existentialism, 147–9

expectations from well-endowed, 200–1
exposition, 89
extension, 123
externality, 7, 76, 79, 107–8, 217
externalization, 65, 68–9, 74–8, 159

faith, 102–3, 121
Fall myth, 50, 193–207, 213, 216, 220, 242; *see also* evil; sick city
false thinking, 24, 94
falsehood, 106, 216, 261
family, 220–1
fear, 230, 240
female principle, 22, 68, 177, 198, 247
Ferguson, A.S., 232, 291
Ferguson, J., 123, 291
festivals, 238–43 *passim*
Ficino, M., 150, 176, 240, 292
Findlay, J.N., 28, 51, 56, 63, 84, 87, 144–5, 150, 156, 163, 256, 292
flattery, 212
Flood myth, 205–6; *see also* alienation
flow, 263; aspectual, 61–6; of consciousness, 21; downward, 205–78, 211, 247; of history, 3; and language, 56; resistance to, 215; sentiment as, 282; upward, 207; *see also* movement
fluidity, *see* flow
formalities, dying to, 187
fragmentation, 125, 197
free choice, 39
Freud, S., 71
Freidlander, Paul, 203, 235, 292
Fung Yu Ian, 256, 292

Gadamer, H.G., 27, 143–4, 292
Gaiser, K., 60, 292
Galileo, 51, 62, 78
Gandhi, M., 215
Gauss, H., 210–11, 292
giving up, 135, 170
Glaucon, xii, 120, 181, 214, 218
Gnana yoga, 30, 39
God: abstract, 101; City of, 4, 106, 134–5; communion with, 228–9; as creator, 283; externalized, 65, 68–9; faith in, 102–4; Hindu, 104, 111, 132, 286–7; and incarnation, 284–5; as neutral currency, 196; reflection of, 176; *see also* One
gods, 195, 197, 245–7
Goethe, J.W. von, 179, 274
Golden Age, 157, 287
Golden Calf, 286
Golden Mean, 143, 235
goodness, *see* virtue
Gosling, J.C.B., 184, 292
Govinda, Lama A., 78, 292
grasping, 87, 107, 111–16, 120, 137, 179, 183
Gregory, St, of Nyssa, 197, 292
Guthrie, W.,.C., 84, 123, 236, 246, 292

Habermas, Jurgen, 28, 37, 151, 292
Hamilton, W., 50, 61
harmony, 78, 105, 180, 197, 222–6, 231
Haruvastra, 30
Hatha yoga, 228
head, 30
healthy city, 137–9, 166, 204; *see also* city
heart, 30, 129–40
heaven, 29, 68, 143–4; *see also* City of God
Hegel, F. : on absolute, 203; dialectic of, 22–3; on duality, 22, 49; on idealism, 85–6, 143, 147, 149; on knowledge, 37; and Marx, 68, 110
Heidegger, Martin, 33, 50, 101, 131, 147, 177, 199, 223
Heisenberg, W., 53, 77–8, 85, 94, 97, 142, 148, 259–60
heliocentricity, 62, 64, 212, 255, 262; *see also* astronomy
hell, 279
Heraclitus, 20, 55–6, 89, 104, 131, 180, 205, 223, 244, 267, 273
high-dwellers, 205–7
Hinduism: caste system, 112; on city, 138; on evil, 110, 219; on God, 104, 111, 132, 277–8; on grasp, 222; on identity, 229; on immortality, 275; on incarnation, 284, 286; on knowing, 120–1, 151; on language, 93; on microcosm/macrocosm, 76; on Nature, 29; on non-violence, 134; paradox in, 48; on perfection, 5; psychological divisions, 112; and psychotherapy, 29; on reincarnation, 275; on self, 41; on seven celestial odies, 218; on soul, 28–30; on thought, 22, 26; on turning around, 185; on universe, 264; on virtue, 197;

on Word, 282–4; on world order, 106; *see also* Bhagavad Gita; Krishna; Upanishads; Vedas
Hobbes, Thomas, 31, 168, 174
Homer, 214, 216, 292
horizontal dimension, 89–90, 108–16, 123–4, 134
Hoyle, Fred, 1, 5, 76, 292
hubris, 2, 195
Hume, David, 102
Husserl, E., 32–3, 41, 83, 148, 263, 292
Hyle, 3, 143, 162

I, the, 40–3, 66, 120, 197, 202; ideal world, 141–58
idealism and materialism, 71–5, 143
ideas, 92, 141–58; *see also* thought, conceptual
identity, *see* self
idolatry, 211–12
ignorance, 105
illiteracy, 12–13, 85
immortality, 98, 155–6, 159, 162, 195, 265, 272–5, 277–81
inactivity, 216; *see also* walls
incarnation, 284–7; *see also* reincarnation
indirect description, 89
individual, *see* I; perfect man; self
insight, religious, 132–3
instantiation, 86
instants, 95, 97, 113
interests of social man, 31
internal study, 76
intuition, 107, 179, 183
inversion, 68, 193–202, 249
'Is', 93
Isherwood, C., 275, 293
Islam: aspectuality in, 30; duality in, 130; and falsehood, 106; and God, 101; and idolatry, 211; on mercy, 132; on morality, 133; paradox in, 48–9, 57; and spiritual vision, 185; rhythm in, 21, 24, 222, 232–3, 284–5; ritual in, 240; on virtue, 47; on Word, 284–5; *see also* Koran; Mohammad

Jaeger, W., 45, 293
James, E.O., 238–9, 293
Haspers, K., 34, 147, 293
Jesus Christ: on adultery, 46; body of, 150; on death, 168, 186–7; disciples, 100–1, 132; and dualism, 131–3, 177; fasting, 185; on giving up, 135; on ideal, 144; on loss of self, 273; as Name, 286; parables of, 57, 200; on psychological conflict, 74; on reincarnation, 275–6; on social ties, 188; on work, 242; and writing, 24; *see also* Christianity; perfect man
Jivatman, 228
John, St, 166, 187, 218, 236, 284–5; *see also* Christianity
Jowett, B., 86, 293
Judas, 132, 171, 276–7
justice, 132

Kama, 26, 29
Kanga, S.N., 284, 293
Kant, I., 32, 35, 144, 293; on Copernicus, 51; cyclical view of history, 36–7; on duty, 67; on ethics and morality, 44, 46, 240; on inversion, 68–9; on man, 65; on matter, 64, 71–3; on perception, 39, 43; on reality, 152; on self, 38–42, 91, 186; on thought, 197; on universalizability, 221
Karma, 145, 246
Karma yoga, 30, 39
Kephr, 44
Kierkegaard, S., 39, 50, 58, 101–2, 131, 147, 149, 278, 293
Klein, J., 181, 212, 293
Knothi Seuton, 76
knowing/knowledge, 112–14, 114, 119, 179–80, 182; being as object of, 39; with body, 18, 26–7, 30, 38; and experience, 36; as flow, 62; as perception of one in many, 104–5; three kinds of, 17–32, 54, 66–7; without thought, 121–2; *see also* *Noesis*; thought
Koan, 48
Koinonia, 45, 154
Koran, 21, 24, 47, 75, 106, 132; *see also* Islam
Kotler, Philip, 257–8
Krishna, Lord, 29–30, 58, 74, 101, 104, 120, 132, 184, 219, 275; *see also* Hinduism
Krishnaswami, 29, 293
Krya, 186
Kundalini, 218, 264

labour, *see* division of labour; work
L'adah, 211
language, 37–8, 42, 56–7, 91,, 121, 152, 219, 233, 244, 257, 259–60; *see also* words
Lao Tzu, 12, 255, 267; *see also* Taoism
left/right duality, 22–3, 29, 68, 108, 172, 178, 198, 244, 246
Legge, James, 123, 293
Leibniz, G., 151
leisure, 240
Leonidas myth, 159–60
Levy, G.R., 45
Li, 20, 232
L'ibdah, 211
lie, *see* falsehood
L'ilm, 211
linear philosophy, 11
linear time, 77–8
Linforth, Ivan, 228, 232, 293
liver, 228–9
Locke, John, 32
logic, systems of, 91
logical postivism, *see* postivism
Logisticon, 29, 37–8, 54, 73, 81, 93, 107, 112–16, 125, 164–6
Logos-oriented thought, 3–4, 64, 144, 247; aspectuality in, 19; on autonomy, 39; avoids verification, 74–5; and being, 93; and conceptualists, 46, 57; and duality, 108; ethical faculty, 37–8; and harmony, 222; and I, 175; objectives of, 182–3, 189; on space, 75, 78; on walls, 215; love, 171, 264–5; being as object of, 39; and heart, 37; kinds of, 172–3; knowledge through, 180; as own reward, 67; and self, 151; as synthesizing force, 125
lower-body logic, 26–7, 30, 179
lust, 198

McClain, E.G., 91, 203, 235–6, 239, 293
Machiavelli, N., 263
macrocosm/microcosm, 4, 76, 217–18
Mahabharata, 46, 55
maieutic technique, 24
male/female duality, 22, 68, 177, 198
Manas, 19, 26–7, 29–30
Mania, 53–4
mantra, 21–2
market, *see* merchant
Marx, Karl, 264, 291; on activity, 148; on externality, 108; and Hegel, 68, 110; on labour, 201; on natural laws, 26; on philosopher, 8; on private property, 177; on stages of society, 35
Marxism, 101, 144
materialism, new, 70–87; *see also* merchant
mathematics and number, xii; as art, 181; and astronomy, 44; and *Chora*, 87; and city plans, 235–7; and conceptual thought, 60, 62–3; ethical, 234–5, 237; and evil, 181; and sophism, 212
matter: *Chora* as, 79–81, 118, 125; constitution of, 256, 264; defined, 85–7; and space, 79–83
Maya, 87, 110
mean, 144
measurement, standardized, 234–5
medical analogy, 221
meditation, 8, 74, 142
Menexenus, 200
mental time, 96
merchant thought, xiii, 6, 35–8, 40, 67, 209, 254, 257–8; on division of labour, 162, 174; on God, and I, 40–3, 196; State, 208–9; *se also* materialism
Merlan, P., 11, 150, 293
Metanoia, 185
Metastrophe, 185
Michell, John, 236, 293
microcosm/macrocosm, 4, 76, 217–18
mind: and body, 167–8; correctly functioning, 180–1; knowing with, 18, 38
Mohammad, 13, 24, 57–8, 101, 117; *see also* Islam
Moira, 125, 143, 163; *see also Theia Moira*
Moksha, 185
Morrall, J.B., 180, 213, 240, 244, 293
Moses, 57
movement, 124, 148, 216, 226–31, 244, 265–6; *see also* flow; vertical
Murti, T.R.V., 97, 192
Muslims, *see* Islam; Koran; Mohammad
music, 21, 55, 223–4, 227, 231–2, 272
myths, 49–50, 84, 89, 101–2, 157–8, 161–2, 177, 193–249

Namas, 44
names, 130; rectification of, 38, 259
Nasr, S.H., 130, 294
nature, 26, 29
needs, sets of, 26–7
negative description, 89
negative, double, 93, 98
negative mania, 54
negative movements, 244
negative sentiments 172–5; *see also* evil
negative soul, 75
newness, 254–5
Newton, Isaac, 78, 236, 254
Nietzsche, F., 68–9, 286
Noesis and noetic thought, 19, 107, 249; and concepts, 57, 59–68; defined, 120; on dualism, 44; on ethics, 31; on falsity of positivism, 32; on ideas, 60; on movement, 207, 230; on reality, 86; on sentiments, 27; on thought, 25; on time, 23, 72, 116–19
non-alienated society, 199
non-conceptual thinking, 51–3
non-violence, 133
norm, 144
Noss, J.B., 106, 294
nothingness, 110–11, 142
notions, 52, 61–2, 90
Nous, 61, 229, 265
number, *see* mathematics

objectivism, conceptual, 141–58
observation, 149
Oehler, K., 120, 199, 294
OM, *see* AUM
One, 103–4; and dyad, 73, 113, 119, 130, 277; in many, 104–5; nature of, 98–9; power of, 287; and Word, 286–7; *see also* God; vertical
ontological realms: of becoming and actuality, 70–87, 111; of being, 88–99, 111
Oppenheimer, J.R., 8, 95, 294
opposites, 171–3; *see also* dualism
oppsition and art, 54
order, 105–6, 238–42
organizaing principle, 28
otherness, 108

pain, 212–13, 258–9
paradox, 2, 48–9, 57, 97, 103, 161
Parekbasis, 173, 243–4
parenthood, 230–1
Parmenides : on being, 39, 88–99; on conceptual objectivism, 141–58 *passim*; on dualism, 244; on habit-conforming, 55–6; on ideas, 60; on One, 73, 98, 103–4, 180
parrot parable, 176
participation, 8, 152–3, 158
Particular Being, 207
passions, 27, 178, 227
Patai, R., 198, 237, 245, 294
Patanjali, 37, 168, 186, 284
Pathos, 19, 133
paths to God, 30
Paul, St, 47, 49, 58, 105, 142, 173, 187, 230, 276, 285; *see also* Christianity
Pausanias, 172
perceptions, 33, 36
perfect city, 4–5
perfect man, 202, 218–19, 256–9, 270
perfect society, 159
Periagoge, 183–5, 229
permanence, 82
personality, 155, 168, 183; *see also* self
persuasion, 219, 221
Pfonos, 171, 208
Philo the Jew, 274
philosopher-poets, 177–8, 180
physical activity, 226–32, 263
physics, 77; *see also* atoms; quantum
Pieper, J., 45, 122, 151, 197, 210, 238, 241, 294
Pindar, 229
Pius X, Pope, 238
plant, man as, 194
Plato and Platonic thought: on ageing, 274; on art, 53; on astronomy, 44, 62–4, 75–6, 78, 162, 218; on being, 39; on children, 231; on *Chora*, 256; on city, xii, 5, 134–9, 199–200, 203–5, 213, 217–19, 237, 239; on Counsellor, 285; on Cronus, 279; and dialectic, 18–24; on dualism, 46, 177–8, 244, 247; on elements, 264; as encyclopaedist, 11–12; on faith, 102, 104; on fear, 230; on flow, 56; on gods, 195, 197, 245–7; on identity, 229; on knowing, 62, 121, 151; on law, 130; on leisure, 240; on *Logisticon*, 37; on mathematics, xii, 60, 143, 181, 234–6, 262; on matter, 79–83, 86, 107–8; on movement, 232,

265; on navy, 214–15; on needs, 26–7; on observation, 149; on order, 239; and Parmenides, 22–3, 88–99, 103; on perception, 72–3, 103; on perfect man, 218; on reincarnation, 155–6, 275–7; on religion, 49; on rivers and flood, 203–6; on ruling, 140, 221; on society, 35, 188; on sophism, 6, 212; on soul, 29–30; on Spartans, 122; on spiritual vision, 183–5; on thought, 62–4, 68; on time, 275; on truth, 45; on two worlds, 141, 144, 150, 152, 174; on walls, 213–15; on work, 241; *see also* Saanthana thought; Socrates
pleasure and pain, 212–13
Pleonexia, 168, 203, 206, 208–9, 248
Plotinus, 11, 98, 150, 152–3, 155, 294
pluralism, 6
Plutarch, 36, 122, 294
Pneuma, 19, 133, 218, 265
poetry, 45, 177–9, 227, 233
Politea, 134–9, 166; *see also* city
politics, 233
positive, 53–5, 244
positivism, xii, 6–8, 53, 59, 119; errors of, 33–47
Prana, 201
priest/Brahmin soul, 28–9
private property, 177–8; *see also* walls
Proclus, 80–1, 107, 112, 150, 184, 218, 232, 265, 286, 294
profit, 257–8; *see also* merchant
progress, 9, 78, 159, 202, 205, 253–6
Protagoras and Protagorean thought, 52, 64–5, 141–58 *passim*
Psellus, 232
Pseudo-Dionysius, *see* Dionysius
Pseudos, 216
Pseudo-Theages, 45
psychological divisions, 112
psychological time, 224
psychotherapy, 29
Ptolemy, 262
punishment, 117, 220
purgatory, 279
Pythagoras and Pythagoreans, 60, 64, 73, 81, 109, 112, 151

Quantilianus, Aristides, 227
quantum theory, 53, 75, 77, 102, 263, 266

Radhakrishnan, D., 41, 294
Rajas, 28, 112, 114, 164
Ramanuja, 11, 72, 149, 168
Ratio, 45, 61
rationalists, *see* thought, conceptual
Ravel, M., 21
reading, *see* writing
reality, 33, 89
reconciliation, 243–7
reincarnation, 40, 155, 159, 272, 275–7
relativistic subjectivism, 141–58
relativity, 146, 262–3, 265
religion, 129–32, 177–8; *see also* Buddhism; Christianity; faith; God; Hinduism; Islam; Taoism
representative precinct, 217
remembering, 270
rhyme, 19–20
rhythm, 20–4, 63, 219, 222, 224, 248; of calendar, 238–42; and exercise, 227–33; loss of, 239
right/left duality, 22–3, 29, 68, 108, 172, 178, 198, 244, 246
Rihd, 112
rituals, 238–42 *passim*
river myths, 201, 205–7, 285
Rolt, C.E., 220, 291
Ross, Sir David, 60, 295
Rta, 106
ruling, 140, 220–1
Rumi, 142
Russell, Bertrand, 100, 151, 295
Rutherford, Ernest, 62, 75, 102

Saanthana thought, 4–5, 10; on ageing, 274; on change, 25; on cosmic Being, 269–70; on division of labour, 12; on duality, 29; on free choice, 39; on external and internal, 76, 217; on harmony, 222; on ideal, 143–7; on knowledge, 234; on participation, 152–3, 158; on perfect society, 159; on progress, 78; on punishment, 220; on rhythm, 248; on sentiments, 197–8; on soul, 75; on time, 276; on unity, 171; *see also* Hinduism; *Logos*; Saanthana thought; Taoism; Zoroastrianism

Sachs, Mendel, 97, 295
sages, 267–8
Samadhi, 5
Samkara, 41
Samsara, 87, 93, 116
Sartre, J.-P., 33–4, 149
Sat-Asat, 90–2
satori, 48
Sattva, 28–9, 112, 114, 263
Schopenhauer, A., 35
Schuon, F., 224
self:-abuse, 218; -assertion, 195; attachment to, 210; as blank, 163; concepts of 40–3; -consciousness, 155, 199; -creator, man as, 144; and death, 168, 186–7; deception, 211; denial, 162; duality in, 169–75, 217; gratification, 211; -identity, 277–8; -limitation, 203; loss of, 273; and love, 151; and many, 155–7; paradigmatic, 159; perceived, 159, 167–8; as pivot, 263–4; purification, 224; -regeneration, 265–7; sacrifice, 159; and soul, 28–9; survival of, 277–81; two, 260–2; unity of, 169–71; unselfish, 185; *see also* I; individual; personality; soul
seasons, 239–42
Seligman, P., 195, 295
sentiments, 19, 282–8; and aspectuality, 63; and emotion, 140; and ideas, 141–58; and movement, 229; and number, 87; and passions, 27, 227; six, 246; and spirit, 133; and synthesis, 44–7; and thought, 65, 121, 123–4; *see also Logos; Pathos; Pneuma*; Tao
seven celestial bodies, 218; *see also* astronomy
seven days, 239
seven evils, 181, 198; *see also* evil
seventh movement, 244
shape of space, 80–2
Shariah, 106, 230–1, 240, 284
Shirk, 211
sick aristocrat, 208
sick city, 137–9, 166, 173–5, 210–12, 271; *see also* Atlantis; city; evil; Fall
silence, 122–3, 266
Simplicius, 109, 195, 286
Simploke, 18, 44
sin, *see* evil; Fall; sick city
Sinaiko, Herman, 27, 39, 46, 134, 146, 295
Sinkresis, 167, 243–4
six sentiments, 246
Smart, Ninian, 285
Smith, Adam, 168
Smith, D.H., 231, 295
society, duality in, 169–75
Socrates, 267; on art, 232; on astronomy, xii, 64; on belief, 205; on city, 139, 145, 199–200, 214; on Counsellor, 285; on death, 185; on decay, 238; dialectic, 20, 23–4, 27; on emotions, 45; on evil, 117, 271; on God, 65; on ideal, 143–4; illiterate, 12, 85; on immortality, 156–7; on labour, 162; on law, 230; maieutic technique, 24; on mathematics, 181; on matter, 80; on mind and body, 221–2; on music, 232; on names, 130; on order, 239, 261; on perception, 32, 34; on possessions, 235; on reincarnation, 286; silence of, 123, 266; on social ties, 188; on sophism, 211–12; on thought, 52, 56, 60–1; on tyranny, 225; on walls, 216; on war, 214; on words, 121, 233; on writing, 135; Xenophon on, 121; and Zeno, 96; *see also* Saanthana thought; Plato
Solmsen, F., 64, 237, 295
Soma, 186
'something', 142
sophism, 68, 205, 210–12, 223–4, 255; *see also* positivism
Sophocles, 283
soul, 18, 74–5, 136, 228; aspects of, 28–30; and division of labour, 164–6; and thought, 38, 112; *see also* self
space, 75–9; and matter, 79–83; shape of, 80–2; and time, 83–5, 97; *see also* astronomy
Spartans, 122
specialization, 162
speech, *see* language; words
Speussipus, 109
spiral, 21, 160
Spirit, 133
spiritual vision, 183–5
Stalin, 178
Stapp, H.P., 43, 295

star, death of, 261–2; *see also* astronomy
statesman, ideal, 139, 228
Stasis, 124, 224
Stenai, 56
Stenzel, J., 59, 167, 295
Stevens, P.S., 26, 83, 295
Stewart, J.A., 45, 195, 295
Stewart, T.C., 237
stillness, 122–3, 266
stomach, 30, 179; *see also Manas*
stream of consciousness, 161
Stumpf, S.E., 34, 295
subjectivism, 141–58
Sufism, 133, 185; *see also* Islam
Suzuki, D.T., 242, 295
symbols, 18
Symphonia, 223
synthesization, 44–7, 125, 167
Syrianus, 150

Tai Chi acupuncture, 29
Tamas, 29, 112, 114
Tao, as sentiment, 19
Taoism: and Confucianism, 131, 177; on death, 187; and dialectic, 20–3, 57; dualism in, 108–9, 111, 177, 244; on Fall, 195; on music, 9; newness of, 255; on non-conceptualization, 53; on nothingness, 142; on order, 106; as organizational principle, 4; rhythm in, 222; on sage, 46; and silence, 123; on work, 185; *see also* Lao Tzu
Tariquah, 130–1, 285
Tasawurf, 211
Taylor, A.E., 82, 84, 86, 92, 233, 295
Tchaikovsky, P., 260
Techne, 235
technology, 202
temple, city as, 226–42
Tenos, 48, 133
terrorist, 224
Thales, 103
Theia Moira, 54, 136, 185; *see also Moira*
therapeutic city, *see* healthy city
things, 64, 118
thinking, *see* thought
third city, the, 129–249
Thompson, D'Arcy, 108, 295
Thorax, 26, 142
thought: conceptual, 37–69, 72, 91, 142–3, 189; parasitic, 179–80; and sentiments, 65, 121, 123–4; and soul, 38, 112; types of, 26–8, 38; as understanding, 111–12, 114–15, 119, 124
three, 274; *see also* triunity
thumetikoid desire, 38
Thumos, 29, 112, 114–16, 124, 164–6, 179, 211
Tien, 106
Tillich, Paul, 104, 295
time: and becoming and changing, 92–6; biological, 96, 116; in conceptual thinking, 50; conjectural, 175; continuity in, 162; cosmic, 96, 116, 224; and immortality, 272–5; linear, 77–8; mental, 96; out of, 5, 23, 72, 95, 272, 275, 278–80; seasons, 239–42; and space, 83–6, 97; types of, 96–7, 116–19, 224, 272–5
To Metron, 235
To Peras, 22–3, 73, 109, 113–14, 265
transconceptual reality, 142
Trasymachus, 212
tree symbol, 194
Trethowan, I., 224
triunity, 110, 129, 243–4, 260
truth, 100–25, 131, 180–1, 210
turning around, 183–5
two cities, 271
two selves, 260–2; *see also* dualism
two-world interpretation, 141, 144, 150, 152, 174
tyrant, 170, 224

ugliness, 216
understanding, *see* thought
unity, 2, 4, 94–6, 169–71, 217
Universal Being, 207
universalizability, 220–1
'universals', 60
Upanishads, 22, 30, 104, 110, 185, 286; *see also* Hinduism
upward movement, 207
Urwick, E.J., 129, 272, 295
Usia Ontos Usa, 104
Utopia, 138–40

Vedas, 29, 93, 106, 109, 287; *see also* Hinduism
verification, 74–5
Versenyi, L., 211, 295

vertical dimension, 89–90, 108–16, 123–4
vice, *see* evil
Victor, Pope, 239
vision, spiritual, 183–5
virtue, 132–3, 175–6, 197–8, 207, 231–2, 244
vision of city, 179–89
Vohu Manu, 133, 218–19; *see also* Zoroastrians
Voltaire, 237

walls, 188, 213–16
Waltham, Clae, 195, 272, 295
Weil, Simone, 198, 295
Weyl, H., 84, 296
wheel, 21
Wheeler, J.A., 77, 83
Whitehead, A.N., 150–2
wholeness, 108
Wild, J., 193, 296
Wittgenstein, L., 32, 42–3, 56, 152
Word, the, 282–6
words: as charms, 121, 233; written, 24, 91, 135, 182; *see also* language
work, 185, 201; *see also* division of labour
world order, 105–6
writing, *see* words
Wundt, Wilhelm, 227, 296

Xenocrates, 24
Xenophon, 12, 85, 121, 296

yin/yang duality, 22–3, 68, 111, 130, 177, 244, 247, 259, 274
Yoga, 5–6, 29–30, 201, 228–9, 260, 274

Zaehner, R.C., 185, 195, 284, 296
Zen, 5, 7, 48, 131
Zeno, 94, 96, 98, 160
Zoroastrians, 11–12, 160, 267; on choice, 39; on city, 138; commands, of, 30; and future age, 279; and Greeks, 78; on movement, 232; on natural order, 106; on other, 110; on soul, 29–30; on thought, 26; on two world souls, 244; on virtue, 133, 218–19; on Word, 284